INTERPRETING
THE GOSPELS
AND ACTS

Handbooks for New Testament Exegesis
John D. Harvey, series editor

Interpreting the Gospels and Acts: An Exegetical Handbook
David L. Turner

Interpreting the Pauline Letters: An Exegetical Handbook
John D. Harvey

Interpreting the General Letters: An Exegetical Handbook
Herbert W. Bateman IV

Interpreting Revelation and Other Apocalyptic Literature: An Exegetical Handbook
C. Marvin Pate

INTERPRETING THE GOSPELS AND ACTS

An Exegetical Handbook

David L. Turner
AUTHOR

John D. Harvey
SERIES EDITOR

Interpreting the Gospels and Acts
© 2019 by David L. Turner

Published by Kregel Academic, an imprint of Kregel Publications, 2450 Oak Industrial Dr. NE, Grand Rapids, MI 49505-6020.

The Greek font GraecaU and the Hebrew font New JerusalemU are both available from www.linguistsoftware.com/lgku.htm, +1-425-775-1130.

ISBN 978-0-8254-2760-2

Printed in the United States of America
19 20 21 22 23 / 5 4 3 2 1

CONTENTS IN BRIEF

CONTENTS

SERIES PREFACE

THE AUTHORS OF THE NEW TESTAMENT communicated their witness to the good news of Jesus Christ using a variety of types of literature (literary genres). Those different types of literature require different principles and methods of interpretation and communication. Those principles and methods are best understood in the context of a series of handbooks that focus on the individual types of literature to which they apply. There are three basic literary genres in the New Testament: narrative, letter, and apocalypse. Other subgenres are present within those basic types of literature (e.g., parable), but narrative, letter, and apocalypse provide the framework for those subgenres.

The four volumes in this series will offer the student of Scripture the basic skills for interpreting and communicating the message of the New Testament in the context of the various literary genres. The four volumes are:

- *Interpreting the Gospels and Acts (Matthew–Acts)*
- *Interpreting the Pauline Letters (Romans–Philemon)*
- *Interpreting the General Letters (Hebrews–Jude)*
- *Interpreting Revelation and Other Apocalyptic Literature*

Each volume is designed to provide an understanding of the different types of literature in the New Testament, and to provide strategies for interpreting and preaching/teaching them. The series is intended primarily to serve as textbooks and resources for seminary and graduate-level students who have completed at least a year of introductory Greek. However, because an English translation is always provided whenever

Greek is used, the series is also accessible to readers who lack a working knowledge of Greek. For that reason, upper-level college students, seminary-trained pastors, and well-motivated lay people should also benefit from the series.

The four volumes cover the twenty-seven books of the New Testament. Each volume (a) includes a summary of the major themes present in the New Testament books it covers; (b) sets methods of interpretation in the context of the New Testament books to which those methods apply; (c) goes beyond exegesis to exposition by providing strategies for communicating each type of New Testament literature; (d) provides step-by-step examples which put into practice the methods and strategies set out in each volume in the context of an overall exegetical-homiletical framework.

In order to enhance the usefulness of the series, the length, style, and organization of each volume is consistent. Each volume includes the following elements:

- *The nature of the literary genre (including important subgenres)*
- *The background of the books (historical setting)*
- *The major themes of the books*
- *Preparing to interpret the books (textual criticism, translation)*
- *Interpreting passages in the context of their genre*
- *Communicating passages in the context of their genre*
- *From exegesis to exposition (two step-by-step examples)*
- *A list of selected resources and a glossary of technical terms*

Authors are given freedom in how they title each chapter and in how best to approach the material in it. Using the same basic organization for each book in the series, however, makes it possible for readers to move easily from volume to volume and to locate specific information within each volume.

The authors in this series represent a variety of theological backgrounds and educational institutions, but each is committed to handling God's Word accurately. That commitment reflects a key element in living the Christian life: the functional authority of Scripture. Whatever theological position we might hold, we submit ourselves to the authority of the Bible and align our understanding of life and doctrine to its teaching. It is the prayer of the authors and the publisher that these handbooks will enable those who read them to study the Bible, practice its teachings, and share its truth with others for the advance of Christ's kingdom purposes.

—JOHN D. HARVEY
Series Editor

PREFACE

The publication of Interpreting the Gospels and Acts: An Exegetical Handbook completes Kregel's four-volume set of Handbooks for New Testament Exegesis, which complements the six-volume set of Handbooks for Old Testament Exegesis. I thank John Harvey and Herb Bateman at Kregel for the opportunity to contribute to a series devoted to biblical exegesis, the central passion of my professional life.

A prerequisite for doing good exegesis is realizing that it does not occur in a vacuum. Exegetes must be self-conscious of the subtle ways in which their own historicity influences their methods and conclusions. Accordingly, brief comments about my background and goals should be useful to those who exegete this book about exegesis. I came to know the Lord Jesus Christ personally during a Bible study in Romans when I was a senior in high school. My first teachers in the faith soon made sure that I received a *Scofield Reference Bible.* When I look at that treasured Bible today, I notice that the especially worn pages in one section reveal that the Pauline corpus was my canon within the canon. My first formal studies in Bible and theology at both the undergraduate and graduate level also stressed Paul and led ultimately to a ThD dissertation on Romans 5:12–21. I came to love Paul's thought and the genre in which he expressed it, his letters. The classical dispensational theology I received early on also lionized Paul, and it tended to relegate the Gospels and Acts to the status of an appendix to the Old Testament that provided the *historical* setting for Paul's theology of grace. All this to say that I acquired my interest in the Gospels and the other narrative books of the Bible later in my life and ministry.[1]

The furor generated among evangelicals by the publication of Robert Gundry's Matthew commentary in 1982 first drew my attention to the genre of the Gospels and their *theological* message. A study trip to Israel soon afterward led me to love the land of the Bible and to resolve to understand more accurately the role played by historical geography and social history as a complement to grammatical-syntactical exegesis. Reflection on dispensationalism led me to what has become known as its "progressive" version and a greater appreciation of the theological unity of the whole Bible, centering in the life, ministry, and teachings of Jesus (not Paul).[2] Early work on the Gospel according to Matthew showed me that my grasp of Second Temple Judaism was totally inadequate, leading me to PhD studies at Hebrew Union College. Perceptive readers will note all these influences in the pages of this book.

In 1539, when he was only thirty years old, John Calvin published his commentary on Romans. Calvin's letter to his friend Simon Grynaeus forms a sort of preface to the commentary, one that expresses Calvin's basic approach to biblical exegesis. At the beginning of the letter, Calvin says,

> I remember that three years ago we had a friendly discussion about the best way of interpreting Scripture. The plan which you particularly favoured was also the one which at that time I preferred to any others. Both of us felt that *lucid brevity* constituted the particular virtue of an interpreter. Since it is almost his only task to *unfold the mind of the writer whom he has undertaken to expound*, he misses the mark, or at least strays outside his limits, by the extent to which he leads his readers away from the meaning of his author.[3]

Calvin went on to say near the end of the letter, "It is, therefore, presumptuous and almost blasphemous to turn the meaning of Scripture

---

1. My experience was much like that of Jonathan Pennington, who candidly explains why he once preferred the straightforward doctrinal teaching in Paul's letters to the often implicit "moral of the story" in the Gospels. See *Reading the Gospels Wisely* (Grand Rapids: Baker, 2012), 36–38. Pennington's discussions of why we need the Gospels (38–49) and why they are the keystone in the archway of the biblical canon (229–58) are highly recommended.

2. David L. Turner, "Matthew among the Dispensationalists," *JETS* 53 (2010): 697–716.

3. John Calvin, *The Epistles of Paul the Apostle to the Romans and to the Thessalonians*, trans. Ross Mackenzie (Grand Rapids: Eerdmans, 1973), 1. Italics added. For further discussion of Calvin's exegetical method, see T. H. L. Parker, *Calvin's New Testament Commentaries* (Grand Rapids: Eerdmans, 1971), 49–68.

around without due care, as though it were some game that we were playing."[4] It is my hope that these exegetical ideals—brevity, clarity, and accuracy—are furthered and modeled in this exegetical handbook.

I am grateful for the good providence of God that has brought many gifted people into my life. First and foremost, I am continually reminded of the loving and sacrificial support of my wife Beverly in all that I do, including the writing of this book during a very hectic season of our life together. I am thankful to all those who taught me Greek grammar and exegesis through the years, including George L. Lawlor, Homer A. Kent Jr., James L. Boyer, John A. Sproule, S. Lewis Johnson Jr., and Adam Kamesar. I have been blessed with the opportunity to teach the Gospels to great students in a positive, collegial setting at Grand Rapids Theological Seminary. I dedicate this book to those GRTS students, especially to those who have served as my teaching assistants in recent years: Todd Frederick, Jennifer McCormick-Bridgewater, Chris McKnight, Kyle Rouse, Seth Stadel, and Leta Von Klompenberg.

—DAVID L. TURNER
Passion Week, 2018

---

4. Calvin, *Romans and Thessalonians*, 4.

ABBREVIATIONS

REFERENCE WORKS AND PERIODICALS

ABD	Freedman, D., ed. *The Anchor Bible Dictionary.* 6 vols. New York: Doubleday, 1992.
AJT	*American Journal of Theology*
ANRW	*Aufstieg und Niedergang der römischen Welt*
BBR	*Bulletin for Biblical Research*
BDAG	Danker, F. W., et al., eds. *A Greek-English Lexicon of the New Testament and Other Early Christian Literature.* 3rd ed. Chicago: University of Chicago, 2000.
BDB	Brown, F., S. Driver, and C. Briggs, eds. *A Hebrew and English Lexicon of the Old Testament.* Oxford: Clarendon, 1906.
BDF	F. Blass and A. DeBrunner. *A Greek Grammar of the New Testament and Other Early Christian Literature.* Translated and revised by R. W. Runk. Chicago: University of Chicago Press, 1979.
Bib	*Biblica*
BSac	*Bibliotheca Sacra*
CBR	*Currents in Biblical Research*
CTQ	*Concordia Theological Quarterly*
CTR	*Criswell Theological Review*
DBSJ	*Detroit Baptist Seminary Journal*
GTJ	*Grace Theological Journal*
HTR	*Harvard Theological Review*
IDB	*Interpreter's Dictionary of the Bible*

Jastrow	Marcus Jastrow, *A Dictionary of the Targumim, Talmud Babli and Yerushalmi, and the Midrashic Literature* (reprinted, New York: Judaica, 1992).
JBL	*Journal of Biblical Literature*
JETS	*Journal of the Evangelical Theological Society*
JSNT	*Journal for the Study of the New Testament*
LSJ	Liddell, H. G., and R. Scott. *A Greek-English Lexicon with a Supplement.* Revised by H. S. Jones and R. McKenzie. Oxford: Clarendon, 1968.
NA$^{28\text{rev}}$	Barbara and Kurt Aland, et al., eds. *Novum Testamentum Graece.* 28th rev. ed. Stuttgart: Deutsche Bibelgesellschaft, 2012.
NIDOTTE	Willem A. Van Gemmeren, ed. *The New International Dictionary of Old Testament Theology and Exegesis.* 5 vols. Grand Rapids: Zondervan, 1997.
NIDNTTE	Moisés Silva, ed. *The New International Dictionary of New Testament Theology and Exegesis,* 5 vols. (Grand Rapids: Zondervan, 2014).
NovT	*Novum Testamentum*
NTS	*New Testament Studies*
SJT	*Scottish Journal of Theology*
TDNT	Kittel, G., and G. Friedrich, eds. *Theological Dictionary of the New Testament.* 10 vols. Translated and edited by G. W. Bromiley. Grand Rapids: Eerdmans, 1964–72.
TheolSt	*Theological Studies*
TynBul	*Tyndale Bulletin*
UBS$^{5\text{rev}}$	Barbara Aland, et al., eds. *The Greek New Testament.* 5th rev. ed. Stuttgart: Deutsche Bibelgesellschaft, 2014.
USQR	*Union Seminary Quarterly Review*
WTJ	*Westminster Theological Journal*

OLD TESTAMENT

Gen.	Genesis	Nah.	Nahum
Exod.	Exodus	Hab.	Habakkuk
Lev.	Leviticus	Zeph.	Zephaniah
Num.	Numbers	Hag.	Haggai
Deut.	Deuteronomy	Zech.	Zechariah
Josh.	Joshua	Mal.	Malachi
Judg.	Judges	Ps./Pss.	Psalms
1–2 Sam.	1–2 Samuel	Prov.	Proverbs
1–2 Kgs.	1–2 Kings	Song	Song of Solomon
Isa.	Isaiah	Eccl.	Ecclesiastes
Jer.	Jeremiah	Lam.	Lamentations

Ezek.	Ezekiel	Esth.	Esther
Hos.	Hosea	Dan.	Daniel
Obad.	Obadiah	Neh.	Nehemiah
Mic.	Micah	1–2 Chr.	1–2 Chronicles

OLD TESTAMENT APOCRYPHA

1–2–3 Macc.	1–2–3 Maccabees	Sir.	Sirach (Ecclesiasticus)
Bar.	Baruch	Tob.	Tobit
Jdt.	Judith	Wis.	Wisdom of Solomon

NEW TESTAMENT

Matt.	Matthew	1–2 Thess.	1–2 Thessalonians
Rom.	Romans	1–2 Tim.	1–2 Timothy
1–2 Cor.	1–2 Corinthians	Phlm.	Philemon
Gal.	Galatians	Heb.	Hebrews
Eph.	Ephesians	Jas.	James
Phil.	Philippians	1–2 Peter	1–2 Peter
Col.	Colossians	Rev.	Revelation

JEWISH PSEUDEPIGRAPHA

Apoc. Abr.	*Apocalypse of Abraham*
2 Bar.	*2 Baruch (Syriac Apocalypse of Baruch)*
1 En.	*1 Enoch (Ethiopic Apocalypse of Enoch)*
Jos. Asen.	*Joseph and Aseneth*
Jub.	*Jubilees*
Let. Aris.	*Letter of Aristeas*
Pss. Sol.	*Psalms of Solomon*
Sib. Or.	*Sibylline Oracles*

PHILO

Contempl.	*De vita contemplative (On the Contemplative Life)*
Flacc.	*In Flaccum (Against Flaccus)*
Prob.	*Quod Omnis probus liber sit (That Every Good Person is Free)*
Legat.	*Legatio ad Gaium (On the Embassy to Gaius)*
Spec. 1, 2, 3, 4	*De specialibus legibus (On the Special Laws)* I, II, III, IV

JOSEPHUS

A. J.	*Antiquitates judaicae* (*Jewish Antiquities*)
B. J.	*Bellum judaicum* (*Jewish War*)
C. Ap.	*Contra Apionem* (*Against Apion*)
Vita	*Life*

DEAD SEA SCROLLS

The customary abbreviations are used, with 1–11Q portraying the number of the Qumran cave, the number following Q portraying the number of the manuscript; superscript a, b, c, etc. multiple copies of a text in one cave. Multiple fragments of the same manuscript are enumerated f. 1, f. 2, f. 3, etc. The final numbers in an abbreviation (e.g., 5.12) refer to the column and line. Individual abbreviations follow:

1QS	*Serek Hayachad* (1Q28, *Rule of the Community*)
1QS^a	*Serek Hayachad* (1Q28^a, appendix to 1QS)
4Q176	4QTanhumim (comments on passages about consolation)
4Q259	4QRule of the Community, a partial copy of 1QS with a calendar
4Q266	Damascus Document (4QD^a)
CD	Cairo Genizah copy of the Damascus Document

MISHNAH, TALMUD, AND RELATED RABBINIC LITERATURE

General abbreviations:

m.	Mishnah	*y.*	Jerusalem Talmud
t.	Tosefta	*b.*	Babylonian Talmud

Individual tractates:

Ber.	*Berakot*	*Sanh.*	*Sanhedrin*
Ketub.	*Ketubot*	*Shabb.*	*Shabbat*
Mak.	*Makkot*	*Ta'an.*	*Ta'anit*
Meg.	*Megilla*	*Yad.*	*Yadayim*
Mid.	*Middot*	*Yebam.*	*Yebamot*
Neg.	*Nega'im*		

Other Rabbinic Works:

S. Olam Rab.	*Seder Olam Rabbah*

EARLY CHURCH AUTHORS

2 Clem.	*2 Clement* (debatably attributed to Clement of Rome)
Comm. Matt.	Origen, *Commentarium in evangelium Matthaei* (*Commentary on the Gospel of Matthew*)
Cons.	Augustine, *De Consensu evangelistarum* (*Harmony of the Gospels*)
Dial.	Justin Martyr, *Dialogus cum Tryphone* (*Dialogue with Trypho*)
Did.	*Didache*
Doctr. chr.	Augustine, *De Doctrina Christiana* (*Christian Instruction*)
Eph.	Ignatius, *To the Ephesians*
Hist. eccl.	Eusebius, *Historia Ecclesiastica* (*Ecclesiastical History*)
Incomp. Nupt.	Augustine, *De Incompetentibus nuptiis* (*On Adulterous Marriages*)
Haer.	Irenaeus, *Adversus Haereses* (*Against Heresies*)
Hom. Matt.	Chrysostom, *Homiliae in Matthaerum* (*Homilies on Matthew*)
Marc.	Tertullian, *Adversus Marcionem* (*Against Marcion*)
Mart. Pol.	*Martyrdom of Polycarp*
Praep. ev.	Eusebius, *Praeparatio evangelica* (*Preparation for the Gospel*)
Praescr.	Tertullian, *de Praescriotione haereticorum* (*Prescription against Heretics*)
Quaest. ev.	Augustine, *Quaestionum evangelicarum libri II*
Scorp.	Tertullian, *Scorpiace* (*Antidote for the Scorpion's Sting*)
Serm.	Augustine, *Sermones* (*Sermons*)
Smyrn.	Ignatius, *To the Smyrnaeans*
Stom.	Clement of Alexandria, *Stromata* (*Miscellanies*)

NEW TESTAMENT PSEUDEPIGRAPHA

Acts Paul	*Acts of Paul*
Gos. Pet.	*Gospel of Peter*
Gos. Thom.	*Gospel of Thomas*

ANCIENT GRECO-ROMAN AUTHORS

Cleom.	Plutarch, *Cleomenes*
Diog. L.	Diogenes Laertius, *Vitae philosophorum* (*Lives of Philosophers*)
Geogr.	Strabo, *Geographica* (*Geography*)
Hist. plant.	Theophrastus, *Historia plantarum* (*Enquiry into Plants*)
Inst.	Quintilian, *Institution oratoria* (*Institutes of Rhetoric*)
Nat.	Pliny the Elder, *Naturalis historia* (*Natural History*)

Od.	Homer, *Odyssea* (*Odyssey*)
Rust.	Varro, *De re rustica* (*On Agriculture*)
Thuc.	Dionysius of Halicarnassus, *Thucydides*

TEXT-CRITICAL SIGLA

Abbreviations relating to the text of the Hebrew Bible are those used by and explained in *Biblia Hebraica Stuttgartensia*, ed. K. Elliger and W. Rudolph (Stuttgart: Deutsche Bibel Gesellschaft, 1967–77), xliv–lv. Abbreviations relating to the text of the New Testament are those used by and explained in Barbara Aland, et al., eds., *The Greek New Testament*, 5th rev. ed. (Stuttgart: Deutsche Bibelgesellschaft, 2014).

ENGLISH VERSIONS OF THE BIBLE

CEV	Contemporary English Version
CSB	Christian Standard Bible
ESV	English Standard Version
JPS	The Jewish Publication Society Tanach
KJV	King James Version
LB	The Living Bible (Kenneth Taylor)
Message	The Message (Eugene Peterson)
NAB	New American Bible
NASB	New American Standard Bible
NET	New Electronic Translation
NIV	New International Version
NJB	New Jerusalem Bible
NLT	New Living Translation
NRSV	New Revised Standard Version
REB	Revised English Bible
RSV	Revised Standard Version

1

THE GENRE AND STRUCTURE OF THE GOSPELS AND ACTS

The Chapter at a Glance

Although other theories of Gospel genre have been promoted, it seems most likely that the Gospels and Acts are quite similar to ancient Greco-Roman *bioi*. The Gospels and Acts creatively present historical events in terms of their theological and pastoral relevance for the church. The narratives of the Gospels and Acts contain other types of literature embedded as subgenres. The Gospels and Acts must be related to the narrative of the Old Testament.

NEW TESTAMENT NARRATIVE GENRE IN GENERAL

"GENRE" AS AN ENGLISH LEXEME DERIVES FROM FRENCH, and in turn from the Latin *genus*. Typical glosses for the word genre include "type," "sort," "kind," or "class." Plato and Aristotle spoke of literary genre in ancient times. Today, genre theory is a vast area of scholarship as it relates to literature, let alone other communicative endeavors such as spoken discourses, prayers, dramatic performances, and film. Literary genres are abstract mental conceptions of entities one encounters empirically; situations give rise to genres. Genres entail conventional features that readers have come to expect in various situations. Discussions of genre are thus descriptive rather than prescriptive. Taxonomies vary from one theorist to another when it comes to classifying genres, super-genres, and subgenres. Current genre theory emphasizes the social and ideological context of the process or action of writing as well as its end product or form.[1]

The complexity of genre theory aside, it seems clear that the understanding of a text's genre is crucial for its interpretation. As E. D. Hirsch put it, "An interpreter's preliminary generic conception of a text is constitutive of everything that he subsequently understands."[2] One's understanding of *what* a text means (exegesis) is to a great degree determined by one's understanding of *how* that text conveys meaning (genre). Cooperative competence in generic conventions and expectations is necessary for effective acts of literary communication; both the original author and the subsequent readers of a text need to be aware of how such a text should be interpreted, given its internal literary features.[3]

Here is a helpful way of construing genre's role in the interpretive process:[4]

Broad Genre
(imprecise, heuristic, open to refinement)

Intrinsic Genre
(a set or contract of expectations)

Expectations further refined by reading

Textual meaning
(reader shares semantic content intended by author)

---

1. Carolyn R. Miller, "Genre as Social Action," *Quarterly Journal of Speech* 70 (1984): 151–76. For an overview of current studies, see Anis Bawarshi and Mary Jo Reiff, *Genre: An Introduction to History, Theory, Research, and Composition* (Anderson, SC: Parlor, 2010); Amy Devitt, *Writing Genres* (Carbondale: Southern Illinois University, 2008).

2. E. D. Hirsch, *Validity in Interpretation* (New Haven, CT: Yale University Press, 1967), 74. Plato (*Republic* 392d) and Aristotle (*Poetics* 1447a–1448a) spoke of various types of writings and the appropriate characteristics of each.

3. Kevin J. Vanhoozer, *Is There a Meaning in This Text?* (Grand Rapids: Zondervan, 1998), 337–38.

4. Adapted from R. A. Burridge, *What Are the Gospels? A Comparison with Graeco–Roman Biography,* 2nd ed. (Grand Rapids: Eerdmans, 2004), 39. Burridge is summarizing Hirsch, *Validity,* 80–81.

VARIOUS VIEWS OF GOSPEL GENRE

Literary scholars present widely diverging approaches to the question of genre. Views range from the idea that every communicative textual act represents its own genre (*sui generis*) to the approach that insists that all communicative acts are intertextual: Each must of necessity be understood in light of its similarities and differences from other textual communications.[5] Those who believe the biblical account of the creation of Adam and Eve might be inclined to the latter approach, viewing human creation in God's image as enabling effective cooperative communication between God and humans. Such communication is hampered by sin after humans rebel against God (Gen. 3), yet it is still possible by the grace of God.

The question of the genre or genres of the Gospels and Acts has been debated for centuries. Currently the view that the Gospels are to be related to Greco-Roman biographies (βίοι) has been accepted by many scholars, but through the history of New Testament interpretation many views have surfaced, including the following more prominent ones:

Sui Generis

The view that the uniqueness of the person, teaching, and redemptive work of Jesus Christ necessitates a new and unique kind of literature, the Gospels, is rather common.[6] Kee described Mark as a unique literary creation, "a new genre of literature for which, as a whole, there was no precedent."[7] Among the problems with the *sui generis* view is the generic resemblance of the Gospels to other ancient forms of literature, including the narratives of the Hebrew Bible and Greco-Roman biographies. Perhaps the most serious problem with the view is linguistic: the necessary interrelatedness of literary genres, what E. D. Hirsch called "the genre-bound character of understanding."[8] A unique genre cannot be imagined by an author, and even if it could be imagined, it would be impossible for a reader to understand it. In the end the *sui generis* view is a **non sequitur**, since unique subject matter does not logically require its own unique communicative genre.

---

5. E. D. Hirsch, *The Aims of Interpretation* (Chicago: University of Chicago, 1976), 69–71.

6. Robert Guelich, "The Gospel Genre," in *The Gospel and the Gospels*, ed. P. Stuhlmacher (Grand Rapids: Eerdmans, 1991), 173–208.

7. H. C. Kee, *Jesus in History: An Approach to the Study of the Gospels,* 2nd ed. (New York: Harcourt, 1977), 139.

8. Hirsch, *Validity*, 76.

Loose Collections of Oral Traditions

Some who held the *sui generis* view understood the Gospels to be relatively random collections of smaller units of orally transmitted traditions or snippets of written traditions about Jesus. Such vignettes would be arranged somewhat loosely with little or no attention to literary concerns. K. L. Schmidt influentially distinguished the Gospels as naively assembled folk tales (*Kleinliteratur*) from compositions with literary sophistication (*Hochliteratur*).[9] Rudolf Bultmann spoke of the Gospels as *Kleinliteratur* that developed from Christian proclamation. Mark as the first Gospel began a unique literary phenomenon, one so dominated by Christian faith that the Gospels are only with difficulty described as a genre at all.[10] The onset of redaction critical studies of the Gospels, which demonstrated the creative editorial work of the respective evangelists, showed that the Gospels were truly literary documents. The rise of narrative criticism only confirmed what redaction criticism had begun to show. The results of these methods led most scholars to abandon the view that the Gospels were merely loose collections of Jesus traditions.

Aretalogies

Ancient accounts of the exploits and miracles of a heroic divine-human figure (θεῖος ἀνήρ) are known as aretalogical literature. In such accounts, the protagonist has been imbued with extraordinary virtue (ἀρετή) and manifests divine power through miracles. In ancient times, such works were found in Egypt, Mesopotamia, and the wider Greco-Roman world. They included such details as the hero's conspicuous birth, asceticism, wisdom, trials, and martyrdom. A commonly discussed aretalogy is Philostratus's *Life of Apollonius of Tyana* (c. A.D. 225), a work about a philosopher and teacher who flourished in the late first and early second centuries. Morton Smith and other scholars attempted to understand the Gospels as dependent on such works, but several critiqued the association of the two.[11] Clearly the miracles of Jesus were an important part of the Gospels' witness to Jesus, and no

---

9. K. L. Schmidt, "Die Stellung der Evangeliien in der allgemeinen Literaturgeschichte," (1923), reprinted as *The Place of the Gospels in the General History of Literature*, trans. B. R. McCane (Columbia: University of South Carolina Press, 2002), 24, 27, 68.

10. Rudolph Bultmann, *The History of the Synoptic Tradition*, trans. J. Marsh, Rev. ed. (Oxford: Blackwell, 1972), 371–74; Bultmann, *Theology of the New Testament*, trans. K. Grobel, 2 vols. (London: SCM, 1952), 1.86.

11. See e.g., Morton Smith, "Prolegomenon to a Discussion of Aretalogies, Divine Men, the Gospels, and Jesus," *JBL* 90 (1971): 174–99, and the critique by H. C. Kee, "Aretalogy and Gospel," *JBL* 92 (1973): 402–22.

doubt some early readers of the Gospels were familiar with aretalogical literature, but there is much debate over what constitutes aretalogy as a genre and whether such a genre actually existed, let alone whether this putative genre served as a model for the Gospels.

Midrash

The term *midrash* comes from דָּרַשׁ, which describes seeking or asking. It has come to refer to a wide spectrum of textual interpretation.[12] Jewish *midrashim* are typically categorized as *halakhic* (close textual exegesis of details in Torah texts) and *haggadic* (a homily based on a biblical text or figure).[13] The origins of midrash are perhaps as early as the Chronicler's reworking of 1–2 Samuel and 1–2 Kings. In terms of the genre of the Gospels, the haggadic or homiletical *midrashim* are most relevant.

Those who attempt to connect the Gospels with midrash draw an analogy between the imaginative retelling of biblical stories in Jewish midrash and the way in which the Gospels allude to the OT, as well as the way in which (assuming Markan priority) Matthew and Luke use Mark in composing their respective narratives. Similarity of *method*, however, even if it is granted, does not amount to identity of *genre*. The Gospels are not as a whole interpretations or elaborations of the OT.[14] Certain scholars argued, however, that individual pericopes within the Gospels were created without historical basis. Goulder argued that pericopes were creatively composed as a lectionary to correspond to the three-year cycle of OT texts read in the synagogue.[15] Gundry held that Matthew created certain pericopes as counterparts to stories found in Mark or Luke. For example, he understood the story of the magi (Matt. 2:1–12) as a fictional embellishment of Luke's narrative of the angelic annunciation to the shepherds (Luke 2:8–20).[16] As an evangelical with a

---

12. Marcus Jastrow, *Dictionary of the Targumim, Talmud Babli, Yerushalmi, and Midrashic Literature,* reprinted (New York: Judaica, 1992), s.v. דָּרַשׁ (325)and s.v. מִדְרַשׁ (735–36).

13. H. L. Strack and G. Stemberger, *Introduction to the Talmud and Midrash* (Minneapolis: Fortress, 1992), 254–68. Jacob Neusner's functional taxonomy differs in that he views midrash as prophecy, paraphrase, or parable. See his *What Is Midrash?* (Philadelphia: Fortress, 1987). Neusner wryly comments that the word midrash "presently stands for pretty much anything any Jew in antiquity did in reading and interpreting Scripture" (xii).

14. Craig L. Blomberg, *The Historical Reliability of the Gospels,* 2nd ed. (Downers Grove, IL: InterVarsity, 2007), 77–78.

15. M. D. Goulder, *The Evangelists' Calendar* (London: SPCK, 1978); Goulder, *Midrash and Lection in Matthew* (London: SPCK, 1974). See the response by Leon Morris, "The Gospels and the Jewish Lectionaries," in *Gospel Perspectives III: Studies in Midrash and Historiography*, eds. R. T. France and D. Wenham (Sheffield: JSOT, 1983), 129–56.

16. Robert H. Gundry, *Matthew: A Commentary on his Narrative and Theological Art* (Grand Rapids: Eerdmans, 1982), 26–31. Gundry supported his approach in a theological postscript (623–

high view of Scripture, Gundry argued that Matthew's audience would have known which parts of Matthew were rooted in historical tradition and which were midrashic embellishments. This contention, however, was unproven, if not unprovable. Gundry's analogy between Jewish midrash on ancient canonical texts and Matthew's use of recent synoptic tradition was not widely persuasive.[17]

Quasi-Old Testament Narratives

Since the authors of the Gospels were familiar with the Old Testament (OT) and viewed Jesus as its fulfillment, it seems plausible that the Gospel narratives would resemble the OT narratives. Further, since the authors of the Gospels viewed Jesus as fulfilling in some sense the roles of Moses and the prophets, it would not be surprising if their accounts of Jesus resembled OT accounts of prophetic figures. Various scholars have written to demonstrate such similarities.[18] Although some OT books contain sections that narrate the lives of noteworthy individuals, there are no clear parallels to the lengthy Gospel narratives as entire compositions wholly devoted to the words and deeds of Jesus.

Apostolic Recollections

The oral testimony of eyewitnesses (αὐτόπται) and early ministers (ὑπηρέται) of Jesus traditions was important to the author of the Gospel according to Luke 1:2. The early church likewise highly valued such sources. According to Eusebius (c. A.D. 325), Papias (c. A.D. 125) placed higher value on testimony received from contemporaries of Jesus's apostles than from books (*Hist. eccl.* 3.39.4).[19]

---

40) and responded to critics in the preface of his second edition, *Matthew: A Commentary on His Handbook for a Mixed Church under Persecution* (Grand Rapids: Eerdmans, 1994), xix–xxx.

17. A great deal of debate arose in response to Gundry's views, especially in evangelical circles. See e.g., David L. Turner, "Evangelicals, Redaction Criticism, and the Current Inerrancy Crisis," *GTJ* 4 (1983): 263–88; Turner, "Evangelicals, Redaction Criticism, and Inerrancy: The Debate Continues," *GTJ* 5 (1984): 37–45. See also R. T. France, "Jewish Historiography, Midrash, and the Gospels," in *Gospel Perspectives III,* 99–127.

18. See e.g., Meredith G. Kline, "The Old Testament Origins of Gospel Genre," *WTJ* 38 (1975): 1–27. One might add that the biographical material in rabbinic sources can arguably be rooted alongside the Gospels in the OT narratives. On this view see Philip Alexander, "Rabbinic Biography and the Biography of Jesus," in *Synoptic Studies: The Ampleforth Conferences of 1982 and 1983*, ed. C. M. Tuckett (Sheffield: JSOT, 1984), 19–50. Burridge supplies literary and Christological reasons for the absence of anything resembling a sustained biography of any of the esteemed rabbinic sages (*What Are the Gospels?* 331–40).

19. In this text Papias spoke of such traditors as those who had "followed" the presbyters (παρηκολουθηκώς τις τοῖς πρεσβυτέροις) and of their testimony as a living and abiding

Eusebius speaks of the Gospels according to Matthew and John as recollections (ὑπομνήματα) written down only after attention was first given to preaching and teaching (*Hist. eccl.* 3.34.5). Similarly Eusebius cites Irenaeus (c. A.D. 180) to the effect that Mark as Peter's interpreter composed his Gospel from Peter's preaching, and Luke as Paul's companion recorded Paul's preaching in Acts (*Hist. eccl.* 5.8.3). The oral transmission of Jesus's words and deeds has been much discussed of late, with emphasis on both original eyewitness testimony and subsequent community control of Jesus traditions.[20] Scholars tend to distinguish between an earlier oral period and a later period when written Gospels were produced, but recently Walton and Sandy have argued that oral and written Gospels existed side by side into the second century.[21]

Greco-Roman Biographies

Although previous scholars had drawn attention to the similarities between the Gospels and Greco-Roman biographies,[22] the work of R. A. Burridge has more recently brought this view into near consensus. Burridge compares the Gospels to Greco-Roman biographies, including works earlier than the NT by Xenophon and Isocrates (fourth century B.C.) and works later than the NT by Tacitus and Plutarch. His study compares four generic features of each:

1. Opening features (whether there is a title, nature of the prologue of preface)

2. Subject (how the protagonist is portrayed, verbal subjects, allocation of space)

---

voice (τὰ παρὰ ζώσης φωνῆς καὶ μενούσης). See Eusebius, *The Ecclesiastical History*, Loeb Classical Library, 2 vols. with ET by K. Lake (Cambridge: Harvard University Press, 1926), 293.

20. Kenneth Bailey, "Informal Controlled Oral Tradition and the Synoptic Gospels," *Themelios* 20 (1995): 4–11; Richard Bauckham, *Jesus and the Eyewitnesses* (Grand Rapids: Eerdmans, 2006); James D. G. Dunn, *Jesus Remembered* (Grand Rapids: Eerdmans, 2003).

21. John H. Walton and D. Brent Sandy, *The Lost World of Scripture* (Downers Grove, IL: InterVarsity, 2013), 241–47.

22. See e.g., Clyde Votaw, "The Gospels and Contemporary Biographies," *AJT* 19 (1915): 45–73, 217–49, reprint *The Gospels and Contemporary Biographies in the Graeco-Roman World*, introduction by J. Reumann (Philadelphia: Fortress, 1970); Philip Shuler, *A Genre for the Gospels: The Biographical Character of Matthew* (Philadelphia: Fortress, 1982); Charles A. Talbert, *What Is a Gospel? The Genre of the Canonical Gospels* (Philadelphia: Fortress, 1977); Talbert, "The Gospel and The Gospels," in *Interpreting the Gospels*, ed. James L. Mays (Philadelphia: Fortress, 1981), 14–26; Lawrence M. Wills, *The Quest of the Historical Gospel* (London: Routledge, 1997).

3. External features (mode of presentation, length, structure, scale, literary units)

4. Internal features (style, tone, quality, content, social setting, purpose)[23]

Burridge concludes that the similarity of all four Gospels to ancient biographies demonstrates that they should be viewed as a subgenre, βίοι Ἰησοῦ, that has affinities with βίοι of ancient philosophers. The differences between the four Gospels are not generic; all four Gospels resemble each other sufficiently to view them as of one genre. Mark represents the initial stage of the subgenre, with Matthew and Luke as a second stage adding infancy narratives and clearer structure. John with its emphasis on Jesus's discourses and dialogues may also be viewed as part of this second stage. Certain of the noncanonical "gospels" (e.g., the unpreserved "Jewish-Christian" gospels of the Nazarenes and the Ebionites) represent a third stage, while others that lack narrative (e.g., the *Gospel of Thomas*) represent another genre altogether.[24]

One may grant the impact of the OT narratives on the way the respective evangelists wrote their Gospels. It is also important to note the crucial role played by eyewitnesses and community **tradents** in passing on reliable testimony of Jesus's words and deeds. Yet as ancient *written* literature, the Gospels should be viewed as βίοι Ἰησοῦ. Others before Burridge argued for this view, and his refinement of the view has merited generally positive reviews. The biographical nature of the Gospels will be assumed in this handbook.

The Genre of Acts

Acts presents generic complexities that continue to divide scholarly opinion. The intentional pairing of Acts with Luke implies some sort of generic unity or at least compatibility of the two books. Their respective plots, points of view, and theological themes are closely related. Yet the books circulated separately, and each can be understood as a discrete composition in its own right. Some scholars have viewed Acts along with Luke as βίος, yet a greater number take it as a history or monograph.[25] Burridge acknowledges that Acts is similar to the

---

23. Burridge, *What Are the Gospels?*, 105–232.

24. Ibid., 240–47.

25. Craig Keener explores at some length various views of the genre of Acts, including travel narrative, biography, novel, and epic. He concludes that Acts is a work of ancient historiography. See *Acts: An Exegetical Commentary*, 4 vols. (Grand Rapids: Baker, 2012–15),

Gospels in certain ways, but also notes how Acts focuses on more than one individual and covers a wider scene.[26] On the other hand, it seems clear that the internal linkage of the two books renders any generic differences to secondary importance. Acts presents the sequential exploits of the followers of Jesus, the subject of the Third Gospel's βίος. Acts is a quasi-biography of the church, a corporate protagonist in literary terms. In a theological sense, Acts presents the ongoing βίος of Jesus, who from heaven sends the Spirit to empower his followers, just as the Father had empowered him at his baptism. As Luke's Gospel presented what Jesus empowered by the Spirit *began* to do and teach (Acts 1:1), so Luke's Acts presents what Jesus *continued* to do and teach through his Spirit-empowered followers, the church. "The conjunction of the Gospel and Acts in a single work does at least suggest a biographic emphasis in much of the larger historic project."[27]

Relating the Historical, Literary, and Theological Features of the Gospels and Acts

Scholars who view the Gospels as imaginative documents produced to meet the later church's needs rather than to transmit historically reliable Jesus traditions are featured from time to time in popular news accounts. Such scholars think the Gospel stories tend to reflect the situations and controversies of the post-A.D. 70 church rather than the historical Jesus. At the opposite end of the theological spectrum, conservative evangelicals have at times been reluctant to view the Gospels as theologically motivated, because of apologetic concerns over the historicity of the Gospel traditions. Evangelicals have rightly responded in defense of the historical reliability of the Gospels,[28] but stressing historicity alone may diminish the theological import of the Gospels.

Others have neglected the theological witness of the Gospels and derived theology from the epistles of the NT, especially those of Paul. This history vs. theology dichotomy is false, whether in a conservative de-theologizing context or in a liberal de-historicizing context. The Gospels narrate what really happened but do so for theological and pas-

---

1.51–89. David Aune took a similar view in *The New Testament in Its Literary Environment* (Philadelphia: Westminster, 1987), 77–11, 116–41.

26. Burridge, *What Are the Gospels?*, 237–39.

27. Keener, *Acts*, 1.61. For additional discussion on the genre of Acts as it relates to Hellenistic literature, see Todd C. Penner and Carolyn Vander Stichele, eds., *Contextualizing Acts: Lukan Narrative and Greco-Roman Discourse* (Atlanta: SBL, 2003); Thomas E. Phillips, "The Genre of Acts: Moving toward a Consensus," in *Acts within Diverse Frames of Reference* (Atlanta: Mercer, 2009), 46–77.

28. E.g., Blomberg, *The Historical Reliability of the Gospels*; Blomberg, *The Historical Reliability of John's Gospel* (Downers Grove, IL: InterVarsity, 2001).

toral reasons. According to Luke's prologue, Luke did careful research in order to ascertain the reliability of oral and written traditions so that Theophilus might be taught reliable truths about Jesus. If one may extrapolate from Luke to the Gospels in general, their procedure was to transmit the Jesus traditions they had received with a view to meeting the needs of the church, which included the historical basis of faith in Christ.

The Gospels are not comprehensive biographies or exhaustive histories of Jesus. A perusal of any Gospel synopsis or harmony dispels that notion. The Gospels are theological interpretations of selected traditions that the authors accepted as reliable accounts of historical events that occurred during the life and ministry of Jesus. Historical fidelity leads to the overall continuity in the Synoptic Gospels' accounts. Literary creativity and theological selectivity account for the differences between the accounts. If John 20:30–31 provides a model, the theological purposes of the evangelists guided their editing of tradition, leading to literary narratives, not historical chronicles. Their purpose was not to satisfy intellectual curiosity by compiling historical data but to disciple the church by bringing selected episodes from the life of Jesus to bear on the church's needs. The Gospels continue to teach the church today by narrating reliable words and deeds of Jesus. The Gospel authors faithfully present story as history and creatively interpret history as story.[29]

EMBEDDED GENRES

The narratives found in the Gospels and Acts contain examples of several other conventional genres. Such embedded genres (or subgenres) include parables, apocalyptic, discourses or speeches, psalms, wisdom, and letters. Before considering these embedded genres it is also appropriate to look into two other related matters that are basic to understanding the Gospels.[30]

Prosaic and Poetic Language

One of the most basic ways of speaking about language and discourse is to distinguish between prose and poetry or, more broadly, between prosaic and poetic language. Distinguishing between the two is not primarily a matter of whether there are formal features such as meter and rhyme. Theories vary, and the difference may not be hard and fast, but a key point is the extent to which vivid images occur. Such images are drawn from the physical world shared by the author and readers,

---

29. Samuel Byrskog, *Story as History—History as Story* (Tübingen: Mohr-Siebeck, 2000).

30. Chapter 2 will include discussion of form-critical categories (e.g., pronouncement stories, conflict stories, miracle stories) that describe Jesus-stories that circulated orally.

and influence readers to supplement their rational capacity with their imaginations. Aristotle thought that poetic imagery engaged common people and made learning more enjoyable to them (*Poetics* 4.1). Even the most bland, prosaic discourse will eventually use picturesque speech or figurative language to make a point. Commonly prose includes metaphorical language in which an abstract idea is compared to a concrete image. In many literary genres, including narrative, readers extend to authors the freedom to write with poetic license

For the most part, narratives in general and the Gospels in particular are written in expository, linear prose. Poetic "flashes," however, heighten the prose when the authors utilize word pictures, perhaps better described as picture-words. Students of the Gospels will do well to read with alertness and sensitivity to such poetic flourishes. The following surveys commonly encountered figures from the standpoint of the logic of the play between the words:

- Comparison: A *metaphor* describes one entity in terms of another (Matt. 5:14; 7:6; Mark 1:17; John 10:7, 11). A *simile* does so by using "like" or "as" (Matt. 3:16; Mark 6:34; Luke 11:44; John 15:6).
- Substitution: *Metonymy* describes an object by using something closely associated with it (Matt. 16:19; Luke 16:29). *Synechdoche* does so by substituting a part for the whole or *vice versa* (Matt. 6:21; 8:20; 16:17).
- Understatement: *Euphemism* uses subtle language for something that is harsh or profane (Luke 1:34; John 11:11). *Litotes* or *meiosis* uses a double negative to understate the corresponding positive idea (Acts 1:5; 20:12; 21:39; 27:14).
- Overstatement: *Hyperbole* speaks with intentional exaggeration to make the point strongly (Matt. 5:29; 7:3–5; 19:24; 23:24; John 21:25). *Personification* overstates the capacity of inanimate objects by attributing human characteristics to them (Matt. 6:24; 11:19; Luke 19:40). *Apostrophe* directly addresses such objects as if they were human (Matt. 23:37; Mark 11:14).
- Interrogation: *Rhetorical questions* are asked not to acquire answers but to invite the reader to join the discourse (Matt. 21:40; Mark 3:23; 8:37; Luke 15:4; John 11:9).
- Opaqueness: Occasionally writers or speakers intend to be mysterious or difficult to understand (Mark 4:11; John 6:52–65).
- Reversal: Through *irony* and *sarcasm* what is apparently meant turns out to be the opposite of what is really intended (Matt. 22:15–16; 23:32; 27:29; Mark 7:9).[31]

---

31. Thorough hermeneutics textbooks treat the distinction between prose and poetry. On biblical imagery see Leland Ryken, et al. eds., *Dictionary of Biblical Imagery* (Downers Grove,

Intertextuality

The OT is the seminal text for the NT. It is apparent from even a casual reading of the Gospels that they regularly refer to the OT in various ways in order to ground their narratives in the larger biblical metanarrative of the Bible. All four Gospels connect with the metanarrative in their first chapters. Apart from the history of Israel, with its covenants and prophetic promises, the Gospels would be unintelligible. Competence in working with the various ways the authors of the Gospels embed the OT in their narratives is essential.[32]

Richard Hays provides a simple yet helpful summary of the spectrum of the use of the OT in the Gospels, whether overt (quotations), implicit (allusions), or faint (echoes).[33] Quotations are often introduced by an introductory formula (e.g., "as it is written," or "in order that it might be fulfilled") and involve a complete OT clause. Allusions do not use introductory formulas and contain less of the OT, often just a phrase or an explicit reference to a key person, place, or event. Echoes are even less clear and therefore are more subjective and debatable. Echoes may involve subtleties of wording or phraseology that suggest analogies or other similarities between the OT and NT characters, contexts, or events.

Identifying intertextual references is a matter of reading the NT alertly with knowledge of the OT. English study Bibles will supply marginal notes that point to intertextual references in both the OT and NT. Both editions of the Greek NT commonly used in academic contexts, the United Bible Societies' edition and the Nestle-Aland edition, provide marginal notes as well as comprehensive tables of intertextual relationships. Beale writes helpfully on the basic issues and complexities involved in the NT use of the OT.[34] The following points summarize the nine-step method he suggests for studying this material:

IL: InterVarsity, 1998). The classic work of E. W. Bullinger, *Figures of Speech in the Bible*, was first published in 1898 and has been reprinted many times.

32. One way to determine the credibility of commentaries and other resources for the study of the Gospels is to examine the degree of their awareness and the skill of their treatment of intertextuality. An indispensable resource for this material is G. K. Beale and D. A. Carson, eds., *Commentary on the New Testamant Use of the Old Testament* (Grand Rapids: Baker, 2007).

33. Richard B. Hays, *Echoes of Scripture in the Gospels* (Waco, TX: Baylor University Press, 2016), 10–13. In this work Hays explains and advocates a "figural reading" of the OT in light of the gospel of Jesus. This approach is sometimes described as reading the Bible backwards to discern how the OT narrative, with its characters, institutions, and events, anticipates or prefigures the NT. The approach appears to be similar to what has traditionally been called typological hermeneutics.

34. G. K. Beale, *Handbook on the New Testament Use of the Old Testament: Exegesis and Interpretation* (Grand Rapids: Baker, 2013), 1–40.

- Identify the OT passage and determine whether it is a quotation or allusion.
- Analyze the broad NT context in which the OT reference occurs, as well as the broad and immediate context of the OT reference itself.
- Survey how the OT text was understood in Second Temple and later Jewish writings and compare that to the NT use.
- Carefully note the textual differences, including variant readings, between all the examples of the OT reference in the Greek NT, the Hebrew Masoretic text, the LXX, the DSS, the Targums, and the ancient Jewish literature.
- Analyze the text form used by the NT author and why it likely was chosen, as well as the NT author's hermeneutical approach to the OT, the theological point being made, and the way in which the usage functions rhetorically.[35]

Parables

Parables are perhaps the most familiar of the genres embedded in the Gospels. Aristotle described parables as realistic fictional comparisons, as opposed to fables, which he viewed as unrealistic or impossible (*Rhetoric* 2.20). Typically defined in literary terms as extended metaphors, they have been aptly described in countless Sunday schools as "earthly stories with heavenly meanings." Snodgrass's term "stories with intent" is succinct and helpful."[36] The two parts of the definitions above imply two basic qualities of parables—as *earthly* stories they are *realistic* and as stories intended to convey *heavenly* meaning they are *symbolic*. Parables vary in length, but even the shorter ones imply a comparative story or narrative that furthers the author's purpose. In the OT one encounters parabolic texts occasionally; Isaiah's song of the vineyard is used by Jesus as a springboard for the parable of the wicked tenant farmers (Isa. 5:1–2/Matt. 21:33; cf. Judg. 9:7–15; 2 Sam. 12:1–4; 2 Kgs. 14:9; Isa. 28:23–29; Ezek. 19:1–14; 31:2–9). The word *mashal* (מָשָׁל) is commonly used for riddles and proverbs; less frequently it introduces a parabolic text (e.g., Ezek. 17:2–8). Rabbinical writings from times after the NT also commonly use parables to explain the Torah and to teach wisdom.[37]

---

35. Beale, *Handbook*, 41–54, 133–48.

36. Klyne R. Snodgrass, *Stories with Intent: A Comprehensive Guide to the Parables of Jesus* (Grand Rapids: Eerdmans, 2008).

37. See e.g., Gary Porton, "The Parable in the Hebrew Bible and in Rabbinic Literature," in *The Historical Jesus in Context,* eds. Amy-Jill Levine, et al. (Princeton, NJ: Princeton University Press, 2006), 206–21; Brad H. Young, *Jesus and His Jewish Parables* (Mahwah, NJ: Paulist Press, 1989), 55–128.

In the Gospels, Jesus frequently used parables to explain various aspects of the kingdom of God. The word παραβολή occurs forty-six times in the Gospels, usually referring to Jesus's parabolic teaching.[38] His parables are not always explicitly called parables in their immediate contexts (e.g., Matt. 11:16; 18:12; 20:16; 21:28; 25:1, 14). Parables are often introduced with the formula "the kingdom is like . . . ."[39] Parables are fictional, yet apart from occasional hyperboles they are true to the life of first-century Israel. Blomberg has shown that the distinction attempted by some biblical scholars to distinguish rigidly between parables and allegories is misguided.[40] As will be seen below, the question of genre is crucial for interpretation.

Depending on how a few difficult texts are understood, there are around thirty parables in the Gospels. They are listed below based on where they occur:

- *Parables of the Triple Tradition* (4)
    1. The Sower (Matt. 13:3–23; Mark 4:1–20; Luke 8:5–15; cf. *Gos. Thom.* 9)
    2. The Mustard Seed (Matt. 13:31–32; Mark 4:30–32; Luke 13:18–19; cf. *Gos. Thom.* 20)
    3. The Wicked Tenants (Matt. 21:33–46; Mark 12:1–11; Luke 20:9–18; cf. *Gos. Thom.* 65)
    4. The Budding Fig Tree (Matt. 24:32–36; Mark 13:28–32; Luke 21:29–33)

- *Parables of Matthew and Luke* (6)
    5. The Children in the Market (Matt. 11:16–17; Luke 7:31–32)
    6. The Leaven (Matt. 13:33; Luke 13:20–21; cf. *Gos. Thom.* 96)
    7. The Lost Sheep (Matt. 18:12–14; Luke 15:3–7; *Gos. Thom.* 107)
    8. The Wedding Feast (Matt. 22:1–14; Luke 14:15–24; cf. *Gos. Thom.* 64)
    9. The Head of the House and the Thief (Matt. 24:43; Luke 12:39; cf. *Gos. Thom.* 21, 103)
    10. The Steward (Matt. 24:45–51; Luke 12:42–48)

---

38. At times παραβολή has a different nuance, as in Luke 4:23. Cf. Heb. 9:9; 11:19.

39. See Matt. 13:24, 31, 33, 44, 45, 47, 52; 18:23; 20:1; 22:2; 25:1; Mark 4:30; Luke 13:18, 20. Cf. other " . . . is like . . ." parabolic formulas in Matt. 7:24, 26; 11:16–17; Luke 7:31–32; 12:36.

40. Craig S. Blomberg, *Interpreting the Parables,* 2nd ed. (Downers Grove, IL: InterVarsity, 2012), 33–81; Leland Ryken, *How to Read the Bible as Literature* (Grand Rapids: Zondervan, 1984), 145–50, 199–203.

- *Parables of Matthew Alone* (9)
  11. The Wheat and the Tares (Matt. 13:24–30; cf. *Gos. Thom.* 57)
  12. The Hidden Treasure (Matt. 13:44; cf. *Gos. Thom.* 109)
  13. The Pearl (Matt. 13:45–46; cf. *Gos. Thom.* 76)
  14. The Net (Matt. 13:47–50; cf. *Gos. Thom.* 8)
  15. The Unmerciful Servant (Matt. 18:23–35)
  16. The Laborers in the Vineyard (Matt. 20:1–16)
  17. The Two Sons (Matt. 21:28–31)
  18. The Ten Virgins (Matt. 25:1–12)
  19. The Talents (Matt. 25:14–30)

- *Parables of Luke Alone* (8)
  20. The Two Debtors (Luke 7:41–42)
  21. The Good Samaritan (Luke 10:30–37)
  22. The Rich Fool (Luke 12:16–21; cf. *Gos. Thom.* 63)
  23. The Alert Slaves (Luke 12:36–38)
  24. The Lost Coin (Luke 15:8–10)
  25. The Prodigal Son (Luke 15:11–32)
  26. The Unjust Steward (Luke 16:1–8)
  27. The Rich Man and Lazarus (Luke 16:19–31)

- *Parables of Mark Alone* (2)
  28. The Quickly Growing Seed (Mark 4:26–29)
  29. The Master's Journey (Mark 13:34–36)

- *Parables of John Alone*[41]
  30. The Good Shepherd (John 10:1–5)
  31. The Vine and the Branches (John 15:1–6)
  32. The Woman in Labor (John 16:21)

When it comes to interpreting parables, the history of the church is instructive.[42] In the early church, parables were often interpreted in an atomized fashion, with each detail understood spiritually with inadequate attention to the context. A commonly cited example of this tendency is Augustine's exegesis of the Parable of the Good Samaritan in Luke 10:25–37. Ignoring the contextual setting of the parable as

---

41. Scholars debate to what degree παροιμία in John (10:6; 16:25, 29; cf. 2 Peter 2:22) overlaps with παραβολή in the synoptics, and whether John's figurative stories are to be linked with the synoptic parables. Other texts in John that arguably might be included in the list above include 3:8, 29; 4:35–38; 8:35; 11:9–10; 12:24.

42. See especially Warren S. Kissinger, *The Parables of Jesus: A History of Interpretation and Bibliography* (Metuchen, NJ: Scarecrow/ATLA, 1979).

Jesus's answer to a self-aggrandizing lawyer (Luke 10:24–29, 36–37), Augustine understood the parable as an extended metaphor of redemptive history, with Adam falling from celestial glory into the clutches of the devil and his angels, who strip him of his immortality. The religion of the OT cannot help Adam, but Jesus comes along, binds up Adam's sin-induced wounds, pours baptismal grace on him, exhorts him to spiritual fervency, seats him on faith in the incarnation, and ultimately brings him to Paul and the church for safekeeping until he returns.[43]

Three Ways of Interpreting Parables

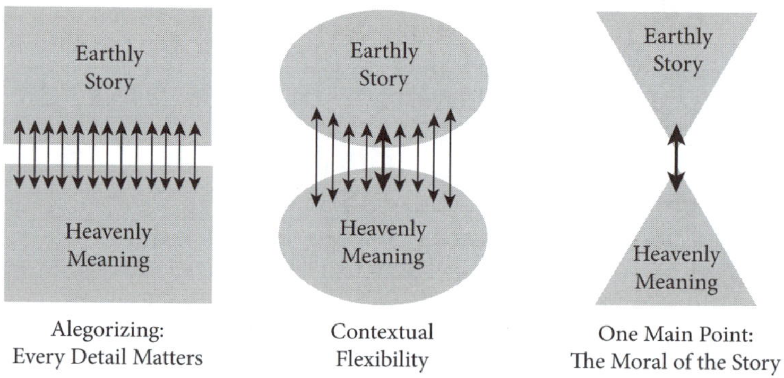

Around the turn of the twentieth century Adolf Jülicher (1857–1938) took a diametrically opposite view, arguing for a position that is still commonly held today, that parables were intended to convey only one main point that was embodied in a single central correspondence between the parable and the kingdom.[44] Yet context renders this view dubious just as it did the atomizing interpretations commonly found in the early church. While the Gospels do not contain Jesus's interpretation for many of his parables, some are interpreted by him with attention to detail (e.g., Matt. 13:36–43, 49–50 and parallels) and others with a simple generalizing conclusion (e.g., Matt. 24:33, 42, 44; 25:13). These differing contextual indicators show that the interpretation of parables must be sensitive to the context and be open to a spectrum of correspondences ranging from one "big idea" or "moral" to multiple correspondences between the story and kingdom realities, as illustrated below.

---

43.   Augustine, *Quaest. ev.* 2.19; *Serm.* 69.7; 81.6

44.   Adolf Jülicher, *Die Gleichnisreden Jesu* 2 vols. (Tübingen: Mohr Siebeck, 1888, 1899).

Apocalyptic

Describing apocalyptic. The term "apocalyptic" comes from Greek lexemes referring to the unveiling or disclosure of divine secrets, often pertaining to the future.[45] The term "apocalypticism" describes a worldview that is focused on such disclosure. The worldview thrives when God's people are oppressed and have no human relief in sight. Prophetic admonition has been rejected and reform seems impossible. In such a dualistic view of history, hope is focused solely on God's promise to some day reward the faithful and punish their oppressors in cataclysmic fashion. A great deal of literature, both canonical and noncanonical, portrays this worldview. Frequently, such literature reveals the future through symbolic dreams or visions experienced by one of the faithful. Often the seer is confused by the revelation, but God sends an angel to explain the meaning. In the Bible, apocalyptic is most clearly seen in Daniel and in Revelation, which describes itself as an apocalypse (Ἀποκάλυψις Ἰησοῦ Χριστοῦ; Rev. 1:1). These biblical books are similar to many outside the canon, such as *1, 2, and 3 Enoch, 2 Esdras (4 Ezra), 2 Baruch, Testament of Levi,* and various other apocalypses attributed to biblical figures.[46]

There is an ongoing debate over the relationship between prophecy and apocalyptic. Broadly speaking, the biblical prophets confronted Israel about its disobedience to the law of Moses after they received verbal oracles from God. The same prophets occasionally also received apocalyptic visions that dealt not with present ethical reform but with ultimate judgment and renewal (e.g., Isa. 24–27, 34–35; Ezek. 38–48; Hag. 2:1–9; Zech. 1–6). Apocalyptic visions in the biblical prophets are one of the ways the divine message was conveyed to God's people. In other words, apocalyptic is one of several ways that prophecy was conveyed.[47] Daniel, whose visions are apocalyptic in nature, is called a prophet by Jesus (Matt. 24:15). The author of the NT book

---

45. The verb ἀποκαλύπτω occurs twenty-six times in the NT. The noun ἀποκάλυψις occurs eighteen times. Both words refer at times to revelation in a more general or non-eschatological sense (Matt. 11:25, 27; Luke 2:32; Eph. 1:17). At other times both describe an end-time revelation of God in which Jesus as Son of Man brings reversal to the earth (Luke 17:30; 2 Thess. 1:7; cf. Dan. 7:13), blessing the oppressed people of God and humbling their enemies (Rev. 1:1).

46. A standard collection of such books, along with those broadly categorized as apocrypha, is James H. Charlesworth, ed., *The Old Testament Pseudepigrapha,* 2 vols. (Garden City, NY: Doubleday, 1983). This helpful work contains introductions, annotations, and English translations of the material by numerous specialists.

47. Years ago George Ladd spoke to the question of the relationship of prophecy to apocalyptic, and his ideas are still helpful. See "Why Not Prophetic–Apocalyptic," *JBL* 76 (1957): 192–200.

of Revelation first calls it an apocalypse (1:1) and then speaks of it in terms of prophecy afterward (1:3; 10:11; 22:7, 9–10, 18–19).

There are embedded sections of the NT that exhibit *some* of the characteristics of apocalyptic that are found in books that are otherwise of a different genre. Passages in Paul such as 1 Thessalonians 4–5, 2 Thessalonians 2, and 1 Corinthians 15:50–57 are examples of embedded apocalyptic. In the Gospels, one can point to the quotations in Mark 1:2–3 of Malachi and Isaiah regarding the restoration of Israel in preparation for the coming one as mildly apocalyptic. John the Baptist's explicit warnings of fiery judgment on sinners are apocalyptically oriented (Matt. 3:7–12; Luke 3:9), as is Jesus's interpretation of parable of the wheat and tares (Matt. 13:37–43). The most obvious apocalyptic passage in the Gospels is Jesus's Olivet or eschatological discourse, found in Matthew 24–25, Mark 13, and Luke 21. The basic content of this discourse appears below in synopsis form.

Segment Synopsis of the Olivet Discourse			
Content	**Matthew**	**Mark**	**Luke**
1. Setting: Jesus leaves the temple.	24:1–3	13:1–4	21:5–7
2. Beginning of birth pains: coming wars, persecution, apostasy, require perseverance.	24:4–14	13:5–13	21:8–19
3. Abomination of desolation: temple sacrilege signals great tribulation.	24:15–28	13:14–23	21:20–24
4. Coming of the Son of Man: cosmic signs accompany the gathering of the elect.	24:29–31	13:24–27	21:25–27
5. Lesson of the fig tree: signs precede the coming of the Son of Man.	24:32–41	13:28–32	21:28–33
6. Thief in the night: the necessity of alertness.	24:42–44	13:33–37	21:34–36
7. Parable of the servant: be ready to meet the master sooner than expected.	24:45–51		
8. Parable of ten virgins: the bridegroom may delay his arrival.	25:1–13		
9. Parable of the talents: faithful stewardship of the master's resources	25:14–30		
10. Judgment of the nations: compassionate treatment of Jesus's little brothers and sisters	25:31–46		

Understanding the genre of apocalyptic literature is essential for its interpretation. This literature is intended to provide hope for the persecuted people of God, not a timetable of future events for curious speculators. Interpreting apocalyptic requires familiarity with the ancient agrarian world of the Bible, because that world—not the modern technological world—is the source of the symbols encountered. Self-awareness is also crucial, because one's view of difficult apocalyptic texts will unavoidably be influenced by one's prior view of eschatology.[48] When it comes to Jesus's eschatological discourse in Matthew 24–25, Mark 13, and Luke 21, one should note that its impetus was the disciples' concern about the future of the temple because of Jesus's ominous prophecy (Matt. 23:27–39; 24:2; Mark 13:2; Luke 21:6). Whatever one believes about this passage's teaching about yet-future events, Jesus was speaking about events that would come in the near future—the temple was destroyed by the Romans in A.D. 70. The question is whether the events of A.D. 70 complete the prophecy.[49]

Wisdom

Definitions of biblical wisdom tend to agree that wisdom is practical intelligence enabling skillful navigation of the complexities of life in a fallen world. Yet wisdom is difficult to classify formally as a *literary* genre. The OT books generally classified as "wisdom books" are quite different, ranging from the compressed pithiness of Proverbs to the gritty realism of Ecclesiastes to the complicated narrative of Job, whose battered protagonist asks in his response to Bildad:

> But where can wisdom be found?
>> Where does understanding dwell?
> No mortal comprehends its worth;
>> it cannot be found in the land of the living.
> (Job 28:12–13, NIV)

After explaining that wisdom *cannot* be found on earth, Job points to its one and only source:

> God understands the way to it
> and he alone knows where it dwells. (Job 28:23, NIV)

---

48. For a thorough discussion of the genre and interpretation of apocalyptic, see C. Marvin Pate, *Interpreting Revelation and Other Apocalyptic Literature* (Grand Rapids: Kregel, 2016).

49. I have summarized various views of the future in Matthew 24 and argued for an approach that understands the A.D. 70 destruction of the temple as prefiguring an ultimate time of tribulation in *Matthew*, Baker Commentary on the New Testament (Grand Rapids, Baker, 2008), 565–611.

Despite the pessimism found near the beginning of Ecclesiastes,

> I applied my mind to study and to explore by wisdom all that is
> done under the heavens. What a heavy burden God has laid on
> mankind! I have seen all the things that are done under the sun; all
> of them are meaningless, a chasing after the wind. (1:13–14, NIV)

at the end of the book the Teacher counsels his readers,

> Now all has been heard;
> here is the conclusion of the matter:
>   Fear God and keep his commandments,
>   for this is the duty of all mankind.
>   For God will bring every deed into judgment,
>   including every hidden thing,
>   whether it is good or evil.
>   (12:13–14, NIV)

Early in the book of Proverbs an antithetical poetic strophe bluntly
states the two alternatives regarding wisdom:

> The fear of the LORD is the beginning of knowledge,
>   but fools despise wisdom and instruction. (Prov. 1:7,
>   NIV)

It seems then that wisdom is more of a God-centered mindset than a
formal type of book, and that books of whatever sort that focus on this
elusive mindset are "wisdom books."

In the Gospels, Jesus grows in wisdom as a youth (Luke 2:40, 52),
and later during his ministry he contrasts proud human "wisdom" with
humble reception of his kingdom (Matt. 11:25). Later Paul and James
alike affirm a similar contrast between what seems wise to humans (cf.
Prov. 14:12) and what is truly wise in God's sight (1 Cor. 1:18–31;
Jas. 1:5; 3:13–18). Paul's comment that wisdom is centered in Jesus (1
Cor. 1:24) is based in the teaching of Jesus. Jesus's fellow residents of
Nazareth cannot understand how he got his wisdom (Matt. 13:54; Mark
6:2; Luke 4:22), a wisdom that Jesus describes as being greater than the
legendary wisdom of Solomon (Matt. 12:42; Luke 11:31). The identification of Jesus and God's wisdom is strikingly shown when one compares Jesus's words in Matthew, "I am sending you prophets" (23:34)
with their parallel in Luke "the wisdom of God said, 'I will send you
prophets'" (11:49). Of course, in Matthew's version of this text Jesus
speaks not only of sending prophets but also of sending wise people,
showing that his wisdom is carried on by his followers (cf. Luke 21:15).

The Gospel texts that most clearly tie into the OT wisdom tradition are the proverbial or aphoristic sayings of Jesus. As a literary form, proverbs are the distillation of many experiences into a few words. Such sayings induce wisdom because they succinctly present lessons from the wise observation of life. The following are among the proverbial statements of Jesus, whose wisdom is greater than that of Solomon:

- "People cannot serve two masters,
    for they will either hate the one and love the other,
    or they will be loyal to the one and despise the other.
  You cannot serve both God and money." (Matt. 6:24, author's trans.)

- "Therefore do not worry about tomorrow,
    for tomorrow will worry about itself.
  Each day has enough trouble of its own." (Matt. 6:34, NIV)

- "Do not give dogs what is sacred;
    do not throw your pearls to pigs.
  If you do, they may trample them under their feet,
    and turn and tear you to pieces." (Matt. 7:6, NIV)

The above texts are examples of proverbial wisdom couched in metaphor, personification, and poetic parallelism (cf. Matt. 12:33; 15:14; 19:24). The examples below are shorter and more prosaic.

- "If a house is divided against itself, that house cannot stand." (Matt. 12:25; Mark 3:25; Luke 11:17)
- "Do to others as you would have them do to you." (Matt. 7:9; Luke 6:31, NIV)
- "No prophet is accepted in his hometown." (Matt. 13:57; Mark 6:4; Luke 4:24)
- "One sows and another reaps." (John 4:37)

An aphorism of Jesus that continues to puzzle is found in both Matthew and Luke. From the standpoint of tradition history it is not clear whether these are two accounts of the same historical saying or two separate though similar sayings:

- ἐδικαιώθη ἡ σοφία ἀπὸ τῶν ἔργων αὐτῆς. (Matt. 11:19)
- καὶ ἐδικαιώθη ἡ σοφία ἀπὸ πάντων τῶν τέκνων αὐτῆς. (Luke 7:35).

In both contexts Jesus has been speaking about the rejection of both John's and his own kingdom ministries. In Luke's version wisdom is vindicated[50] by her own children, evidently the converts mentioned in 7:29, in contrast to the children in the mini-parable of 7:32 (explained in 7:33–34) who would not cry when John sang a dirge or dance when Jesus played the flute. Matthew's version is more enigmatic in that wisdom is said to be vindicated by its works (ἀπὸ τῶν ἔργων αὐτῆς). Matthew may refer to the ultimate vindication of Jesus, whose wisdom is validated by the results he produces (cf. 11:2, τὰ ἔργα τοῦ Χριστοῦ).[51]

Speeches

As will be discussed below, the teachings of Jesus are occasionally presented in lengthy discourses in the synoptics. Although the Gospel of John frequently presents Jesus's teaching in dialogues, occasionally more lengthy teachings are found (John 5:19–47; 14–17).

In common with other ancient historiographical works, the book of Acts emphasizes the speeches of its major characters. Speeches comprise roughly one-third of the content of Acts. The major speeches in Acts are the following:

- Acts 2:14–40   Peter to the Pentecost pilgrims in Jerusalem
- Acts 7:1–60   Stephen to the council in Jerusalem
- Acts 10:28–48   Peter to the household of Cornelius in Caesarea
- Acts 13:16–41   Paul to the synagogue in Antioch of Pisidia
- Acts 15:13–21   James to the church leaders in Jerusalem
- Acts 17:22–34   Paul to the philosophers on Mars Hill in Athens
- Acts 20:18–35   Paul to the Ephesian church elders at Miletus
- Acts 22:1–21   Paul to the crowd at the temple
- Acts 23:1–10   Paul to the council in Jerusalem
- Acts 24:1–9   Tertullus accuses Paul before Felix in Caesarea
- Acts 24:10–22   Paul before Felix in Caesarea
- Acts 26:1–29   Paul before Festus and Agrippa in Caesarea

Citing ancient sources, Keener identifies the basic outline or components of ancient Hellenistic speeches as prologue, narrative, proof, and epilogue.[52] One may find these elements in the above speeches.

---

50. The aorist verb ἐδικαιώθη occurs in both versions. Evidently it should be taken in a gnomic or timeless sense, one that fits a proverbial saying.

51. See further on Jesus and wisdom Alan P. Winton, *The Proverbs of Jesus* (Sheffield: JSOT, 1990); Ben Witherington III, *Jesus the Sage* (Minneapolis: Fortress, 1994).

52. Keener, *Acts*, 1.263–64.

The speeches in Acts can be categorized in terms of their audiences and purposes. The evangelistic speeches by Peter and Paul vary based on their audiences' ethnicity and background. Such speeches to Jewish audiences seek to demonstrate through biblical quotations and allusions how Jesus is linked to the history of Israel. One of Paul's speeches is pastoral (Acts 20); his later speeches are legal defenses of his ministry. The harsh tone of Stephen's indictment speech in Acts 7 and its tragic outcome anticipate the opposition later experienced by Paul. All in all, the speeches in Acts should be viewed in the context of ancient persuasive rhetoric. Their content involves historical events presented with literary creativity for theological purposes. They provide insight into the theological point of view that informs the narrative. The fact that several of them are depicted as being interrupted before they conclude indicates their pivotal role in the volatile world depicted in Acts.[53]

Psalms

Psalms are found in the Gospels and Acts as quotations from the OT psalms and as songs of praise embedded or inset in the Gospel narratives. Both uses of psalms occur somewhat regularly, requiring the student of the Gospels to be familiar with the features of Hebrew poetry, especially its parallelism.[54] The way the Psalms were used in Israel's worship is another key feature in understanding their use in the NT.[55]

As displayed below, there are nearly forty quotations of the Psalms in the Gospels and Acts.[56] Acts contains the most quotations (11), followed by Matthew (9), Luke and John (7 each), and Mark (5). The most frequently quoted is Psalm 118. As would be expected, nearly all the quotations are applied to Jesus, especially to his Davidic roots, his crucifixion, and his resurrection. Jesus is depicted as quoting the Psalms around a dozen times. He finds Judas in Psalm 41 (John 13:18), as does Peter in Psalms 69 and 108 (Acts 1:20). Remarkably, the devil is portrayed as quoting Psalm 91 in Matthew's and Luke's narratives of Jesus's temptation.

---

53. For a succinct summary of the nature and role of the speeches in Acts, see Darrell Bock, *Acts* (Grand Rapids: Baker, 2007). Keener discusses the relation of the speeches in Acts to other ancient speeches at some length (*Acts,* 1.258–319).

54. C. F. Burney, *The Poetry of Our Lord* (Reprinted, Eugene, OR: Wipf and Stock, 2008). The book was originally published in 1925.

55. For a thorough approach to interpreting the Psalms, see Mark D. Futato, *Interpreting the Psalms* (Grand Rapids: Kregel, 2007).

56. This number and the table above are based on the "Index of Quotations" found in the UBS⁵ Greek NT, 858–59. The Psalms chapter numbers come from the English Bible.

Quotations of the Old Testament Psalms in the Gospels and Acts		
Psalm	**Gospel/Acts Passage**	**Content**
2:1–2	Acts 4:25–26	Rulers are gathered together against the Lord's anointed.
2:7	Acts 13:33	God endorses his son.
8:2	Matt. 21:16	God ordains praise from infants.
16:8–11	Acts 2:25–28, 31	God's holy one will not undergo decay.
16:10 LXX	Acts 13:35	God's holy one will not undergo decay.
22:1	Matt. 27:46 Mark 15:34	Why have you forsaken me?
22:18	John 19:34	Casting lots for Jesus's garments.
31:5	Luke 23:46	Into your hands I commit my spirit.
35:19; 69:4	John 15:25	They hated me without a cause.
41:9	John 13:18	He who eats my bread lifts his foot up against me.
69:9	John 2:17	Zeal for your house consumes me.
69:25	Acts 1:20	Let his home be desolate.
78:2	Matt. 13:35	Parables and things long hidden.
78:24	John 6:31	He gave them bread from heaven to eat.
82:6	John 10:34	I said, "You are gods."
89:20	Acts 13:22	David the servant of God.
91:11–12	Matt. 4:6 Luke 4:10–11	Angels will guard and prevent striking a foot on a stone.

Quotations of the Old Testament Psalms in the Gospels and Acts		
Psalm	**Gospel/Acts Passage**	**Content**
109:8	Acts 1:20	Let another man take his office.
110:1	Matt. 22:44; 26:64 Mark 12:36; 14:62 Luke 20:42–43; 22:69 Acts 2:34–35	The LORD says to my Lord, "sit at my right hand."
118:22	Luke 20:17 Acts 4:11	The rejected stone becomes the cornerstone.
118:22–23	Matt. 21:42 Mark 12:10–11	The rejected stone becomes the cornerstone.
118:25–26	Matt. 21:9 Mark 11:9–10 John 12:13	Hosanna to the one who comes in the name of the Lord.
118:26	Matt. 23:39 Luke 13:35; 19:38	Blessed is the one who comes in the name of the Lord.
132:11	Acts 2:30	One of his descendants will be set on his throne.

Psalms also appear in the Gospels and Acts in the form of songs by people in the narrative. Such psalms are seen in the OT as well, in texts such as Moses's songs (cf. Rev. 15:3) of the sea (Exod. 15:1–21) and of Israel's history (Deut. 32:1–43), Deborah's song (Judg. 5:1–31), and Hannah's song, which seems to be the model for Mary's *Magnificat* (1 Sam. 2:1–10; Luke 1:46–57).[57] It seems that the inset songs in the Apocalypse are also instances of this literary technique.[58] As shown below, Luke skillfully embeds four songs into his infancy narrative (Luke 1–2). The songs apparently function theologically to make explicit what is implicit in the narrative—God is faithfully fulfilling his promises to Israel.

---

57. James W. Watts, *Psalm and Story: Inset Hymns in Hebrew Narrative* (Sheffield: Sheffield Academic, 1992). Watts also discusses inset songs in 2 Samuel 22, Isaiah 38:9–20, Jonah 2:3–10, Daniel 2:20–23, and 1 Chronicles 16:8–36. His study closes with historical, literary, and methodological conclusions.

58. E.g., Revelation 4:8, 11; 5:9–10, 12, 13; 15:3–4.

Narrative Inset Psalmody in Luke 1–2

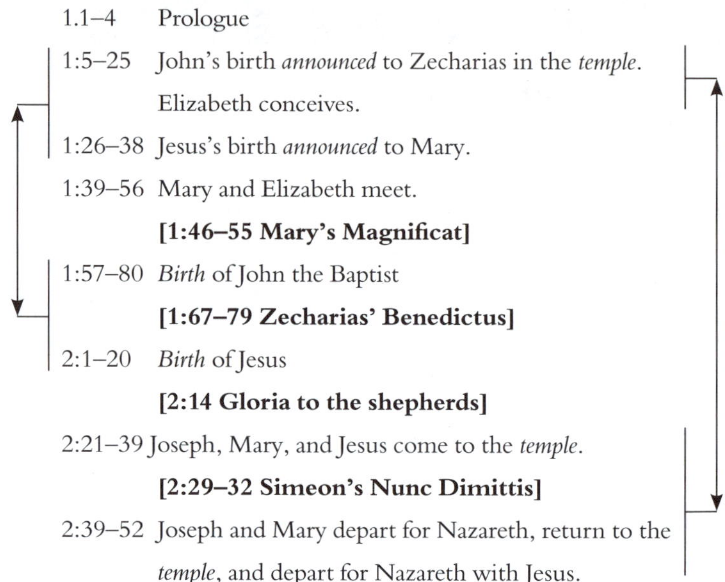

Letters

One typically would not think of letters playing a role in the Gospels and Acts, but there are three references to letters in Acts. According to 9:2, Paul sought letters from the high priest in Jerusalem to the synagogues of Damascus to authorize persecution of Jewish followers of Jesus. There are also two actual letters in Acts, one from the Jerusalem church leaders to recent Gentile converts (Acts 15:22–30), and another from Claudias Lysias, the Roman commander in Jerusalem, to Felix the governor in Caesarea (Acts 23:26–30). The Acts 15 letter is relevant for understanding the process of assimilation of Gentiles into the early church and Pauline theology. The Acts 23 letter is a window into the power struggles of the Romans and the Jewish leaders of the province of Judea. Exegetical commentaries on Acts will introduce these issues in more depth. The typical structure and function of Hellenistic letters is well known and has been discussed by other volumes in this series.[59] A structural analysis of these two letters follows:

---

59.   Herbert W. Bateman IV, *Interpreting the General Letters* (Grand Rapids: Kregel, 2013), 19–56; John W. Harvey, *Interpreting the Pauline Letters* (Grand Rapids: Kregel, 2012), 21–44.

Two Hellenistic Letters in Acts		
Letter Structure	**Acts 15:22–29**	**Acts 23:26–30**
Opening (author, recipients, greetings)	15:23—χαίρειν, the greeting used here and in Acts 23:26, is also found in James 1:1.	23:26
Body (opening, middle, ending)	15:24–29—The opening identifies the occasion of the letter as unauthorized "Judaizing" of Gentile converts (cf. Acts 15:1–5). The rest of the body describes the Spirit-led solution to the matter.	23:27–30—The letter acknowledges that Paul as a Roman citizen deserves protection from a murder plot caused by a Jewish legal disagreement. It also mentions the likelihood of further accusations against Paul in Caesarea.
Closing (Final comments, greetings, benediction)	At the end of 15:29, the word Ἔρρωσθε ends the letter as a farewell wish.	This abrupt letter likely had no closing, although some ancient manuscripts include the closing Ἔρρωσθε or Ἔρρωσο the end of 23:30.

NARRATIVE GENRE AND THE INDIVIDUAL FEATURES OF THE GOSPELS AND ACTS

Burridge points out that the opening of a literary work contains the initial features (e.g., title, opening words, prologue or preface) that get the reader's attention and begin to convey the genre of the work. Additional features such as the topics chosen and how they are structured contribute to the reader's process of construing (decoding) the author's intended (encoded) genre and meaning.[60] In this section, we survey the openings, structure, and content of the Gospels and Acts in order to gain heuristic insight into their distinct ways of telling the story of Jesus.

Mark

Mark begins by describing his project as the beginning of the gospel of Jesus Christ (1:1). Mark's mention of the name of his protagonist,

---

60. Burridge, *What Are the Gospels?* 107–9, 115.

Jesus, is in keeping with the openings of many Greco-Roman βίοι.[61] The word "gospel" is not a title referring to the genre of his book[62] but rather to its contents: the book is about the good news centering in Jesus Christ, which more likely speaks of the good news *about* him than of the good news he preached.[63] This good news is immediately validated and contextualized by its linkage to a composite prophetic text (Mal. 3:1; Isa. 40:30; cf. Exod. 23:20) about a messenger who would prepare the way of the Lord in the wilderness. This messenger is abruptly introduced (asyndeton) in 1:4 as John the Baptist. John's ministry in 1:4–8 is the gospel-beginning spoken of in 1:1, and 1:14–15 forms an inclusio when John's imprisonment leads to Jesus beginning to preach the gospel of God. Taken as a whole then, Mark's opening portrays John's ministry as the beginning of the prophesied good news about Jesus. This good news entails a sort of new exodus that restores the historic people of God to his favor by repentance and baptism. Judging from this opening, one would expect Mark's composition to show how Jesus accomplishes the restorative agenda of the biblical prophets.[64]

After a rather abrupt opening, Mark's narrative proceeds to emphasize the works of Jesus more than his words. This focus on action leads to the near-absence (see the eschatological discourse in Mark 13) of teaching discourses. Mark's focus on action is often triggered by the adverb εὐθύς,[65] commonly translated "immediately," which summons the reader's attention to a new episode or a surprising turn of events. Mark is oriented to geography,[66] with Jesus's Galilean ministry (1:14–9:50) concluding with a trip to Judea east of the Jordan (10:1–31), leading to entering Jerusalem and the events of the passion week (11:1–16:8). The pivotal point of the entire Gospel is 8:27–38, where at Caesarea Philippi near the end of the Galilean ministry, Jesus asks his disciples two ques-

---

61.   Burridge, *What re the Gospels?* 129–30, 189.

62.   The four Gospeis were first described by the term εὐαγγέλιον in the middle of the second century of the common era. See BDAG, s.v. εὐαγγέλιον, #3; R. H. Gundry, "Εὐαγγέλιον: How Soon a Book?" *JBL* 115 (1996): 321–25.

63.   Despite 1:14, Mark emphasizes the works of Jesus more than his words, so the genitives in the phrase Ἀρχὴ τοῦ εὐαγγελίου Ἰησοῦ Χριστοῦ should be understood respectively as subjective and objective: the good news about Jesus Christ began (1:1) just as Malachi and Isaiah indicated it would with a wilderness messenger (1:2–3) who turned out to be John the Baptist (1:4–8). See further R. H. Gundry, *Mark: A Commentary on His Apology for the Cross* (Grand Rapids: Eerdmans, 1993), 31–32.

64.   See further Rikk E. Watts, "Mark," in *Commentary on the New Testament Use of the Old Testament*, 111–20.

65.   See 1:10, 12, 18, 20, 21, 23, 28, 29, 42; 2:8, 12; 3:6; 4:5, 15, 29; 5:2, 29, 42; 6:25, 27, 45, 50, 54; 7:25; 8:10; 9:15, 20, 24; 10:52; 11:12; 14:43, 45, 72; 15:1.

66.   See e.g., 1:9, 14, 28, 39; 3:7–8; 4:35; 5:1, 20, 21; 6:21, 45, 53; 7:24, 31; 8:10, 13, 27; 9:30; 10:1, 32–33, 46; 11:1, 11, 15, 27; 14:3, 26, 28, 32; 16:7.

tions about his identity. The first concerns who people think Jesus is, and the second who the disciples themselves think he is. The disciples' response to the first question shows that Jesus was generally perceived to be a prophetic figure. Peter's response to the second question is direct and simple: "You are the Messiah." At this point, Jesus for the first time plainly tells the disciples that he will be rejected and killed by Israel's leaders, but will rise again.[67] He responds caustically to Peter's objection to this new teaching, telling the disciples that they as well as he must take up the cross if they are to expect eschatological reward from God. This teaching leads to the trip to Jerusalem and the narrative of Jesus's final days there. If that narrative ends at 16:8 instead of 16:20, as will be discussed in chapter 4, Mark is the only Gospel with no postresurrection appearances of Jesus.

The contents of Mark may be analyzed as follows:

I. Opening (1:1–13)
II. Galilean ministry (1:14–9:50)
III. The trip to Jerusalem via Judea east of the Jordan (10:1–52)
IV. The Passion Week in Jerusalem (11:1–16:8)

Matthew

Matthew opens with a genealogy that roots Jesus in Israel's history, and in so doing, roots Israel's destiny in Jesus. Focus on the ancestry of the protagonist is also a common feature of Greco-Roman βίοι.[68] Matthew 1:1 points explicitly back to Abraham and David and implicitly to the promises associated with them (e.g., Gen. 12:1–3; 2 Sam. 7:8–17). This initial identification of Jesus prepares the reader for Matthew's stress on Jesus as the fulfillment of Israel's history, law, and prophets (Matt. 5:17–21). The historical and theological importance of Abraham and David is underscored by the *inclusio* structure of 1:1–17, as the visual below indicates. Reaching even further back into the OT, the genealogy begins with a formula (Βίβλος γενέσεως) that echoes the first two genealogies of the book of Genesis (LXX Gen. 2:4; 5:1). As 1:17 makes clear, Matthew depicts Israel's history as three sets of fourteen[69] generations:

---

67. This initial passion prediction is anticipated in Mark 3:6, 22, and leads to additional predictions in 9:31; 10:33–34, 45; 14:22–25.

68. Burridge, *What Are the Gospels?* 141.

69. Matthew's choice of the number fourteen to organize his genealogy is explained in various ways. Matthew might have chosen the number to approximate the time involved in the periods he summarizes. Fourteen is twice seven and may take on the sense of completion

Genealogy of Jesus the Messiah
   Son of David, Son of Abraham (1:1)
      from Abraham to David (1:2–6) *Promise Enacted*
      from David to the exile (1:7–11) *Promise Delayed*
      from the exile to Jesus, David's son (1:12–16) *Promise Fulfilled*
   Abraham to David to the exile to the Messiah (1:17)
Generations of Jesus the Messiah

Matthew's first few scenes show how the birth and early days of Jesus's life actually transpired, with additional emphasis on Jesus's Davidic lineage (1:20) and biblical fulfillment (1:23; 2:6, 15, 18, 23). None of the material in Matthew 1–2 has parallels in Mark. By Matthew 3, however, the story begins to be roughly parallel to Mark's account of a Galilean ministry (Mark 1:14–9:50) leading to a trip to Jerusalem and the stress on the final week of Jesus's life (Mark 11:1–16:8).

One way of looking at the structure and content of Matthew calls attention to its similarity to Mark. Matthew uses the pivotal expression "from that time Jesus began" (ἀπὸ τότε ἤρξατο ὁ Ἰησοῦς) to signal two key transitions in the narrative, the beginning of Jesus's public ministry in 4:17 (cf. Mark 1:14–15) and the move toward Jerusalem and the passion in 16:21 (cf. Mark 8:31). With this pivotal expression in mind, Matthew may be analyzed simply as follows:

I.   Preliminaries (1:1–4:16)
II. Public ministry in Galilee (4:17–16:20)
III. Movement toward Jerusalem and the passion (16:21–28:20)

The above approach helpfully depicts chronological and geographical aspects of the life of Christ, but it overlooks a key difference between Matthew and Mark.

Matthew's narrative is unlike Mark's in that Matthew greatly stresses the teaching of Jesus in five discourses,[70] each ending with the transitional expression "and it happened when Jesus had finished" (καὶ ἐγένετο ὅτε ἐτέλεσεν ὁ Ἰησοῦς; 7:28; 11:1; 13:53; 19:1; 26:1). This

---

or fullness sometimes associated with the number seven. If ancient gematria is involved, one arrives at the number fourteen by adding the numerical values of the letters of David's name in Hebrew. In any event, it is clear that Matthew's genealogy of Jesus is primarily a theological statement.

70.   In Burridge's analysis, the five discourses amount to 31.5 percent of Matthew's content (*What Are the Gospels?* 191). Acknowledging the importance of these discourses for the structure of Matthew does not necessarily lead to the conclusion of Bacon that Matthew's five discourses correspond to the five books of Moses. See B. W. Bacon, "The 'Five Books' of Matthew against the Jews," *The Expositor* 15 (1915): 56–66.

expression leads the reader from the previous discourse back into the flow of the narrative. Recognizing that Matthew alternates narratives that feature Jesus's deeds with discourses that feature Jesus's words results in a more detailed outline of Matthew:

    I.   Prologue: background for Jesus's ministry (1:1–2:23)
    II. Early days of kingdom word and deed (3:1–7:29)
        A. Narrative: transition from John to Jesus (3:1–4:22)
        B. Discourse: Sermon on the Mount (4:23–7:29)
    III. Kingdom ministry continues (8:1–11:1)
        A. Narrative: miracles and discipleship (8:1–10:4)
        B. Discourse: mission and suffering (10:5–11:1)
    IV. Growing opposition to the kingdom (11:2–13:52)
        A. Narrative: unbelief increases (11:2–12:50)
        B. Discourse: parables of the kingdom (13:1–52)
    V.   Opposition continues in Galilee (13:53–19:2)
        A. Narrative: the passion looms (13:53–17:27)
        B. Discourse: values of the kingdom (18:1–19:2)
    VI. Opposition culminates in Jerusalem (19:3–26:2)
        A. Narrative: controversy in Judea and Jerusalem (19:3–23:39)
        B. Discourse: judgment on Jerusalem and Christ's return (24:1–26:2)
    VII. Epilogue: Jesus's death, resurrection, and commission (26:3–28:20)

The literary interdependence of Matthew and Mark (discussed in the next chapter) factors into the matter of Matthew's structure. If, as many scholars believe today, Matthew depended on Mark, it seems clear that Matthew diminished Mark's stress on Jesus's deeds in order to emphasize Jesus's teachings. If the opposite dependence is held, Mark deleted much of Jesus's teaching in order to portray Jesus as a man of action. Either way, Matthew's emphasis on Jesus as a teacher is a distinctive that should be recognized in any attempt to outline or describe its structure.[71]

Luke–Acts

The opening of Luke's Gospel is a formal preface describing the book and its agenda. As such, Luke's opening is unlike the openings of Mark and Matthew. Other ancient works, including Hellenistic Jewish books,

---

71. Likewise, it is appropriate that any analysis of Mark should stress its depiction of Jesus as a man of action. Craig Blomberg attempts to synthesize the two approaches to Matthew's structure presented here. See *Matthew* (Nashville: Broadman, 1992), 22–25, 49.

have similar prefaces (e.g., Josephus, *C. Ap.* 1.1–4; 2 Macc. 2:19–32; Sir. prologue; *Let. Aris.* 1–8). Luke 1:1–4 is carefully and skillfully written in dense, elevated prose intended to explain the setting of the Gospel, Luke's painstaking approach to writing it, and his goal in doing so. Luke makes it clear that his Gospel is not the first such book to be written. Rather, he writes after many have undertaken to compile an "account"[72] of events related to Jesus. Further, such narratives have been written in light of the oral testimony of eyewitnesses to the events. Luke adds his own contribution to this previous oral and literary corpus only after his carefully investigating the matter. His goal to provide an accurate account, one leading to certainty for Theophilus[73] regarding what he has been taught. One other area of the preface deserves comment—the way Luke describes the contents of his and the other accounts as "things that have been accomplished among us" (Luke 1:1, ESV). The term "accomplished"[74] may well imply that Luke regards his content as the unfolded or fulfilled plan of God. A hint about fulfillment here would be in keeping with the emphasis on the fulfillment of God's promises elsewhere in Luke-Acts, beginning with Luke's infancy narrative (e.g., 1:17, 20, 31–32, 55, 57, 70–73; 2:25–26, 29–32, 34, 38).

Acts 1:1–5 links Luke's second volume to his first by referring again to Theophilus and recounting several events from the Gospel. It is noteworthy that this prologue or dedication begins by styling Luke's Gospel as "all that Jesus began to do and teach." This expression provides insight into the genre of the Gospels as Jesus's words and deeds that proclaimed and demonstrated the reign of God. The expression may also imply that as Luke's Gospel narrates what Jesus began to do and teach while he was on earth, so Acts narrates what Jesus continues to do and teach after his ascension through the gift of the Spirit to the church.

Acts 1:6–11 continues the narrative of 1:1–5 by depicting Jesus's reiteration of his instruction for the disciples to wait in Jerusalem for the promised coming of the Spirit (Luke 24:49; Acts 1:4) that would empower them for witness to all the nations (Luke 24:47–48; Acts 1:8). The narrative also reiterates Jesus's ascension from Bethany and the disciples' return to Jerusalem (Luke 24:50–53; Acts 1:9–12). Acts 1:10–11 adds the words of two angels who promise the disciples that

---

72. The word is διήγησις, which commonly refers to an orderly historical narrative (BDAG, s.v. διήγησις, 245). The word may refer to either oral or written narratives, but here the latter may be in view since the narrative is apparently based on orally transmitted eyewitness reports.

73. Although the description of Theophilus as "most excellent" may not in itself imply elevated social status (BDAG, s.v. κράτιστος, 565), the word does convey status in Acts 23:26; 24:3; 26:25. Luke dedicates his Gospel as well as Acts to this man, evidently a Christian who needed assurance about his previous Christian instruction. Theophilus was likely Luke's patron.

74. The word is πεπληροφορημένων, a perfect passive participle, implying God's agency in fulfilling the divine plan. BDAG, s.v. πληροφορέω, 1. a., 827.

they will see Jesus will come again from heaven just as they have seen him go into heaven.

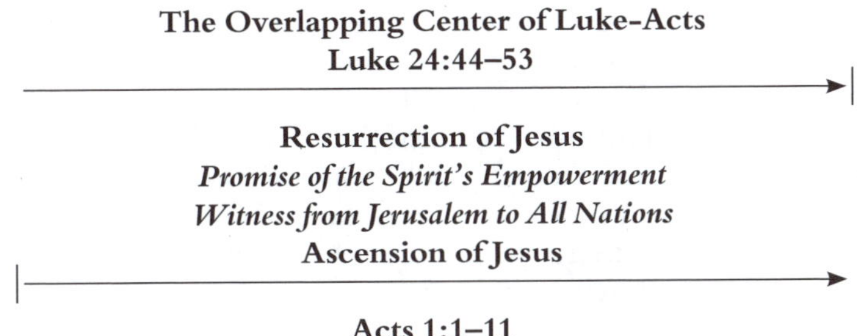

The compositional unity of Luke-Acts is shown by their interwoven openings and by their overlapping center. These factors, along with the content of the two volumes, lead us to discuss the overall structure of Luke-Acts as well as the individual structures of Luke and Acts.

Luke's brief preface is followed by a background narrative that leads to the birth of John the Baptist and Jesus (Luke 1–2) and prepares the reader for the ministry of John. As in Mark and Matthew, John's ministry transitions into Jesus's ministry following Jesus's baptism and reception of the Spirit. After his temptation, Jesus public ministry begins in Galilee. Relatively soon in that ministry Jesus asks the crucial question about his identity (9:18–20; cf. Mark 8:27–29; Matt. 16:13–19), predicts his passion (9:22), and sets his face for Jerusalem (9:51). Luke's unique extended travel narrative ensues (9:51–19:27).[75] Jesus eventually enters Jerusalem for the events of the passion (19:28). This analysis leads to the following outline:

Preface (1:1–4)
I. Preliminaries: Jesus and John the Baptist (1:5–4:13)
II. Galilean ministry (4:14–9:50)
III. Journey to Jerusalem (9:51–19:44)
IV. Passion and postresurrection appearances in Jerusalem (19:28–24:53)

Readers of Acts who take its full title (The Acts of the Apostles) at face value will be misled. It is clear that the book does not cover the ministries of the apostles as a whole (although see 1:13–26). Two major protagonists stand out, Peter in Acts 1–12 and Paul in Acts 13–28. Paul is mentioned as early as Acts 7:58, and his dramatic turn to Jesus

---

75. In contrast to Matthew's and Mark's relatively brief treatment, Luke devotes over a third of his Gospel to the travel narrative. This section of Luke contains a great deal of his distinctive theology.

is narrated in Acts 9. His mission begins in Acts 13, and it is endorsed by Peter in 15:7. Despite this emphasis on Peter and Paul, it is doubtful that their respective ministries are key to the structure and content of Acts. Luke's stress on the spread of the gospel from Jerusalem to the end of the earth transcends the human messengers who spread it. The theme of expansion begins in 1:8 (cf. Luke 24:47) and it is reinforced by additional texts in the ensuing narrative (2:41; 6:7; 9:31; 12:24; 16:4; 19:20). The expansion is not simply *biographical* (from Peter to Paul) and *geographical* (Jerusalem, Judea, Samaria, the ends of the earth). It is also *ethnic*, from Jews to Samaritans to Gentiles. Keeping all these factors in mind leads to the following analysis:

I.   Opening: review of Luke (1:1–11)
II. The Promised Spirit arrives: Peter leads the church (1:12–2:42)
III. Witness in Jerusalem: growth and persecution (2:43–8:3)
IV. Witness expands: Samaritans, Paul, and Gentiles (8:4–12:25)
V.   Witness in Asia and Greece: Paul's three mission trips (13:1–21:16)
VI. Witness in Rome: Paul's arrest and trials (21:17–28:20)

The overall content and structure of Luke-Acts is shown by literary ties and parallels between the two books. Acts 1:1 intentionally connects with Luke 1:1, and Acts 1:1–11 recapitulates the narrative of Luke, especially 24:44–53. Comparison of the story lines of the two books yields a number of parallels. The following lists some of the more obvious parallels:

- Connected prefaces (Luke 1:1–4; Acts 1:1)
- Overlapping center (Luke 24:44–53; Acts 1:1–11)
- Descent of the Spirit (Luke 3:21–22; Acts 2:1–4)
- Fulfilled prophecy (Luke 4:18–19/Isa. 61:1–2; Acts 2:17–21/Joel 2:28–32)
- Rejection and persecution (Luke 4:24, 28–29; Acts 12; 22:22)
- Jerusalem temple (Luke 19:45–48; Acts 4:13–18)
- Gentiles (Luke 2:32; 4:25–27; Acts 13:47; 28:28)
- Samaritans (Luke 9:52; 10:33; 17:16; Acts 8:5–25)
- Miracles (Luke 4:31–37; 7:22; Acts 3:2–10)
- Use of Isaiah 6 (Luke 8:10; Acts 28:26–27)
- Use of Isaiah 49:6 (Luke 2:32; Acts 13:47)

The role of Jerusalem in the overall composition is another important factor in Luke-Acts. Luke's Gospel's infancy narrative begins in Jerusalem with Zecharias in the temple and ends with Jesus there

(1:8; 2:46). Jesus's temptations culminate at the temple in Jerusalem (Luke 4:9–12). Jesus focuses on Jerusalem beginning in Luke 9:51, and arrives there in 19:41, and Luke's narrative remains focused on Jerusalem until Acts 8:3. Accordingly, Jerusalem is at the heart of twenty-four consecutive chapters of Luke-Acts, and it remains the hub of the church even after Paul's mission emanates from Antioch in Syria.[76] As will be developed more fully in chapter 3, the centrality of Jerusalem is rooted in Luke's theology of promise and fulfillment (e.g., Luke 1:54–55, 68–75; 2:11, 25–32, 38), based on such OT texts as Micah 4:2 (NIV):

> "The law will go out from Zion,
> the word of the LORD from Jerusalem."

John

Luke Timothy Johnson's description of the Fourth Gospel as "stylistically simple yet theologically dense"[77] goes double for the prologue to the Gospel. The prologue resembles the form and function of a proem or exordium in Greco-Roman rhetorical schemes.[78] As such, it does not simply begin the Gospel but gains the readers' attention by winsomely introducing them to the main themes that are to come. John's prologue is commonly compared to the entry hall or foyer of a magnificent edifice. Its beauty engages those who enter the building, yet it hints that the best of the architect's work remains to be seen.

The Synoptic Gospels' openings all have reference to a beginning of sorts—Matthew to Jesus's genealogy, Mark to the beginning of the good news about Jesus, and Luke to the initial eyewitnesses who have handed down the Jesus traditions. John's reference, however, is to the very beginning of the world and to Jesus as the one who began it (1:1–5). John's initial statement, Ἐν ἀρχῇ ἦν ὁ λόγος (1:1), combines an allusion to Genesis 1:1 with a key term (ὁ λόγος) that would be suggestive for Jewish and Greek readers alike. Jewish readers would likely associate ὁ λόγος with God's creative and redemptive power (Gen. 1:3, 6, 9; Ps. 33:6; 148:5; Isa. 45:23; 55:10–11; Prov. 8:22–31). Greeks familiar with philosophical thought would

---

76. Among the numerous references to Jerusalem later in Acts, see especially 8:14–25; 9:26–30; 11:2–18, 22–30; 12:25; 15:2; 16:4; 19:21; 20:16, 22; 21:4–13; 21:15–23:30.

77. Luke Timothy Johnson, *The Writings of the New Testament* (Minneapolis: Fortress, 1999), 532.

78. Quintilian, *Inst.* 4.1.1; Dionysius of Halicarnassus, *Thuc.* 19. See the discussion and additional ancient sources cited by Craig Keener, *The Gospel of John: A Commentary*, 2 vols. (Peabody, MA: Hendrickson, 2003), 1.338–39.

understand ὁ λόγος as the rational principle that gave structure to the world.[79] To varying degrees, Jews were aware of and influenced by Greek thought, and perhaps under its influence had begun to associate God's wisdom and the preexistent Torah with God's creative action.[80] In any case, John's teaching about Jesus would transcend the reader's preunderstanding. Jesus is both the transcendent, eternal creator of the world and the human revelator of the glory of God.

Jesus's forerunner, John the Baptist, is mentioned twice; the dual reference (1:6–8, 15) frames the center of the prologue (1:12–13) and prepares the reader for the first scenes of the narrative where John's followers become Jesus's followers (1:19–51). At the conceptual center of the prologue, 1:12–13, John shows that the irony of unbelief (1:9–11) is offset by God's act of giving life to those who do believe in him. The allusion to Moses (1:14, 17; cf. Exod. 33:12–34:8) adds to the intrabiblical texture of the prologue. Jesus reveals fully the God whom Moses only glimpsed. God's gracious revelation through Moses's Torah is completed by God's ultimate gracious revelation through the Word-become-flesh who is in the closest imaginable relationship with the Father (1:17–18).

John's unique narrative of Jesus is framed by two texts that speak of belief and unbelief in Jesus, 1:12–13 and 20:30–31. The individual episodes of John's plot provide examples of people who follow Christ in faith (e.g., 1:34–51; 2:11; 4:7–42; 9:35–38) and those who do not (e.g., 2:18–20; 5:16–18; 10:31–39). There is also an ambiguous middle ground occupied by those who do not fully follow Jesus (2:23–3:15; 6:66; 7:12–13, 40–41, 50–52; 12:42–43; 19:38–39). As John 20:20–31 indicates, there is a relationship between Jesus's miraculous deeds (called "signs" and "works") and faith. Jesus insists that his miracles are simply the Father's working through him (5:17; 17:4). Some are enraged by this claim (5:18), and others seem to misunderstand it, seeing the miracle but not understanding the message it demonstrates (3:2; 6:2, 14, 26). As John's narrative comes to the end of Jesus's public ministry, the irony of many people seeing Jesus's many signs but not believing in him is palpable, recalling that of Isaiah's ministry to Israel (12:37–50; cf. Isa. 6:1–10; 53:1).

Unlike the synoptics, John's Gospel has Jesus make multiple trips to Jerusalem, and Jesus clears the temple on the first trip, not the last one. This difference is visualized in the following chart:

---

79. E.g., Heraclitus, according to *Diog. L.* 9.1.1; Cleanthes, *Hymn to Zeus*; Stoicism, according to *Diog. L.* 7.1.134.

80. See the adept discussion of the background of the Johannine λόγος in Keener, *The Gospel of John*, 1.339–63.

Genre and Geography in the Gospels			
	The Synoptics	**John**	
Preliminaries	Mark 1:1–13 Matt. 1:1–4:11 Luke 1:1–4:13	1:1–18	
Galilean Ministry	Mark 1:14–9:50 Matt. 4:12–20:34 Luke 4:14–19:27	**Cycles from Galilee to Jerusalem**	
		Galilee 1:19–2:12 4:1–54 6:1–7:9	**Jerusalem** 2:13–3:36 5:1–47 7:10–10:39
Trip to Jerusalem	Mark 10:1–52 Matt. 19:1–20:34 Luke 9:50–19:40	11:1–12:11	
Passion Week	Mark 11:1–16:8 Matt. 21:1–28:15 Luke 19:1–24:43	12:12–20:31	
Meeting in Galilee	Mark 16:7 Matt. 28:7, 16–20	21:1–25	

Analyses of the Fourth Gospel typically note the transitions from Jesus's public signs and works (John 1–12) to his private farewell discourse (John 13–17) to his passion (John 18–20). The story proper seems to end at 20:31 where Jesus's post-resurrection appearance to Thomas leads to an editorial comment on the role of Jesus's signs in the purpose of the book. However, there is an epilogue of sorts in John 20 where Peter is restored to ministry following his denials and the relationship between Peter and the beloved disciple is clarified.

The following outline incorporates key themes of John as discussed above:

   I.   Prologue (1:1–18)
  II. The book of signs (1:19–12:50)
 III. The book of glory (13:1–20:31)
      A. Farewell discourse (13:1–17:26)
      B. Passion (18:1–20:31)
 IV. Epilogue (21:1–25)

THE FOURFOLD GOSPEL TRADITION

Modern scholarly analysis has tended to emphasize the differences between the four Gospels. Although it is helpful to discern the individual voices of each Gospel, it is also necessary to stress how this diversity oc-curs in an overall unity—"the Gospel."[81] Around A.D. 180 Irenaeus com-pared the four Gospels to the four zones and four winds of the world and spoke of the Gospels as four pillars supporting the church. He viewed the four Gospels as the Gospel in four aspects bound together by one Spirit.[82] This ancient testimony resonates with evangelical Christians who value the theological unity and canonical authority of the Bible.

Each of the four Gospels presents a narrative about Jesus that begins in Galilee and culminates in Jerusalem. A forerunner promised in the OT points the way to Jesus the Messiah. Endowed by the Spirit, Jesus begins a ministry of proclaiming and demonstrating the reign of God. He chooses his inner circle of twelve apostles who walk in his steps and begin their own ministries. There is much resistance, especially among the entrenched leaders of Israel, the Torah-experts, and those who con-trol the temple. Jesus announces that he will be arrested and crucified in Jerusalem, but that he will rise again. He will meet his disciples and renew their commission for ministry all over the world. The following points are among the key areas emphasized by the fourfold tradition, albeit in a manner unique to each Gospel:

- John the Baptist's ministry (Matt. 3:1–15; Mark 1:2–11; Luke 3:2–17; John 1:6–8, 19–28; 3:22–30)
- The wilderness voice (Isa. 40:3 in Matt. 3:3; Mark 1:3; Luke 3:4; John 1:23)
- Jesus endowed with the Spirit (Matt. 3:16; Mark 1:10; Luke 3:22; John 1:32–34)
- Jesus's twelve apostles (Matt. 10:1–4; Mark 3:16–19; Luke 6:14–16; John 6:70–71; 20:24)
- Hearing without understanding (Isa. 6:9–10 in Matt. 13:14–15; Mark 4:12; Luke 8:10; John 12:40)
- The kingdom of God (Matt. 3:2; 4:17; Mark 1:15; Luke 4:43; John 3:3, 5)
- Feeding the multitude (Matt. 14:13–21; Mark 6:32–44; Luke 9:10–17; John 6:1–13)
- Jesus enters Jerusalem (Matt. 21:1–11; Mark 11:1–10; Luke 19:29–38; John 12:12–19)
- Blessing the one who comes in the name of the Lord (Ps. 118:25–26 in Matt. 21:9; Mark 11:9–10; Luke 19:38; John 12:13)
- Jesus's temple action (Matt. 21:12–17; Mark 11:15–19; Luke 19:45–48; John 2:13–22)

---

81. For various essays on the unity and diversity of the Gospels, see Peter Stuhlmacher, ed., *The Gospel and the Gospels* (Grand Rapids: Eerdmans, 1991).

82. Irenaeus, *Haer.* 3.11.8; cf. *Did.* 8:2; 15:4; *2 Clem.* 8:5; *Mart. Pol.* 4:1.

- Judas betrays Jesus (Matt. 10:4; 26:14–16, 25, 47; 27:3; Mark 3:19; 14:10–11, 43; Luke 22:3–6; John 18:1–11)
- Jesus arrested and tried by the Jerusalem leaders (Matt. 26:47–68; Mark 14:43–65; Luke 6:16; 22:47–53; John 6:71; 12:4; 13:2, 21–30; 18:3)
- Peter denies the Lord three times (Matt. 26:31–35, 69–75; Mark 14:26–31, 66–72; Luke 22:31–34, 55–62; John 13:36–38;18:16–18, 25–27)
- Jesus tried and condemned by Pilate and crucified by Roman soldiers (Matt. 27:2, 11–35; Mark 15:1–24; Luke 23:1–33; John 18:28–19:23)
- Jesus's resurrection (Matt. 28:1–10; Mark 16:1–8; Luke 24:1–12; John 20:1–10)

By the fourth century the church had distilled the fourfold Gospel into the second paragraph of what is known today as the Apostles' Creed:

> *I believe in Jesus Christ, [God's] only Son, our Lord,*
> *who was conceived by the Holy Spirit*
> *and born of the virgin Mary.*
> *He suffered under Pontius Pilate,*
> *was crucified, died, and was buried;*
> *he descended to hell.*
> *The third day he rose again from the dead.*
> *He ascended to heaven*
> *and is seated at the right hand of God the Father almighty.*
> *From there he will come to judge the living and the dead.*

Scholars commonly analyze the similarities and differences between the Gospels, especially those of Matthew, Mark, and Luke, in word-for-word detail. Although such close microanalysis of the individual Gospels undoubtedly has its place, it is also helpful to look at the Gospels from a wide angle, so to speak, as a sort of literary scenic vista, taking in their similarities and differences at a macro level.[83] Microanalysis of the synoptic problem will be explained in the next chapter. The following macroanalytical chart displays both the differences between the individual Gospels and the unity of the fourfold Gospel testimony to Jesus, the Gospel in four aspects bound together by one Spirit.

---

83. Burridge's analysis (*What Are the Gospels?* 194–96) is again helpful. His conclusion concerning the structure of the Gospels notes their overall chronological sequence and geographical progression, interspersed with topical material inserted for literary reasons. In the case of John, the geographical progression is clearly more complex.

The Structure of the Four Gospels: A Comparative Chart				
MARK	"Title" 1:1	Preliminaries 1:1–13 John the Baptist (1:2–8) Baptism of Jesus (1:9–11) Temptation of Jesus (1:12–13)	Public Ministry 1:14–10:52 Galilee (1:14–9:50) To Jerusalem (10:1–52)	Passion 11:1–15:47 Triumphal Entry (11:1–11) Temple Events (11:12–13:37) Last Supper, etc. (14:1–42) Arrest/Trials (14:43–15:15) Crucifixion/Burial (15:16–47)	Resurrection, etc. 16:1–8 [9–20] Appears to Women (16:1–8) [Appearances (16:9–14)] [Commission (16:15–18)] [Ascension, etc. (16:19–20)]
MATTHEW	Genealogy / Infancy 1:1–17 / 1:18–2:23	Preliminaries 3:1–4:11 John the Baptist (3:1–12) Baptism of Jesus (3:13–17) Temptation of Jesus (4:1–11)	Public Ministry 4:12–20:34 Galilee (4:12–18:35) To Jerusalem (19:1–20:34)	Passion 21:1–27:66 Triumphal Entry (21:1–11) Temple Events (21:12–26:16) Last Supper, etc. (26:17–46) Arrest/Trials (26:47–27:26) Crucifixion/Burial (27:27–66)	Resurrection, etc. 28:1–20 Appears to Women (28:1–10) Cover-Up (28:11–15) Commission (28:16–20)
LUKE	Preface /Infancy 1:1–4 / 1:5–2:52	Preliminaries 3:1–4:13 John the Baptist (3:1–20) Baptism of Jesus (3:21–22) Genealogy of Jesus (3:23–38) Temptation of Jesus (4:1–13)	Public Ministry 4:14–19:27 Galilee (4:14–9:50) To Jerusalem (9:51–19:27)	Passion 19:28–23:56 Triumphal Entry (19:28–44) Temple Events (19:45–22:6) Last Supper, etc. (22:7–46) Arrest/Trials (22:47–23:25) Crucifixion/Burial (23:26–56)	Resurrection, etc. 28:1–20 Appears to women (24:1–12) More Appearances (24:13–44) Commission (24:45–49) Ascension (24:50–53)
JOHN	Prologue 1:1–18	Preliminaries 1:19–34 John's Identity (1:19–28) John's Testimony (1:29–34)	Public Ministry 1:35–12:11 Galilee (1:35–2:12) Jerusalem (2:13–3:36) Galilee (4:1–54) Jerusalem (5:1–47) Galilee (6:1–71) Jerusalem (7:1–10:39) Transjordan (10:40–42) Judah/Bethany (11:1–12:11)	Passion 12:12–19:42 Triumphal Entry (12:2–19) Belief/Unbelief (12:20–50) Last Supper/ Upper Room (13:1–17:26) Arrest/Trials (18:1–19:16) Crucifixion/Burial (19:17–42)	Resurrection, etc. 20:1–21:25 Appears to Mary (20:1–18) More Appearances (20:14–31) Epilogue Appearance (21:1–14) Peter Reinstated (21:15–19) Beloved Disciple (21:22–25)

Chapter in Review

In this chapter we discussed noteworthy views of the genre of the Gospels and Acts, concluding that the Gospels are quite similar to ancient Greco-Roman biographies (*bioi*), while Acts is much like Greco-Roman histories. Further discussion of this narrative genre addressed the hole of historical events, pastoral theology, and literary techniques in the composition of the Gospels. We concluded that the Gospels and Acts creatively present historical events in terms of their theological and pastoral relevance for the church. Sub- or embedded genres such as poetry, parables, and apocalyptic were also addressed, as was the prominence of OT citations and allusions in the Gospels' and Acts' presentations of the words and deeds of Jesus. We also presented distinctive features of each Gospel and Acts individually and discussed how the story line of the Gospels and Acts must be related to the overall narrative story line of the OT.

2

THE HISTORICAL SETTING OF THE GOSPELS AND ACTS

The Chapter at a Glance

The Gospels' milieu can be described as Jewish and near-eastern, and the book of Acts brings into play the wider world of the Roman Empire, including its geography, its governmental structure, and its cultural, religious, and philosophical complexity. The setting of the Gospels and Acts is illumined by several types of ancient sources, including the OT, Second Temple Jewish literature, and Greco-Roman literature, as well as by inscriptions and other archaeological discoveries. The Gospels and Acts are rooted in the world of Second Temple Judaism, a world in which the Jewish people are influenced by Hellenistic culture and ruled by Rome. The Gospels and Acts come to us through a complex oral and literary history.

SOURCES

The Bible

THE SEMINAL RESOURCE FOR THE SETTING of the Gospels and Acts is the OT. The NT authors view the narrative of Israel's history as their heritage, resulting in the pervasiveness of the OT in NT historical reflection and teaching. The NT authors and the characters they depict are convinced of their religious continuity with the OT and that the

OT is the primary source for their own history and religious identity (Matt. 1:1–17; 5:17; 22:29; Luke 3:23–38; John 4:20; 5:46–47; Rom. 1:1–2; 15:4; 1 Cor. 10:6–11; 1 Peter 1:10–12). The church's story can be correctly understood only as the continuation of Israel's story. The God of Adam, Abraham, Moses, David, and the prophets in the OT is the God of Jesus, Peter, John, and Paul in the NT.

Second Temple Judaism

The period of time from the rebuilding of Solomon's temple in the days of Ezra and Nehemiah under the authority of Cyrus king of Persia to the time of that temple's destruction by the Roman general Titus, roughly 538 B.C. to A.D. 70, is known as the Second Temple era. The historical outline below provides an overview of the key periods and persons during that time span. Ancient Jewish sources for the Second Temple era include the Apocrypha, Pseudepigrapha, Dead Sea Scrolls, Josephus, Philo, and the Mishnah.

The Apocrypha. The common term Apocrypha is of dubious usefulness. Its etymology implies hiddenness or mystery, and the adjective "apocryphal" implies lack of credibility. Protestants use the term to describe the deuterocanonical books of the Roman Catholic Bible. None of these books are included in the Hebrew Bible, but they are found in the Greek translation of the OT, the Septuagint (LXX), and are cited at times by ancient church authors as authoritative. These books include the historical narratives 1 Esdras, 1 Maccabees, and 2 Maccabees (which is called pathetic history because of its bombastic rhetoric). More imaginative narratives akin to novels are Tobit, Judith, Susanna, and Bel and the Dragon. The Apocrypha also contains books classified as wisdom: Sirach (Ecclesiasticus) and the Wisdom of Solomon. The Prayer of Manasseh, the Prayer of Azariah, containing the Song of the Three Young Men, are poetic books of devotional content. There is also a letter, the Letter of Jeremiah, and the apocalyptic work 2 Esdras. Similar books not found in the above group are 3–4 Maccabees and Psalm 151. The Authorized (King James) Version of the Bible (1611) originally contained the Apocrypha, and Protestants today can profit from the historical, theological, and devotional aspects of the books without according them normative doctrinal authority.

The Pseudepigrapha. The term Pseudepigrapha, although somewhat familiar, is also problematic because it is typically taken to imply deceptive, counterfeit literature. Pseudepigraphic works are indeed later works attributed piously to earlier heroes, but in all likelihood such works were understood to be unhistorical in their own day—no deception was intended. Numerous ancient books are known as pseudepigraphic and there is some disagreement as to which books should be categorized as such. The standard English edition today contains fifty-two ancient books.[1] The Pseudepigrapha include apocalyptic works such as *1–2–3 Enoch*, the *Sibylline Oracles*, *4 Ezra*, and *2–3 Baruch*. Testamentary literature, containing the solemn last words of a notable biblical figure such as Adam, the twelve patriarchs, Job, Moses, and Solomon, is also included. Some pseudepigrapha are legendary works that expand the Bible to various degrees. Such works include the *Letter of Aristeas, Jubilees, Joseph and Aseneth, Pseudo-Philo*, the *Martyrdom and Ascension of Isaiah*, and *4 Baruch*. There are also poetic works such as the *Psalms of Solomon* and *Odes of Solomon*.

The Dead Sea Scrolls. The Dead Sea Scrolls could be described as the rock stars of Second Temple literature. The discovery (c. 1947) of these texts from eleven caves near Khirbet Qumran near the northwest shore of the Dead Sea has led to a huge amount of scholarly literature and not a few books that can only be described as crackpot. The "scrolls" comprise thousands of fragments of hundreds of texts, dated mainly to the second and first centuries B.C. Although some scholars differ, there is something of a consensus that the manuscripts were the library of an Essene settlement.[2] The Qumran texts comprise copies of biblical texts that have greatly enhanced the textual criticism of the OT. Manuscripts (or fragments) of pseudepigraphic texts such as 1 Enoch and Jubilees have been found there. More to the focus of this book are the sectarian works that functioned to guide the community's thought and life as a sort of super-canon. These sectarian texts contain interpretations of the OT, instruction for the community, hymns and prayers, and eschatological writings. These books contain historical allusions and other material that may be compared and contrasted in helpful ways to the Gospels and Acts.

Josephus. The writings of Josephus may well be the most important source of historical information for the period of the Gospels and Acts. According to his writings, Josephus was a well-to-do Pharisaic Jew from a priestly family. He was the commander of Jewish forces in Galilee during the first Jewish revolt against Rome (A.D. 66–70). After his defeat at Jotapata, he joined the Roman side and ingratiated himself to Vespasian and his son Titus during the siege of Jerusalem. He went back to Rome under the patronage of the Flavian dynasty and wrote several books to explain the Jewish people to the Romans. His work *The Jewish War* was

---

1. James H. Charlesworth, ed., *The Old Testament Pseudepigrapha* (Peabody, MA: Hendrickson Publishers, 2010). The forewords to this two-volume set, as well as Charlesworth's introduction, provide helpful introductory insights for this literature. See 1.1x–xiii, xxi–xxxiv.

2. Ancient references to the Essenes are found in Josephus *A. J.* 15.371; 18.18–22; *B. J.* 2.151; Philo, *Prob.* 75–91; *Contempl.* Philo also mentions the Essenes in his apology for the Jews cited in Eusebius *Praep. ev.* 8.11–12. See also Pliny the Elder, *Nat.* 5.18.73.

probably published around A.D. 75, followed by his *Antiquities of the Jews*, a summary of OT history, around twenty years later. Near the end of his life he produced two short works, *Against Apion* (a defense of the Jews) and *The Life of Flavius Josephus*. Although he was far from objective in his accounts, his works contain valuable historical information. It is noteworthy that his writings refer to the deaths of John the Baptist (*A. J.* 18.109–19), James (as the brother of Jesus who was called Messiah; *A. J.* 20. 199–201), and Jesus himself (*A. J.* 18.63–64). This last passage, known as the *Testimonium Flavianum*, is somewhat notorious because of likely Christian interpolations.

Philo. Philo was an Alexandrian Jew who lived from c. 20 B.C. to c. A.D. 50. Philo was an admirer of Greek philosophy, and his writings deal with metaphysics and view the OT as compatible with Greek thought. He wrote on biblical and philosophical themes, producing allegorical commentaries that were admired in some circles of the early church. His books *In Flaccum* and *Legatio ad Gaium* describe the persecution of Jews in Alexandria that led to a journey he and other influential Alexandrian Jews made to the Emperor Caligula (c. A.D. 40) to petition him for better treatment. Philo claims the Roman Prefect Flaccus persecuted the Jews and confiscated their homes and synagogues because they refused to worship Caligula (*Flacc.* 41–52). He also refers to Caligula's plan to erect a statue of himself in the Jerusalem temple (*Legat.* 346–48; cf. Josephus *A. J.* 18.257–88), and his outrage that the Jews refuse to worship him or eat pork (*Legat.* 349–73). Such accounts are relevant for understanding the tensions between the Jerusalem leaders and Pilate that are alluded to in the Gospels. They also have implications for Jesus's teaching about a future temple sacrilege (Matt. 24:15/Mark 13:14/Luke 21:20).

The Mishnah. The Mishnah is the earliest written edition of the oral rabbinic teaching that augmented the written Torah (תורה שבכתב). This oral Torah (תורה שבעל פה) was redacted around A.D. 200 into a book containing sixty-three tractates, topically arranged in six divisions loosely relating to agriculture, festivals, marriage and divorce, damages, the temple, and purity. Chapters in the tractates typically teach by alluding to concrete examples where rabbinic teaching on how to apply the written Torah may differ. Commonly disputes between the followers of Hillel and Shammai are adjudicated in favor of Hillel's reading. The growing rabbinic commentary (Gemara) on the Mishnah led to the Babylonian Talmud by around A.D. 500. The Tosefta and Jerusalem Talmud represent teaching between the time of the Mishnah and the Babylonian Talmud. Since the Mishnah was not redacted until c. A.D. 200, there is the danger of anachronism when using it for study of the Gospels and Acts, but it contains teaching of the earliest rabbis (the Tannaim), many of whom flourished during the first century A.D.

When used with caution, it can be helpful in aiding the understanding of disputes over the OT Law in the Gospels and Acts.

Greek Sources. Polybius (c. 200–120 B.C.) and Diodorus Siculus (c. 90–30 B.C.) obviously do not speak of the period of the Gospels and Acts. Their accounts of events during the Hellenistic period leading up to the time of Jesus and the apostles are useful, however, in reconstructing the period between the Testaments. Polybius's *Histories* describe the rise of the Roman Republic from the mid-third to the mid-second centuries B.C., particularly Rome's battles with Carthage. Less than half of Diodorus's comprehensive *Bibliotheca Historica* has been preserved, but what survives includes his treatment of the rise of Alexander the Great and the successors to Alexander's empire. The works of Suetonius (c. A.D. 75–150) and Tacitus (c. A.D. 56–120) are more directly related to NT times. Suetonius wrote a series of biographies of the twelve Caesars from Julius to Domitian entitled *De Vita Caesarum.* His work *Claudius* 25.4 refers to the decree of Claudius that expelled Jews from Rome, plausibly due to strife over Christ.[3] This decree led to Priscilla and Aquila meeting Paul and Apollos in Corinth (Acts 18:2–3, 26). Among the writings of Tacitus that partially survive are his *Annals and Histories* that cover the times of Augustus to the Jewish Wars of A.D. 66–70. His discussion of the great fire in Rome of A.D. 64 (*Ann.* 15.38–44) is of interest for the setting of Paul in Rome in Acts 28. Tacitus relates how Nero shifted suspicion for the fire from himself to the Christians and persecuted them severely. Tacitus's negative view of Jews and Christians, as well as Nero, is clear from his description of the interrogation, torture, and death of Christians at Nero's whim. Tacitus also describes the cruelty of the procurator Felix (Acts 23), stating that Felix exercised the power of a king with the mind of a slave (*Hist.* 5.9).

Archaeology and the Physical World

St. Jerome is reported to have said, "Five gospels record the life of Jesus. Four you will find in books and the one you will find in the land they call holy. Read the fifth gospel and the world of the four will open to you." This point is well taken, whether or not it can be traced to Jerome.[4] Students who are able to take a serious study tour of Israel

---

3. The Latin text is *"Iudaeos impulsore Chresto assidue tumultuantis Roma expulit." Chrestus* could be an alternate or mistaken spelling of Christus, or there may have been an otherwise unknown person named Chrestus.

4. Jerome's references to Isaiah as the fifth gospel are well known. Ernst Renan spoke of the land as a fifth gospel (*un cinquième Évangile*) in *Vie de Jésus*, 13th ed. (Paris: Michel Levi Freres, 1867), XXIV. I thank my colleague Dr. Byard Bennett for this reference.

and other NT lands will learn a great deal about the world of Jesus and the apostles. Until that is possible, an up-to-date detailed atlas of the historical geography of Israel is a very helpful tool for understanding the Gospels and Acts.[5]

Additionally, archaeological data derived from coins, inscriptions, ostraca, and other artifacts help illumine the text of the Gospels and Acts. It must also be noted that such data sometimes seem to contradict biblical texts, at least as they have been previously interpreted.[6] There is no space here to go into detail about such matters, but as an example of a helpful find, note the discovery of the "Pilate stone" at Caesarea Maritima in 1961. A damaged limestone block, the stone has a partially intact inscription that apparently indicates its original use as a memorial to Pilate's dedication of a building to the emperor Tiberias. The inscription is the earliest known historical reference to Pilate; it describes him as a prefect, not a procurator.[7] The current dig at Magdala, north of Tiberias on the western shore of the Sea of Galilee, is an example of the ongoing potential of archaeology. Apparently there are extensive first-century remains, including those of a synagogue.[8] Students of the Gospels and Acts are well advised to keep up on the latest archaeological information by looking into publications such as *Biblical Archaeology Review.*[9]

THE GOSPELS AND ACTS IN GRECO-ROMAN HISTORY

Overview. Christians often describe the historical period that led up to the time of Jesus and the writing of the Gospels later in the first century A.D. as the intertestamental period. This period began with the return of some of the exiled Jews to their land (c. 539 B.C.) under the authority of the Persian Empire, which had defeated the Neo-Babylonian Empire.[10] The temple was rebuilt (c. 516 B.C.) despite the opposition

---

5. Among the better atlases are Yohanan Aharoni, et al. *The Macmillan Bible Atlas*, 2nd ed. (New York: Harper, 1993); Carl G. Rasmussen, *The Essential Atlas of the Bible* (Grand Rapids: Zondervan, 2013); Bill Schlegel, *The Satellite Bible Atlas* (by the author, 2013).

6. Christopher M. M. Brady summarizes the difficulties in analyzing archaeological information as it relates to biblical studies in "What Do the Stones Cry Out?" Sept. 1, 2003, http://www.christianitytoday.com/ct/2003/septemberweb-only/9-22-33.0.html.

7. For additional discussion, see Helen K. Bond, *Pontius Pilate in History and Interpretation* (Cambridge: Cambridge University Press, 1998), 11–12, 38–39; Craig A. Evans, *Jesus and the Ossuaries* (Waco, TX: Baylor University Press, 2003), 45–47.

8. See Marcela Zapata-Meza, "Magdala 2016: Excavating the Hometown of Mary Magdalene," July 8, 2016, Bible History Daily, https://www.biblicalarchaeology.org/daily/archaeology-today/magdala-2016-excavating-the-hometown-of-mary-magdalene.

9. https://www.biblicalarchaeology.org.

10. It was probably during the period of exile in Babylon that the synagogue originated.

of the Samaritans.[11] The Greeks under Alexander the Great defeated the Persians (331 B.C.), and at the premature death of Alexander his empire was divided among four successors (323 B.C.). Ptolemy, one of Alexander's inner circle, was appointed to rule Epypt, and his dynasty did so until conquered by the Romans in 30 B.C. The Ptolemies also ruled over Israel until 200 B.C., when they were defeated by the rulers of Syria, the Seleucid dynasty.

When Alexander died, Seleucus received control of a huge area, ranging from Syria in the west to India in the east. The Seleucids viewed themselves as the guardians of Greek culture and language (Hellenism) and promoted it throughout their empire. This program led to persecution of the Jews by the Seleucid ruler Antiochus IV, who destroyed Torah scrolls, banned circumcision, and sacrificed a pig in the Jerusalem temple (1 Maccabees 1; Josephus, *A. J.* 12.246–256). Under the leadership of Mattathias and his sons, the Jews revolted against their Syrian overlords and the Maccabean[12] kingdom arose (1 Macc. 2:1–4).[13] Their purification and dedication of the temple along with reinstitution of sacrifices (c. 164 B.C.) is the basis of the Hanukkah festival, the Feast of Dedication (1 Macc. 4:59; John 10:22). After about a hundred years of Hasmonean rule, the Romans conquered them after their kingdom had been weakened by civil war (63 B.C.). Rome itself soon underwent a governmental transition from a republic to an empire. The Herodian dynasty arose (37 B.C.) to rule as clients of Rome, alongside various Roman provincial governors.[14]

Synagogues existed alongside the Second Temple and after its destruction became the central institution of Jewish civic and religious community.

11. The Samaritans are in tension with observant Jews in the Gospels, yet some of them are responsive to Jesus and the apostles in the Gospels and Acts.

12. The word "Maccabean" is derived from the Hebrew word for hammer. Mattathias's most prominent son Judah was nicknamed "the hammer" (יהודה המכבי; 1 Macc. 3:1) and the term came to describe the ensuing dynasty.

13. It was probably during Hasmonean rule that the Jewish sects of the Pharisees and Sadducees originated. The Pharisees were Torah-specialists, experts in the ancestral oral traditions that were later redacted as the written Mishnah around A.D. 200. The Sadducees were mainly the priestly hierarchy entrenched in Jerusalem. They did not accept the oral traditions of the Pharisees.

14. For the history of the period between the Testaments, see further Elias J. Bickerman, *The Jews in the Greek Age* (Cambridge: Harvard University, 1988); F. F. Bruce, *Israel and the Nations*, 3rd ed., rev. by D. F. Payne (Downers Grove, IL: InterVarsity, 1998); Schaye D. Cohen, *From the Maccabees to the Mishnah* (Philadelphia: Westminster, 1987); E. Schürer, *The History of the Jewish People in the Age of Jesus Christ 175 B.C.–A.D. 135*, new ed., rev. by Geza Vermes and Fergus Miller, 3 vols. (Edinburgh: Clark, 1973); James C. VanderKam, *An Introduction to Early Judaism* (Grand Rapids: Eerdmans, 2001).

Historical Outline of the Second Temple Era

I. The Persian Period (539–331 B.C.)
II. The Hellenistic Period
   • Greek Rule under Alexander the Great (331–323 B.C.)
   • Egyptian Rule under the Ptolemaic Dynasty (323–198 B.C.)
   • Greek Rule under the Seleucid Dynasty (198–167 B.C.)
III. The Maccabean Revolt and the Hasmonean Dynasty (167–63 B.C.)
   • Mattathias (died 165 B.C.)
   • Judas Maccabeus (165–161 B.C.)
   • Jonathan (160–142 B.C.)
   • Simon (142–134 B.C.)
   • John Hyrcanus (134–104 B.C.)
   • Aristobulus I (104–103 B.C.)
   • Alexander Jannaeus (103–76 B.C.)
   • Alexandra (76–67 B.C.)
   • Aristobulus II vs. Hyrcanus II (67–63 B.C.)
IV. The Roman Period (63 B.C.–A.D 117)
   • Pompey conquers Jerusalem (63 B.C.) and Roman control begins
   • Hyrcanus II (A.D. 63)
   • Parthian Rule (A.D. 40–37)
   • Herodian Dynasty (37 B.C.–A.D. 92)
      – Herod the Great (37–4 B.C.)
      – Archelaus (**Ethnarch** of Judea, Samaria, and Idumea; 4 B.C.–A.D. 6)
      – (**Tetrarch** of Galilee and Perea; 4 B.C.–A.D. 39)
      – Philip (Tetrarch of Iturea and Trachonitis; 4 B.C.–A.D. 34)
      – Agrippa I (succeeded Antipas; A.D. 41–44)
      – Agrippa II (Cholcis, Lebanon; A.D. 49–92)
   • Roman Emperors
      – Augustus (27 B.C.–A.D. 14) ⎤
      – Tiberias (A.D. 14–37)   ⎥ Julio-Claudian
      – Gaius (Caligula, A.D. 37–41) ⎥ Dynasty
      – Claudius (A.D. 41–54)   ⎥
      – Nero (A.D. 54–68)   ⎦
      – Civil War: Galba, Otho, Vitellius, and Vespasian (A.D. 68–69) ⎤
      – Vespasian (A.D. 69–79)   ⎥
      – Titus (A.D. 79–81)   ⎥ Flavian Dynasty
      – Domitian (A.D. 81–96)   ⎦

- Nerva (96–98 A.D.) ⎤ Nerva-Antonine
- Trajan (98–117 A.D.) ⎦ Dynasty
- Selected Roman Governors of Judea
  - Pontius Pilate (**Prefect**, A.D. 26–36)
  - Marcellus Ambivulus (Prefect, A.D. 36–37)
  - Marullus (Prefect, A.D. 37–41)
  - Agrippa I (Herodian king, A.D. 41–44)
  - Cuspius Fadus (**Procurator**, A.D. 44–46)
  - Tiberius Julius Alexander (Procurator, A.D. 46–48)
  - Ventidius Cumanus (Procurator, A.D. 48–52)
  - Marcus Antonius Felix (Procurator, A.D. 52–60)
  - Porcius Festus (Procurator, A.D. 60–62)
  - Lucceius Albinus (Procurator, A.D. 62–64)
  - Gessius Florus (Procurator, A.D. 64–66)
  - Marcus Antonius Julianus (Procurator, c. A.D. 66–70)
  - Sextus Vettulenus Cerialis (**Legate**, A.D. 70–71)

Key Historical References in the Gospels and Acts

The Gospels and Acts were not primarily intended to be neutral chronicles of ancient history so much as literary narratives that explained the significance of historical events for the church. As such there are occasional historical references that support the point of the narratives, especially Luke-Acts. One may be surprised at the number of such references to people and institutions of the Roman world when they are collected:

- Augustus Caesar's decree (Luke 2:1)
- Quirinius the governor of Syria (Luke 2:2)
- Herod, Archelaus, and the magi (Matthew 2)
- Tiberias Caesar's fifteenth year (Luke 3:1)
- Pilate the Roman governor of Judea (Luke 3:1; 13:1/ Matthew 11/Mark 15:1/Luke 23:1)
- The Herodian Dynasty, including
  - Herod I (the Great; Matt. 2:1, 7, 12, 19; Luke 1:5)
  - Antipas (Luke 3:1, 19; 8:3; Matt. 14:1–12/Mark 6:14–29/Luke 9:7–9; 13:31; 23:7–15; Acts 4:27; 13:1)
  - Philip (Matt. 14:3/Mark 6:17/Luke 3:19; cf. Matt 16:13/Mark 8:27); his ex-wife Herodias later married his half-brother Antipas (Matt 14:3, 6; Mark 6:17, 19, 22; Luke 3:19)

- – Agrippa I (Acts 12:1, 6, 11, 19, 21)
- – Agrippa II (with Bernice his sister, Acts 25:13–26:32)
- The Herodians (Matt. 22:16; Mark 3:6; 12:13; cf. Rom. 16:11)
- Lysanias the tetrarch (Luke 3:1)
- Annas and Caiaphas, high priests (Luke 3:2; cf. Matt 26:3; John 11:49; Matt 26:57/Mark 14:53/John 18:13, 24, 28; Acts 4:6; 23; cf. Acts 23:2; 24:1).
- The Decapolis (Matt. 4:25; Mark 5:20; 7:31)
- Roman centurions (Matt. 8:5–13/Luke 7:1–10; Matt. 27:54/Luke 23:47; Acts 10:1, 22; 21:32; 22:25–26; 23:17, 23; 24:23; 27:1, 6, 11, 31, 43)
- A royal official at Capernaum (John 4:46)
- Joanna, the wife of Herod's official Chuza (Luke 8:3)
- Matthew the tax collector (Matt. 9:9/Mark 2:14/Luke 5:27)
- Synagogues, governors, and kings (Matt. 10:18)
- Tyre and Sidon (Matt. 15:21/Mark 7:24–30; Mark 3:8)
- Caesarea Philippi (Matt. 16:13/Mark 8:27/Luke 9:18)
- The Samaritans (Matt 10:5; Luke 9:52; 10:33; 17:11, 16; John 4:5; Acts 8:5–25)
- The **Feast of Dedication** (John 10:22)
- Zaccheus the chief tax collector (Luke 19:1–10)
- The rulers of the Gentiles (Matt. 20:25/Mark 10:42/Luke 22:25)
- Jerusalem surrounded by armies (Luke 21:20)
- The praetorium or governor's residence (Matt. 27:27/Mark 15:16/John 18:28; cf. John 18:33, 19:9; Acts 23:35; Phil. 1:13)
- Simon of Cyrene pressed into service by Roman soldiers (Matt. 27:32/Mark 15:21; cf. Matt. 5:41)
- Theudas and Judas, insurrectionists against Rome (Acts 5:36–37)
- Candace, queen of Ethiopia (Acts 8:27)
- Sergius Paulus and Gallio the provincial governors of Cyprus and Achaia (Acts 13:7–12; 18:13–17; 19:38)
- Macedonia the Roman colony (Acts 16:12)
- Epicurean and Stoic philosophers (Acts 17:18)
- The temple of Artemis, the Asiarchs, and the CEO of Ephesus (Acts 19:23–41)
- Lysias the commander of the Roman cohort at the temple (Acts 21:31–23:30; 24:22; cf. Matt. 27:27/Mark 15:16/John 18:3, 12; Acts 10:1; 27:1)

- Felix the procurator of Palestine (Acts 23:24–24:27; cf. Tacitus, *Hist.* 5.9; his wife Drusilla was the daughter of Herod Agrippa I; Acts 24:24)
- Festus the governor (Acts 24:27–26:32)
- Paul's Roman citizenship and appeal to Caesar (Acts 16:35–40; 22:25–29; 23:27; 25:8–12, 21, 25–27; 26:32; 28:19)

THE GOSPELS AND ACTS AND SECOND TEMPLE JUDAISM

The Second Temple Period (530 B.C.– A.D. 70) began with the decree of Cyrus the Great, permitting the Jews to return to their homeland and rebuild the temple.[15] The period featured several major political transitions, from the Persians (530–331 B.C.), to the Greeks (331–323 B.C.), to the Ptolemies (323–198 B.C.), to the Seleucids (198–167 B.C.), to the Jewish Hasmonean rulers (167–63 B.C.), and finally to the Romans (63 B.C.–A.D. 70), who appointed Herod the Great as their client king to rule Judea around 40 B.C. Technically, the period ends with the destruction of Herod's temple by the Romans, but in many ways it extends through several additional decades of political and religious tension leading to the second major Jewish revolt under Simon Bar Kosiva (A.D. 132–135).[16] The Romans had renamed Jerusalem Aelia Capitolina, dedicating the city to the emperor Hadrian and the god Zeus. After crushing the revolt, the Romans forced the Jews out of Jerusalem, and carried out an extensive rebuilding project, including the colonnaded north-south street known as the Cardo, pictured on the Madaba Map (c. A.D. 550) and seen by many tourists today.[17]

Our discussion here will focus on the religious aspects of this setting. The Jews of the Second Temple period had learned the bitter lesson of God's punishment for idolatry, and monotheism was certainly their hallmark (Deut. 4:35, 39; 6:4; Matt. 22:34–40/Mark 12:28–34; cf. Luke 10:27). Allegiance to God alone was expressed through faithfully obeying the Mosaic covenant, the Torah (Matt. 19:16–22; Luke 1:6; 10:25–28; Rom. 2:17–23; Phil. 3:6). Foundational Torah instructions involved

---

15. See many OT texts, including Jer. 25:12; 29:1–14; Daniel 9; 2 Chron. 36:21–33; Ezra; Nehemiah; Esther; Haggai; Zechariah; and Malachi.

16. He is often called Bar Kochba, Hebrew for "son of the star," a messianic title (Num. 24:17) evidently conferred upon him by Rabbi Akiva. See *y. Ta'an.* 4:8 68d. It is unclear whether the name Bar Kosiva refers to his father or hometown, or is a slur meaning "son of a lie," coined by Yose ben Halaphta, a contemporary of Akiva (*S. 'Olam Rab.* 30).

17. Cassius Dio, 69.12.1–14; Eusebius *Hist. eccl.* 4.6.4.

the circumcision of male infants and Gentile proselytes,[18] the observance of the weekly Sabbath and other festivals,[19] and keeping to a diet free from forbidden or ritually impure foods.[20] Jesus did not always agree with the traditional interpretations of these Torah teachings.[21]

The Temple and the Priesthood

The turbulent period beginning with the building of the Second Temple (Ezra 3:8–13; 6:14–22) stretches to its renovation and expansion by Herod the Great (John 2:20), and sadly, to its destruction, as prophesied by Jesus (e.g., Luke 21:6, 20–24; 23:27–31). The Jewish world, centered on the temple, is the setting of the Gospels, and the temple is in some ways the base for the world of the book of Acts. The setting of Acts expands from Jerusalem northward to Syrian Antioch and westward to Rome. The following table shows how prominent the temple is in the Gospels and Acts.

The Temple in the Gospels and Acts				
	Matthew	**Mark**	**Luke–Acts**	**John**
Chapters	4, 5, 12, 21, 23, 24, 26, 27	11, 12, 13, 14, 15	Luke 1, 2, 4, 11, 18, 19, 20, 21, 22, 23 Acts 2, 3, 4, 5, 21, 22, 24, 25, 26	2, 5, 7, 8, 10, 11, 18

In the OT God's presence traveled with Israel through the tabernacle.[22] David's wish to build a permanent sanctuary for God was realized by Solomon (1 Kings 5–9), but the subsequent disobedience of David's descendants and of Israel as a whole led to the destruction of the first

---

18.   Gen. 17:12–14; Lev. 12:3; Luke 1:59; 2:21; John 7:22; Acts 7:8; 10:45; 11:2–3; 15:1, 5; 16:3; 21:21; Rom. 2:25–29; 3:30; 4:9–12; 15:8; Gal. 2:7; Eph. 2:11; Phil. 3:1–5; Col. 2:11; 3:11.

19.   On the Sabbath, see Exod. 20:8–11; 31:13–16; Lev. 19:3, 30; Deut. 5:12–15; Neh. 13:15–22; Isa. 56:2, 4, 6; 58:13–14; Jer. 17:21–27; Ezek. 20:12; Amos 8:5; Matt. 12:1–14/Mark 2:23–3:6/Luke 6:1–11; Luke 4:16; 13:10–17; 14:1–6; John 5:9–10, 16–18; 7:22; 9:16; Acts 13:14, 27, 42, 44; 15:21; 16:13; 17:2; 18:4.

20.   Lev. 11; Deut. 14:3–21; Isa. 65:4; 66:17; Ezek. 4:14; Matt. 15:10–20/Mark 7:14–23; Acts 10:9–16; 11:3; 15:20, 29; Rom. 14:14.

21.   E.g., Matt. 12:1–14/Mark 2:23–3:6/Luke 6:1–11; Matt. 15:1–20/Mark 7:1–23; John 5:1–18.

22.   Exod. 25–30; 35–40; Lev. 8–9; Num. 1:50–54; 3:5–9; Ps. 78:60; Ezek. 41:1; Acts 7:44; Heb. 8:5; 9:2, 21; Rev. 21:3.

temple by Nebuchadnezzar in 587 B.C. (2 Kings 25:9–17; 2 Chron. 36:6–21). The building of the Second Temple under Zerubbabel's leadership was a bittersweet occasion for those who had seen the first temple (Ezra 3:8–13; Hag. 2:6–9). Herod the Great renovated the Second Temple and expanded its grounds by leveling the surrounding area and filling in a flat platform for the outer courts. The massive western wall visible today, often called the wailing wall because of its importance as a holy place for prayer, is a retaining wall built by Herod. The grandeur of Herod's construction was stressed by Josephus,[23] but it is somewhat ironic when Jesus's disciples speak of the beauty of the temple just before his eschatological discourse on the Mount of Olives (Matt. 24:1–2/Mark 13:1–2/Luke 21:5–6).

The large outer court of the temple complex, known as the Court of the Gentiles, was accessible to all. An intermediate court known as the Court of the Women was open only to Jews. Jewish males who were ritually pure could enter the next court, the Court of Israel (Acts 21:27–29), but the Court of the Priests was open only for those who offered daily sacrifices on the altar (Matt. 23:35). The sanctuary building itself had an outer chamber, the holy place, where a priest burned incense twice a day (Luke 1:8–10; cf. Exod. 30:7–8). Only the High Priest could enter the inner chamber, the most holy place or Holy of Holies, and that occurred only once a year on the Day of Atonement to offer incense and sprinkle sacrificial blood (Lev. 16:1–19, 29–34; 23:26–32; Num. 29:7–11; Heb. 5:1–4; 7:27–28; 9:7). Jews gathered at the temple not only to offer sacrifices but also for worship (Luke 24:53), singing (1 Chron. 6:31–48; 9:33; 15:16–17, 22; 25:6–7), prayer (Luke 18:11), giving (Mark 12:41–44/Luke 21:1–4), and teaching (Lev. 10–11; Deut. 24:8; 33:10; Mark 14:49).[24]

As Israel was to function in a priestly manner among the nations (Exod. 19:5–6; 1 Peter 2:5, 9), so individuals functioned as priests among the Israelites. The temple priesthood began with the consecration of Aaron and his sons to serve in the tabernacle (Exod. 40:12–16; Deut. 18:1–8). God gave Moses specific instructions regarding the personal holiness of the Aaronic priests (Lev. 21:1–24), their clothing (Exod. 28:1–43), and the appropriate manner of offering sacrifices (Exod. 30:19–21; Lev. 22:1–33). Priests were chosen by lot for temple service

---

23. Josephus, *B. J.* 5.222–24; *A. J.* 15.391–425. See also the account of the Mishnah (*m. Mid.*). Later in the Talmud it was said "Whoever has not seen the Holy Temple built by King Herod, has never seen a beautiful building his entire life" (*b. Sukkah* 51b).

24. For a fine overview of the Jerusalem Temple, including the Second Temple, see Moises Silva, ed., *Zondervan Encyclopedia of the Bible*, rev., ed. 5 vols. (Grand Rapids: Zondervan, 2009), s.v. "temple, Jerusalem," by H. G. Stigers (5.716–52). For lengthy discussion, maps, and skilled drawings of Herod's temple, see Leen Ritmeyer, *The Quest: Revealing the Temple Mount in Jerusalem* (Jerusalem: Carta, 2006).

(1 Chron. 24; Luke 1:9), which involved daily sacrifices and offerings (Lev. 1–8; Num. 15),[25] overseeing and caring for the temple complex and its treasury (Neh. 10:37–38), performing purification ceremonies (Lev. 13–15; Luke 17:14), and blessing Israel (Num. 6:22–27). The high priesthood was to have been based on heredity (Leviticus 16), but this practice was not observed from the Hasmonean dynasty onward. Herod appointed and dismissed high priests as a matter of political expedience.[26] The high priest's responsibilities included the most sacred Day of Atonement sacrifice as well as presiding over the ruling council or Sanhedrin (Mark 14:53, 60–64). The captain of the temple assisted the high priest in sacrificial and administrative duties (Acts 4:1; 5:24, 26). The chief priests were most likely those from aristocratic families who worked under the high priest in various administrative roles. Jesus's action in clearing the temple and subsequently teaching there was especially provocative to them. Ordinary priests like Zechariah numbered in the thousands. When not chosen by lot to serve in the temple they evidently lived at home and subsisted from other labors (Luke 1:5–9, 23). The following table shows the prominence of the priesthood in the NT.

Priests, *Chief Priests*, and the *High Priest* in the Gospels and Acts[27]			
	Matthew	**Mark**	**Luke–Acts**	**John**
Chapters	2, 8, 12, *16*, 20, 21, ***26***, 26, 27	1, 2, *2*, 8, 11, 14, ***14***, 15	Luke 1, 6, *9*, 10, 17, *19*, 20, 22, ***22***, 23, 24 Acts 4, *4*, ***4***, 5, ***5***, 6, *7*, 9, *9*, 19, ***22***, 23, ***23***, ***24***, 25, 26	1, 7, *11*, ***11***, 12, 18, ***18***, 19

The descendants of Jacob's son Levi were consecrated as a special tribe to God in the place of the firstborn from the other tribes (Num. 3:11–13, 41, 45; 8:18; 35:2–3). They did not receive a territorial al-

---

25. The complex system of sacrifices and offerings has been well summarized by A. F. Rainey, *Zondervan Bible Encyclopedia*, s.v. "Sacrifices, offerings" (5.233–52). See further Roger T. Beckwith and Martin J. Selman, eds., *Sacrifice in the Bible* (Grand Rapids: Baker, 1995).

26. On high priests in the Second Temple period, see James C. VanderKam, *From Joshua to Caiaphas: High Priests after the Exile* (Minneapolis; Fortress, 2004).

27. Chapters mentioning priests are in normal font, chief priests are in italics, and the high priest is in bold italics.

lotment but subsisted from their ministry to Israel, which involved caring for the Tabernacle and subsequently the temple (Num. 3:14–4:49; 18:21; Deut. 18:1; Josh. 14:3–4; 1 Chron. 9:14–32). Levites are seldom mentioned by name in the NT. In two texts they appear with priests (Luke 10:32; John 1:19). Barnabas, a prominent person in Acts, was a Levite (Acts 4:36). According to ancient sources they served as the temple police,[28] so they were likely involved in arresting Jesus and the apostles (John 7:32, 45–52; 18:3, 12; Acts 4:1; 5:17–18, 22, 26).

The Synagogue

With the destruction of Solomon's temple and the dispersion of the Jews in the southern kingdom in 587 B.C. came a decentralization of Judaism. The temple with its politically powerful priesthood and daily sacrifices ceased operation until the Jews were permitted to return to the land and build the Second Temple. It is likely that synagogues began during this "between the temples" period in Babylon as Jewish community centers for social, civil, educational, and worship activities.[29] A synagogue could be formed wherever there was a *minyan* (מִנְיָן) of ten males (*m. Meg.* 4:3); informal services were held even when there was no synagogue (Acts 16:13). The prevalence of synagogues in the Gospels and Acts is shown in the table below.

The Synagogue in the Gospels and Acts[30]			
	Matthew	**Mark**	**Luke-Acts**	**John**
Chapters	4, 6, 9, 10, 12, 13, 23	1, 3, 5, 6, 12, 13	Luke 4, 6, 7, 8, 11, 12, 13, 20, 21 Acts 6, 9, 13, 14, 15, 17, 18, 19, 22, 24, 26	6, 9, 12, 16, 18

---

28. Philo, *Spec.* 1.156; *m. Mid.* 1:1–2.

29. According to Josephus, Moses founded the synagogue (*C. Ap.* 2.17). The Mishnah's reference to "the great synagogue" (*m. Avot* 1:1–2) is most likely to a traditional assembly of Torah-authorities dating to the early days of the Second Temple. For a compilation of ancient source material on the synagogue, see Anders Runesson, Donald D. Binder, and Birger Olsson, *The Ancient Synagogue from its Origins to 200 C.E.* (Leiden: Brill, 2010).

30. The word συναγωγή occurs fifty-six times in the NT, fifty-three in the Gospels and Acts. See also Jas. 2:2; Rev. 2:9; 3:9.

NT references (Luke 4:14–30; Acts 13:14–48) provide some of the earliest evidence about synagogue services. A ruler oversaw the synagogue and its services.[31] An attendant assisted the ruler in various ways (Luke 4:20).[32] Services included recitations of the Shema (Deut. 6:4 with accompanying Scripture), the eighteen blessings of the Amidah, and readings from the Scriptures in a three-year cycle, apparently from both the law and the prophets (Acts 13:15). Readings from the Hebrew Bible in Palestine and the east were accompanied by Aramaic paraphrases or targum (cf. Neh. 8:7–8). In the synagogues of the dispersion, the Scriptures may have been paraphrased in Greek. A homily or sermon and a benediction closed the service.[33] Jesus and the apostles frequently carried out ministry in synagogues. The synagogue looms especially large in Acts as the location where Paul preached "to the Jew first" (Rom. 1:16). Gentile God-fearers who attended these synagogues proved to be a ready audience for Paul's message (Acts 13:16, 26, 43, 48; 16:14; 17:4, 17; 18:7; cf. Luke 7:5; Acts 10:2, 22, 35). Synagogues could also become sources of opposition for Jesus and his Jewish followers (Luke 4:28–30; 13:14–17; Acts 6:9–12; 13:44–52; 14:2; 17:5).

Rabbis

It is unclear how and when the term "rabbi" became the title for an ordained Jewish synagogue leader. In the NT ῥαββί occurs fifteen times, but never in the sense in which it is used today. It is a title for a respected leader or teacher, most often John the Baptist (John 3:26) and Jesus (Mark 9:5; 11:21; John 1:38, 49; 3:2; 4:31; 6:25; 9:2; 11:8). Since it was sometimes used ostentatiously, Jesus prohibited its use among his followers (Matt. 23:7–8). Judas called Jesus "Rabbi" when he betrayed him (Matt. 26:25, 49; Mark 14:45). After the destruction of the temple, the sages who carried on the Pharisaic traditions were known as rabbis, but their rabbinate was one of piety, wisdom, and Torah knowledge, not clerical status. By the fifth century the Talmud could speak of qualifications for ordination to the rabbinate (*b. Sanh.* 5b; 7b; 17a).

---

31. The word ἀρχισυνάγωγος occurs in Mark 5:22, 35–36, 38; Luke 8:41 (ἄρχων τῆς συναγωγῆς), 49; 13:14; Acts 13:15 (plural); 14:2 (Western Text); 18:8, 17.

32. The attendant was something of a sexton who cared for various duties and was known as the חַזָּן. See Jastrow, *Dictionary*, s.v. חַזָּן (444). The term used in Luke 4:20 is ὑπηρέτης.

33. The expression λόγος παρακλήσεως may be a technical term for such a homily (Acts 13:15; cf. Heb. 12:22).

GROUPS WITHIN JUDAISM

Pharisees

Legally scrupulous Jews known as *Hasidim* fought against the oppressions of Antiochus Epiphanes during the days of the Maccabean revolt (175–63 B.C.). Such Jews remained wary of the resulting Jewish kingdom led by the Hasmoneaen dynasty because it retained Hellenistic trappings and did not consistently obey and enforce Mosaic Law. These *Hasidim* evidently gave rise to the Pharisees of the NT, whose name implied their separatist values. Josephus speaks of the Pharisees, along with the Sadducees and Essenes, along the lines of the Greco-Roman philosophies (*A. J.* 18.11–25).[34] The most basic tenet of the Pharisees was their adherence to traditional oral laws that supplemented the written Torah. This oral Torah was viewed as originating in principle with Moses, and functioned to guard the written Torah by applying it to specific situations (*m. Avot.* 1:1–2).[35] It seems likely that the Pharisees' attempted to extrapolate the OT priestly purity laws to themselves. The Pharisees figure prominently in the narrative of the Gospels and Acts as opponents of Jesus and his followers. Despite this opposition, Jesus followed Pharisaic tradition to some degree and taught his followers to do likewise (Matt. 23:1–2).[36] Occasionally Pharisees are portrayed positively,[37] and some Pharisees became followers of Jesus (John 12:42). With the demise of the temple in A.D. 70, the followers of the NT Pharisees became the leaders of formative Judaism. All branches of Judaism today trace their origins back to the Pharisees. Even the Talmud (*b. Sot.* 22b) acknowledges with sarcasm that *certain* Pharisees were hypocrites, but also speaks of the one who is a Pharisee out of love. Careful students will avoid negative global stereotypes regarding this group, which border on anti-Semitism.[38]

---

34. Other texts in Josephus bearing on the Pharisees include *A. J.* 13.171–72, 297–98; 17.41–45; 18.16; *B. J.* 1.110; 2.162–65.

35. The NT term "traditions of the elders" (ἡ παράδοσις τῶν πρεσβυτέρων) refers to the oral Torah. See Matt. 15:2–3, 6; Mark 7:3, 5, 8, 13. Paul expressed his loyalty to Pharisaism similarly: περισσοτέρως ζηλωτὴς ὑπάρχων τῶν πατρικῶν μου παραδόσεων (Gal. 1:14). Josephus notes that these traditions are a key difference between the Pharisees and the Sadducees (*A. J.* 13.297–98; 17.41).

36. Noel S. Rabbinowitz, "Does Jesus Recognize the Authority of the Pharisees and Does He Endorse their *Halakhah?" JETS* 46 (2003): 423–47; Harvey Falk, *Jesus the Pharisee* (Eugene, OR: Wipf and Stock, 2003).

37. Matt. 22:34–40/Mark 12:28–34; Luke 13:31; John 2:23–3:2; 7:50–51; Acts 5:34–39; Acts 23:9.

38. The facile equation of Pharisee and hypocrite should be avoided. Anthony J. Saldarini seeks to avoid dubious generalizations in *Pharisees, Scribes, and Sadducees in Palestinian Society* (Grand Rapids: Eerdmans, 2001).

The Pharisees in the Gospels and Acts			
	Matthew	**Mark**	**Luke–Acts**	**John**
Chapters	3, 5, 9, 12, 15, 16, 19, 21, 22, 23, 27	2, 3, 7, 8, 10, 12,	Luke 5, 6, 7, 11, 12, 13, 14, 15, 16, 17, 18, 19 Acts 5, 15, 23, 26	1, 3, 4, 7, 8, 9, 11, 12, 18

Of course, Jesus's teaching conflicted with the traditional Pharisaic teachings on many matters, including ritual purity (Matt. 15:1–20/ Mark 7:1–23), Sabbath observance (Matt. 12:1–14/Mark 2:23–3:6/ Luke 6:1–11), and divorce (Matt. 5:31–32; 19:3–12/Mark 10:1–12). Jesus's popularity with the masses exacerbated such conflicts because it threatened the Pharisees' status and authority (John 11:47–53; 12:19). Their hubris (Matt. 27:18; Mark 15:10; cf. Acts 5:17; 13:45) led to the charge that Jesus collaborated with Satan (Matt. 9:34; 12:24) and their plan to kill him. The leaders of the Pharisees aligned with the Sadducean chief priests against their common enemy (e.g., Matt. 16:1; 21:45; John 7:32, 45; 11:47, 57; 18:3), which led to the Sanhedrin's condemnation of Jesus. In the book of Acts, opposition to Jesus's followers seems to come mainly from the chief priests. Paul cleverly utilized Pharisaic belief in the resurrection when he appeared before the Sanhedrin (Acts 23:6–9). Many of the early followers of Jesus in Jerusalem were Pharisees. Their loyalty to the ancestral traditions led to serious disputes about assimilating Gentiles into Christian communities (Acts 10:1–11:18; 15:1–5; 21:20–21). In those days the question was not whether Jews who believed in Jesus should abandon Torah observance, but whether Gentiles who believed in Jesus should adopt it.[39]

Scribes

Scribes (γραμματεύς) appear sixty-two times in the Gospels and Acts and only once elsewhere in the NT (1 Cor. 1:20). Their origin is commonly traced back to the early days of the Second Temple, particularly to Ezra (Ezra 7:6, 11, 10:3; Neh. 8:1–9, 13–18). Scribes were professional legal scholars who were active in studying and teaching the

---

39. On the Pharisees see Jacob Neusner's extensive discussion of ancient tradition about the Pharisees in *Rabbinic Traditions about the Pharisees*, 3 vols. (Leiden: Brill, 1971). Scholars address various questions about the Pharisees in Jacob Neusner and Bruce Chilton, eds., *In Quest of the Historical Pharisees* (Waco, TX: Baylor University Press, 2007).

law. Perhaps the teachers alluded to in Luke 2:46 were scribes. Their guild likely expanded during the Second Temple period when more scrupulous attention was paid to the law, both written and oral. Their awareness of and focus on traditional teaching is contrasted to the approach of Jesus, who commonly spoke on his own authority, but cited the OT when questioned (Matt. 5:21–48; 7:28–29; Mark 1:22). Those who called Jesus "teacher" viewed him in a quasi-scribal role (e.g., Matt. 8:19; 9:11; 12:38; 17:24; 19:16).

The Scribes in the Gospels and Acts

	Matthew	Mark	Luke–Acts	John
Chapters	2, 5, 8, 9, 12, 13, 15, 16, 17, 20, 21, 23, 26, 27	1, 2, 3, 7, 8, 9, 10, 11, 12, 14, 15	Luke 5, 6, 9, 11, 15, 19, 20, 22, 23 Acts 4, 6, 23	8

In the Gospels and Acts scribes are often linked to the Pharisees (cf. Mark 2:16; Acts 23:9), leading to the likelihood that scribal expertise went hand in hand with Pharisaic sympathies. They are also portrayed as being associated with the high priests and elders. Jesus had severe words for the scribes at times, and scribes were part of the Sanhedrin that condemned Jesus. Yet Matthew refers to scribes more often than the other Gospels, occasionally depicting them in a more positive light (8:19–20; 17:10) and citing Jesus speaking of his own disciples as scribes (13:52; 23:34). Scribal opposition to Jesus continued into the book of Acts (4:5; 6:12), but their belief in the resurrection opened their minds a bit to Paul's message (23:9). After the destruction of the temple it seems likely that the scribes' unique expertise would have rendered them prime candidates for early rabbinic roles in formative Judaism.[40]

Elders

The elders of Israel who appear in the Gospels and Acts apparently play a role in Israel that can be traced back to the seventy elders chosen by Moses (Num. 11:16–17), or even to the days before the exodus from Egypt (Exod. 3:16–18; 4:29; 12:21). In ancient cultures generally, aged men were accorded respect as heads of families and clans in various villages and cities. With age came experience, and with experience wisdom.

---

40. See further Christine Schams, *Jewish Scribes in the Second Temple Period* (Sheffield: Sheffield Academic, 1998).

Such respected leaders appear throughout the OT on occasions involving communal and legal decisions.[41] In rabbinic Judaism the term was associated with aged persons who had attained wisdom through much study.[42]

<table>
<tr><td colspan="5" align="center">Elders in the Gospels and Acts</td></tr>
<tr><td></td><td>Matthew</td><td>Mark</td><td>Luke–Acts</td><td>John</td></tr>
<tr><td>Chapters</td><td>15, 16, 21, 26, 27, 28</td><td>7, 8, 11, 14, 15</td><td>Luke 7, 9, 20, 22
Acts 4, 6, 22, 23, 24, 25</td><td></td></tr>
</table>

In the Gospels and Acts elders are seldom portrayed in a neutral fashion as local village leaders (Luke 7:3). They are mentioned at times in connection with the ancestral tradition of the oral Torah. Most frequently they are associated with other Jewish leaders in Jerusalem such as chief priests and scribes in speaking and acting in opposition to Jesus and his followers. Apparently such elders were respected leaders who represented influential families of Pharisaic, Sadducean, and priestly backgrounds on the Sanhedrin. They participated in the Sanhedrin's decision to seek the death of Jesus, and after the resurrection they continued to oppose the followers of Jesus.

Sadducees

The term "Sadducee" is often linked to the Hebrew word צֶדֶק, which refers to righteousness, and to Zadok, a prominent priest in the days of David and Solomon.[44] The Sadducees' association with the temple and the priesthood probably dates back to Hasmonean times. Josephus styles them as a smaller group of powerful aristocrats as opposed to the more numerous Pharisees who are in touch with the masses. Their views differed from those of the Pharisees on many points because they

---

41. E.g., Deut. 22:15–18; 25:7–9; Josh. 7:6; 8:10; 24:1; Ruth 4:9–11; Isa. 3:14; Jer. 29:1; Ezek. 20:1; Joel 1:2, 14.

42. Jastrow, *Dictionary*, s.v. זָקֵן (409). *M. Yoma* 1:5 speaks of elders of the court and of the priests. *M. Sukkah* 2:7 speaks of both Hillelite and Shammaite elders. The elders of the high court in Jerusalem are mentiones in *m. Sotah* 9:1 (cf. 9:5). *M. Sanh.* 1:6 connects Moses's seventy elders to the Jerusalem Sanhedrin. With Moses the body had seventy-one members.

43. The chapters in Acts include only the elders of Israel. Church elders are mentioned in Acts 11, 14, 15, 16, 20, 21.

44. See 2 Sam. 15:24–37; 19:11; 1 Kings 1:32–40, 44; 2:35; 4:1–4; 1 Chron. 6:8, 53; 15:11–15; 16:39; 24:3, 6, 31; 29:22; Ezek. 40:46; 43:19; 44:15.

did not accept the oral law. In fact, they seem to have accepted only the five books of Moses as fully authoritative. This conservative view of the canon is the reason for the Sadducees' skepticism about the resurrection and life after death (Josephus *A. J.* 13.297–98), and likely their denial of predestination as well. The Sadducees are mentioned relatively infrequently in ancient sources.[45] The Gospels and Acts mention them only fourteen times in six episodes:

The Sadducees in the Gospels and Acts			
	Matthew	**Mark**	**Luke–Acts**	**John**
Chapters	3, 16, 22	12	Luke 20 Acts 4, 6, 23	

The well-known differences between the Pharisees and Sadducees notwithstanding, Matthew portrays the two groups together on two occasions. Members of both groups were among the crowds coming to John's baptism (Matt. 3:7). Later in Galilee they came together to test Jesus by asking for a sign, leading him to warn his disciples about their "leaven" or teaching, which would be rather different on many points (Matt. 16:1–12). When Jesus arrived in Jerusalem and cleared the temple, the high priests who questioned his authority were Sadducees. Later the Sadducees came with a hypothetical question about levirate marriage (Gen. 38:6–30; Deut. 25:5–10; Ruth 3–4; *m. Yebam.*) and marital status in the resurrection (Matt. 22:23–33/Mark 12:18–27/ Luke 20:27–40). Each of the Synoptics prefaces its account of this event by mentioning the Sadducees' denial of life after death. After Pentecost the Sadducean leaders contested the apostles' authority to preach in the temple, just as they had questioned Jesus's authority. (Acts 4:1–22; 5:17, 28, 40; cf. Matt. 21:23/Mark 11:28/Luke 20:2). The final mention of the Sadducees in the NT comes during Paul's hearing before the Sanhedrin (Acts 23:6–10). Realizing that the Sanhedrin contained both Pharisees and Sadducees, Paul linked his preaching of Jesus's resurrection to the Pharisees' belief in the resurrection of the dead. This led to a heated debate between the Pharisees and Sadducees, and the Roman commander took Paul back to his barracks.

Little is known of the Sadducees after the destruction of the temple in A.D. 70. Evidently their identity could not be sustained apart from their social status as custodians of the temple and its cultural network.

---

45. Josephus, *A. J.* 13.171, 173, 293, 297–98; 18.11, 16; 20.199; *B. J.* 2.119, 164–65; *Vita* 2. The Mishnah refers to the Sadducees in *Mak.* 1:6; *Parah* 3:3, 7; *Yad.* 4:6.

The Sadducees are sometimes linked to the Karaite movement that flourished in the ninth and tenth centuries. The Karaites emphasized the written Scriptures and did not accept the authority of the oral law and the Rabbis who expounded it.[46]

Sanhedrin

Although there were local councils (Matt. 5:22; 10:17; Mark 13:9), the NT is concerned with the governing council or Sanhedrin in Jerusalem.[47] It was made up of high priests (Sadducees), elders, and scribes (likely Phariseees). Answerable only to Roman authority (John 18:31), it governed religious and civil matters alike. The roots of the Sanhedrin may be as early as the councils in the time of Ezra and Nehemiah (Ezra 5:5, 9; Neh. 2:16).[48] Herod had conflicts with the Sanhedrin and reportedly killed all its members at one point (Josephus, *A. J.* 14.175). According to Josephus, the Sanhedrin was mainly composed of high priestly individuals, although some prominent Pharisees were also involved (*A. J.* 20:224–51). This evidence is in tension with the Mishnah, which speaks of a Sanhedrin made up of seventy-one Torah experts (*m. Sanh.* 1:6). Tractate Sanhedrin in the Mishnah presents principles and procedures that were calculated to result in exemplary fairness for those undergoing trials, especially those charged with capital crimes. From the perspective of the Gospel accounts of the trial of Jesus—not to mention the trials of Stephen and Paul in Acts—the most egregious miscarriage of justice occurred. Christians who take the Gospel accounts of these matters as true should also acknowledge the wisdom and fairness of the Jewish laws that were disregarded by unworthy leaders at one crucial point in Israel's history. The Gospels present moments where the Sanhedrin's predetermined outcome to do away with Jesus was questioned by honorable people (Luke 23:50–51; John 7:45–52; cf. Acts 5:34–39; 23:9).[49]

---

46. See further Fred Astren, *Karaite Judaism and Historical Understanding* (Columbia: University of South Carolina Press, 2004).

47. The word συνέδριον occurs twenty-two times in the NT, mostly in reference to the governing council in Jerusalem, as in Matt. 26:59; Mark 14:55; 15:1, 43; Luke 22:66; 23:50; John 11:47; Acts 4:15; 5:21, 27, 34, 41; 6:12, 15; 22:30; 23:1, 6, 15, 20, 28; 24:20.

48. Rabbinical tradition viewed the seventy elders appointed by Moses (Num. 11:16) as the origin of the Sanhedrin. See *m. Sanh.* 1:6. Josephus (*A. J.* 12.138) refers to a governing council that existed in the days of the Seleucid ruler Antiochus III (223–187 B.C.). After the Roman victory in 63 B.C., Israel was divided into five regional "sanhedrins" (Josephus, *A. J.* 14.91).

49. For a thorough study of how Jewish scholars have understood this matter, see David R. Catchpole, *The Trial of Jesus* (Leiden: Brill, 1971), esp. 221–60.

Essenes

Although they are not mentioned in the NT, the Essenes warrant mention here because of their likely association with Qumran and the Dead Sea Scrolls.[50] The Essenes might have originated as part of the *Hasidim* movement of the Hasmonean era. Essenes are mentioned by Josephus alongside the Pharisees and Sadducees as one of the three major "philosophies" of Judaism.[51] Philo and the Roman author Pliny the Elder also describe them.[52] The Essenes believed that the Sadducean leaders of the Jerusalem temple were corrupt and they did not offer sacrifices there. Although Josephus speaks of Essenes living in families in various places around Israel, Pliny describes them as sexually abstinent and locates them near En Gedi and Masada, which fits the location of Khirbet Qumran. Such discrepancies lead some scholars to doubt that the Qumran complex was occupied by Essenes. The larger Essene movement, however, might have contained both monastics and people who lived a typical family life. In the Qumran sectarian literature the priests are commonly called the sons of Zadok,[53] and the Sadducean views on ritual purity agreed with those of the Qumran sect on some points. These facts lead some scholars to view the Qumran sect as a split from mainline Sadduceanism.[54] Similar views on some aspects of ritual purity aside, there are major theological differences between the Sadducees and the Essenes on key matters such as predestination and life after death. A majority of scholars argue that the Essene hypothesis has fewer problems than other theories about Qumran.

Speculation that John the Baptist was an Essene is based on a few superficial similarities. John's ministry was centered in the Judean desert, the same region where Qumran was located. Essenes were known to take orphans into their communities, and John's parents were elderly. John's dress and diet are thought to be consistent with the practice of the Essenes. John's baptism is compared to the Qumran ritual immersions. The most significant comparison may lie in the fact that the Qumran sect and John both understood Isaiah 40:3 as their *raison*

---

50. There are of course other views of the Qumran community, but currently the "Essene hypothesis" approaches consensus status. For assessment of various views and defense of the Essene hypothesis, see James VanderKam and Peter Flint, *The Meaning of the Dead Sea Scrolls* (San Francisco: Harper, 2002), 239–54.

51. Josephus, *A. J.* 13.171–72, 298, 311; 15.371–73, 378–79; 17.346; 18.11, 18, 22; *B. J.* 1.78; 2.113, 119–61, 567; 3.11; 5.145; *Vita* 10.

52. Josephus, *B. J.* 2.119–161; 8.119; Philo, *Prob.* 12.75–87. Philo also speaks of *therapeutae* or contemplative Essenes (*Contempl.* 1.1). Pliny the Elder [*Nat.* 5.17 (§73)] identifies the sect as sexually abstinent and locates it near En Gedi and Masada.

53. CD 4:1, 3; 1QSa 5:2, 9; 1QS1:2; 2:3; 3:22; 4Q266 f2, f5.

54. E.g., Lawrence Schiffman, *Reclaiming the Dead Sea Scrolls* (New York: JPS, 1994), 75.

d'etre.[55] John and the Qumran sect, however, understood Isaiah 40 in different ways. The Qumran sect viewed their desert location as a pure place, away from the evils of Jerusalem, where the law could be properly expounded and observed as they waited for the predestined end-time vindication of their community (1QS 8:15–16). John viewed the desert as the place from which to call out a repentant remnant from Israel in preparation for Jesus's messianic rule. Even if John had spent time as a member of the Qumran sect, his aggressive preaching of repentance to the multitudes and his pointing people to Jesus would indicate a parting of the ways with the fatalism and monasticism of the Essenes. Their daily ritual immersions were a matter of maintaining community relationship. John's immersion marked a one-time radical reorientation of one's life and ethics.[56]

Scholars note how such Essene ideas as ethical dualism and apocalypticism have affinities with NT teachings.[57] Jesus and his followers as well as the Essenes represented sectarian approaches to Judaism that stringently critiqued the Jerusalem establishment led by the Pharisees and Sadducees. Similarities between the early Christian movement and the Essenes have led to speculation that there are cryptic references to John the Baptist, Jesus, and the apostles in the Qumran sectarian manuscripts. There is no historical basis for such theories.

Politically Oriented Groups

Politically oriented groups are significant even if seldom mentioned in the NT. The *Herodians*, as their name implies, were loyal to the *status quo* of Herodian kings and Roman governors (Mark 3:6; Matt 22:16/ Mark 12:13). They were evidently in a comfortable socio-economic position and desired things to remain as they were. They likely viewed Jesus's teaching of a coming reign of God as a threat to their standard of living. The wealthy Sadducees and high priests would likely be political bedfellows of the Herodians. The Pharisees likewise accepted Roman rule and the status quo as long as it did not contradict their traditional legal observance. At the opposite end of the political spectrum were various messianic pretenders and pseudo-prophetic insurrectionists who wished to overthrow Roman rule. Peasants who were oppressed

---

55.   Matt. 3:3/Mark 1:2/Luke 3:4/John 1:23. Cf. 1QS 8:13; 4Q176 f1; 4Q259 3:4.

56.   On this question, see further Otto Betz, "Was John the Baptist an Essene?" in *Understanding the Dead Sea Scrolls*, ed. Herschel Shanks (New York: Random House, 1992), 205–14; John C. Hutchison, "Was John the Baptist an Essene from Qumran?" *BSac* 158 (2002): 152–64.

57.   See e.g., John J. Collins and Craig A. Evans, eds., *Christian Beginnings and the Dead Sea Scrolls* (Grand Rapids: Baker, 2006); Mary L. Coloe and Tom Thatcher, eds., *John, Qumran, and the Dead Sea Scrolls* (Atlanta: SBL, 2011).

by wealthy landowners and Roman taxation would gravitate to such leaders who spoke of throwing off the yoke of Rome. Josephus refers to a "fourth philosophy" (in addition to the Pharisees, Sadducees, and Essenes) that viewed Israel's political independence as a corollary of its status as God's people.[58] Simon the *zealot*, one of the Twelve (Matt. 10:4/ Mark 3:18/Luke 6:15; Acts 1:13), likely sympathized with such views. The term "zealot" recalled the heroism of Phinehas (Num. 25:11) and Mattathias (1 Macc. 2:19–27). Gamaliel advised the Sanhedrin to exercise caution in dealing with the apostles in Jerusalem on the grounds that the Jesus movement would likely be another short-lived insurrection like those of Theudas and Judas of Galilee (Acts 5:36–38).[59] The *sicarii* mentioned in Acts 21:38 were willing to assassinate not only the Romans but also their Jewish political opponents.[60] The "thieves" (λησταί) crucified with Jesus (Matt. 27:38/Mark 15:27) were likely bandits whose thievery was designed to destabilize Roman rule and foment revolt.[61] Barabbas, the murderous insurrectionist released by Pilate (Mark 15:7–15; Luke 23:19), is described in John 18:40 as a ληστής.

JEWISH FEASTS AND FESTIVALS

The Jewish feasts or festivals are another aspect of the Jewish background of the Gospels and Acts. In Leviticus 23 and other OT passages Israel is commanded to observe appointed times as holy convocations to the Lord. The common thread tying these festivals together is the absence of labor, reminding Israel to focus on their covenant relationship with God. The festivals are as follows:

- Sabbath/*Shabbat* (Exod. 20:8–11; 31:12–17; Lev. 23:3; Matt. 12:1–14; 28:1; Luke 4:16; Acts 13:14, 27, 42; 16:13)
- Passover/*Pesach* (Exod. 12; Lev. 26:5; cf. Matt. 26:2–19/Mark 14:12–16/Luke 22:1–20; Luke 2:41–42; John 2:13–23; 6:64;

---

58. *A. J.* 18.4–10, 23–25. Josephus attributed the origin of the fourth philosophy to Judas of Galilee, and he attributed the Jewish revolt and the destruction of the Second Temple to the fourth philosophy.

59. The reference to Theudas raises a chronological question when compared to Josephus, *A. J.* 20.97–99. On Judas of Galilee, see Josephus, *A. J.* 18.4–20, 23–25; 20:102; *B. J.* 2.118, 433; 7.253.

60. BDAG, s.v. σικάριος (923). The word is etymologically related to the means of their assassinations—a dagger. Cf. Josephus, *B. J.* 2.254–57.

61. BDAG, s.v. ληστής (594). Josephus (*B. J.* 2.254; cf. 2.271) describes the *sicarii* as another sort of ληστής. He goes on to describe other quasi-prophetic revolutionaries in 2.258–65. Jesus warned against such impostors in Matt 24:25/Mark 13:21–23. See further Richard A. Horsley and John S. Hanson, *Bandits, Prophets, and Messiahs* (Harrisburg, PA: Trinity Press International, 1999).

        11:55; 12:1; 13:1–30; 18:28, 39; 19:14; Acts 12:4; 1 Cor. 5:7;
        Heb. 11:28)
  • Unleavened bread/*Chag HaMotzi* (Exod. 12:15–20; 13:6–10;
        Lev. 23:6–8; Matt. 26:17; Mark 14:1, 12; Luke 22:1, 7; Acts
        12:3; 20:6; 1 Cor. 5:8)
  • Firstfruits/*Reshit Katzir* (Lev. 23:9–14; Rom. 8:23; 1 Cor.
        15:20–23)
  • Pentecost/Weeks/*Shavu'ot* (Lev. 23:15–22; Deut. 16:9–12; Acts
        2:1; 20:16; 1 Cor. 16:8)
  • Trumpets/*Rosh HaShana* (Lev. 23:23–25)
  • Day of Atonement/*Yom Kippur* (Lev. 16:29–34; 23:26–32; 25:9;
        Acts 27:9)
  • Tabernacles/Booths/*Succot* (Lev. 23:33–43; Deut. 16:13–17;
        Neh. 8:13–18; Zech. 14:16–19; John 7:1–14; Acts 18:21)

Two additional festivals were observed during NT times:
  • *Purim* (Esther 9:18–32; *m. Meg.*)
  • Dedication/Lights/*Hannukah* (1 Macc. 4:36–61; Josephus, *A. J.*
        12.323; John 10:22)

The Jewish calendar is lunar, beginning in the spring with Passover,
Unleavened Bread, Firstfruits, and Pentecost. Trumpets, Day of
Atonement, and Tabernacles come in the fall.[62] As observant Jews,
Jesus and his apostles participated in the Jewish feasts (see NT references above). There is not space for extended discussion, but students
of the Gospels and Acts realize that proper Sabbath observance was an
occasion of major conflict between Jesus and the Pharisees. Passover
looms large in the NT as the setting for the Last Supper, the institution
of the Lord's Table, and the crucifixion. Lamb-typology closely related
to Passover is an important aspect of NT theology (e.g., Isa. 53:7; John
1:29; Acts 8:32; 1 Peter 1:19; Rev. 5:6). The unleavened bread festival,
closely related to the Passover, also has typological implications (Matt.
16:6, 11–12; 1 Cor. 5:6–8; Gal. 5:9). The Jewish feasts are especially
important for the understanding of the Fourth Gospel. The mention of
three different Passovers in John is a major reason for believing Jesus's
public ministry lasted three years.[63]

---

62. See the accessible discussion of David Feinstein, *The Jewish Calendar: Its Structure and Laws*
     (Brooklyn: Mesorah, 2004).

63. See further Michael Daise, *Feasts in John: Jewish Festivals and Jesus's "Hour" in the Fourth Gospel*
     (Tübingen: Mohr Siebeck, 2007); Gary Wheaton, *The Role of the Jewish Feasts in John's Gospel*
     (Cambridge: Cambridge University Press, 2015); Gale A. Yee, *Jewish Feasts in the Gospels of
     John* (Wilmington, DE: Glazier, 1989).

THE INDIVIDUAL SETTINGS OF THE GOSPELS AND ACTS

The Historical Setting of Matthew

Authorship. The Gospel of Matthew is technically anonymous, as are the other Gospels. And yet Hengel's argument that the titles of the Gospels are very early, perhaps even original with each Gospel, is plausible.[64] Ancient custom tended to identify books by their authors (cf. Tertullian, *Marc.* 4.2). It should not be assumed that the Gospels originally circulated anonymously, with their titles being added in the second century. The nearly unanimous attribution of the Gospels to their traditional authors in the second century A.D. implies that their titles were early and based on oral tradition.

The grammar, syntax, literary style, and distinctive themes of the Gospel of Matthew lead most scholars to conclude that its author was a Jew who understood Hebrew and Judaism. This conclusion supports the traditional view of Matthew's authorship, but of course it does not prove it. When it comes to external evidence, the titles of many ancient manuscripts ascribe the book to Matthew; none ascribe it to another author. Ancient church tradition likewise attributes the book to Matthew. Eusebius's *Ecclesiastical History* (c. A.D. 320) cites three authorities to this effect, Papias (c. A.D. 130) in 3.39, Clement of Alexandria (c. A.D. 200) in 6.14, and Origen (mid-third century A.D.) in 6.25.4. Irenaeus (late second century A.D.) agrees (*Haer.* 3.1.1; cf. Eusebius, *Hist. eccl.* 5.8.2), as do several later sources. This unanimous ancient tradition is at least plausible, and arguments against it are not convincing.

Matthew, the traditional author of the First Gospel, is mentioned five times in the NT (Matt. 9:9; 10:3; Mark 3:18; Luke 6:15; Acts 1:13). Jesus's call of Matthew the tax collector at Caesarea is found in Matt. 9:9–13/Mark 2:13–17/Luke 5:27–32. In these calling texts Mark and Luke speak of Levi, not Matthew, although in the texts that list the names of the twelve apostles, Mark 3:18 and Luke 6:15 agree with Matthew 10:2 in speaking of Matthew. Some Jews had two names (Acts 4:36; Josephus *A. J.* 12.285; 18.35, 95; 20.196). Jesus gave Simon the name Peter (Matt. 16:18), so it is plausible that Matthew the apostle was also called Levi, perhaps because of his ancestry. Only Matthew 10:3 mentions that Matthew was a tax collector (τελώνης), a subordinate customs official who was responsible to collect revenue on goods moving through a particular area. Such officials were generally despised, and pious Jews particularly distrusted them due to their daily contact with Gentiles (cf.

---

64. Martin Hengel, *Studies in the Gospel of Mark*, trans. J. Bowden (Philadelphia: Fortress, 1985), 64–84; Hengel, *The Four Gospels and the One Gospel of Jesus Christ* (Harrisburg, PA: Trinity Press International, 2000), 48–53, 77.

Matt. 5:46; 9:10; 11:19; 18:17; 21:31).[65] Assuming the traditional view of authorship, the detail that Matthew was a tax collector would be a subtle way of the author saying he was thankful for the Jesus's grace and mercy.

Occasion and Purpose. Matthew's presentation of Jesus as one who fulfills biblical law and promise requires his readers to come to a conclusion about the relationship of this Gospel to Judaism. Some scholars are convinced that Matthew is written from the perspective that the church is primarily a Gentile community that is out of touch with the synagogue, and others think that Matthew assumes the church still has a strong Jewish element and is still engaged with the synagogue. Still others believe that Matthew can be satisfactorily explained only when it is viewed against the background of an embattled minority in the process of leaving the synagogue. The first view seems least likely for several reasons, including Matthew's inclusion of Jesus striking instruction in Matthew 23:2–3.

Proposed locations for Matthew's writing and reception include Antioch, Phoenicia, Galilee, Alexandria, Caesarea, and even Pella. Grasping the message of the book does not depend on knowing the location of its original recipients. Bauckham's arguments that Matthew as well as the other Gospels were intended for a wide audience should not be taken lightly.[66] Matthew wants the entire church, not just Christian Jews, to understand how its foundational OT heritage informs its ongoing mission to Jews and Gentiles. Matthew's occasion and purposes can only be approximated by inferences from the text itself. Matthew's audience needs to understand how Jesus fulfilled and interpreted Moses's law (Matt. 5:17–48). This audience needs to understand how occasional Gentile receptivity to Jesus (e.g., Matt. 8:10; 15:28; 27:54) anticipates Jesus's climactic commission that the community teach Jesus's message to all the nations (28:19).

Since the date of Matthew is not mentioned in the Gospel itself, it must be inferred from its contents and relation to the other Gospels. There may well be allusions to Matthew in Ignatius (c. A.D. 105) and in the Didache (late first or early second century A.D.).[67] When these allusions are taken in conjunction with Papias's testimony (see below), it seems clear that Matthew was well known by the early second century. The current scholarly consensus, based on the Markan priority view of Gospel relationships, places Matthew's origin in the A.D. 80s or 90s. Some argue for such a date by connecting Matthew's occasion with that of a rabbinic council in Jamnia (Jabneh), but this theory is increasingly

---

65. BDAG, s.v. τελώνης, 999.

66. Richard Bauckham, "For Whom Were the Gospels Written?" in *The Gospels for All Christians*, ed. R. Bauckham (Grand Rapids: Eerdmans, 1998), 9–48.

67. Ignatius, *Eph.* 19; *Smyr.* 1; *Did.* 1:3–5; 8:2; 9:5.

disputed. On the other hand, if one accepts the traditional testimony to apostolic authorship and Matthean priority, the date is earlier. Many scholars affirm a pre-A.D. 70 date for Matthew.

Papias and a Hebrew Matthew.[68] A foundational question regarding the origins of Matthew's Gospel is whether it arose as an Aramaic or Hebrew text that was later translated into the present Greek version. The key text is Eusebius's (c. A.D. 330) *Ecclesiastical History* 33.39.16, which cites Papias (c. A.D. 130) as follows: "περὶ δὲ τοῦ Ματθαίου ταῦτ᾽ εἴρηται: 'Ματθαῖος μὲν οὖν Ἑβραΐδι διαλέκτῳ τὰ λόγια συνετάξατο, ἡρμήνευσεν δ᾽ αὐτὰ ὡς ἦν δυνατὸς ἕκαστος.'" This text affirms that Matthew collected the oracles (of Jesus) in the Hebrew language (or perhaps "Hebraic style") and everyone translated (perhaps "interpreted") them as they were able. At first glance this text implies that any Greek editions of Matthew have been translated from an original Hebrew document, but the present Greek Matthew does not read like a translation of a Hebrew original. Some have argued that Matthew wrote both a Hebrew Gospel and a Greek Gospel.[69] Others think that Papias's λόγια were not a Gospel at all but sayings of Jesus that modern source critics call Q, or even Jesus's discourses that are found in canonical Matthew. There are no ancient manuscripts, however, that exemplify the putative Hebrew Matthew mentioned by Papias. For these and additional reasons, others propose that Ἑβραΐδι διαλέκτῳ does not mean the Hebrew language but Semitic rhetorical style, and that ἡρμήνευσεν does not refer to translation but to interpretation. If such is the case, Papias speaks of Matthew's Jewish style of composition, which subsequent readers interpreted to the best of their ability. Perhaps such features as Matthew's genealogy and stress on "fulfillment" are indicative of his Jewish compositional style.[70]

The Historical Setting of Mark

Authorship. Mark, along with the other Gospels and Acts, is anonymous. Its title, "The Gospel according to Mark," was added early on because of its association with Mark's testimony and authority. In early

---

68. On Papias's general impact on NT studies, see Monte A. Shanks, *Papias and the New Testament* (Eugene, OR: Pickwick, 2013). See also Richard Bauckham, "Papias on Mark and Matthew," in Bauckham, *Jesus and the Eyewitnesses*, 202–39.

69. Additional references to a Hebrew Matthew include Irenaeus, *Haer.* 3.1.1; Origen, cited by Eusebius in *Hist. eccl.* 6.25.4, and Eusebius in *Hist. eccl.* 3.24.6; 5.10.3.

70. For more detailed treatment of Matthew's historical setting, see D. A. Carson and D. J. Moo, *An Introduction to the New Testament*, 2nd ed. (Grand Rapids: Zondervan, 2005), 140–62; W. D. Davies and Dale C. Allison, *A Critical and Exegetical Commentary on the Gospel according to Matthew*, ICC, 3 vols. (Edinburgh: Clark, 1988–91), 1.1–148; 3.692–738; John Nolland, *The Gospel of Matthew* (Grand Rapids: Eerdmans, 2005), 1–62.

church tradition Mark is closely associated with Peter. The most strik-ing text[71] is a citation of Papias (c. A.D. 130) by Eusebius (*Hist. eccl.* 3.39.15), to the effect that Mark was not a hearer and follower of the Lord but of Peter, and, as Peter's interpreter, Mark wrote his Gospel as an accurate if not orderly account of all that Peter remembered.[72]

John Mark in the NT is traditionally and likely correctly identified as the author of this Gospel. Unless Mark 14:51–52 is regarded as a cryptic reference to John Mark,[73] he is not mentioned as a follower of Jesus in the Gospels. John Mark comes to light in Acts. His mother's house in Jerusalem was the site of the prayer meeting when Peter was miraculously freed from prison (Acts 12:12). John Mark accompanied Paul and Barnabas on the first mission trip, but his departure led to tension between them and their parting of ways (Acts 12:25; 13:5, 13; 15:36–41). More than ten years later, assuming Colossians and Philemon were written from Rome during Paul's two-year house ar-rest there (Acts 28:30–31), Mark appears as one of Paul's trusted fellow workers (Philem. 24). Perhaps the difficulties of the first mission trip led to Paul's instructions that Mark should be welcomed at Colossae (Col. 4:10). In any event, Paul's final word about Mark is positive— Paul instructs Timothy to bring Mark when Timothy comes to Paul because Mark is helpful for Paul's ministry (2 Tim. 4:11). Mark was also a ministry associate of Peter, likely in Rome, and is mentioned en-dearingly by Peter as his son (1 Peter 5:13). This last text supports the Peter-Mark connection affirmed several times in early church tradition.

Occasion and Purpose. As noted above, both Paul and Peter place Mark in Rome. Likewise, early church tradition associates Mark with Peter in Rome and depicts Mark's Gospel as a collection of Peter's individual memories, or of Mark's memories of Peter's teaching. There is also the idea that as Peter's life was drawing to an end his followers wanted a

---

71.   See also Justin Martyr, *Dial.* 106.3; Irenaeus *Haer.* 3.1.1; Clement of Alexandria, cited in Eusebius, *Hist, eccl.* 6.14.6–7; Origen, cited in Eusebius, *Hist. eccl.* 6.25.5; Tertullian, *Marc.* 4.5; Eusebius, *Hist. eccl.* 2.16–17.

72.   For a lengthy discussion of Eusebius's citation of Papias and a defense of authorship by John Mark, see R. H. Gundry, *Mark: A Commentary on His Apology for the Cross* (Grand Rapids: Eerdmans, 1993), 1026–45. See also Eusebius *Hist. eccl.* 2.15.1–2; 6.14.5–7.

73.   Mark 14:51–52 depicts a brief scene following the arrest of Jesus. All the disciples have fled, but an unnamed young man follows the arrest party and is apprehended. He then runs away naked, leaving behind his linen garment. William L. Lane, among others, takes this obscure passage as an autobiographical reference to John Mark. See *Mark* (Grand Rapids: Eerdmans, 1974), 527–28. For a lengthy discussion of this text, see Raymond E. Brown, *The Death of the Messiah*, 2 vols. (New York: Doubleday, 1994), 1.294–304. Brown speaks of the "extraordinary amount of speculation" on the passage. It is worth noting that, if this interpretation is correct, the early tradition that John Mark was not a follower of the earthly Jesus is mistaken. It seems more likely that the purpose of this text is to emphasize the shame of the disciples in abandoning Jesus (Mark 14:27–31, 40, 50, 51–52, 66–72).

written record of his teaching. Mark's tendency to translate Aramaic expressions into Greek (Mark 3:17; 5:41; 7:34; 14:36; 15:34), explain Jewish customs (Mark 7:2–4; 15:42), and use Latin terms (Mark 4:21; 12:14, 42; 15:15, 21) is consistent with the idea that he wrote for a largely Gentile audience in a place like Rome, although his Gospel would soon be circulated well beyond that center of the church's life.

Like Matthew (and unlike Luke and John), Mark does not explicitly state its purpose. From the content of Mark one may deduce an interest in presenting Jesus more as a man of action than as a teacher. Generally speaking, this approach is the opposite of Matthew's emphasis, and it helps explain the redactional interests of both books. Mark puzzles readers by juxtaposing its presentation of Jesus as the promised Messiah who does great miracles with its presentation of Jesus as a victim of persecution and crucifixion, who was often misunderstood even by his own disciples. This perplexity likely points to Mark's teaching that the way of suffering that leads to the cross is surprisingly the path to glory.[74] This theme will be explained in chapter 3.

Date. The date of Mark is obviously a matter of great debate. If we assume the reliability of the early tradition of Mark writing the Gospel while he was Peter's companion in Rome, the Gospel would have been written before Peter's martyrdom during the persecution of Nero around A.D. 64–68.[75] Peter was in Corinth during the mid-50s A.D. (1 Cor. 1:12; 3:22; 9:5), so he did not arrive in Rome until the late 50s A.D. at the earliest. This circumstance would leave a span from the late 50s A.D. to late 60s A.D. for the book to be written.

The Historical Setting of Luke–Acts

Authorship. As are the other Gospels, Luke and Acts are anonymous, but early and unanimous tradition attributes both of these books to Paul's companion Luke. Irenaeus (*Haer.* 3.1; 3.14.1–4; late second century A.D.), Clement of Alexandria (*Strom.* 5.12; c. A.D. 200), Tertullian (*Marc.* 4.2; c. A.D. 208), and Eusebius (*Hist. eccl.* 3.4; 3.24.15; c. A.D. 320) all speak to this point, as do the **Muratorian Canon** (c. A.D. 200?) and the **Anti–Marcionite prologues** (c. A.D. 300). Internally, the echoing of Luke's preface (Luke 1:1–4) in Acts 1:1, as well as the recapitulation of Luke 24:44–53 in Acts 1:1–11, give every indication that they were written by the same author to the same recipient, Theophilus. The elevated vocabulary and writing style of Luke–Acts

---

74. If this is the case, Mark becomes an apologist for the cross. See Gundry, *Mark*, 1–15. The passion is itself a success story (2).

75. For ancient tradition on Peter's martyrdom, see Tertullian, *Praescr.* 26; *Scorp.* 15; Eusebius, *Hist. eccl.* 3.1.2.

indicates a well-educated author. The common theological emphasis of the two books also supports their common authorship.

Luke is mentioned by name only three times in the NT (Col. 4:14; Phlm. 24; 2 Tim. 4:11), each time as a companion of Paul in the closing of a letter. In Colossians 4:14 he is called "the beloved physician" (Λουκᾶς ὁ ἰατρὸς ὁ ἀγαπητὸς).[76] In Philemon 24 he is mentioned last in a group of four co-workers (συνεργοί) of Paul who greet Philemon. In 2 Timothy 4:11 he is mentioned as Paul's only companion (Λουκᾶς ἐστιν μόνος μετ᾽ ἐμοῦ). Assuming that the "we-sections"[77] in Acts are not a literary device and actually refer to the narrator's physical presence with Paul,[78] Luke also accompanied Paul on portions of the second and third mission trips and on the voyage to Rome, including the shipwreck at Malta. Colossians and Philemon are commonly believed to have been written (along with Ephesians and Philippians) during Paul's two-year house arrest in Rome mentioned in Acts 28:30–31. If such is the case, and if the "we-sections" are taken as historical references to Luke as Paul's traveling companion, Luke was with Paul during the writing of these "prison epistles." By entirely plausible inference then, Luke was the writer of Acts, and, therefore, of the Third Gospel as well.

Little is known about Luke outside these few NT references. That church tradition connects him with Syrian Antioch is likely the result of the dubious identification of Luke with Lucius (Λούκιος) of Cyrene in Acts 13:1. It is tempting to view Luke as a Gentile God-fearer, one whose background was not unlike some of the people in his writings (Luke 7:1–10; Acts 10:1–2, 22, 30–35; 13:16, 43, 48; 16:14; 18:7). Paul's description of his companions in Colossians 4:10–14, that seems to distinguish Jews from Gentiles, is another indication that Luke was a Gentile.

---

76. Vivid descriptions of illnesses (e.g., Acts 28:8) are consistent with Luke the physician's authorship of Acts.

77. The use of first person pronouns and verbs in the "we-sections" appear to place the narrator as a companion of Paul during various periods of his ministry. In Acts 16:10 the narrative noticeably shifts from the previous third person plural pronouns and verbs to first person plural forms. See Acts 16:10–13, 16; 20:5–8, 13–15; 21:1–8, 10–12, 14, 15–18; 27:1–8, 15–16, 18, 20, 27, 29, 37; 28:1, 10–14, 16. If this understanding is correct, Luke accompanied Paul from Troas to Macedonia and then on to Philippi during Paul's second mission trip (16:10–17; note the shift back to third person forms in 16:19). He is with Paul again at Philippi in Acts 20:5 on Paul's journey back to Jerusalem at the end of the third mission trip, accompanying him to Troas, Assos, Miletus, and from there on to Tyre, Ptolemais, Caesarea, and Jerusalem (20:5–21:18). Finally, he appears again with Paul at the end of Paul's imprisonment at Caesarea (27:1) and accompanied Paul on the voyage to Rome, enduring the shipwreck at Malta (27:1–28:16). None of Paul's other companions are mentioned between 21:19 and 26:32, so it may well be that Luke was with Paul during this time as well.

78. This is the conclusion of Craig S. Keener after an extensive discussion in *Acts: An Exegetical Commentary*, vol. 3 (Grand Rapids: Baker, 2014), 2350–74.

Occasion and Purpose. There is no real evidence of where Luke-Acts was written, or of its specific audience. To the degree that it can be inferred from the preface in 1:1–4, the occasion and purpose of Luke has been discussed in the previous chapter. Acts 1:1 implies that Acts is a continuation of Luke as the former account of all that Jesus began to do and teach. Accordingly, Luke's goal for the two-volume project was to provide an accurate narrative of the Jesus movement from its earliest days in Palestine to its recent expansion to Rome. He wrote so that his patron Theophilus (and no doubt a much broader audience) could be assured of the accuracy of what he had been taught as a follower of Jesus. The distinctive emphasis of Luke-Acts on historical authenticity, the fulfillment of OT promises in Jesus, the work of the Holy Spirit, the evangelization of undesirables, and the validity of Paul's mission are certainly at the heart of this two-part composition's purpose. We will turn more fully to such matters in the next chapter.

Date. Comparing Acts 1:1–4 and Luke 1:1–2 indicate that Luke was written before Acts. The somewhat abrupt ending of Acts, with Paul still waiting for the emperor to resolve his case, leads many to think that Acts was written at the end of that two-year period as a defense of Paul's ministry, perhaps one intended to be submitted to the emperor Nero. In a plausible chronology of Paul, this time in Rome would have occurred around A.D. 62. Unless Luke chose to omit later events in Paul's life, such as those reflected in the pastoral letters 1–2 Timothy and Titus, this early date for Acts seems best. On the other hand, if Acts was written to show the expansion of the gospel message from Jerusalem to Rome, as implied in Acts 1:8, the plot of the book had reached its goal with Paul preaching in Rome and the outcome of his case was not important for Luke's literary agenda. On this reading Acts was likely written later. How much later is difficult to determine. If the silence of Acts on such matters as Nero's persecution of the church (c. A.D. 64–68) and the Jewish revolt against Rome leading to the destruction of the temple (A.D. 66–70) is taken to mean those events had not yet occurred, it was not much later.[79]

The Historical Setting of John

Authorship. At first glance, the Gospel of John is anonymous, although the author claims to be an eyewitness of Jesus (John 1:14; 19:35; 21:24–25; cf. 1 John 1:1–4). The details included in the narrative (e.g., John 2:6; 18:10; 21:11) as well as the author's familiarity with place

---

79. For more detailed discussions of the provenance of Luke-Acts, see Darrell L. Bock, *Luke*, 2 vols. BECNT (Grand Rapids: Baker, 1994, 1996), 1.4–18; Darrell L. Bock, *Acts*, BECNT (Grand Rapids: Baker, 2007), 1–32; Carson and Moo, *Introduction*, 290–321; and especially the magisterial discussion of Keener, *Acts*, 1.43–458.

names and Jewish festivals (e.g., John 4:3–5; 7:37–39; 10:22) support this claim. The book ends with an oblique reference to its authenticity and authorship, ascribing it to "the disciple whom Jesus loved, who had leaned on his breast at the supper" (John 21:20–24; cf. 13:23; 18:15–16 [?]; 19:26, 34–35; 20:2, 8; 21:7). Answers to the question as to who this mysterious disciple might be include Lazarus (John 11:3, 5, 36) and Thomas (19:35; 20:24–29), but it appears that neither Lazarus nor Thomas were close associates of Peter, as was the beloved disciple (John 13:24; 20:2–10; 21:7, 20–24).

Ancient church tradition identifies the beloved disciple as John, but not without introducing additional ambiguity into the matter. Irenaeus (*Haer.* 3.1.2; late second century) says that John, the disciple who reclined on Jesus's breast, published a Gospel while he lived in Ephesus. According to Eusebius (*Hist. eccl.* 6.14.6–7; c. A.D. 320), Clement of Alexandria said that John, at the encouragement of his associates, composed a spiritual Gospel (πνευματικὸν ποιῆσαι εὐαγγέλιον) because he perceived that the previous Gospels had emphasized external matters (τὰ σωματικὰ). Eusebius (*Hist. eccl.* 3.39.4–6) also cites a perplexing word from Papias (c. A.D. 110) who speaks of his interest in hearing traditions from "elders" who were passing through Hierapolis. In this passage Papias apparently mentions two individuals named John, one associated with other disciples from Jesus's original apostolic circle, and another associated with Aristion.[80] Papias refers to both of these individuals as "elders." It might be, however, that Papias refers only to John the apostle, mentioning him first in conjunction with the original twelve apostles and the second time because he was the last surviving apostle. In any event, this ambiguity does not call into question the other early traditions that identify the beloved disciple who wrote the Fourth Gospel as John.

It is interesting that the Fourth Gospel does not mention John by name, although several other apostles are so mentioned. This factor, along with the book's repeated oblique references to the beloved disciple, imply that if John is the author, he is being modest. Elsewhere in the NT John appears as one of Jesus's original twelve apostles, who along with his fellow son of Zebedee, James, immediately left their work as fishermen when Jesus called them (Mark 1:19–20). John seems to be a part of an inner circle of Jesus's disciples who accompany him as significant times, including his transfiguration and agony in Gethsemane (Mark 9:2; 14:33). John and his brother James could be headstrong and volatile (Mark 10:35–41; Luke 9:51–55). John was a bold preacher in the early days of the Jerusalem church (Acts 3:1–11; 4:1, 13, 19–20), and later ministered to the Samaritans

---

80.   This is how Eusebius understood Papias, as he comments in *Hist. eccl.* 3.39.5–6.

(Acts 8:14–25). His brother James was martyred (Acts 12:2), but John lived a long life and was regarded by Paul as a pillar of the Jerusalem church (Gal. 2:9).

Occasion and Purpose. John does not provide any explicit internal clues as to where his Gospel was written and to whom it was sent. The late-second-century tradition of Irenaeus (cited above) places John in Ephesus. According to a citation of Irenaeus in Eusebius (*Hist.eccl.* 3.28.6; 4.14.6; cf. Irenaeus *Adv. Haer.* 1.16.1; 3.2.1, 77–8), one day John fled from the public baths in Ephesus because he heard that the heretic Cerinthus was there and feared the roof would cave in. Cerinthus was an early gnostic who apparently believed that Jesus was only a man on whom a divine spirit came at his baptism and left before his crucifixion. It is plausible that the emphasis on Jesus as God in human flesh in John's Gospel (e.g., 1:14; cf. 1 John 4:2; 2 John 7) was intended to counter the views of Cerinthus. J. Louis Martyn[81] and others argued that the texts in John that refer to fear of being put out of the synagogue (9:22; 12:42; 16:2; cf. 7:13; 19:38; 20:19) reflect a decision of the purported early rabbinic council of Jamnia around A.D. 85 to ban heretics from the synagogue. This rather speculative view has been widely challenged.

The purpose of John's Gospel is implied in the prologue (1:12–13) and stated explicitly at the end (20:30–31). Many traditions about Jesus were omitted from this Gospel (20:30), and those that were selected for inclusion were especially calculated to lead people to life-giving faith in Jesus Christ. The reader of John is confronted repeatedly with the claims of Christ through signs (σημεῖα; 20:30) that signal Jesus's messianic identity and divine status.[82]

Date. Scholars once confidently dated John to the middle of the second century A.D. because they viewed its theologically sophisticated content as a late development. The publication in 1934 of the small papyrus manuscript 𝔓[52] caused many to doubt this view. This fragmentary manuscript contains part of John 18:31–33 on one side and John 18:37–38 on the other. This manuscript is generally dated by paleographers to around A.D. 130 This discovery, along with ongoing scholarship that examines John alongside the Qumran documents and other Second Temple Jewish literature, has led to something approaching a new consensus about the origins of John in the context

---

81. J. Louis Martyn, *History and Theology in the Fourth Gospel*, 3rd ed. (Louisville: Westminster John Knox, 2003).

82. D. A. Carson argues that the syntax of John 20:31 implies that the purpose of the book is not to assure Christians that Jesus is the Messiah but to prove to a Jewish audience that their Messiah is Jesus. See "The Purpose of the Fourth Gospel: John 20:30–31 Reconsidered," *JBL* 108 (1987): 639–51.

of Judaism in the late first century A.D. Today mainstream scholars tend to date John in the last decade of the first century A.D. and take it much more seriously as a viable witness to the historical Jesus, as summarized in the table below.[83]

	The Old Perspective	The New Perspective
The New Perspective on John[84]		
Author	Out of touch with the historical Jesus	Eyewitness
Date	Mid second century A.D.	Late first century A.D.
Milieu	Hellenistic	Jewish
Content	Secondary, dependent	Primary, independent
Historicity	Dubious	Plausible

Chapter in Review

In this chapter we surveyed four aspects of the historical setting of the Gospels and Acts. First, we provided an overview of the ancient sources that illumine the world of the Gospels and Acts. Second, we surveyed the historical period that led up to the time of Jesus and the writing of the Gospels and Acts later in the first century A.D. Third, we discussed key aspects of the background of the Gospels and Acts in Second Temple Judaism. Finally, we looked at the likely first-century origins of each of these books individually.

---

83. For more detailed discussions of the provenance of John, see Carson and Moo, *Introduction*, 229–76; Keener, *John*, 1.81–232.

84. See e.g., Paul N. Anderson, et al., eds., *John, Jesus, and History*, vol. 1, *Critical Appraisals of Critical Views* (Atlanta: SBL, 2007); *John, Jesus, and History*, vol. 2, *Aspects of Historicity in the Fourth Gospel* (Atlanta: SBL, 2009).

3

THE THEOLOGY OF THE GOSPELS AND ACTS

The Chapter at a Glance

Biblical theology is a vital discipline that synthesizes the innate themes of the Gospels and Acts, showing how their distinct voices contribute to a unified overall witness to the story of God, redemptive history. The Gospels and Acts present John the Baptist as Jesus's prophetic forerunner. The Gospels and Acts present Jesus as the Son of God, who through the Spirit embodies and enacts the reign of God as he teaches Israel. The Gospels and Acts present Jesus's disciples as his chosen successors who are mandated to continue his ministry by discipling the nations until his coming at the end of the age.

INTRODUCTION

IT IS POSSIBLE TO APPROACH AN INTRODUCTION to the theology of the Gospels and Acts in many ways. One might aim for comprehensiveness, summarizing a wide number of themes. The limited space available here, however, would necessitate brevity, leading to superficial discussions that sacrifice depth for breadth. In this chapter we have taken a different approach. First, there is a discussion of the nature and methods of theology. Then we take a crucial theme, Jesus and the Spirit, and trace it throughout the Gospels and Acts. Next we look at Matthew, Mark, Luke-Acts, and John individually, highlighting distinctive teachings of each. Although this approach sacrifices comprehensiveness, it provides better treatment of the selected themes and provides a model for readers who wish to address themes not treated here.

UNDERSTANDING THE DISCIPLINE OF BIBLICAL THEOLOGY

To understand the theology of the Gospels and Acts we must decide what theology is and how we should go about it. In the broadest sense, theology is reasoned discourse about God. For people of faith in Christ, who believe the Bible is God's revelation, discourse about God is not merely an academic discussion of ancient religious beliefs but worshipful engagement with one's Redeemer, made possible by saving grace. Theology in this sense is covenantal and therefore personal and relational, an exercise of faith and love as well as intellect. Vanhoozer put it well:

> To know God as the author and subject of Scripture requires more than intellectual acknowledgment. To know God is to love and obey him, for the knowledge of God is both restorative and transformative. The saving knowledge of God results in the transformation of the reader into the likeness of Jesus Christ.[1]

There are many branches and ways of describing theology, but for the purposes of this chapter we will simply speak of biblical and systematic theology and how these two approaches relate to other relevant disciplines in biblical studies and to each other. As will become clearer, our focus on exegetical method in this book leads to biblical rather than systematic theology.

Theological Disciplines

Students of the Bible should acknowledge the basic non-negotiable assumptions they bring with them to the text. These *presuppositions* profoundly influence how they read the Bible, the questions they ask of it, how they arrive at the answers, and what they do about those answers. Students should also be aware that their goals for studying the Bible, such as personal enrichment or ministry enactment, influence their study. The disciplines of biblical studies logically begin with biblical *criticism* or *introduction*, which relates to the social history of any biblical book, including its geography, time period, original text, culture,

---

1. Kevin J. Vanhoozer, in the Introduction to Kevin J. Vanhoozer, ed., *Theological Interpretation of the New Testament: A Book-by-Book Survey* (Grand Rapids: Baker, 2005, 2008), 24.

political climate, and the specific occasion that gave rise to the book, as best it can be understood. *Survey* provides a synthetic summary of the content of biblical books. *Exegesis* analyzes the details of selected segments of biblical books to ascertain their specific teachings. After synthesizing the teachings of a biblical book's segments into what the book teaches as a whole, *biblical theology* begins. Biblical theology continues the work of exegesis by relating one book's key teachings or themes to those of other books, beginning with other books by the same author, from the same time period, or of the same genre. We can speak of the theology of each Gospel as well as Acts, but it is arguably better to work with Luke and Acts together. One's view of literary interdependence will influence one's view of the theology of the Synoptic Gospels. It is common to distinguish between the theology of the synoptics and that of the Fourth Gospel, as well as to link the theology of the Fourth Gospel to the Johannine letters. This approach builds a corpus of teaching descriptively and incrementally, consisting of the main themes that emerge from the Bible when it is studied historically.

Biblical and Systematic Theology

Descriptive biblical theology is to be distinguished from dogmatic or *prescriptive systematic* theology. Historians commonly tie this distinction to an address by J. P. Gabler (1753–1826) at the University of Altdorf in Germany in 1787.[2] One might also cite in this regard the agenda John Calvin set for his biblical commentaries in the dedication of his Romans commentary to Simon Grynaeus in 1539. Calvin spoke of the tendency of his contemporaries to write commentaries that handled the biblical text unevenly and that contained lengthy digressions on topics of dogmatic theology. Satisfied that he had covered theological doctrines topically in his *Institutes of the Christian Religion*, Calvin did not seek to write biblical commentaries as pretexts for topical digressions to prove his doctrines. Rather, he sought in his commentaries to unfold the mind and meaning of the biblical authors with lucid brevity.[3]

Systematic theology ideally builds upon biblical theology by relating biblical teaching to current issues. Systematics also employs other relevant disciplines to provide teaching for the church in a given situation. In this way systematic theology attempts to prescribe sound

---

2. For a summary of Gabler's work, see M. Elliott, "Gabler, Johann Philipp," in *Dictionary of Major Biblical Interpreters* (Downers Grove, IL: InterVarsity, 2007), 452–56.

3. John Calvin, *The Epistles of Paul to the Romans and to the Thessalonians*, trans. R. Mackenzie (Grand Rapids: Eerdmans, 1960), 1–4. See the discussion of the key term "lucid brevity" (*perspicua brevitas*) in T. H. L. Parker, *Calvin's New Testament Commentaries* (Grand Rapids: Eerdmans, 1971), 49–56.

doctrine and by implication godly behavior for the church. Systematic theologians traditionally organize their work comprehensively under ten topics, sometimes called *loci,* that cover all the areas of theological knowledge. Systematic theology when done well is done with awareness of the development of doctrine (historical theology) in different branches of the church in various parts of the world through various time periods, beginning with the early church. Systematic theology goes astray when it utilizes the Bible anachronistically to prove doctrines developed centuries after the Bible was written, or to answer obscure questions that were never on the mind of the biblical author and are of no real value for the church.[4] Basic distinctions between biblical and systematic theology appear in the chart below.[5]

Biblical and Systematic Theology	
Biblical Theology	**Systematic Theology**
Reconstructs the past	Addresses the present
Descriptive	Prescriptive
Progressive (diachronic) canonical revelation	Ahistorical (synchronic) use of the Bible
Themes taken from the Bible itself	Comprehensive logical arrangement of topics
God spoke through the prophets	Bibliology
The kingdom of God	Theology proper
The words and deeds of Jesus	Christology
The Comforter	Pneumatology

---

4. The classic case is the storied debate over how many angels could dance on the head of a pin. Evidently the question was never put quite like this, although Aquinas did discuss whether several angels could occupy the same space at the same time (*Summa Theologica* Question 3.2). Perhaps better examples would be debates among dispensational theologians over precise eschatological details, like whether Armageddon is a battle or a campaign, or debates among reformed theologians over the precise covenantal manner in which Adam's first sin was imputed to his posterity. Whether or not such questions should occupy theologians, the point here is that theologians should not make it a priority to press biblical texts into service for debates that are foreign to the intrinsic agendas of those texts.

5. On the relationship of biblical and systematic theology, see further D. A. Carson, "Systematic Theology and Biblical Theology," *New Dictionary of Biblical Theology*, eds. T. Desmond Alexander, et al. (Downers Grove, IL: InterVarsity, 2000), 89–104, esp. 100–3.

Biblical and Systematic Theology	
Biblical Theology	**Systematic Theology**
Cosmic warfare, ethical dualism	Angelology
Image of God	Anthropology
Rebellion and alienation in Adam	Hamartiology
Election and reconciliation in Christ	Soteriology
The people of God	Ecclesiology
Promise and fulfillment	Eschatology
Redemptive history from Genesis to Revelation	Doctrines from A to Z

Problems with Biblical Theology

According to Balla, there are two major academic challenges to biblical theology. The first relates to the legitimacy of privileging a collection of certain texts (the canon of Scripture) and excluding others, and the second relates to the basic conceptual unity of those privileged canonical texts.[6] Those who argue against limiting the authoritative texts used in NT theology to the canon appear to argue that NT theology should not be based on the NT. This approach dismisses the church's process of considering the apostolicity, consistency, and reception history of the books that were eventually deemed canonical. The canon did not suddenly appear in the fourth century by episcopal fiat simply due to political considerations. Jesus charged his earliest followers to reproduce themselves by teaching others to observe his teachings. Their mission, aided by the coming of the Spirit, led to their writings. Their mission and their writings alike came with Christ's unique authority and spiritual empowerment. After these earliest followers of Jesus died, the church recognized their foundational authority in distinguishing between authentic teaching and teaching that departed from Jesus. There were lengthy disputes over some books, but these disputes do

---

6. Peter Balla, "Challenges to Biblical Theology," in *New Dictionary of Biblical Theology*, 20–27. Balla refers mainly to Heikki Räisänen, *Beyond New Testament Theology* (London: SCM, 1990, 2000). Balla's more lengthy treatment of the issue is *Challenges to New Testament Theology* (reprinted, Peabody, MA: Hendrickson, 1998). See further Michael. J. Krueger, *The Question of Canon: Challenging the Status Quo in the New Testament Debate* (Downers Grove, IL: InterVarsity, 2013).

not justify disregarding the primacy of the canonical writings of the NT. There are likewise difficulties in understanding the theological unity of the distinct voices found in the canon, but the church has long held to the one gospel of Jesus found in the fourfold Gospel tradition. Accordingly, it is historically appropriate to limit NT theology to the NT. Beyond the discipline of NT theology, it is also appropriate to study early Christianity in all its literature, no matter how aberrant that literature may be.[7]

Three additional problems with biblical theology involve hermeneutics. One approach to biblical theology emphasized the study of Hebrew and Greek words etymologically and diachronically as a means of revealing complex theological concepts. James Barr and others have exposed the linguistic naiveté of this approach, and its use has dwindled.[8] A more difficult problem is that many practitioners of the discipline, influenced by enlightenment rationalism, have supposed themselves as *historians* to be neutral and objective in describing the NT, in contrast to *theologians* who subjectively seek to develop prescriptive doctrines from the NT.[9] Yet it is commonplace in recent hermeneutics to acknowledge that it is impossible for human beings to approach the Bible with sheer disinterested objectivity.[10] Accordingly, it is vital to be aware that one's personal background and pragmatic goals influence one's choice of methods as well as the conclusions one reaches. A third hermeneutical problem is how the historical methods and data of biblical theology translate into authoritative values for the world today. Liberal practitioners of biblical theology might be content to leave what the Bible *meant* in the past if that ancient meaning conflicts with current values. Evangelicals who are confessionally bound to biblical authority cannot sever what the text *meant* from what it *means* today. This commitment means reading the Bible in sympathy with its original authors' agenda rather than with suspicion of that agenda. The Bible in general and the

---

7.   See further, Balla, *Challenges to New Testament Theology*; Krueger, *The Question of Canon*.

8.   James Barr, *The Semantics of Biblical Language* (Oxford: Oxford University Press, 1961). Moisés Silva provides a linguistically-informed approach to studying biblical words in *Biblical Words and their Meaning* (Grand Rapids: Zondervan, 1983). A similar approach to words is the comprehensive lexical work edited by J. P. Louw, *Greek-English Lexicon of the New Testament: Based on Semantic Domains*, 2nd ed., 2 vols. (New York: United Bible Societies, 1999).

9.   This problem goes back to Gabler. A classic statement of the view is that of Krister Stendahl, "Biblical Theology, Contemporary," in *IDB*, eds. G. A. Buttrick and K. Crim, 4 vols. with Supplement (Nashville: Abingdon, 1962): 1.418–32.

10. E.g., see Rudolf Bultmann, "Is Exegesis without Presuppositions Possible?" in *New Testament and Mythology*, ed. and trans. S. Ogden (Philadelphia: Fortress, 1984), 145–53. The original lecture dates from 1957. For Bultmann, sadly, presuppositions came from historical-critical skepticism and existential philosophy, not from a worldview consistent with that of the biblical text that Bultmann sought to describe.

Gospels and Acts in particular originally were intended to be read by the people of God in faith. When biblical theologians today read the Bible in faith, their descriptive work provides the basis for prescriptive teaching. What the text meant to Matthew, Mark, Luke, and John ought to determine what it means to the church today.

Biblical Theology and the Theological Interpretation of the Bible

The somewhat recent trend in hermeneutics known as theological interpretation of the Bible (TIB)[11] seems at first blush to be an unlikely partner of biblical theology. Biblical theology's goal, describing the Bible's teaching in the Bible's own terms, seems to collide head-on with TIB's aim of reading the Bible with the church's tradition in mind. After all, Gabler sought to free biblical theology from the accretions of ecclesiastical dogmatics. Although the ecclesial focus of TIB seems to make full *rapprochement* with biblical theology unlikely at best, there are areas on which evangelical biblical theologians and advocates of TIB can agree. Foundationally, both biblical theology and TIB are interested in a word from God for the church—*theology*—not just ancient religious ideas. The unity and authority of the Bible is a fundamental assumption of both evangelical biblical theologians and practitioners of TIB. Another point of agreement is that biblical theology should mediate historical-critical exegesis and systematic theology.[12] As such, biblical theology provides a welcome alternative to the atomistic tendencies of historical criticism and the **scholasticism** that sometimes has characterized systematic theology. Evangelicals should agree with Vanhoozer that biblical theology can partner with TIB "in the attempt to free the Bible from its recent captivity in the cold ivory towers of academia."[13]

Conclusion

An evangelical approach to the biblical theology of the Gospels and Acts reads these texts in faithful sympathy with their original Spirit-led agendas. As the authors of these books based their own normative

---

11. For discussion of the origins, main tenets, and burgeoning literature of this movement, see Daniel J. Treier, *Introducing Theological Interpretation of Scripture* (Grand Rapids: Baker, 2008); Kevin J. Vanhoozer, gen. ed., *Dictionary for Theological Interpretation of the Bible* (Grand Rapids: Baker, 2005).

12. Vanhoozer, "Introduction," in *Dictionary for Theological Interpretation*, 20–22. D. A. Carson agrees. See his essay "Systematic Theology and Biblical Theology," in *New Dictionary of Biblical Theology*, 95.

13. Kevin J. Vanhoozer, "Four Theological Faces of Biblical Interpretation," in *Reading Scripture with the Church*, eds. A. K. M. Adam, et al. (Grand Rapids: Baker, 2006), 131.

theological discourse on previous biblical revelation (the OT), so we today depend on these NT Scriptures for our own biblical theology. As we ascertain and describe the distinctive voices of the Gospels and Acts and combine these into an overall theology, we are as it were following the route prescribed by redemptive history. Our historic grasp of the symphonic fourfold Gospel witness will result in a composition characterized by diversity without disparity, resulting in unity without uniformity. Such a biblical theology should aid the church in providing an accurate record of its earliest canonical tradition, a tradition that should guide the church in evaluating all subsequent theological discourse.

JESUS AND THE SPIRIT IN THE THEOLOGY OF THE GOSPELS AND ACTS

The Gospels and Acts depict the work of God progressively and incrementally through the Spirit's ministry to John the Baptist, to Jesus, and to the followers of Jesus, the church.[14] John the Baptist is the promised prophetic voice who prepares the way. Jesus is the Son of God who through the Spirit embodies and enacts God's reign and instructs Israel concerning it.[15] After the ascension, Jesus and the Father send the Spirit to the church, led by Jesus's chosen successors, the Twelve. Jesus commissions the church to continue his ministry until his coming, expanding the scope of his ministry to all the people groups of the earth. As the table below shows, the Spirit of God is the empowering presence who actualizes the entire process.

---

14. Systematic theologians tend to subsume these texts under the loci of Christology, pneumatology, and ecclesiology. Although the logic of this arrangement is obvious and somewhat helpful, the categories seem to divide what the Bible unites and obscure the historical flow of the biblical narrative. This grand story unfolds the perichoretic, interrelational mission of the Father, Son, and Spirit in engendering the community of the kingdom and empowering its witness to the kingdom. If umbrella terms or categories are necessary to describe this story, the best may be inaugurated eschatology as creation renewal, as expounded by G. K. Beale in *A New Testament Biblical Theology* (Grand Rapids: Baker, 2011).

15. On the work of the Spirit in the Gospels and Acts, see Beale, *A New Testament Biblical Theology*, 559–78; James D. G. Dunn, *Jesus and the Spirit* (London: SCM, 1975); John Harvey, *Anointed with the Spirit and Power* (Phillipsburg, NJ: Presbyterian & Reformed, 2008); Gerald F. Hawthorne, *The Presence and the Power* (1991; reprinted, Eugene, OR: Wipf and Stock, 2003); Thomas R. Schreiner, *New Testament Theology: Magnifying God in Christ* (Grand Rapids: Baker, 2008), 435–73. For the work of the Spirit in Luke-Acts, see Max Turner, *Power from on High: The Spirit in Israel's Restoration and Witness in Luke-Acts* (Sheffield: Sheffield Academic, 1996). For the work of the Spirit in John, see Gary M. Burge, *The Anointed Community: The Holy Spirit in the Johannine Tradition* (Grand Rapids: Eerdmans, 1987).

Overview of Key Texts

Jesus and the Spirit in the Gospels and Acts				
Spirit's ministry	**Matthew**	**Mark**	**Luke–Acts**	**John**
Fills John the Baptist while still in Elizabeth's womb			Luke 1:15, 41	
Conception of Jesus	1:18		Luke 1:35	
Fills Elizabeth			Luke 1:41	
Fills Zechariah			Luke 1:67	
Messianic revelation to Simeon			Luke 2:25–27	
John the Baptist's promise: Jesus will baptize with the Spirit	3:11	1:8	Luke 3:16; Acts 1:5, 8; 11:16; 19:4	1:31
Visibly descends upon Jesus	3:16	1:10	Luke 3:22	1:32–33
Given to Jesus without limit				3:34
Remains on Jesus			Luke 4:1	1:33
Leads Jesus into the wilderness	4:1	1:12	Luke 4:1	
Empowers Jesus after the wilderness temptations			Luke 4:14	
Brings new birth through Jesus				3:5–6, 8; 6:63
Enables authentic worship				4:23–24
Enables disciples to witness during persecution	10:19	13:11	Luke 12:12	
Brings joy to Jesus	11:25		Luke 10:21	
Upon/anoints Jesus for ministry	12:17–21 (Isa. 42:1–4)		Luke 4:18–19 (Isa. 61:1–2) Acts 10:38	
Empowers Jesus's exorcisms	12:28			
Slandered by unbelievers	12:31–32	3:29	Luke 12:10	
Spoke through David about Jesus's exaltation	22:43–44 (Ps. 110:1)	12:36	Luke 22:42	
To be "given" after Jesus's glorification				7:37–39;
Continues Jesus's ministry to the disciples after Jesus's glorification				14:16–17

Jesus and the Spirit in the Gospels and Acts				
Spirit's ministry	**Matthew**	**Mark**	**Luke-Acts**	**John**
Testifies about Jesus after Jesus's glorification				15:26
Convicts the world				16:8–10
Guides the disciples into all the truth				16:13
"Given" to disciples by Jesus				20:22
To be invoked with the Father and Son by disciples at baptisms	28:19	16:16	Acts 2:38, 41; 8:12, 16, 36–38; 9:18; 10:47–48; 16:15, 33; 18:8; 19:5 22:16	
A gift promised by the Father, awaited by the disciples			Luke 24:49; Acts 1:4; 15:8	
Spoke through David about Judas			Luke 1:16–20 (Ps. 69:25; 109:8)	
Filled the disciples and enabled glossolalia			Luke 2:4	
Poured out by Jesus upon Jews and Gentiles			Luke 2:17–21, 33 (Joel 2:28–32) 10:44	
Promised to those who repent and are baptized			Luke 2:38	
Repeatedly fills Peter, Stephen, Paul, Barnabas, and other disciples			Luke 4:8, 31; 6:3, 5; 7:55; 9:17; 11:24; 13:9, 52	
Spoke through David about persecution			Luke 4:25–26 (Ps. 2:1–2)	
Lied to and tested by Ananias and Sapphira			Luke 5:3, 9	
Witnesses to Jesus, given by God to those who obey him			Luke 5:32	
Empowers Stephen's witness			Luke 6:10	

Jesus and the Spirit in the Gospels and Acts				
Spirit's ministry	**Matthew**	**Mark**	**Luke–Acts**	**John**
Resisted by Stephen's audience			Luke 7:55	
Falls/comes upon believers			Luke 8:16; 10:44; 11:15; 19:6	
Received by the Samaritans, Cornelius's household, et al.			Luke 8:14–24; 10:47; 19:1–7	
Spoke to Philip, Peter, et al.			Luke 8:29; 10:19; 11:12; 13:2; 20:23; 21:4, 11	
Carried Philip away			Luke 8:39	
Comforted the church			Luke 9:31	
Sent out Paul and Barnabas			Luke 13:4	
Guided decisions of the Jerusalem elders and Paul			Luke 15:28; 19:21; 20:22	
Prevented ministry in some Asian provinces			Luke 16:6–7	
Places overseers in the church			Luke 20:28	
Spoke through Isaiah			Luke 28:25–27 (Isa. 6:9–10)	

Three Phases[16]

The Spirit in the OT. The work of the Spirit in the Gospels and Acts did not occur in a vacuum. Although we should take care not to read the developed Christian doctrine of the Trinity back into the OT, the activity of the divine Spirit in the OT leads to the NT ministries. Only a very brief summary of the work of the Spirit in the OT is pos-

---

16. The three phases or stages of the work of the Spirit laid out here correspond roughly to Conzelmann's scheme of Luke's theology as set out in three periods or epochs, that of Israel (concluding with John), Jesus (the center of history), and the church. See Hans Conzelmann, *The Theology of St. Luke*, trans. G. Buswell (London: Faber and Faber, 1960), 16, 150, 170–234.

sible here. In the OT, the Spirit is active in creating and sustaining the world (Gen. 1:2). The Spirit enables the interpretation of dreams (Gen. 41:38). The Spirit equips temple artisans for their work (Exod. 28:3; 31:3; 35:31). The Spirit enables the leaders of Israel,[17] including Moses and the seventy elders of Israel (Num. 11:17, 25–26, 29), Caleb and Joshua (Num. 14:24; 27:18; Deut. 34:9), the judges (Judg. 3:10; 6:34; 11:29; 13:25; 14:6, 19; 15:14), the kings Saul and David (1 Sam. 10:6, 10; 11:6; 16:13–14; 2 Sam. 23:2; Ps. 51:10–12). The Spirit's ministry upon Israel's prophets is also clear in the OT (2 Chron. 24:20; Neh. 9:20, 30; Ezek. 2:2, 12; Mic. 3:8).[18]

The Psalms speak of the Spirit in the context of sustaining the creation (104:30), repentance from sin (51:10–12), worship (139:7), and seeking guidance from God (143:10). Closer to the work of the Spirit in the Gospels, the prophets speak of the eschatological work of the Spirit on the stem of Jesse (Isa. 11:1–5; cf. Acts 13:22–23) and on the servant of the Lord (Isa. 42:1–4; cf. Matt. 12:18–21; cf. Isa. 61:1–3; Luke 4:18–19). There is also remembrance of the past work of the Spirit with Israel as a nation (Isa. 63:10–11, 14; Hag. 2:5; Zech. 4:6) and anticipation of a time when the Spirit is poured out again on the nation (Isa. 32:15; 34:16; 44:3; 59:21; Ezek. 11:19; 36:26–27; 37:14; 39:29; Joel 2:28–32; cf. Acts 2:16–21). These OT examples of the Spirit's work indicate that NT references to God's Spirit would not seem novel in the least.[19]

Phase One: The ministry of John. According to Luke, the Spirit was active in the life of John the Baptist before he was born (Luke 1:15, 41). The fourfold Gospel and Acts unite to stress the pivotal nature of the baptism of John, culminating in Jesus's receiving the Spirit when John baptized him. This baptism prepared Israel for Jesus's ministry and corresponding baptism with the Spirit, and it prepared Jesus for his own special anointing by the Spirit for ministry (Matt. 3:11/Mark 1:8/Luke 3:16/Acts 1:5; cf. John 1:31; Acts 1:8; 11:16; 19:4). When the imprisoned, discouraged John sent messengers to inquire about Jesus's identity, Jesus emphasized the pivotal role of John the Baptist in redemptive history (Matt. 11:2–19/Luke 7:18–35). After answering John's question with an appeal to biblical prophecy, Jesus said no prophet was greater

---

17. For a study of the Spirit's ministry to Israel's leaders, see Harvey, *Anointed with the Spirit and Power*, 13–28.

18. For discussion of the Spirit's ministry to Israel's prophets, see Harvey, *Anointed with the Spirit and Power*, 29–50.

19. See further James M. Hamilton, *God's Indwelling Presence* (Nashville: B&H, 2006); Leon J. Wood, *The Holy Spirit in the Old Testament* (Grand Rapids: Zondervan, 1976); Christopher J. H. Wright, *Knowing the Holy Spirit through the Old Testament* (Downers Grove, IL: InterVarsity, 2006). Against Wood and others, Hamilton argues that the Spirit did not indwell believers in the OT.

than John. John's prophetic ministry constituted the apex of biblical revelation leading up to Jesus and the kingdom.[20]

Phase Two: The ministry of Jesus. According to Matthew (1:18) as well as Luke (1:35), the Holy Spirit was active in Jesus's miraculous conception. One should probably assume that the Spirit's ongoing activity in Jesus's human development led to Jesus's early wisdom and realization of God's plan (Luke 2:40, 46–49, 52).[21] Jesus's reception with the Spirit at his baptism equipped him for ministry to Israel. Matthew's account indicates that John was reluctant to baptize Jesus, but he did so when Jesus insisted it was necessary "to fulfill all righteousness" (Matt. 3:15), evidently linking himself to the repentant remnant of Israel.[22] In direct response to Jesus's righteous obedience to the Father's plan, the Spirit comes upon him as the visible demonstration of the Father's approval. Only Luke describes Jesus as being full of the Spirit after his baptism by John (Luke 4:1); this description is similar to the statement in John 1:33 that John the Baptist would see the Spirit descending and *remaining* on Jesus. All three synoptics speak of the Spirit leading Jesus into the desert to be tempted by the devil (Matt. 4:1/Mark 1:12/Luke 4:1), but only Luke speaks of Jesus after the temptation as returning to Galilee in the power of the Spirit (Luke 4:14).

Luke is also alone in depicting Jesus as beginning his ministry at the synagogue in Nazareth by reading Isaiah 61:1–2 ("the Spirit of the Lord is upon me . . .") and declaring himself to be its fulfillment (Luke 4:16–21; cf. Acts 10:38). Later in Luke, the Spirit brings joy to Jesus in the midst of heavy opposition (Luke 10:21). The citation of Isaiah 42:1–4 in Matthew 12:17–21—also coming as a response to opposition—has much the same effect as the citation of Isaiah 61 in Luke 4: God's placing the Spirit upon Jesus is the impetus for his ministry to those who need justice. Jesus's opponents slander the

---

20. For discussion of the Spirit's activity in the life and ministry of John the Baptist, see Harvey, *Anointed with the Spirit and Power*, 51–62.

21. At this point and in the following comments it should be noted that I am assuming (in agreement with Hawthorne, *The Presence and the Power*, 199–226) the full humanity of Jesus, and that his self-humbling in the incarnation involved his constant reliance upon the Spirit for every aspect of his ministry. Accordingly, his miracles should be uniformly attributed to the perichoretic work of the Father through the Spirit's empowerment of Jesus, as implied in texts like John 1:18; 3:35; 5:19–26, 36; 10:18, 25, 32, 37–38; 12:49–50; 14:8–11; Acts 2:22; 10:38.

22. The many views of Jesus's words about fulfilling all righteousness can be sorted out in the exegetical commentaries. It may be a bit of a stretch to see Jesus as the second Adam beginning a new humanity here (Beale, *A New Testament Biblical Theology*, 416). Jesus as the representative of Israel or at least its remnant seems more likely, although there are overtones of Jesus as the second Adam in Luke's account of the temptation of Jesus (Luke 4:3 taken with 3:38; Beale, *A New Testament Biblical Theology*, 222, 422).

work of the Spirit (Matt. 12:31–32/Mark 3:29/Luke 12:10) in empowering Jesus to demonstrate the presence God's kingdom (Matt. 12:28).[23]

Phase Three: The ministry of the church. Acts speaks in detail about the ministry of the Spirit to the church, but that ministry is implied and previewed in the Gospels, especially in John. Jesus's teaching about the work of the Spirit in the new birth is as relevant for the church's ministry as it was for his own (John 3:3–9). John explains that Jesus's teaching about rivers of living water relates to the coming of the Spirit after Jesus's glorification (John 7:37–39).[24] Jesus's teaching in the upper room (John 13–17) shows that this discourse is not ultimately about farewell but about what Johnson calls "transformation of presence."[25] Jesus will soon be physically absent (John 13:33, 36; 14:28; 16:5, 28–29), but the greater point of the discourse is that he will continue to be present with his disciples through the Spirit (John 14:16–23). Jesus goes so far as to tell the disciples that his departure is advantageous for them because it will lead to the fuller work of the Spirit in their lives and ministries (John 16:7). The Spirit whom the Father and Jesus send (14:16, 26; 15:26) will remind them of his teachings (14:26), guide them into further insight about Jesus (14:26; 16:12–15), and convict the world through their testimony (15:26–16:11).[26]

The final mention of the Spirit in John occurs in Jesus's first post-resurrection appearance to the disciples as a group (John 20:19–23). He greets them, shows them the marks of crucifixion on his body, and commissions them as the Father had commissioned him. He then breathes on them and says, "Receive the Spirit." Jesus's comparison of him sending them to the Father sending him just before they receive the Spirit may be intended to recall Jesus's receiving the

---

23. For discussion of the Spirit's empowerment of Jesus's ministry, see Harvey, *Anointed with the Spirit and Power*, 63–92.

24. Against many scholars and translations, it seems that Jesus, not the believer, is the one from whose innermost being the living water (Holy Spirit) flows. Although one may say the Spirit flows from believers in a derivative sense, that would not be true if the Spirit did not flow first to them from Jesus (John 4:14; cf. 1:33; 3:34; 15:26; 20:22; Acts 2:33). For this minority view and different punctuation of the text that leads to it (as in NLT), see Burge, *The Anointed Community*, 88–93; Craig L. Keener, *The Gospel of John: A Commentary*, 2 vols. (Peabody, MA: Hendrickson, 2003), 1.728–30..

25. Luke Timothy Johnson, *The Writings of the New Testament*, 3rd ed. (Minneapolis: Fortress, 2010), 195. Johnson is speaking of the ascension in Acts 1, but in light of such texts as John 14:16–18, 25–26, his point holds just as well with Jesus's teaching in John 13–17.

26. The synoptic tradition joins with John 15:26–16:11 in promising the disciples that they will be led by the Spirit in speaking for Jesus when they are persecuted (Matt. 10:19/Mark 13:11/Luke 12:12).

Spirit from the Father (John 20:21–22 with 1:32–33). If so, the passage implies that just as the Spirit's descent upon Jesus initiated and enabled his ministry for the Father, so Jesus's breathing the Spirit upon his disciples initiates and enables their ministries for him.[27] If one were reading only the Gospel of John, one would assume that on this occasion the disciples experienced the reception of the Spirit that Jesus promised in John 7:37–39; 14:16–17. In terms of canonical biblical theology, if John 20:22 is intended to echo Genesis 2:7 and Ezekiel 37:9, it implies a renewal of creation/Israel theology. In terms of relating John 20:22 to Luke 24–Acts 2, some have argued that the two texts are different perspectives on the same historical reality. It appears from John 21, however, that the disciples do not yet have the sort of boldness for witness characterized by the aftermath of Acts 2. Others take the reception of the Spirit in John 20:22 as a partial or preliminary endowment intended to support the disciples until Pentecost. More likely, John 20:22 should be interpreted as a prophetic act symbolizing the coming of the Spirit at Pentecost. Since the semantic range of רוּחַ/πνεῦμα includes breath and wind (cf. John 3:8; Acts 2:2) as well as the Spirit, perhaps there is a sort of visual pun here.[28]

The work of the Spirit in the church is obviously a focus of Acts, as previewed in Jesus's promise that the disciples would be clothed with power from on high (Luke 24:49; cf. Luke 1:35; 4:14; Acts 1:8; 2 Chron. 24:20).[29] Jesus, exalted to the right hand of God, pours out the Spirit upon the disciples on the day of Pentecost, fulfilling Joel 2:28–32 (Acts 2:16–21, 33). Those who repent and receive baptism receive the gift of the Spirit (Acts 2:38; 10:45; 15:8). Beginning at Pentecost, the Spirit sovereignly fills various disciples for missional tasks on a regular basis (Acts 2:5; 4:8, 31; 6:3, 5; 7:55; 9:17; 11:24; 13:9, 52). Unfortunately, on one occasion two disciples test the Spirit, with disastrous consequences that bring fear upon the church (Acts 5:1–11). The Spirit's testimony to Jesus confirms the apostolic evangelistic testimony (Acts 5:32; 6:10; cf. John 15:26–27). The Holy Spirit occasionally speaks to disciples, prompting them to perform specific ministries (8:29; 10:19; 11:12; 13:2; 20:23; 21:4, 11). The Spirit guides the disciples both positively, leading them into certain activities (Acts 8:39; 9:31; 13:4; 15:28; 19:21; 20:22) and hindering

---

27. See further Frederick Dale Bruner, *The Gospel of John: A Commentary* (Grand Rapids: Eerdmans, 2012), 1176–79; Burge, *The Anointed Community*, 114–49; James D. G. Dunn, *Baptism in the Holy Spirit* (Philadelphia: Westminster, 1970), 173–82.

28. For discussion of how Jesus's departure leads to the Spirit's future ministry, see Harvey, *Anointed with the Spirit and Power*, 93–122.

29. On the Spirit in Luke-Acts, see further Harvey, *Anointed with the Spirit and Power*, 211–26.

them from others (16:6–7). Acts also depicts the Spirit's past (Acts 1:16–20 [Ps. 69:25, 109:8]; 4:25–26 [Ps. 2:1–2]; 28:25–27 [Isa. 6:9–10]) and present (11:28; 20:23; 21:4, 11) work in prompting prophetic speech. Additionally, the Spirit is active in qualifying and appointing leaders for local congregations (Acts 6:3, 5; 20:28). As the gospel is preached, the Spirit's activity is variously described as coming upon, falling upon, being poured out upon, or being given to new converts (Acts 10:44–45; 11:15; 15:8; 19:6), who are said to receive the Spirit (Acts 2:38; 8:15–19; 10:47; 19:2).[30]

The four featured occasions of the giving/coming/receiving of the Spirit in Acts align in their basis in personal faith of the recipients in the crucified, risen, and exalted Jesus. Beyond this constant, there is considerable diversity in the circumstances surrounding the reception of the Spirit. Perhaps this is instructive for the church today (John 3:8).

Faith, Baptism, and the Reception of the Spirit in Acts			
	Acts 2:1–42	**Acts 8:5–25**	**Acts 10:1–48**	**Acts 19:1–7**
Recipients	Jesus's disciples, numbering about 120 people	Samaritans	Household of Cornelius; Gentile God-fearers	Disciples of John the Baptist
Relation to baptism	Possibly prior recipients of John's baptism (?)	Faith/baptism in Jesus's name did not immediately lead to receiving the Spirit.	Faith immediately resulted in reception of the Spirit. Baptism followed.	Prior recipients of John's baptism

---

30. For discussion of the Spirit's ministry in the early church, see Harvey, *Anointed with the Spirit and Power*, 123–42. For further discussion of the Luke's teaching on the Holy Spirit in light of the OT, see Roger Stronstad, *The Charismatic Theology of St. Luke*, 2nd ed. (Grand Rapids: Baker, 2012).

Faith, Baptism, and the Reception of the Spirit in Acts			
	Acts 2:1–42	**Acts 8:5–25**	**Acts 10:1–48**	**Acts 19:1–7**
Additional circumstances	Longtime disciples of Jesus receive the Spirit promised by Jesus.	Spirit is eventually received after Jewish apostles from Jerusalem arrive and lay on hands.	Amazement that the Spirit was poured out on the Gentiles as on the Jews in Acts 2.	Spirit is received after baptism in Jesus's name, and Paul lays on hands.
Theological implications	Foundational eschatological movement of the Spirit.	Samaritans acknowledge that salvation is from the Jews. Jews acknowledge Samaritans as true Christians.	Jewish believers acknowledge that Gentiles received the Spirit just as they did at Pentecost.	Followers of John acknowledge that Jesus is the one who baptizes with the Spirit.
Relevant biblical texts	Luke 24:49; Acts 1:8	Luke 10:33; 17:16; Acts 8:25; John 4:9, 22	Acts 10:45; 11:1–26; 14:27; 15:7–11	Luke 3:15; 7:24–29; Acts 1:5; 11:16; 13:24–25; 18:25–26

Summary. The Holy Spirit, active in John the Baptist even before he was born, comes from God to Jesus when John baptizes him. This pneumatic endowment enables Jesus to represent the Father perfectly while on earth. Exalted to the right hand of the Father, Jesus sends the Spirit to the church at Pentecost. This endowment constitutes the church as a messianic/pneumatic community, enabling it to represent, genuinely yet imperfectly, the Father on earth. The church's activity is attributed directly to the Spirit's empowerment, but the Spirit's powerful work is attributed to the exalted Jesus, who has poured out the Spirit to continue the work he began on earth (Acts 1:1). The Spirit is the Spirit of Jesus (Acts 16:6; cf. 1 Cor. 6:11; 12:3; 2 Cor. 3:17–18), and the book of Acts is best understood as the Acts of Jesus.

**The Acts of the Ascended Messiah
through His Pneumatic Community**

John   →   Jesus   →   Church   →

Jesus as Pneumatic Messiah   The Church as Messianic/Pneumatic Community

| God sends the Spirit to Jesus at his baptism | Jesus sends the Spirit to the church at Pentecost | Jesus continues his mission through the Spirit-enabled church |

Matthew,   Mark,   John,   Luke   →   Acts   →

THE DISTINCTIVE THEOLOGY OF MATTHEW

*Do not think that I have come to abolish the Law or the Prophets;
I have not come to abolish them but to fulfill them.*
(Matt. 5:17, NIV)

In many ways Matthew 5:17 is the keynote of both the Sermon on the Mount and the entire Gospel of Matthew. The parallel form of the text first prohibits divorcing Jesus and Moses and then affirms Jesus as the fulfillment of Moses (Matt. 17:1–6; cf. John 1:14–18; 5:45–47). This emphatic double statement means that any legitimate theology of Matthew must affirm the basic loyalty of Jesus to Moses. From this statement follows the theological continuity of the OT and the NT, and of Israel and the church. Matthew characteristically depicts Jesus in a manner that recalls Moses.[31] Even the language of Jesus's mandate for world mission—"teaching them to observe all that I commanded you" (διδάσκοντες αὐτοὺς τηρεῖν πάντα ὅσα ἐνετειλάμην ὑμῖν)—harks back to the language about the authority of the prophet like Moses in Deuteronomy 18:18 (cf. Josh. 1:7; Jer. 1:7). This graphic pictures the relationship of Jesus and Moses as it pertains to the canon:

---

31.   Dale C. Allison, *The New Moses: A Matthean Typology* (Minneapolis: Fortress, 1993).

The Torah of Moses and the Torah of Jesus

"Old Testament"

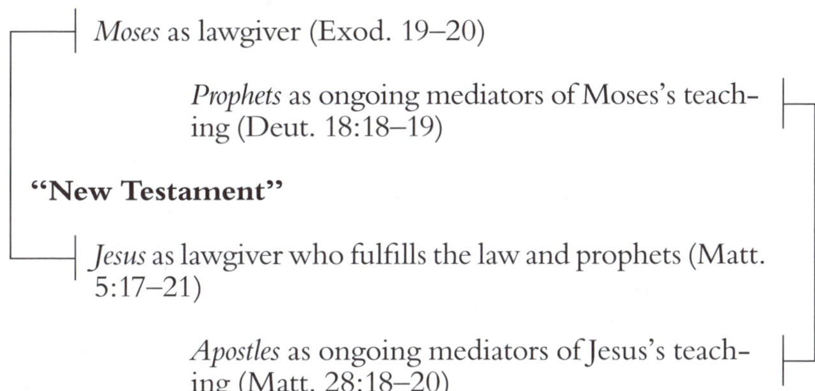

Moses as lawgiver (Exod. 19–20)

Prophets as ongoing mediators of Moses's teaching (Deut. 18:18–19)

"New Testament"

Jesus as lawgiver who fulfills the law and prophets (Matt. 5:17–21)

Apostles as ongoing mediators of Jesus's teaching (Matt. 28:18–20)

We will approach Matthew's distinctive theology by examining how Matthew (1) understands the OT, (2) presents Jesus's teaching on the kingdom of God, and (3) equips the church for world mission.

Matthew and the Old Testament

Matthew's pervasive use of the Bible is one of the major reasons why many interpreters note the Jewish orientation of this Gospel.[32] The prevalence of this **intertextuality** calls into question the very notion of an "Old Testament" in Matthew's theology. If Matthew's Jesus came not to abolish but to fulfill the Law and the Prophets (Matt. 5:17), it is doubtful that Matthew conceived of the Jewish Scriptures as "old," at least in the connotative senses of antique, outmoded, or quaint. Instead, Matthew viewed both the historical patterns and prophetic oracles of the Hebrew Bible as filled with ultimate significance through the ministry and teaching of Jesus. In addition to numerous informal allusions that are difficult to count, there are around fifty formal quotations. It is possible to categorize these quotations in various ways, such as by introductory formula (e.g., "in order that it might be fulfilled," "for it is written") or speaker (e.g., Jesus, Matthew as narrator).

The idea that fulfillment involves a specific biblical prediction being "fulfilled" (occurring) in a NT event is simplistic at best. This notion

---

32. Among the voluminous literature on Matthew's use of the OT, see especially Robert H. Gundry, *The Use of the Old Testament in St. Matthew's Gospel* (Leiden: Brill, 1967); John Nolland, *The Gospel according to Matthew* (Grand Rapids: Eerdmans, 2005), 29–36; Graham Stanton, *A Gospel for a New People: Studies in Matthew* (Edinburgh: Clark, 1992), 346–63.

is largely the result of a mistaken reduction of prophecy to prediction. The use of the word and its cognate in Matthew shows that fulfillment has as much to do with historical patterns as it does with prophetic predictions.[33] Prophetic prediction involves the prophet's revelational foresight of a future event (cf. 2:4–6), but Matthew's fulfillment quotations more often involve the Christian hindsight that a historical event from the OT serves as a pattern for a NT event that it providentially anticipated. Historical events, whether past, present, or future, are viewed as the providential outworking of God's plan. Biblical prophecy is not primarily prediction but covenantal admonition that utilizes the rehearsal of past events as well as the prediction of future events as motivation to effect present covenant loyalty. Fulfillment in Matthew involves ethical and historical matters as well as predictive prophecy. These categories are not discrete but overlapping; individual fulfillments might contain elements of all three aspects. At times the ethical element is preeminent (3:15; 5:17). At other times, fulfillment of biblical prediction is primary (4:14; 8:17; 12:17; 21:4; 26:54, 56). Probably the most prevalent aspect of fulfillment in Matthew, however, concerns historical patterns (1:22; 2:15, 17, 23; 13:14, 35; 23:32; 27:9). Events in biblical history anticipate events in Jesus's ministry in that Jesus fills them with new significance. Even Jesus's opponents have their precursors in the Bible (Matt. 23:32).[34] By recapitulating these biblical events Jesus demonstrates the providence of God in fulfilling his promises to Israel. As implied in the genealogy, Jesus the Messiah, who is Abraham's son and David's son, fulfills biblical history.[35]

The Kingdom of God in Matthew

The word βασιλεία (kingdom) occurs fifty-four times in Matthew, fifty-five if the Byzantine reading in 6:13 is included. The kingdom of God/heaven is undoubtedly at the center of the message of Matthew. The discussion here will only summarize (1) Matthew's use of "kingdom," (2) the relationship of the kingdom of heaven and the kingdom of God, and (3) the presence and future of the kingdom.

The expression *kingdom of heaven* (hereafter KoH) is literally "the kingdom of the heavens" (ἡ βασιλεία τῶν οὐρανῶν). This expression

---

33. See especially the fulfillment formula texts 1:22; 2:15, 17, 23; 4:14; 8:17; 12:17; 13:35; 21:4; 27:9, as well as 13:14; 26:54, 56.

34. David L. Turner, *Israel's Last Prophet: Jesus and the Jewish Leaders in Matthew 23* (Minneapolis: Fortress, 2015).

35. See further David L. Turner, *Matthew*, BECNT (Grand Rapids: Baker, 2008), 17–32, and the sources cited there. For Matthew 1–4, see Joel Kennedy, *The Recapitulation of Israel* (Tübingen: Mohr Siebeck, 2008).

occurs thirty-three times in Matthew and nowhere else in the NT (3:2; 4:17; 5:3, 10, 19[2x], 20; 7:21; 8:11; 10:7; 11:11, 12; 13:11, 24, 31). In four instances where Matthew uses the expression *kingdom of God* (ἡ βασιλεία τοῦ θεοῦ; hereafter KoG), which is common in the other Gospels (12:28; 19:24; 21:31, 43).[36] It is difficult to grasp why Matthew uses KoG in these texts instead of KoH.[37] The word "kingdom" occurs nineteen other times in Matthew. Two refer to human kingdoms (4:8; 24:7), and two refer to Satan's kingdom (12:25, 26). The remaining fifteen describe the KoG.[38] The word βασιλεύς (king) occurs twenty-two times in Matthew. Eight times, the word describes human kings, one referring to David (1:6), three referring to Herod (2:1, 3, 9) and four referring to others (10:18; 11:8; 14:9; 17:25). The other fourteen times refer to the Father (5:35/Ps. 48:2; 18:23; 22:2, 7, 11, 13) or to Jesus (2:2; 21:5/Zech. 9:9; 25:34, 40; 27:11, 29, 37, 42). It should also be noted that the references to Jesus as the Son of David have regal overtones (1:1, 6, 16, 17, 20; 9:27; 12:3, 23; 15:22; 20:30, 31; 21:9, 15; 22:42–43, 45).

Matthew's use of kingdom terminology occurs in various important connections in his Gospel. The kingdom is at the heart of John's, Jesus's, and the church's proclamation (3:2; 4:17; 10:7; 13:19; 24:14). Jesus's miracles demonstrate the authority of the kingdom (4:23–25; 8:9–13; 9:6–8; 12:28; 20:30–34). His teaching on the ethical life of disciples prominently features the kingdom (5:3, 10, 19, 20; 6:10, 33; 7:21). His parables picture the work of the kingdom in redemptive history (13:11, 19, 24, 31, 33, 38, 43–45, 47, 52; 18:23; 22:2; 25:1). As king, Jesus judges the world (25:34, 40).

While Matthew speaks of the "kingdom of God" occasionally (12:28; 19:24; 21:31, 43), his unique term "kingdom of heaven" oc-

---

36. The expression also occurs in the Byzantine text of Matthew 6:33.

37. Most scholars see no difference in meaning between kingdom of God and kingdom of heaven in Matthew. Explanations for the occasional use of "kingdom of God" include literary variation or its opposite—Matthew did not change his source's "kingdom of God" to his typical "kingdom of heaven." Mark Saucy proposes that the kingdom of God refers to the present, mysterious reign of God that is unknown to the world. This secret kingdom is not introduced until Israel has rejected the kingdom of heaven, which is understood as God's physical, national rule over Israel in Palestine. See "The Kingdom-of-God Sayings in Matthew," *BSac* 151 (1994):175–97. See also Margaret Pamment, "The Kingdom of Heaven according to the First Gospel," *NTS* 27 (1980–81): 211–32.

38. Of this group, eight use the word βασιλεία absolutely, without grammatical modifiers (4:23; 6:33, though there are modifiers in variant readings; 8:12; 9:35; 13:19, 38; 24:14; 25:34). Four texts use βασιλεία with nouns or pronouns referring to the Father (6:10; 13:43; 26:29; also 6:13 *Byz*), and three with nouns or pronouns referring to Jesus (13:41; 16:28; 20:21). In addition to speaking sometimes of the kingdom as the Father's or Jesus's, these texts also speak significantly of the gospel or word of the kingdom (4:23; 9:35; 13:19; 24:14) and of those who respond to this message as the children (υἱοὶ) of the kingdom (8:12; 13:38).

curs thirty-two times. The purported distinction between the two is untenable for at least three reasons. First, Matthew 19:23–24 uses both expressions in a synonymous fashion. Second, a comparison of parallel synoptic texts indicates that Matthew often uses the expression kingdom of heaven when Mark and/or Luke use the expression kingdom of God (e.g., Matt. 13:31 with Mark 4:30; Matt. 19:14 with Mark 10:15 and Luke 18:17). Third, Matthew's terminology is likely an instance of metonymy, the figural association of heaven as God's realm with God himself (cf. the prominence of this association in Dan. 2:18–19, 28, 37, 44; 4:34–35, 37; 5:23; 12:17). Matthew's use might be influenced by reverence for the name of God in Matthew's Jewish context (cf. Luke 16:18, 21).[39] Matthew's four kingdom of God texts are probably just stylistic variations for literary purposes.

The question of the presence and future of the kingdom is closely tied to the question of its nature. It would seem that a kingdom would require a ruler, subjects who are ruled, the exercise of that rule, and a realm in which the rule occurs. Those who prefer to think of the kingdom as present emphasize the dynamic "rule" aspect of kingdom, while those who prefer to think of it as future emphasize the concrete "realm" aspect. The modern debate in its larger context has been between advocates of "consistent eschatology" (*konsequente Eschatologie*) and "realized eschatology." Traced back to Johannes Weiss,[40] consistent eschatology holds that Jesus was a prophet who predicted imminent apocalyptic catastrophe that would usher in the reign of God. In this view, the KoG is future. On the other hand, realized eschatology[41] argues that the kingdom reached its zenith on earth during the ministry of Jesus. In American evangelical circles a similar debate occurs between dispensationalists, who tend to think of the kingdom as the future millennium on earth, and amillennialists, who tend to think of the kingdom as the present rule of Christ in believers through the Spirit, although these categories should not be viewed as mutually exclusive.

George Ladd demonstrated that the kingdom must be understood as both present and future.[42] The usage of βασιλεία in the NT, as well

---

39. See further Jonathan Pennington, *Heaven and Earth in the Gospel of Matthew* (reprinted, Grand Rapids: Baker, 2009), 279–330. Pennington discounts the idea that KoH is a reverential circumlocution of kingdom of God views the terminology as a piece of Matthew's theology of the tension between God's heavenly reign and earth's present sinfulness (331–48).

40. Weiss's 1892 book *Die Predigt Jesu vom Reiche Gottes* was edited and translated by R. H. Hiers and D. L. Holland as *Jesus's Proclamation of the Kingdom of God* (Philadelphia: Fortress, 1971).

41. The term and idea are often linked to C. H. Dodd, *The Parables of the Kingdom*, rev. ed. (London: Nisbet, 1961).

42. George E. Ladd, *The Presence of the Future* (Grand Rapids: Eerdmans, 1974). See also Dale C. Allison, *The End of the Ages Has Come* (Philadelphia: Fortress, 1985), 101–14; G. R. Beasley-Murray, *Jesus and the Kingdom of God* (Grand Rapids: Eerdmans, 1986).

as the usage of מַלְכוּת (rule, dominion) in the OT, connotes dynamic rule more than material realm, though the two concepts should not be separated. Insistence that the kingdom is essentially a realm leads to viewing it as strictly future as well, and a strictly future kingdom will not do in Matthew. John, Jesus, and the disciples announce the dawning of the kingdom (3:2; 4:17; 10:7). Those who repent at this message of God's rule already possess the kingdom (5:3, 10). The royal power of God is dynamically present in Jesus's words and works (Matt. 12:28 especially). God endows the church with this dynamic power for ministry through its confession of Jesus as the Son of God (16:18–19; 28:18–20).

This stress on the kingdom as the present dynamic rule of God exists alongside eschatological hope for a full manifestation of God's rule on earth (6:10). Those who have already experienced the kingdom's power (5:3, 10) will someday receive it in full measure (5:3–9). In the meantime, their quest is for a greater approximation of kingdom righteousness on earth (6:33). At the return of Jesus the Son of Man, the entire world will come under God's rule (7:21–23; 25:31, 34). So, the kingdom is a spatial, physical realm, existing today as a microcosm and in the future when Jesus returns as a macrocosm. Today the lives of believers exhibit the rule of God individually, corporately, and as they relate to the world. In that day God's rule will be extended to all humankind in judgment or redemption.

Generally, the kingdom of heaven refers to the nearness or even presence of the rule of God in the person, works, and teaching of Jesus (3:2; 4:17; 10:7; 11:12; cf. 12:28). There are, however, times when it implies (5:19; 7:21; 13:24, 47; 25:1) or clearly describes (8:11; cf. 6:10; 13:38–43; 25:34; 26:29) the future reign of Jesus upon the earth. Perhaps the best way to describe the dynamic nature of God's reign is to say that it has been *inaugurated* at Jesus's first coming and will be *consummated* when he returns. Matthew characterizes the preaching of Jesus, John, and the apostles as centered on the kingdom (Matt. 3:2; 4:17; 10:7). References to the present experience of the kingdom (Matt. 5:3, 10) frame the beatitudes, which otherwise speak of future kingdom blessings. Jesus's kingdom involves a radical righteousness greater than that of the legal experts (5:19–20); it requires disciples to seek it first, before their daily needs (6:33). Even John's greatness as a prophet of the kingdom is eclipsed by the least one who experiences eschatological kingdom realities (11:11–12). The preaching of the kingdom and responses to it are presented figuratively in the parables of the kingdom in Matthew 13, and the keys of Matthew 16:10 further symbolize its authority. Entrance into this kingdom requires childlike humility (18:3–4; 19:14), and the unknown time of its future arrival mandates constant alertness (24:36–25:13).

The Church and Mission to All the Nations

The Gospel of Matthew, while often and accurately described as the most Jewish of the Gospels, is also the only Gospel that uses the word "church" (ἐκκλησία; 16:18; 18:17). As in Daniel 7, so in Matthew—the Son of Man is linked to a community of saints that confesses his identity. The identity of this community can be gleaned by reading Matthew from the beginning and noting the hints dropped by Matthew concerning the type of people who are followers of Jesus. It can also be ascertained by taking note of the final triumphant commission Jesus leaves with his disciples (28:18–20).

The two texts in Matthew that refer to the church are quite different. In 16:16–19 Jesus promises to build his church on Peter, who has spoken out for his fellow apostles in affirming Jesus's identity as the Messiah, the Son of the living God. With the metaphor of the keys, Jesus also promises kingdom authority to Peter, implying that the church is the agency through which kingdom authority is exercised. In this text Jesus speaks of the church broadly in terms of its origin and authority. The other church-text in Matthew, 18:17, is different in that it provides the church with instructions for maintaining interpersonal harmony in a community context of humility (18:3), hospitality (18:5), and forgiveness (18:21–35). Taken together, the two texts speak respectively about the church in global and local terms, about its foundational identity in Christ and its functional values.

From the beginning Matthew begins to make it clear that the community of the Messiah is formed from unexpected sources. The mention of Tamar, Rahab, Ruth, and Bathsheba (1:3, 5, 6), all evidently Gentiles with overtones of scandal in their backgrounds, prepares the reader for Jesus's association with the sinners of his own day. The inexplicable arrival of the mysterious wise men from the east who wish to worship Jesus (2:1–12) augurs the power of the message of the kingdom to summon Jesus-followers in surprising ways. Jesus's amazement at the faith of the Roman officer (8:10–12) and his acknowledgement of the faith of the Canaanite woman (15:28) encourage the readers of this Gospel to believe that the message of the kingdom is able to engender faith from unlikely sources in their own day. The Roman soldier's amazed confirmation of Jesus's true identity at the crucifixion (27:54) has a similar effect. All of these episodes from the narrative collectively influence Matthew's original Jewish readers to expand their vision of the people of God. It is not that they are to abandon their fellow Jews, but the message of the kingdom must be taken to "*all* the nations" (28:19).[43]

---

43. See further Matthias Konradt, *Israel, Church, and the Gentiles in the Gospel of Matthew* (Waco, TX: Baylor University Press, 2014). Konradt argues that the promises first made to Israel are extended to the Gentiles by the church.

Jesus's final commissioning of his disciples rests on his now exalted status. Having received all power (28:18), he sends the eleven to all the nations to make disciples who will obey all his commands (28:20). The reference to all of Jesus's commands likely recalls the five discourses that figure prominently into Matthew's distinctive portrayal of Jesus's teaching for the church as the agency that extends God's kingdom on earth:

- The *ethics* of the kingdom (Matt. 5–7)
- The *mission* of the kingdom (Matt. 10)
- The *reception* of the kingdom (Matt. 13)
- The *values* of the kingdom (Matt. 18)
- The *future* of the kingdom (Matt. 24–25)

Through these five discourses Matthew equips the church for the ongoing mission to Israel and for the burgeoning mission to the Gentiles. They are to inculcate the Torah-fulfilling teaching of Jesus on righteous living, on handling opposition during mission, on the mixed reception of the message, on the internal values that characterize his community, and on how to live in light of his coming. Jesus arms his disciples with the promise that he will be with them all the days until the end of the age (28:20; cf. 1:23; 18:20). His all-powerful presence enables them to accomplish his daunting universal commission until the end of the age.[44]

THE DISTINCTIVE THEOLOGY OF MARK

*"The time has come. . . . The kingdom of God has come near.
Repent and believe the good news!"*
(Mark 1:15, NIV)

Mark's account of the Jesus's first words amount to an electrifying keynote for this Gospel. These words affirm that a decisive moment of redemptive history has arrived, God's promises are being fulfilled, and God's saving reign has arrived. This eschatological indicative leads to an ethical imperative involving discipleship. Those who hear of the arrival of God's reign must turn their lives over to Jesus and follow his teachings. As Mark's narrative unfolds, however, surprisingly few people recognize Jesus's true identity, and even his disciples often turn out to be less than perceptive. In the end he is crucified. These perplexities and others lead Luke Timothy Johnson to comment that

---

44. See further on mission in the Gospels and Acts, Michael F. Bird, *Jesus and the Origins of the Gentile Mission* (Edinburgh: Clark, 2006); William F. Larkin Jr. and Joel Williams, eds., *Mission in the New Testament: An Evangelical Approach* (Maryknoll, NY: Orbis, 1998); Eckhard J. Schnabel, *Early Christian Mission*, 2 vols. (Downers Grove, IL: InterVarsity, 2004).

"In some ways, the shortest of the Gospels is also the strangest and most difficult to grasp."[45]

A Passion Narrative with an Extended Introduction?

Martin Kähler's attempt to grasp Mark led him to describe it as a passion narrative with an extended introduction.[46] This statement about the genre of Mark is also telling for the theology of Mark, because it implies that everything in Mark before the passion narrative is of secondary importance. In this approach, Jesus's life, including his compassionate miracles and exorcisms as well as his ethical teaching, appear to be pointless since they are not tied directly to the cross. Kähler's view has affinities with some segments of contemporary conservative evangelicalism that focus on preaching the cross to achieve personal conversions. This emphasis is laudable but incomplete since it can result in "converts" who do not become disciples. At the opposite end of the theological spectrum are those who emphasize what some call "the social gospel," stressing Jesus's lofty ethical ideals but minimizing the cross. N. T. Wright addresses this problem in terms of "the missing middle," his term for the gap between theological reflection on Christ's incarnation and Christ's passion.[47] Wright argues correctly that a truly biblical theology must integrate the life of Christ, his words and deeds, into its understanding of the incarnation and the passion.

For Mark, Jesus's identity as Messiah is tied directly to the cross. No sooner has Peter acknowledged that Jesus is the Messiah than Jesus begins to teach about the necessity of the passion (Mark 8:29–31). Of course, this teaching is counterintuitive for Peter, and for us as well. Jesus's rebuke of Peter implies ominous consequences for any theology that does not link Jesus's messianic life with his passion, and vice versa (8:32–33). Jesus's cross is not simply a place where Jesus once provided personal salvation. The cross is a sacred symbol that eternally epitomizes sacrificial denial, the antithesis of self-centered living. Those who claim to be followers of Jesus must take up their own crosses (Mark 8:31–38). Jesus taught that those who wish to rule must learn to serve. His cross provided not only a ransom for many but also a model for the Christian

---

45. Johnson, *The Writings of the New Testament*, 143.

46. Martin Kähler's *Der sogenannte historische Jesus und der geschichtliche, biblische Christus* (Leipzig: Deichert, 1892). ET by Carl E. Braaten, *The So-Called Historical Jesus and the Historic Biblical Christ* (Philadelphia: Fortress, 1964), 80 n. 11. In fairness to Kähler, he emphasized the power of the passion in continuity with the ancient church in opposition to the liberal historical critical scholars of his day.

47. N. T. Wright, *How God Became King: The Forgotten Story of the Gospels* (New York: HarperCollins, 2012), 3–24.

life (Mark 10:35–45). Agonizing self-denial led Jesus to the cross while his oblivious disciples slept. They had not yet learned that Jesus's death provided the model for his disciples' lives (Mark 14:32–42).

Kähler's view seems to compartmentalize the life and death of Jesus in a way that runs counter the way in which Mark links Jesus's death to the disciples' lives. Far from being a mere introduction to the passion, Mark's story of Jesus is the story of a sacrificial life leading to a sacrificial death. Both are crucial (pun intended) for properly understanding Mark's depiction of the identity of Jesus and his disciples. Mark's traditional mentor Peter came to understood this well, judging from his words in 1 Peter 2:20–21 (NIV): "[I]f you suffer for doing good and you endure it, this is commendable before God. To this you were called, because Christ suffered for you, leaving you an example, that you should follow in his steps."

Limited Recognition of Jesus

A key factor in understanding Mark's theology is coming to terms with the limited recognition accorded Jesus in this gospel. Mark begins by acknowledging the messianic identity and divine sonship of Jesus (1:1). Prophetic confirmation of Jesus's forerunner John follows immediately (Mark 1:2). Yet as the narrative proceeds, the characters do not necessarily share the information and point of view regarding Jesus that the narrator has given the reader. The author intends this disparity between 1:1–2 and the ensuing narrative to impress the reader that relatively few people really "get" Jesus. Jesus's significance is immediately acknowledged by his forerunner John the Baptist in 1:4–8 and John's insight is confirmed by the words from heaven at Jesus's baptism, "you are my beloved son; with you I am well pleased." The coming of the Spirit upon Jesus at that point is a further indication of the Father's endorsement, and Jesus now enters his public ministry.

From this point on recognition of Jesus is sporadic. Occasionally there are scenes involving healing or other actions that imply there is something extraordinary about Jesus (e.g., 1:1:17–18, 20, 22, 27, 29, 32–34, 39, 41), but on these occasions there is no clear testimony to what has been disclosed about Jesus in 1:1. Surprisingly, demons whom Jesus is casting out acknowledge he is the holy one of God (1:24) or the Son of God (3:11; 5:7). When Jesus asks his disciples about his identity, Peter acknowledges that Jesus is the Messiah (8:29). At Jesus's transfiguration the Father's voice from heaven echoes the words which marked Jesus's baptism (9:7). Blind Bartimaeus addresses Jesus as the son of David as he begs to be healed (10:46–47; cf. Mark 2:25; 11:10; 12:35–37). The Roman centurion who oversaw Jesus's crucifixion exclaims that Jesus was the Son of God (15:39). Jesus's parable of the tenants metaphorically and ominously alludes to his divine sonship (12:6–9). Jesus's self-designation "Son of Man" regularly occurs (2:28; 8:31, 38; 9:9, 12, 31; 10:33, 45; 13:26; 14:21, 41; cf. Dan. 7:13), but it culminates in the high priest's charge of blasphemy and precipitates the crucifixion (14:60–64).

Adding further perplexity to the lack of recognition of Jesus in Mark are the occasions where Jesus forbids testimony to that identity. This phenomenon occurs on occasions where demons whom Jesus casts out are aware of Jesus's identity (1:25, 34; 3:12). Jesus also forbids people he has healed from talking widely about it (1:44–45; 5:19, 43; 7:36; 8:26). As soon as Peter has confessed that Jesus is the Messiah, and the disciples have observed Jesus's transfiguration, Jesus forbids the disciples to tell people about him (8:30; 9:9). Despite Jesus's attempts to suppress the news about him, he is regularly pressed by multitudes who desire to be healed and by Pharisees who dispute his teaching. Jesus's name becomes so well-known that Herod Antipas becomes aware of him (6:14). On occasions where his notoriety leads to extreme crowd pressure or danger from the Pharisees, Jesus withdraws to a remote place (1:38, 45; 3:7; 6:31; 7:24; 8:13; 9:30). He teaches his disciples privately at times (4:13, 34; 7:17; 9:28–32; 10:10–11; 13:3) and uses parables to conceal his teaching from the multitudes (4:10–12, 33–34).

Since the 1901 publication of Wilhelm Wrede's monograph, scholars have referred to this perplexing motif as the messianic secret.[48] It is most prominent in Mark, but it also occurs in Matthew and Luke. Wrede's explanation was that the historical Jesus did not teach that he was the Messiah, and that pre-Markan tradition did not contain this teaching either. Wrede held that the author of Mark invented the secrecy motif and added it to pre-Markan tradition to explain why more people did not believe in Jesus during his lifetime. Once the church had come to believe that Jesus had risen from the dead, it needed the secrecy motif to validate Jesus's messianic status.

The messianic secret is a real problem in understanding Mark, but few believe that Wrede has solved it. Perhaps the most obvious problem with Wrede's theory is that Jesus's commands for secrecy are seldom followed. Typically, those he healed made it known widely (1:45; 5:20; 7:36–37) and people are somehow able to find him even in remote or private places (1:37, 45; 2:1–2; 3:8; 6:33–34; 7:24; 10:1). Several additional factors converge to explain how this seemingly strange Markan motif is an authentic part of Jesus's teaching. Jesus did not want or need the testimony of evil demons—he would experience a slanderous accusation of collaboration with them (3:22). He counseled people he

---

48. *Das Messiasgeheimnis in den Evangelien* (Göttingen: Vandenhoeck & Ruprecht, 1901). ET by J. C. G. Grieg, *The Messianic Secret* (London: Clarke, 1971). For extended discussion of this motif, see C. M. Tuckett, ed., *The Messianic Secret* (Philadelphia: Fortress, 1983).

healed to moderate their enthusiasm to avoid drawing even more of a curious mob than was already following him. Such a following would only arouse the suspicions and jealousies of the Jewish leaders more rapidly, and the Roman authorities would most likely understand such a following as politically subversive. This concern is also why Jesus strategically withdrew to remote places from time to time. Since he knew his destiny was tied to Jerusalem, he did not let things get out of hand in Galilee. Even the strangest silence, that of his own disciples, grew out of their lack of understanding of his office as a suffering, crucified, yet risen Messiah (8:30–32; 9:9–13, 30–32; 10:32–34; 14:27–31; 16:6–8). Mark Strauss sums it all up well: "The messianic secret is better understood as Jesus's attempt to define his messiahship on his own terms, which means in light of the cross."[49]

The Failure of the Disciples and the Ending of Mark

Related to the Messianic secret theme is another perplexing matter: the pervasive weakness of Jesus's disciples in Mark. All four Gospels, as well as Acts,[50] present the disciples realistically, showing their foibles as well as their faithfulness, but Mark especially features the foibles, almost to the extent that the disciples appear to be Jesus's antagonists along with the religious leaders. Twenty-five scenes stand out to varying degrees when one reads through Mark:

- The disciples fearfully ask Jesus whether he cares that they are about to drown in a storm on the Sea of Galilee (4:38–41).
- The disciples ask Jesus to dismiss the hungry multitude at the end of the day, and respond incredulously to Jesus's command that the multitude be fed (6:35–37; cf. 8:4).
- The disciples respond in fear when they see Jesus walking on the water during another storm on the Sea of Galilee. They did not learn from Jesus's miraculous feeding of the multitude (cf. 6:35–37), and their hearts were hardened (6:49–52).
- The disciples, like the scribes and Pharisees, do not understand Jesus's teaching about the heart as the true source of purity and impurity (7:17–23).
- As in 6:35–37, the disciples lack compassion for the multitude and forget that Jesus is able to feed them miraculously (8:4).
- The disciples surprisingly mistake Jesus's warning for them to beware the leaven of the Pharisees and Herod as criticism of

---

49. Mark L. Strauss, *Four Portraits, One Jesus* (Grand Rapids: Zondervan, 2007), 180.
50. See Acts 5:1–11; 6:1; 8:9–24; 9:13–14, 26; 11:1–18; 12:15; 15:1–2, 5; 15:37–39; 20:29; 21:20–26.

their forgetting to bring bread on their journey. Jesus asks them why they do not understand and if their hearts are hardened. His allusion to Ezekiel 12:2 and Isaiah 6:5 is particularly ominous (8:14–21; cf. 3:5; 4:12; 6:52; 10:5; [16:14]).

- Peter responds to Jesus's first passion prediction by rebuking Jesus, only to receive Jesus's scathing words "Get behind me, Satan" in reply (8:32; cf. 1:13).
- After the transfiguration, Peter, James, and John discuss what Jesus meant when he spoke of his resurrection, and they ask him about the coming of Elijah (9:9–13).
- The disciples are unable to perform a particularly difficult exorcism (9:14–29).
- The disciples do not understand Jesus's passion prediction, but are afraid to ask him about it (9:30–32).
- The disciples do not want to admit to Jesus that they had been discussing who was the greatest (9:33–37).
- The disciples mistakenly attempt to hinder an exorcist (9:38–40).
- The disciples question Jesus about his teaching on divorce (10:10).
- The disciples rebuke people who are bringing children to Jesus, leading to Jesus's indignation and teaching on children as a model of those who receive his kingdom (10:13–16).
- The disciples are astonished at Jesus's teaching that personal wealth hinders entrance into his kingdom (10:23–27).
- James and John ask Jesus if they may sit at his right and left hand in glory, leading to the indignation of the other disciples when they hear of it (10:35–45).
- The disciples seem to be more impressed with the beauty of the temple architecture than with Jesus's teaching about the poor widow (13:1).
- Peter, James, and John want inside information on the time and signs of the temple's destruction (13:3–4).
- Some of the disciples scold a woman who pours a very expensive vial of perfume on Jesus's head, opining that the perfume could have been sold and the money given to the poor (14:3–9).
- The disciples find it difficult to believe Jesus's word that one of them would betray him (14:17–21).
- Peter and the other disciples disagree with Jesus's word that they will fall away or disown him (14:27–31; cf. Zech. 13:7).
- Peter, James, and John sleep during Jesus's agonized prayers in the garden of Gethsemane (14:32–42).
- As Jesus predicted, the disciples flee when he is arrested (14:50–51; cf. 14:27–29).

- As Jesus predicted, Peter denies the Lord three times (14:66–72; cf. 14:30–31).
- Mary Magdalene, Mary the mother of James, and Salome are overawed by the angel at the empty tomb and run away, disregarding the angel's instructions to tell the disciples and Peter that Jesus will meet them in Galilee, as he had promised (16:8; cf. 14:28).[51]

It is clear from the above texts that Mark is not **hagiography**—idealism and adulation are not found in this narrative. In Mark Jesus is the sole protagonist; the disciples rarely appear in a positive light. And yet, it is apparent from Mark's editorial point of view and overall content that the disciples are truly (albeit weakly and haltingly) committed to Jesus and his kingdom, and Mark assumes that they will remain so in the future. For example, Jesus picks twelve of them and gives them special authority to represent him and his ministry to renew Israel (3:13–19). His parable of the sower depicts fruitful results from the proclamation of the kingdom message (4:20). He patiently explains his parabolic teaching to his disciples (4:34). They tell him about their current ministry accomplishments (6:30). He promises them rewards for their faithful service (10:28–31), and he reveals that their future ministries will reach all the nations despite much peril (13:9–13; 14:9).

Arguably, Mark's abrupt ending in 16:8 that emphasizes the disciples' failure also implies their eventual faithfulness.[52] Mark has repeatedly narrated Jesus's promises that he would be raised from the dead (8:31; 9:9, 31; 10:33–34; 14:28; 16:6–8), and that he would return to rule the earth (8:38; 13:24–27; 14:62/Dan. 7:13). Mark's account of the Last Supper shows that even though Jesus may be "going," he will one day drink new wine in the kingdom of God (14:21–25). Mark takes his readers right into the empty tomb with the three women to hear the angel's testimony to the resurrection (16:1–8) before ending without a narrative of Jesus's postresurrection appearances (Matt. 28:1–17; Luke 24:1–45; Acts 1:1–8; John 20:1–21:23) and final commissions (Matt. 28:18–20; Luke 24:46–48; Acts 1:8; John 20:21–23). As Jesus predicted, the Twelve have scattered (14:27–31, 50–52), and none of them is present to hear the angel tell the women to remind the disciples of Jesus's promise to meet them

---

51. It should be noted that the long ending of Mark, [16:9–20], continues the theme of the disciples' unbelief in Mary Magdalene's ([16:11] cf. Luke 24:11) and the two disciples' ([16:12–13] cf. Luke 24:13–35) reports of the resurrection, as well mentioning Jesus's rebuking them for their unbelief ([16:14] cf. Luke 24:36–43).

52. In the next chapter our treatment of textual criticism will feature discussion of the controversy over the ending of Mark, concluding that Mark originally ended at 16:8. The discussion here assumes the conclusion reached there; Mark 16:9–20 will not be considered here.

in Galilee (14:28; 16:7). The women, gripped by fear,[53] flee from the tomb and as Mark closes, they don't say anything to anybody.

As odd as it seems at first blush, Mark's abrupt and starkly sad ending is altogether in keeping with his depiction of the disciples' foibles throughout this Gospel. Their lack of compassion, understanding, and obedience all come to a head here. They have slept when Jesus struggled over the prospect of the cross (14:32–42), and they have run away when its shadow loomed (14:50). Since they did not witness the agony of Jesus's crucifixion, it is oddly fitting that they do not experience the joy of his resurrection. Yet after all this failure, there is, by the grace of God, a glimmer of hope. What if the women get over their fear, come to their senses, and tell Peter and the disciples that Jesus will meet them in Galilee, just as he had promised? And what if Peter, last seen weeping after denying the Lord three times (14:54, 66–72), takes heart and sets out afresh to follow Jesus?

Mark has evidently left these questions open to engage his readers in terms of their own fidelity to Jesus. God has confirmed and endorsed his son the Messiah (1:1) by raising him from the dead. The question remains for all readers of Mark: Will they turn to God in repentance and faith because the resurrection of Jesus is the ultimate demonstration of the arrival of God's kingdom? What Mark omits for his unique literary purposes, the remainder of the fourfold Gospel and the book of Acts make clear. The women told Peter and the disciples that Jesus would meet them in Galilee (Matt. 28:8; Luke 24:9). The disciples met him there (Matt. 28:16; John 21), and the rest is redemptive history.

THE DISTINCTIVE THEOLOGY OF LUKE-ACTS

For my eyes have seen your salvation,
which you have prepared in the sight of all nations:
a light for revelation to the Gentiles, and the glory of your people Israel.
(Luke 2:30–32, NIV)

Simeon's words betray a remarkable degree of perception of the plan of God, a perception resulting from special revelation by the Holy Spirit (Luke 2:25–27). Simeon's brief, prayerful words, occurring early in Luke's Gospel, distill and augur the central theological agenda of the entire two-volume composition Luke-Acts. Simon understands God's plan in Isaianic terms. He is waiting for the *consolation* of Israel (2:25; cf. Isa. 40:1; 49:13; 51:3; 57:18; 61:2) and he *sees* God's salvation (2:30; cf. Isa. 40:5; 52:10) in the baby Jesus. This salvation is *universal*, prepared in the

---

53. The women's lack of immediate obedience should be attributed not to willful rebellion against the angel's directive but to their being emotionally overwhelmed by the empty tomb and the angelic epiphany.

presence all the peoples (2:31; cf. Isa. 55:5; 60:5; 61:9), and it is pictured as *light* (2:32; cf. Isa. 2:5; 9:2; 30:26; 42:16; 50:10), which brings revelation to the Gentiles (2:32; cf. Isa. 42:6; 49:6; 51:4–5) and glory to Israel (2:32; cf. Isa. 4:5; 24:23; 28:5; 46:13; 58:8; 60:1–3, 19–20). Simeon's stress on God's salvation coming to the Gentiles from Israel can be traced back to God's original plan for the descendants of Abraham to be a blessing to all the families of the earth (Gen. 12:1–4; 18:18–19). In fact, many texts in Luke-Acts allude to God's plan for Abraham's descendants as the backdrop for the saving message of Jesus (Luke 1:55, 73; 3:8; 13:16, 28; Acts 3:13, 25; 7:2; 13:26). Such texts prepare the way for a key theme of Pauline theology (Rom. 4:1–18; Gal. 3:7–29).

Undertaking a summary of the theology of Luke-Acts requires a synthesis of the largest body of literature by a single author in the NT. The two volumes of Luke-Acts are somewhat different generically, and evidently arose and circulated individually. In a sense, each volume is complete in itself, but the two compositions were unmistakably intended to be read together as a presentation of the spread of the message of Jesus from Jerusalem to Rome. Accordingly, the tendency to read Acts mainly as a text that provides the background for Paul's life and letters should be resisted. There is a certain spontaneity and unpredictability in Luke-Acts. Although the overall plan is clear, the individual steps are surprising. Writing about the theology of Luke-Acts is somewhat like writing a treatise on dance steps in terms of plane geometry. We have previously presented the emphasis on the work of the Spirit in Luke-Acts. Here we will address two additional emphases: (1) the interplay of Jerusalem and Rome and its theological implications, and (2) the salvation of the outcasts.

Jerusalem and Rome

The prevalence of Jerusalem in Luke-Acts is in keeping with the honor accorded Jerusalem and the temple in the OT. Jerusalem became the capitol of David's kingdom (2 Sam. 5:5), and it was there that Solomon built the temple as the center of God's presence with Israel (1 Kings 6–7). The ark of the covenant was installed in the most holy place, and God's glory filled the temple (1 Kings 8:1–11). Solomon's prayer at the dedication of the temple indicates just how crucial Jerusalem and the temple were to the religious identity of Israel (1 Kings 8:12–61). There are many other biblical texts that allude to the centrality of Jerusalem and the temple in God's plan for his people (e.g., 1 Kings 11:13, 32, 36; 14:21; 15:4; 2 Kings 18:22; 19:31–34; 2 Chron. 6:6). Despite their crucial role in Jerusalem, the Davidic kings were not faithful to God, and Jerusalem became an egregiously sinful city, leading to its destruction by the Babylonians.[54] Yet God's ultimate plan for Jerusalem was not judgment but blessing, and that blessing was not for Israel alone but for all the nations.[55]

It is likely that the focus of Luke-Acts on Jerusalem, and how the gospel came to extend from Jerusalem to Rome, rests on these OT prophecies of a restored Jerusalem that blesses both Israel and the nations. As Luke-Acts begins, Zechariah the priest receives the amazing news of the birth of John the Baptist while burning incense in the Jerusalem temple (Luke 1:8–11). Not long afterward, Simeon meets Jesus in the Jerusalem temple, and speaks of Israel's role as a light to the nations (Luke 2:25–32; cf. Isa. 42:6; 29:6; Acts 13:47; 26:23). Anna also encounters Jesus in this scene, and speaks of him to all who are looking for the redemption of Jerusalem (Luke 2:38; cf. Isa. 52:9; 59:20). Luke's unique travel narrative, beginning in 9:51, begins a section of twenty-eight consecutive chapters that either focus on or center in Jerusalem (Luke 9–Acts 8). As Luke-Acts ends, Paul has preached the gospel in Rome, concluding his sermon with an appeal to Isaiah 6:10, a text that reflects God's message to Isaiah in the waning days of Judah and the first temple in Jerusalem.[56]

As the table below indicates, Jerusalem is the center of Luke-Acts both geographically and theologically. In Luke the plot moves toward Jerusalem, and in Acts the plot moves from Jerusalem to Rome. The biblical prophecies of God's plan to restore Jerusalem and bless the nations through Jerusalem likely provide the theological basis for this literary-geographical motif.[57] The relation of Jerusalem and Rome in Luke-Acts, however, is more complicated than a simple one-way movement. Luke-Acts actually begins in Jerusalem, and there are several additional references to Jerusalem before the travel narrative begins in Luke 9:51. The mention of Roman rule in Luke 3:1–2 has been taken as the beginning of a chiasm reaching all the way to Acts 28,[58] but this suggestion is problematic in the details, not least because Luke's Gospel begins in Jerusalem, not Rome. During the travel narrative, a reminder of Rome's harsh rule over Israel and its impingement on the

---

54. 2 Chron. 36:22–23; Ps. 122, 125, 126; 128:5; 137; Isa. 1:26; 2:1–4; 4:3; 30:19; 31:5; 40:2, 9; 52:9; Jer. 32:36–44; 33:16; Zech. 8:2–13.

55. Isa. 52:7–10; 62:1–12; 65:10–24; Jer. 3:17–19; 4:2–3; 33:9; Mic. 4:1–5; Zeph. 3:8–20; Zech. 2:10–12; 8:19–23; 14:16; Mal. 3:12.

56. For discussion of the literary and theological significance of Acts 28:16–31 for interpreting Luke-Acts, see Charles B. Puskas, *The Conclusion of Luke-Acts* (Eugene, OR: Pickwick, 2009).

57. See further J. Bradley Chance, *Jerusalem, the Temple, and the New Age in Luke-Acts* (Atlanta: Mercer, 1988).

58. Craig L. Blomberg, *Jesus and the Gospels* (Nashville: B&H, 1997), 142–44. Blomberg cites others who have taken this view.

temple mars the focus on Jerusalem. Once Jesus arrives in Jerusalem, its Roman overlords are obviously prominent in the narrative. The italicized entries in the table below show the influence of Rome is not lacking in sections of Acts that focus on Jerusalem. Jews and proselytes from Rome are already present at Pentecost before mission to the end of the earth has even begun. A eunuch from Ethiopia comes *to* Jerusalem before Jerusalem can come to him. Further, the sections Acts that feature movement toward Rome contain frequent references back to Jerusalem. In short, the Jerusalem-focused sections of Luke-Acts contain regular reminders that Rome, not Jerusalem, is currently the center of political power, and, correspondingly, the Rome-focused sections of Luke-Acts contain regular reminders that Jerusalem, not Rome, is the center of spiritual power. In Luke-Acts the church's spiritual power subtly subverts the political power of the Roman Empire.[59]

From Jerusalem to Rome:
The Movement of the Gospel in Luke-Acts

Zechariah, Jesus, Simeon, and Anna in the **Jerusalem** temple (Acts 1:5–8; 2:22–38, 41–50)

John's ministry set in the context of Roman *rule (Luke 3:1–2)*

People from all over, including **Jerusalem**, come to Galilee to see Jesus (5:17; 6:17)

Jesus's upcoming **Jerusalem** "exodus" discussed with Moses and Elijah at his transfiguration (9:31)

Jesus journeys to **Jerusalem** (Luke 9:51–19:40)

Jesus resolutely sets out for **Jerusalem** (9:51)

Samaritans do not welcome **Jerusalem**-bound Jesus (9:53)

Jesus parable has a Samaritan help a person from **Jerusalem** (10:30)

Jesus refers to Pilate*'s harsh and sacrilegious treatment of certain Galileans (13:1–2)*

Jesus refers to the Siloam tower falling and killing people in **Jerusalem** (13:4)

Jesus visits other towns on his way to **Jerusalem** (13:22)

Jesus speaks movingly about **Jerusalem**'s historic rejection of the prophets (13:33–35)

Jesus passes between Samaria and Galilee on his way to **Jerusalem** (17:11)

Jesus tells the Twelve about their **Jerusalem** destination and his passion (17:31–34)

Jesus tells a parable as he nears **Jerusalem** (19:11–27)

Jesus ascends to **Jerusalem** and weeps over the city (19:28, 41–44)

Jesus's ministry, arrest, crucifixion, resurrection, appearances in **Jerusalem** (Luke 19:45–24:43)

Jesus predicts Roman *armies will surround* Jerusalem *and defeat it (21:20–24)*

Pilate *tries Jesus,* Roman *soldiers mock Jesus "the king of the Jews" (23:1–38)*

Jesus tells disciples to remain in **Jerusalem** until the Spirit comes (Luke 24:44–53; Acts 1:1–8)

---

59. See further David Rhoads, et al., eds., *Luke-Acts and Empire* (Eugene, OR: Pickwick, 2011), especially Michael Bachmann, "Jerusalem and Rome in Luke-Acts," 60–83.

Jesus ascends to heaven and disciples remain in **Jerusalem** (Luke 24:50–53; Acts 1:9–26)

The Spirit comes and mission to the ends of the earth begins from **Jerusalem** (2:1–8:4)

Jews and Proselytes from Rome *are present on the day of Pentecost (2:10)*

Jerusalem church leaders endorse the Samaritan converts (8:14–25)

Philip speaks to an Ethiopian eunuch who had worshiped in **Jerusalem** (8:27)

Paul's conversion acknowledged in **Jerusalem** (9:27–30; cf. 8:1; 9:1–2, 13, 21)

Peter recalls Jesus's activities and crucifixion in **Jerusalem** (10:39)

Peter explains the baptism of Cornelius's household to the **Jerusalem** church (11:1–18)

Barnabas sent by the **Jerusalem** church to minister to Gentile Christians in Antioch (11:19–26)

Jerusalem receives an offering from the church in Antioch (11:27–30; 12:25)

John Mark left Paul and Barnabas and returned to **Jerusalem** (13:13)

Paul recalls Jesus's crucifixion and postresurrection appearances in **Jerusalem** (13:27–31)

Jerusalem church council debates assimilation of Gentile converts (15:1–29)

Paul and companions inform Gentile converts of the decision in **Jerusalem** (15:30–31; 16:4)

Roman *emperor Claudius's decress results in Paul meeting Aquila and Priscilla in Corinth (18:1–3)*

Paul reports to **Jerusalem** after the second mission trip (18:22)

Paul's plans to return to **Jerusalem** and prophetic warnings (19:21; 20:16, 22; 21:4–14)

Paul reports to **Jerusalem** after the third mission trip (21:17)

Roman *cohort saves Paul from the mob in the temple (21:31–39)*

Paul has severe problems with the Jews in **Jerusalem** (21:40–22:23; 23:1–16)

The Lord assures Paul that he will bear witness of the gospel in Rome *as he has in Jerusalem (23:11)*

Roman *centurion sends Paul to the governor Felix in Caesarea (23:17–24:27)*

Roman *governor Festus deals with Paul and Paul appeals to Caesar (25:1–27:32)*

Jerusalem leaders request Paul's return to Jerusalem so they can kill him (25:1–3)

Paul's voyage to Rome *under the cohort Julius (27:1–28:15)*

Paul arrives in Rome *where he preaches and teaches for two years (Acts 28:16–31)*

Paul tells the Jews in **Rome** that he was taken into Roman custody due to false accusations by the Jews in **Jerusalem** (28:17–19)

Evangelizing the Outcasts

Nearly all scholars recognize that salvation is a central theme of Luke-Acts.[60] Closely related to this theme is the concept that salvation in Luke-Acts is for everyone, including various outcasts. The first few chapters of Luke focus on humble characters. We are first introduced to an elderly priest and his wife who are childless, then a couple from the obscure Galilean village of Nazareth who lay their newborn child in a manger

---

60.   E.g., Darrell L. Bock, *A Theology of Luke-Acts* (Grand Rapids: Zondervan, 2012), 239–78; Joel B. Green, *The Theology of the Gospel of Luke* (Cambridge: Cambridge University Press, 1995), esp. 22–101.

and offer doves instead of a lamb for the firstborn sacrifice. Shepherds staying out in the fields all night receive a visit from angels who announce that a Savior has been born for them. Soon an elderly man and a widow who frequent the temple meet the baby and show remarkable insight into God's plan of salvation. With these scenes in mind, it should not come as a surprise that Luke will soon depict the impact of Jesus's coming for people who are even more obscure or unsavory. When Jesus announces that he has been anointed with the Spirit to minister to the poor, the captives, the blind, and the downtrodden (Luke 4:17–19, citing Isa. 61:1–2), the agenda of Luke-Acts becomes clearer. The overall movement of the gospel from Jerusalem to Rome will sweep various marginalized people into the kingdom, resulting in "the triumph of inclusiveness."[61]

Jesus's teaching that wealth could keep people out of his kingdom was shocking to his disciples (Luke 18:18–30, especially 18:26). Evidently, they assumed wealth to be a sure sign of God's blessing. Those in economic duress, however, might be more open to God's kingdom and its values. Certainly, Jesus's mother Mary was not wealthy, and it is clear from her *Magnificat* that she believed the promises associated with her son's birth included economic reversal (Luke 1:52–53). Her prayer indicates that poverty can be a result of sinful oppression, and that Christ's followers should begin now to reverse such injustice (Luke 14:12–13). Unlike Matthew, Luke depicts Jesus's beatitudes for poor, hungry, weeping, and hated people with corresponding woes against rich, well-fed, laughing, and popular people (Luke 6:24–26; cf. Matt. 5:1–12). Jesus's parable of the rich fool (Luke 12:16–21) powerfully demonstrates the folly of using wealth for personal aggrandizement. In its context the parable applies both to coveting the wealth of others and using one's wealth solely for one's own benefit (cf. Luke 16:14). Jesus's parable of the rich man and Lazarus (Luke 16:19–31) makes it abundantly clear that rich people who do not use their resources compassionately will one day find themselves seeking—and not finding—compassion from God. In both Luke and Acts it is clear that some financially well-off people are faithful followers of Jesus, and that they use their wealth in consistency with kingdom values (Luke 8:3; Acts 4:32–37; 11:27–30; 12:12). There are negative examples as well (Acts 5:1–11). The scene involving the poor widow who contributed all she had, even though it was a minimal amount, contains perhaps the most striking teaching of Jesus on the use of material possessions (Luke 21:1–4).[62]

---

61. Frank Thielman, *Theology of the New Testament* (Grand Rapids: Zondervan, 2005), 127. See further Bock, *A Theology of Luke-Acts*, 343–59; Robert Tannehill, *The Narrative Unity of Luke-Acts*, 2 vols. (Philadelphia: Fortress, 1986), 1.101–40.

62. See further Walter E. Pilgrim, *Good News to the Poor: Wealth and Poverty in Luke-Acts* (Minneapolis: Augsburg, 1981) and Craig L. Blomberg, *Christians in an Age of Wealth: A Biblical Theology of Stewardship* (Grand Rapids: Zondervan, 2013), 85–87, 104–12, 157–65.

Closely related to economics is social status. In Luke-Acts social outcasts would involve several types of people. All Gentiles would fit here, since they did not keep ritual purity, dietary, and Sabbath laws. Ethnic Jews would also be marginalized for immorality (Luke 7:37), crime (Luke 23:39–43) or lack of observance of Pharisaic traditions (Luke 5:29; 7:34; 15:1). Sicknesses such as leprosy would lead to ritual impurity, but Jesus touched and healed such people (Luke 7:12–16). Another factor that would marginalize individuals would be a questionable occupation, such as tax collecting. Yet Jesus welcomed tax collectors, like Levi and his friends and Zaccheus (Luke 5:27–32; 19:1–10; cf. Luke 3:12; 7:29, 34; 15:1). Jesus also told a parable in which a repentant tax collector went home right with God and a proud Pharisee did not (Luke 18:9–14). Jesus's parable of the prodigal son also shows that God's heart was receptive even to egregious sinners (Luke 15:1–2, 11–32).

Luke-Acts includes many examples of Jesus's positive attitude toward women and of positive contributions of women to the church. Women are prominent in the birth narratives of Luke 1–2. Jesus's compassion for the widow of Nain, whose only son had died, led him to resuscitate the young man (Luke 7:11–17). The poor widow of Acts 21:1–4 has been mentioned above. Other women receive special praise or concern from Jesus (Luke 4:38–39; 7:36–50; 8:43–56; 10:38–42; 13:10–17; 23:27–31). Jesus's strict teaching on divorce would help prevent mistreatment of women as well (Luke 16:18). Women also appear in the narrative of Luke-Acts who made special contributions to Jesus and the apostles. Joanna and Susanna were among the group who were financially able to support Jesus and the apostles (Luke 8:3). Other women had sufficient means to host church meetings and contribute to the ministry (Acts 12:12; 16:14–15; 17:4, 12). Certain women who followed Jesus from Galilee witnessed the crucifixion, announced the resurrection, and were among the disciples in the upper room awaiting the coming of the Spirit (Luke 23:49; 23:55–24:11; Acts 1:14). Luke specifically mentions that early converts included both men and women (Acts 5:14; 8:3, 12; 9:2; 16:1, 14; 17:4, 12, 24; 22:4).

The openness of Jesus and his kingdom to all human beings regardless of their racial heritage is clear in Luke-Acts. Luke and Acts alike show that the notorious historic rift between the Jews and the Samaritans (2 Kings 17:24–41; John 4:7–9; 8:48) could be overcome by the message of the kingdom. Although the Samaritans treated Jesus badly on one occasion (Luke 9:52–56), he rebuked his disciples for wanting to call down fire on them. This scene should be juxtaposed with the later receptivity of Samaria to the gospel, and with the Jerusalem leaders' authentication of the conversion of the Samaritans (Acts 8:5–25). On other notable occasions, Samaritans are positive examples of kingdom values (Luke 10:30–37; 17:11–19). Early in Luke, Simeon through the Spirit was aware of

Isaiah's vision for Israel to be a light to the Gentiles (2:32; cf. Acts 13:47; 26:23). At the end of Luke, Jesus mandates that the gospel be proclaimed to all nations (Luke 24:49). Of course, mission to the Gentiles begins in earnest in Acts with Peter being led to speak to Cornelius's household (Acts 10:1–48). Later Paul continues what began with Peter.

One wonders whether post-Pentecost reflection on the implications of Joel 2:28 ("I will pour out My Spirit *on all mankind*") was influential in the Jerusalem church's view of its immediate mission in Jerusalem and eventual mission to the Gentiles. When Peter cited this text in his sermon on the day of Pentecost (Acts 2:17), he was speaking to Jews and **proselytes** (Acts 2:10) from around the Mediterranean world. There were no Gentiles present, although perhaps "all who are far off" (Acts 2:39) implied the Gentiles (cf. Eph. 2:2:13, 17). There was evidently no clear movement of the Spirit to encourage Gentile outreach until Acts 10 (cf. Acts 13:2). In Acts 15:15–18, James validated Gentile outreach scripturally from Amos 9:11–12. In retrospect, "all flesh" in Acts 2:17/ Joel 2:28 would seem to include all human beings, regardless of their ethnicity, gender, social status, or economic standing. Perhaps Peter preached better than he yet knew on the day of Pentecost.

THE DISTINCTIVE THEOLOGY OF JOHN

He came to that which was his own, but his own did not receive him.
Yet to all who did receive him, to those who believed in his name,
he gave the right to become children of God.
(John 1:11–12, NIV)

The Fourth Gospel begins with a beginning that is unlike those of the first three Gospels. Matthew takes its readers all the way back to Abraham, the father of the nation of Israel, showing that Jesus fulfills Israel's story. Mark explains that the message about Jesus began with his promised forerunner John the Baptist, showing that the comfort Isaiah promised Israel was on its way. Luke wants to be clear that he has looked into the historical traditions handed down from the beginning by eyewitnesses of Jesus, showing, as Paul put it later, that "this has not been done in a corner" (Acts 26:26). We could say that Matthew, Mark, and Luke begin respectively with the ethnic, prophetic, and historic beginnings of Jesus.

How different is the beginning of the Fourth Gospel! It begins not with an aspect of Jesus's beginning but with Jesus as the "Beginner," the eternal creator of the universe. He is divine in the fullest sense of the word, and yet he is personally distinct from the Father. He is divine creator of the world, yet he is also the human revealer of the Father. He not only spoke light into a dark world at its beginning, he also spoke life-giving light into sin-darkened human lives. John bore witness of him, and the grace of Moses's law anticipated the fullness of grace he brought to his people. Attentive readers can only be astounded, when reading John 1:11 with all this in mind, that his own people did not receive him. The **irony** is profound, and it would be shattering if the assertion in John 1:12 that some did receive him, and became God's children, due solely to God's grace did not mitigate it.

The rest of the Gospel of John seems to play off John 1:11–12. Most of the characters that enter the story are defined by their rejection or reception of Jesus. John 20:20–31 seems to echo 1:11–12, explaining that the significant stories selected for this Gospel were calculated to be faith-generating and life-generating. Readers of John, therefore, will either be warned against unbelief or will be encouraged to believe by the scenes included in this Gospel. Of the many Johannine themes that could be discussed here, two that relate to John 1:11–12 have been chosen. In John, signs are a prominent preliminary to faith, and faith in Jesus brings eternal life. Accordingly, the following discussions engage the relation of signs to faith and the eschatological blessings that come to those who believe.

Signs and Faith

The fourfold Gospel testimony frequently speaks of the miracles Jesus performed, and the Fourth Gospel does so in a unique fashion. The narrative of Jesus's public ministry in the Fourth Gospel (1:19–12:50) is replete with references to Jesus's signs (σημεῖα) and works (ἔργα).[63] These signs turn out to be extraordinary deeds performed by Jesus through his reliance on the Father. These deeds bear witness that the Father is at work through Jesus. Scholars commonly point out that there are *seven* signs featured in John 2–12, culminating in the raising of Lazarus:

1. Transformation of water into wine at Cana (2:1–11)
2. Healing the royal official's son (4:46–54)
3. Healing the paralytic at the pool with five porticoes (5:1–18)
4. Multiplication of loaves (6:1–14)

---

63. The word σημεῖον occurs seventeen times in John, sixteen times in John 1–12 (2:11, 18, 23; 3:2; 4:48, 54; 6:2, 14, 26, 30; 7:31; 9:16; 10:41; 11:47; 12:18, 37) and once in the summary of the book's purpose in 20:31. The word ἔργον occurs ten times in reference to Jesus's activities (4:34; 5:20, 36; 7:3, 21; 10:25, 32, 37–38). Signs are the exclusive domain of Jesus in John, but works are not (3:19; 6:28; 7:7; 8:39, 41; 9:3; 14:12; 15:24; 17:4). Jesus frequently says that his works have been given to him by the Father, and in one case he describes them directly as the Father's works (14:10). The verbs ἐργάζομαι (5:17; 6:30; 9:4), ποιέω (2:11, 23; 3:2; 4:34, 45–46, 54; 5:11, 15, 19, 36; 6:2, 6, 14, 30, 38; 7:3, 21, 23, 31; 8:28; 9:16, 30; 10:25, 37–38; 11:37, 45–46; 12:18, 37; 14:12; 15:24; 17:4; 20:30; 21:25), δείκνυμι (2:18; 5:20; 10:32; 20:20), and τελειόω (4:34; 5:36; 17:4) are used to describe Jesus's performance of signs and works.

    5.   Walking on the waters of the Sea of Galilee (6:15–21)
    6.   Healing the young man born blind (9:1–41)
    7.   Raising Lazarus from the dead (11:1–46; 12:9–11)

Jesus's post-resurrection appearance to Thomas and the disciples (20:26–29) is evidently the ultimate sign that transcends even the resurrection of Lazarus, since immediately after that event John concludes the narrative by speaking of many *other* signs Jesus did (20:30).[64]

John clearly teaches that the signs are a God-given means to bring people to faith (1:50; 2:11; 4:48, 53; 7:31; 11:45, 48; 20:20–31). Many who saw the signs, however, did not believe in him (12:37), and Jesus said people could believe in him without seeing signs (20:29)—evidently through the written testimony of this gospel (20:30–31). The relation of signs and faith becomes all the more ambiguous in instances where people apparently "see" Jesus's signs and do believe in him in some sense, only to be later rebuked by him (2:23–3:3; 6:14–15, 22–40). In such cases, people evidently believed in Jesus as a miracle-worker but did not fully grasp the significance of his miracles. Further ambiguity arises in the case of those whose belief in Jesus was private because of their fear of the religious leaders' disapproval (7:13; 12:42; 19:38; 20:19).

The ambiguity of signs and faith comes to a head in the case of Nicodemus. Nicodemus takes the initiative to come to Jesus to acknowledge how Jesus's miracles attest to the divine origin of his teaching (3:1–3, taken with 2:23–25). Yet Jesus's abrupt teaching of the necessity of rebirth from above only leaves Nicodemus confused and questioning Jesus (3:4, 9). Later, Nicodemus appears with the leaders of Jerusalem whose officers have been unsuccessful in arresting Jesus. The leaders scorn their officers and affirm that none of their number has believed in Jesus (7:45–49). When Nicodemus cautions them from the law against making a judgment without evidence, they likewise scorn him (7:50–52). After Jesus's crucifixion, Nicodemus appears for the final time in the company of Joseph of Arimathea to give Jesus a proper burial (19:38–42). Nicodemus even goes to the expense of bringing a large quantity of spices for wrapping Jesus's body. John describes Joseph as a secret believer in Jesus, and if we admit details from the synoptic tradition (Mark 15:43; Luke 23:50–51), he is a member of the ruling council who did not agree to Jesus's crucifixion (cf. John 7:48). What does all this evidence say about Nicodemus's relationship to Jesus? His cautionary words in John 7:51 possibly imply he has come to true faith, but more likely, they simply reflect his sense of justice and a desire that

---

64.   Other acts of Jesus, such as his clearing the temple (John 2:13–23), are arguably intended to be regarded as signs. See Andreas J. Köstenberger, *The Theology of John's Gospel and Letters* (Grand Rapids: Zondervan, 2009), 323–35.

the law be followed (cf. *m. Sanh.* 4.5–5.5). His public act of joining with Joseph, a previously secret believer, in giving Jesus a lavish burial, however, probably indicates that the confusion of John 3 has been resolved and that Nicodemus has become a believer in Jesus. This act by Joseph and Nicodemus likely amounts to a reversal of John 12:42–43—they openly acknowledged their faith, evidently at a time when Jesus's core disciples were afraid to do so (cf. 20:19), because they had come to love the praise of God more than the praise of humans. Jesus's signs clearly aroused Nicodemus's curiosity; Jesus's cross evidently brought him to public faith (cf. John 3:14–15; 12:32–33).[65]

The Future in John

The most basic question facing a study of the future in the Fourth Gospel is whether it addresses the future at all.[66] Ladd bluntly stated that "the most superficial comparison of the Synoptics and John leaves one with the impression that the Johannine Jesus is little interested in eschatology."[67] Certain Johannine teachings stress the present realization of things typically understood as future. For example:

- Jesus the Messiah has already come to reveal God and establish authentic worship (John 1:14–18; 4:21–26; cf. 1 John 4:2; 5:6).
- Jesus has overcome the world; his work of redemption is finished (John 16:23; 17:4; 19:30; cf. 1 John 2:8, 13–14; 3:5; 4:4; 5:4–5; Rev. 1:5; 3:21; 5:5; 12:10–11).
- The "hour" of resurrection is already here: Dead people are hearing the Son of God's voice and coming to life (John 5:25–29).
- Satan, the prince of this world, has already been judged (John 12:31; 16:11; 1 John 3:8; cf. Rev. 12:7–10). Believers in Jesus al-

---

65. See further Craig Koester, *The Word of Life: A Theology of John's Gospel* (Grand Rapids: Eerdmans, 2008), 163–70; Thielman, *Theology of the New Testament*, 162–70.

66. Studies of Johannine eschatology include R. E. Brown, *An Introduction to the Gospel of John*, ed. F. J. Moloney (New York: Doubleday, 2003), 234–48; W. R. Cook, "Eschatology in John's Gospel," *CTR* 3 (1988): 79–99; W. J. Dumbrell, "Johannine Eschatology," in *The Search for Order: Biblical Eschatology in Focus* (Grand Rapids: Baker, 1994), 235–58; L. R. Helyer, *The Witness of Jesus, Paul, and John* (Downers Grove, IL: InterVarsity, 2008), 344–77; Koester, *The Word of Life*, 175–86; G. E. Ladd, *A Theology of the New Testament*, rev. ed., ed. D. A. Hagner, (Grand Rapids: Eerdmans, 1993), 334–44; Frank Thielman, *Theology of the New Testament*, 172–79; David L. Turner, "The Doctrine of the Future in John's Writings," in *Eschatology: Biblical, Historical, and Practical Approaches*, eds. D. Jeffrey Bingham and Glenn R. Kreider (Grand Rapids: Kregel, 2016), 211–26.

67. Ladd, *Theology of the New Testament*, 334. Contrasting John to the Synoptics, Ladd notes John's emphasis on present eternal life rather than the inbreaking kingdom of God and on the coming of the Spirit rather than the apocalyptic *parousia* of Christ.

ready have eternal life;[68] unbelievers are already under judgment (John 3:18, 36; 1 John 5:12–13, 19).

- Antichrists are already in the world (1 John 2:18, 22; 4:3; 2 John 7).

Yet John speaks unequivocally about the future:

- Jesus will go to prepare a place for his disciples and then come for them (John 14:1–3, 18, 28; 21:22–23; cf. 1 John 2:28; 3:2–3; Rev. 1:7; 2:5, 15, 25; 3:3, 11; 16:15; 19:11–16; 22:7, 12, 20).
- Jesus's enemies may be permitted to overcome his people for a time (John 16:32–33; cf. Rev. 6:2; 11:7; 12:11; 13:7), but ultimately Jesus will overcome them (John 5:26–29; Rev. 17:14).
- The hour of resurrection is coming: all people will be raised, either to life or to judgment (John 5:28–29; 6:39–40, 44, 54; cf. Rev. 11:15–18; 20:4–6).[69]

The complexity of John's teaching in this area has led scholars such as C. H. Dodd and Rudolf Bultmann to argue that the "future" in John should be taken as having already been fully realized in the present time. Dodd argued that the delay of Christ's coming led early Christians to sublimate a primitive futuristic apocalyptic eschatology into a nuanced mystical sense of Christ's indwelling through the Spirit.[70] Bultmann's demythologizing existentialist agenda resulted in his denial of all things miraculous, including an apocalyptic end of the world. He understood eschatology as authentic personal existence and attributed futuristic texts in John to later interpolation.[71] The more recent work of Von

---

68. D. E. Aune stated that eternal life is "the primary mode of expressing realized eschatology within the Fourth Gospel." See "The Present Realization of Eschatological Salvation in the Fourth Gospel," in *The Cultic Setting of Realized Eschatology in Early Christianity* (Leiden: Brill, 1972), 82.

69. Additional bits of future eschatology are found in 1 John. Current antichrists demonstrate the reality of the future Antichrist (1 John 2:18; 4:3). It is the last hour (1 John 2:18), and believers in Jesus may anticipate judgment day with confidence (1 John 4:17).

70. See, e.g., Rudolf Bultmann, *The Apostolic Preaching and Its Developments* (London: Hodder & Stoughton, 1936), 155, 170–74; Bultmann, *The Coming of Christ* (Cambridge: University Press, 1954), 6–7.

71. Bultmann internalized eschatology, viewing faith itself as eschatological existence. See *Theology of the New Testament*, 2 vols. trans. K. Grobel (London: SCM, 1955), 2.75–92. D. E. Holwerda counters Bultmann's approach in *The Holy Spirit and Eschatology in the Gospel of John: A Critique of Rudolf Bultmann's Present Eschatology* (Amsterdam: Vrije Universiteit, 1959). Utilizing the theological concept of perichoresis (interpenetration), J. Moltmann critiques Bultmann's (and many others') bifurcation of present and future while arguing for an eschatology in motion— those who are in the risen Christ (cf. John 15:5) are in a sort of anteroom intertwined with and moving toward God's future kingdom. See "God in the World—the World in God: Perichoresis in Trinity and Eschatology," in *The Gospel of John and Christian Theology*, eds. R. Bauckham and C. Mosser (Grand Rapids: Eerdmans, 2008), 378–81.

Wahlde handles things similarly by arguing for three editions of the Fourth Gospel that progressively develop eschatology from (1) possession of eternal life by the believing community to (2) spiritual existence of believers beyond death to (3) future physical resurrection believers at a future time of reckoning.[72]

Traditional dispensationalists typically espouse an opposite view. For them, God's reign is entirely future. Charles Ryrie downplayed the role of the Gospel and letters in the study of Johannine eschatology: "Johannine eschatology is found mainly in the Apocalypse."[73] This statement assumes a strictly futuristic approach. John Walvoord acknowledged that the kingdom of God was present in some sense during Jesus's first advent, but he went on to say, "The hopes and promises and expectations associated with his coming did not take place—the eschatology which included them was not realized."[74] Walvoord's view of a promised advent without even the least realization of promised eschatological blessings is starkly futuristic. Similarly, A. J. McClain's treatment of John 5:25–29 separates the present "hour" of spiritual regeneration from the eschatological "hour" of physical resurrection so strictly that one wonders why Jesus would describe the former in terms of the latter.[75] In the larger context of NT theology, this sort of futurism has affinities with what has been called consistent eschatology.[76]

Most New Testament scholars across the theological spectrum have resisted both of these "all or nothing" approaches, viewing the realized and futuristic aspects of New Testament eschatology as complementary and correlative, not contradictory and corrective. The teaching about eternal life as a present reality assumes the future consummation and rests on it.[77] The differences between John's focus on eternal life and that of the Synoptics on the kingdom of God are commonly understood not as disparate teachings but as distinct emphases. John portrays God's glorious reign neither as fully realized nor fully future, but as

---

72. U. C. Von Wahlde, *The Gospel and Letters of John*, 3 vols. (Grand Rapids: Eerdmans, 2010), 3.459–74; 490–93.

73. Charles C. Ryrie, *Biblical Theology of the New Testament* (Chicago: Moody, 1959), 345. Despite Ryrie's question-begging futurism and lack of engagement with other views, his discussion includes passing references to John 5:24–29; 8:51; 14:1–3; 1 John 2:18; 3:14; 2 John 7 (347–52, 356).

74. John F. Walvoord, "*Realized Eschatology*," *BSac* 127 (1970): 322–23.

75. A. J. McClain, *The Greatness of the Kingdom* (Chicago: Moody, 1968), 489.

76. Consistent eschatology describes the futuristic eschatology (*konsequente eschatologie*) of the German scholar Johannes Weiss (1863–1914). See his *Jesus's Proclamation of the Kingdom of God*, trans. and eds. R. H. Hiers and D. L. Holland (Philadelphia: Fortress, 1971). The editors' introduction (1–51) helpfully surveys the development of various eschatological views.

77. Keener, *The Gospel of John*, 1.323.

both partially realized in the present and yet to be fully experienced in the future. In describing the Johannine teaching, the term "inaugurated" is more appropriate than the term "realized."[78] Strictly futurist eschatology truncates the Johannine stress on the powerful impact of Christ's life, death, resurrection, and his sending the Spirit to empower his people to do his work (John 20:21–23; cf. 1 John 2:8, 13–14, 20, 27). Strict realized eschatology truncates biblical teaching about what God will do to finish what he has begun in Christ. Johannine eschatology links the "already" to the "not yet" in that the eschatological life already experienced by followers of Jesus abides in them by the Spirit and empowers them for the troubles that are ahead (John 15:18–16:11; 16:20–22, 32–33; 17:14; 21:18). In Ashton's view, John's emphasis on the immediate consequences of belief (life) and unbelief (death/judgment) "de-eschatologizes [final] judgement,"[79] but it is truer to John's thought to say that John "eschatologizes" present life, underlining the urgency of belief in Jesus and the reality of true fellowship with God through him.

What does this "life eschatologized" look like? Fundamentally, it is the *abundant* life (John 10:10) engendered by the Holy Spirit through the word of Jesus (John 6:63, 68), who is life (John 14:6; 1 John 1:1–2; 5:11, 20) and who gives life (John 17:2; 20:31). Jesus's life-giving word comes to benighted people in a sin-darkened world, *illumining* them just as God illumined the world he originally created (John 1:1–5; 3:16–21, 36; 8:12). This life is actually of the same sort as that already shared by Jesus, his Father, and the Comforter (John 6:57; 17:3). It is a life of authentic *worship* in Spirit and truth, wherever and whenever it occurs (John 4:23–34). It is a life of *love*, a love for Jesus, fellow Christ-followers, and other humans. This love is actually the same sort of love as that already shared and shown by Jesus, his Father, and the Comforter (John 13:34–35; cf. 1 John 3:14–16). It is a life of *obedience* to Jesus. This obedience is actually the same sort of obedience as Jesus's own obedience to his Father (John 15:10). It is a life of *unity* with fellow believers. This unity is actually the same sort of unity as that shared by the Father, Son, and Holy Spirit, a *missional* unity designed to bring the world to faith in Jesus (John 17:21–23; cf. 4:36). Finally, it is a *surviving* life that anticipates transformed life after death following a resurrection on the last day (John 5:28; 6:40, 54; cf. Rev. 2:10; 20:4). This survival is similar to the survival experienced by Jesus on that first Easter morning (John 6:57; 14:19; cf. Rev 2:8).

---

78. J. Jeremias spoke of *sich realisierende eschatologie*, "eschatology in process of realization." See *The Parables of Jesus*, 3rd rev. ed. (London: SCM, 1972), 229 n. 3.

79. John Ashton, *Understanding the Fourth Gospel* (New York: Oxford University Press, 2007), 409.

SUMMARIZING THE THEOLOGY
OF THE GOSPELS AND ACTS

The theology of the Gospels and Acts is a theology of the *beginning* of the fulfillment of Israel's story, law, and destiny. Through Jesus—sent by the Father and empowered by the Spirit—Israel's history is recapitulated, Israel's law is obeyed, and God's promises to Israel start to come true.

Jesus's promised forerunner, John the Baptist, called Israel to prepare for God's reign by reorienting their lives to Jesus. Jesus demonstrated or performed the kingdom of God through his life, miracles, teaching, and ultimately through his passion. He inaugurated the new covenant by shedding his blood, and after his ascension to the Father's right hand, he poured out the eschatological fullness of the Spirit on his followers. Thus empowered as a renewed Israel, they began the church's age-long mission of extending the blessings of the God of Abraham's to all the nations.

Chapter in Review

This chapter first introduced the discipline of biblical theology. Second, instead of a broad yet shallow overview of many topics, it presented a comprehensive yet brief biblical theology of Jesus and the Spirit in the fourfold Gospel and Acts. Then it discussed selected individual themes of Matthew, Mark, Luke-Acts, and John.

4

PREPARING TO INTERPRET THE GOSPELS AND ACTS

The Chapter at a Glance

Since the first step in exegesis is establishing the text to be interpreted, exegetes must be aware of the history of the transmission of the NT and the rudiments of NT textual criticism. Exegetes should be aware of the rudiments of linguistics so that they can evaluate popular translations of the Bible and compose their own translations. Exegetes need to understand and use critical methods competently in order to understand the historical process that led to the Gospels and Acts as well as their literary features.

ESTABLISHING THE TEXT: TEXTUAL CRITICISM

IN ANCIENT TIMES, THE PROCESS OF HAND-COPYING manuscripts could and did lead to variations from the *exemplar* or base text. Manuscripts were written in continuous text with no breaks between words or sentences. Scribes could err unintentionally because of fatigue or mental lapse. At times scribes might intentionally introduce what they viewed as literary or theological "improvements" into their copies. In light of these considerations, textual criticism is necessary because "(*a*) none of the original documents of the Bible is extant today, and (*b*) the existing copies differ from one another."[1] Metzger's comment can be applied to all works of antiquity, even to texts as recent as the plays of William Shakespeare.[2] Evangelicals who view the original NT documents as divinely inspired texts have all the more reason to be interested in reconstructing those original texts as nearly as possible from the copies that are available today. Although the study of the transmission of the NT text may provide helpful insights into the history of NT interpretation and the social history of early Christianity, reconstructing the original NT text as nearly as possible by comparing its ancient copies must be the primary goal.[3] Here we can only briefly sketch the discipline as it relates to NT studies.[4]

History of New Testament Textual Criticism

The transmission of the text. The NT is by far the best-attested of all ancient documents. In the early days of the church, the apostolic writings were received by local congregations on papyrus sheets or rolls (scrolls) made by sewing sheets together. It is estimated that Luke's Gospel would require a roll of around thirty feet, the maximum advisable length. Papyrus copies were made so that the apostolic teachings could be read more widely (Col. 3:16; 1 Thess. 5:27).[5] Early on, heretical counterfeits were perpetrated (2 Thess. 2:2), and Paul hand-wrote the concluding greetings in at least some of his letters to demonstrate their authenticity (1 Cor. 16:21; 2 Thess. 3:17). As the apostles were passing off the scene, their followers recorded the apostolic traditions in the canonical Gospels. It is generally believed that the majority of variant readings came into the text during these early days. Today, scholars study nearly 100 NT papyrus manuscripts, written from the second to fourth centuries.

---

1. Bruce M. Metzger, *A Textual Commentary on the Greek New Testament,* 2nd ed. (Stuttgart: Deutsche Bibelgesellschaft, 1994), 1.

2. A fascinating yet dated study of the pursuit of ancient manuscripts from all over the world is Leo Deuel's *Testaments of Time* (New York: Alfred Knopf, 1965).

3. Stanley M. Porter and Andrew W. Pitts, *Fundamentals of New Testament Textual Criticism* (Grand Rapids: Eerdmans, 2015), 1–6.

4. Current introductions to NT textual criticism include Kurt and Barbara Aland, *The Text of the New Testament*, 2nd ed., trans. E. B. Rhodes (Grand Rapids: Eerdmans, 1989); David Alan Black, ed., *Rethinking New Testament Textual Criticism* (Grand Rapids: Baker, 2002); Robert F. Hull, *The Story of the New Testament Text* (Atlanta: SBL, 2010); Bruce M. Metzger and Bart D. Ehrman, *The Text of the New Testament*, 4th ed. (New York: Oxford University Press, 2005); Porter and Pitts, *Fundamentals of New Testament Textual Criticism.* More advanced essays on the state of the art are found in Bart D. Ehrman and Michael W. Holmes, eds., *The Text of the New Testament in Contemporary Research* (Leiden: Brill, 2013) and Eldon J. Epp and Gordon D. Fee, *Studies in the Theory and Method of New Testament Textual Criticism* (Grand Rapids: Eerdmans, 1993).

5. Metzger and Ehrman (*Text of the NT*, 3–35) provide a helpful overview of how books were made in ancient times.

By the late second century the Greek NT began to be translated into Syriac, Latin, and Coptic. From the fourth century on, Armenian, Georgian, Ethiopic, Arabic, and other early versions were produced. As the church became more established, all the apostolic writings were gradually recognized, collected, and officially canonized. Beginning in the fourth century, uncial or majuscule manuscripts were produced in book (codex) form, using capital letters written on vellum (treated leather) instead of papyrus. There are 263 NT uncial manuscripts, a few containing the entire NT, or even the whole Bible, with the OT in Greek (the Septuagint or LXX) as well as the NT. In early medieval times the customary majuscule manuscripts gave way to minuscule writing style that used an elegant cursive script. Around 2,500 of these minuscule manuscripts survive today. The church also developed a standard schedule of liturgical Scripture readings, resulting in approximately 2,200 lectionary manuscripts that exist today. Widely recognized bishops and teachers began to write treatises on the Bible or used the Bible in their topical writings. The church in the East continued producing Greek manuscripts, but the Western church typically transmitted the NT in Latin. Accordingly, the majority of Greek NT manuscripts that survive today are minuscule and lectionaries that originated in the East.

As a result of this process, there are about 5,500 manuscripts known to scholars that contain the Greek NT. The great majority of these manuscripts are partial or fragmentary. Less than 3 percent were written in the first five centuries, over 30 percent are from the sixth through tenth centuries, and roughly 65 percent are from the eleventh through fourteenth centuries. There are also around 9,000 manuscripts of the early versions of the NT, around 90 percent of them from the Latin tradition. Patristic citations are also numerous. The sheer magnitude of these manuscripts leads to an embarrassment of riches when it comes to the preservation of the NT. Those who make much of the number of variant readings (perhaps 300,000) seldom admit that this number is high only because the NT has been so well preserved in so many manuscripts, and that the vast majority of the variants are trivial. Michael Holmes comments, "It is practically certain that the original text has been preserved somewhere among the surviving witnesses."[6] With the invention of the printing press (c. 1450), copying of manuscripts by hand began to wane. Erasmus's edition of the Greek NT was first published in Rotterdam in 1516. Cardinal Jiménez de Cisneros's more

---

6. Michael W. Holmes, "Textual Criticism," in David Alan Black and David S. Dockery, *New Testament Criticism and Interpretation* (Grand Rapids: Zondervan, 1991), 106, n. 21; 127–28. On the reliability question, see also Robert B. Stewart, ed., *The Reliability of the New Testament: Bart D. Ehrman & Daniel B. Wallace in Dialogue* (Minneapolis: Fortress, 2011).

ambitious project, the six-volume Complutensian Polyglot, although begun in 1502, was not officially published until 1522.[7]

Classifying Genealogical Relationships

Through the centuries, local texts developed around major ecclesiastical centers such as Rome, Antioch, Constantinople, and Alexandria. Each of these centers tended to circulate its own type of text that contained distinctive readings peculiar to its area. Through painstaking collation of the minutiae of manuscript variations, scholars began to detect that certain distinctive readings were shared among numerous manuscripts, and those that shared distinctive readings began to be characterized into text-types or families that apparently shared genealogical roots. Today scholars speak of three[8] such text-types:

- *Alexandrian text.* This text-type is named Alexandrian because the manuscripts that support it come from Egypt, their preservation owing in part to the arid climate there. It is characterized by shorter readings and unpolished style. This text-type can be traced to the mid–late second century. Its major sources are the papyri (especially $\mathfrak{P}^{46}$, $\mathfrak{P}^{66}$, and $\mathfrak{P}^{75}$); the uncial codices ℵ, B, C, L, and parts of W; the Sahidic and Bohairic versions; and the fathers Origen and Didymus.
- *Western text.* The so-called Western text is viewed by some to be as early as the Alexandrian text, and it is actually more geographically widespread than the Alexandrian. Manuscripts supporting it have come from Italy, North Africa, Syria, Gaul, and Egypt. It is a longer text characterized by freedom, exercised in paraphrase, harmonization, addition, and even occasional omission. The most important witnesses are the papyri $\mathfrak{P}^{38}$ and $\mathfrak{P}^{48}$, Codices Bezae (D) and parts of W, the Old Latin version, and the fathers Irenaeus, Tertullian, and Cyprian. As we will see, it is a crucial issue for the textual criticism of Acts.
- *Byzantine text.* The provenance and value of the Byzantine text are controversial. A majority of scholars attribute its smoothness,

---

7. See further on the history of the transmission of the NT text, Aland and Aland, *The Text of the NT*, 48–71; Metzger and Ehrman, *The Text of the NT*, 3–35, 95–146.

8. Aland and Aland propose five text-types. In addition to the Alexandrian, Western, and Byzantine, they hold to an Egyptian text-type closely related to the Alexandrian but with occasional Byzantine influences. They also argue for an eclectic text with with readings from a wide variety of resources. See *The Text of the NT*, 106–7, 159, 332–37. The existence of the Caesarean text-type is debatable. Originally proposed by B. H. Streeter in 1924, it exists only in the Gospels, if at all. Some view the minuscules categorized as f^1 and f^{13} as subgroups of the Caesarean text. See further Aland and Aland, *Text of the NT*, 66, 172; Bruce M. Metzger, *Chapters in the History of New Testament Textual Criticism* (Leiden: Brill, 1963), 42–72.

completeness, and clarity to its being a collation or **recension** of earlier readings into a secondary, harmonized text in the middle of the fourth century. This suggestion is disputed by a minority of scholars who regard it as the primary witness to the original text of the NT. The Byzantine or Majority text is usually linked to Antioch and Constantinople. It is represented by Codex A (curiously, only in the Gospels, not in the rest of the NT) and the later uncials, and by the minuscule manuscripts as a whole. It was the most widely approved Greek text-type from late medieval times until the invention of printing. The relatively small collection of minuscules used by Erasmus to edit his edition of the Greek NT in 1516 were of the Byzantine text-type. Soon this type of printed NT became known quasi-officially as the received text (*Textus Receptus*), the Greek tradition used in the translation of the Authorized (King James) Version in 1611.[9]

Evaluating the Evidence

Scholarly analysis of the manuscript tradition has led to differing views of how the text-types should be valued and the priority that should be given to internal and external evidence. Four major approaches exist today, although the third and fourth are typically found among evangelicals.

- *Consistent Eclecticism.*[10] Those who espouse consistent eclecticism are skeptical of attempts to reconstruct the history of the transmission of the text of the New Testament. Accordingly, such scholars do not prioritize readings from a particular text-type, from more ancient manuscripts, or from a majority of the manuscripts. They select the reading that makes the best sense in light of the literary context and the author's known vocabulary, style, and theology.[11]

---

9. Many editions followed, including those by Erasmus (1519, 1522, 1527, 1535), Robert Stephens in Paris (1546–1551), Theodore Beza in Geneva (1565–1604), and the Elzivir brothers in Leyden (1624–41). According to the preface of a current *Textus Receptus*, Η ΚΑΙΝΗ ΔΙΑΘΗΚΗ *The New Testament* (London: Trinitarian Bible Society, 1976), these editions "all present *substantially* the same text, and the *variations* are not of *great* significance and *rarely* affect the sense [italics added]." This acknowledgment of variations within the *TR* counters the common impression of its uniformity. The term *Textus Receptus* may have originated in the Latin preface to the 1633 edition of the Elzivir brothers in Leyden: *Textum ergo habes, nunc ab omnibus receptum* . . . (Therefore you have the text, now received by all . . .).

10. Others use the terms "radical" or "thoroughgoing" to describe the strict eclectic and conservative (majority text) positions.

11. The British scholars G. D. Kilpatrick and J. K. Elliott are perhaps the most prominent advocates of sheer eclecticism. See, e.g., Elliott's essay "The Case for Thoroughgoing Eclecticism," in D. A. Black, *Rethinking NT Textual Criticism*, 101–24.

- *Reasoned Eclecticism.* The reasoned eclecticism view is perhaps the consensus view of NT text-critical scholars. The roots of this view reach back to the work of J. A. Bengel (1687–1752), J. J. Griesbach (1745–1812), Karl Lachmann (1793–1851), Constantin Von Tischendorf (1815–1874), and most influentially to B. F. Westcott (1825–1901) and F. J. A. Hort (1828–1892). Westcott and Hort's reconstruction of the history of the transmission of the text of the NT, especially its argument for the secondary and late character of the Byzantine text-type, has been very influential.[12] Their dedication to the Alexandrian text-type has been moderated only slightly by reasoned eclectics today. Those who hold this view prefer the most ancient text, usually found in the Alexandrian text-type, unless that reading is suspect on internal grounds. At that point there is reasoned analysis of readings from the other text-types.[13]
- *Reasoned Conservatism.* This approach is probably the most obscure of the four summarized here; yet it deserves mention among the more prominent approaches. Based on the early existence of local texts in the Christian centers of the ancient world, it holds that a reading with wide geographical distribution should typically be preferred. Those who favor this approach do not accept the near-consensus view that the Byzantine text-type is a late collation of earlier text-types, but hold it should have equal weight with the Alexandrian and Western texts in determining the original reading. Accordingly, the reading found in the majority of text-types is favored unless there is strong internal evidence to the contrary.[14]
- *Consistent Conservatism.* Those who argue for the superiority of the Byzantine or Majority text are the outliers of the textual criticism debate. Their position is that the reading of the majority of manuscripts should be favored because, all things being equal, the earlier the reading, the more copies would be made through time. Advocates explain the absence of early Byzantine manuscripts as the result of heavy use that wore out the manuscripts.

---

12. B. F. Westcott and F. J. A. Hort, *The New Testament in the Original Greek,* 2 vols. (Cambridge: Macmillan, 1881–82). Vol. 1 contains their text of the NT and vol. 2 contains their introduction to how they arrived at that text, along with extensive notes on selected readings.

13. For a helpful statement of the view, see Michael W. Holmes, "The Case for Reasoned Eclecticism," in D. A. Black, *Rethinking NT Textual Criticism,* 77–100.

14. This view is commonly traced to Harry Sturz, *The Byzantine Text-type and New Testament Textual Criticism* (Nashville: Nelson, 1984). Anecdotally, I had the privilege of studying textual criticism with Prof. Sturz. Evangelical text critics Dan Wallace and David Black trace their interest in the discipline to their undergraduate studies with Sturz at Biola University. Wallace has become an advocate of reasoned eclecticism, but Black still favors Sturz's approach. See David Alan Black, *New Testament Textual Criticism: A Concise Guide* (Grand Rapids: Baker, 1994), esp. 40–41.

Conversely, ancient Alexandrian manuscripts survived because they were not highly valued and were not used. Advocates of the Majority Text fall into two groups, those whose evidence-based arguments warrant due respect in scholarly circles[15] and those whose arguments are largely *ad hominem* innuendoes.[16] Our ensuing discussions of Mark 16:9–20 and John 7:53–8:11 will broach the issues raised by the consistent conservatism position.

The following chart summarizes these four major approaches:

Major Approaches to Textual Criticism[17]			
Consistent Eclecticism	**Reasoned Approaches**		**Consistent Conservatism**
Prioritizes **internal** evidence	Weighs **both** internal **and** external evidence		Prioritizes **external** evidence
	Reasoned **Eclecticism**	Reasoned **Conservatism**	
Any single manuscript may preserve the original reading.	Prioritizes the **Alexandrian** text-type. Considers other readings if prompted by internal evidence.	Prioritizes the **majority** of text-types. Considers other readings if prompted by internal evidence.	The **majority** of manuscripts preserve the original reading

---

15. For scholarly arguments in favor of the Majority Text, see Wilbur N. Pickering, *The Identity of the New Testament Text*, rev. ed. (Nashville: Nelson, 1980); Maurice Robinson, "The Case for Byzantine Priority," in D. A. Black, *Rethinking NT Textual Criticism*, 125–140. Zane C. Hodges and Arthur Farstad have produced an edition of the majority text complete with critical apparatus that displays the many variations within that text-type. See *The Greek New Testament according to the Majority Text*, 2nd ed. (Nashville: Nelson, 1985).

16. I am thinking here of those whose dogmatic advocacy of the *Textus Receptus* results in the "King James only" position. Against this view, see D. A. Carson, *The King James Version Debate: A Plea for Realism* (Grand Rapids: Baker, 1979); James R. White, *The King James Only Controversy* (Minneapolis: Bethany, 1995), and more recently White, *King James Onlyism: A New Sect* (published by the author in 2006).

17. This chart has been adapted from a similar chart by John D. Harvey, *Interpreting the Pauline Letters* (Grand Rapids: Kregel, 2012), 104. Terminology is adapted from Black, *NT Textual Criticism*, 36–40.

Much of the debate in evangelical circles today is between advocates of reasoned eclecticism and consistent conservatism. This debate is one of quality versus quantity. Reasoned eclectics *weigh* the value of manuscripts largely based on their age, presuming that, all things being equal, the more ancient the manuscript the better chance it has of preserving the original. This approach results in assigning greater value to relatively few more ancient manuscripts. Consistent conservatives *count* the number of manuscripts, presuming that, all things being equal, a more ancient reading will have been copied more frequently. The problem is that all things are not equal in the history of the transmission of the NT.[18]

Principles of Textual Criticism

Unless one is convinced that certain external evidence—a particular text-type such as the Alexandrian or Byzantine—is automatically authoritative and must be mechanically followed, there is an important place in textual criticism for eclecticism. Perhaps the most important principle for thinking through variant readings is that one should *prefer the reading that best explains the existence of the other readings* in a hypothetical reconstruction of the history of the text's transmission. This approach involves both external and internal evidence. We have already discussed external evidence, which involves the age, geographical distribution, and text-type of manuscripts supporting a reading. Now we turn to internal evidence.

There are two aspects of internal evidence: *intrinsic probability* and *transcriptional probability*. Intrinsic probability has to do with what can be determined about what any given *author* most likely would have written, given what is known of the author's vocabulary, style, and content from the rest of the author's corpus of writings. Transcriptional probability has to do with what a given *scribe* most likely would have copied, given what can be known about scribal habits and tendencies. Scribes sometimes erred unintentionally. At times multiple scribes would copy a manuscript as it was read, which could occasion errors by misreading or mishearing. If a scribe was copying by glancing back and forth from the exemplar to the in-process copy, the scribe's eyes might overlook a segment of the exemplar or repeat a section if the same word occurred more than once in the exemplar. Letters with similar shapes could be confused, and the lack of spaces between words only complicated matters further. The scribe's relative alertness and competence would also figure into the accuracy of the copy.

At other times scribes intentionally added to texts in order to smooth their grammar, conflate or harmonize them with similar texts, adapt

---

18.   On weighing external evidence, see Porter and Pitts, *Fundamentals*, 100–9.

them for liturgical use, or even "improve" their theology.[19] By all accounts scribes were more open to "improving" texts by adding words than by omitting words. Their marginal notes could eventually be incorporated into texts. Although exaggerated charges are sometimes made, based on intentional scribal changes, the sheer volume of copies of the NT ensures that no real theological aberrations have been incorporated into the NT.[20]

In addition to preferring the reading that best explains the other readings, two additional principles come into play. The first is that, generally, one should *prefer the more difficult reading*. The more difficult reading is likely preferable because intentional scribal changes were attempts at clarifying the meaning of an obscure text. The second principle is that generally one should *prefer the shorter reading*. The shorter reading is more likely to be original because scribes tended to add what they viewed as clarifying words to manuscripts rather than deleting words from them. These two rules need to be applied wisely and artfully, not mechanically, in individual cases. The two principles sometimes are contradictory on the surface, as when the longer reading is more difficult. Preference for the more difficult reading does not apply when that reading is an unintentional scribal blunder. Preference for the shorter reading likewise does not apply when there is reason to believe the scribe misread the exemplar and missed some of its words.[21]

Suggestions for Text-critical Analysis

Coming to a reasoned decision about a given textual variant begins with the use of the critical apparatus of a Greek NT. Two editions are widely available today, one commonly known as the United Bible Societies' edition (UBS),[22] the other as the Nestle-Aland edition (NA).[23] The two testaments have nearly identical texts, determined

---

19. Origen lamented both unintended and intended scribal changes to the text, attributing them respectively to negligence and audacity. See his *Comm. Matt.* 15.14.

20. See most recently Bart D. Ehrman, *The Orthodox Corruption of Scripture*, updated ed. (New York: Oxford University, 2011). Ehrman argues that scribes intentionally altered NT manuscripts in order to infuse them with later orthodox Christological doctrine. For a response, see Daniel B. Wallace, ed., *Revisiting the Corruption of the New Testament* (Grand Rapids: Kregel, 2011).

21. On weighing internal evidence, see further Porter and Pitts, *Fundamentals*, 129–36.

22. The current edition is Barbara Aland et al., eds., *The Greek New Testament*, 5th rev. ed. (Stuttgart: Deutsche Bibelgesellschaft, 2014). This testament is available with a useful Greek-English dictionary prepared by Barclay Newman.

23. The current edition is Barbara and Kurt Aland, et al., eds., *Novum Testamentum Graece*, 28th rev. ed. (Stuttgart: Deutsche Bibelgesellschaft, 2012). It is also available with the Greek-English dictionary.

by a committee of scholars on the basis of rational eclecticism, but differ in format, paragraphing, punctuation, and critical apparatus. Editions of the NA text began in 1891; UBS editions began in 1965 with the needs of translators in mind. Accordingly, the UBS format is more welcoming and its apparatus is more accessible to nonspecialists. The NA apparatus includes more variant readings than UBS's, whose discussions key on variants that affect the meaning of the text. Both editions have extensive introductions that summarize the manner in which ancient manuscripts are cited in the apparatus. The textual notes in NA provide information on variants before citing the manuscripts that support the text; UBS reverses this order. Both NA and UBS cite the evidence in the following order: papyri, majuscules (uncials), minuscules, lectionaries, early versions, and patristic citations. Both NA and UBS use space-saving sigla for the preponderance of the Byzantine minuscules—NA uses a Gothic M (𝔐) and UBS uses *Byz*. Each entry in the UBS apparatus follows either {A}, {B}, {C}, or {D}, letters reflecting the editors' view of the degree of certainty that their reading is the original text.[24]

Bruce Metzger's *Textual Commentary on the Greek NT* is a helpful tool in evaluating textual variants. Metzger explains the editorial committee's thought process and decision on each textual variant cited in the fourth edition of UBS. Roger Omanson's *Textual Guide* popularizes and somewhat expands Metzger's commentary. Consulting Metzger and/or Omanson helps students understand how expert analysis of internal evidence augments the external evidence cited in the apparatus of the UBS[4]. Exegetical commentaries will also occasionally discuss variant readings.

Certain online resources are also helpful. Daniel Wallace's online study center provides current information on textual criticism as well as images of many manuscripts.[25] High definition images of many manuscripts, including Sinaiticus (א) and Vaticanus (B) can be viewed online.[26] Ongoing discussion of text-critical issues and an extensive archive of previous discussions can be engaged at the evangelical textual criticism website.[27] The Institute for New Testament Textual Research at the University of Münster also has an extensive website devoted to the NT textual criticism.[28]

---

24. Porter and Pitts provide a substantial introduction to the apparati of both NA[28] and UBS[5rev] in *Fundamentals*, 146–76.

25. The Center for the Study of New Testament Manuscripts (http://www.csntm.org).

26. Sinaiticus may be viewed at http://www.codexsinaiticus.org/ and Vaticanus at http://digi.vatlib.it/view/MSS_Vat.gr.1209.

27. http://evangelicaltextualcriticism.blogspot.com.

28. http://egora.uni-muenster.de/intf/index_en.shtml.

Suggested Methodology

How one analyzes the external and internal evidence for a given textual variant is based on one's overall approach to the evidence. Consistent eclectics will pay little attention to the date or geographical distribution of the manuscripts containing the various readings and will instead focus on intrinsic and transcriptional probabilities. Consistent conservatives will tend to disregard non-Byzantine external evidence and will use internal evidence to ascertain the probable original reading when the Byzantine witnesses do not agree on a given reading.[29] Reasoned eclectics and reasoned conservatives will find the following scheme more helpful.

Students may find it helpful to lay out the evidence for variant readings of a given verse with a simple worksheet[30] like the following:

Variant Reading Worksheet				
Variants	**Alexandrian**	**Western**	**Byzantine**	**Comments**

Variants in a given text are listed in the left column. Supporting manuscripts are listed in their respective text-type columns in chronological order starting with the most ancient.[31] Comments on the strength of the external evidence for each reading as well as internal considerations are placed in the right column.

The Ending of Mark

Whether Mark ends at 16:8 or 16:20 is probably the most well-known textual problem in the Bible. On a casual reading, the ending at 16:8 seems too abrupt to be correct, and the mention of handling snakes and drinking poison is odd if not bizarre. Contemporary versions typically enclose Mark 16:9–20 in brackets and include notes that acknowledge its debatable authenticity. Congregants often ask pastors about this passage.

---

29. NA signifies a split in the Byzantine tradition with *pm* (*permulti*, very many) or *Byz*[pt]. Such a split is signified by *Byz*[pt] in UBS. See also Hodges and Farstad, *Greek NT*, xi–xxiii.

30. See also the worksheets suggested by Black in *NT Textual Criticism*, 67–71.

31. Various sources list manuscripts by text-type and/or age. See e.g., Aland and Aland, *Text of the NT*, 159–62; Black, *NT Textual Criticism*, 63–65.

The various readings. The NT textual tradition contains two main options to the ending of Mark—either the abrupt "short ending" with the women fleeing the empty tomb at 16:8,[32] or the "long ending," 16:9–20, which depicts Jesus's post-resurrection appearances, commission, and ascension, followed by the disciples' early ministry.[33] There are many variants in the textual tradition after 16:8, but two additions are notable. The first is a sort of brief appendix immediately following 16:8 in which the women report to Peter and the apostles what the angel told them, and subsequently Jesus sends out through them "from east to west the sacred and imperishable proclamation of eternal salvation."[34] Another notorious addition comes after 16:14. In it the disciples excuse their unbelief by blaming it on Satan's power over the present age. They ask Jesus to reveal his glory immediately. He acknowledges Satan's power and states that he was handed over to death for sinners so that they might sin no more and "inherit the spiritual and incorruptible glory of righteousness that is in heaven."[35] Both of these additions are dubious on internal grounds because they use non-Markan expressions. Their external evidence is also questionable, especially that of the addition to 16:14. Accordingly, we will discuss the merits of only the short (16:8) and long (16:9–20) endings.

The arguments. Choosing between the short and long endings of Mark is fairly simple if one has been convinced of either of the standard theories of textual authenticity. If one prefers the more ancient manuscripts in keeping with rational eclecticism, all other things being equal, one will rule out 16:9–20 on external grounds alone since it is not supported in the most ancient sources. The style and vocabulary of Mark 16:9–20, as well as its awkward connection to 16:8, render it dubious on internal grounds as well. Most NT scholars today hold this view. On the other hand, if one is convinced that a reading supported by the most manuscripts is more likely to be original (consistent conservatism), all other things being equal, one will rule out the short ending in 16:8 because relatively few manuscripts support it. The short ending can also be opposed on internal grounds due to its abruptness and omission of Jesus's promised postresurrection ap-

---

32. Mark ends at 16:8 in relatively few sources: ℵ, B, 304, and a few early versions. Eusebius, Epiphanius, Hesychius, and Jerome also attest to this ms. tradition.

33. Mark 16:9–20, with variants, is found in the great majority of manuscripts: A, C, D, W (with addition to 16:14), Δ, Θ, f^{13}, many minuscules (*Byz*), lectionaries, early versions, and patristic sources. It appears with critical notes or signs in f^1, 205, and others. It also appears in certain mss. that contain the short addition to 16:8, sometimes called the "shorter ending."

34. Mark ends with this "shorter ending" in it[k]. Additional mss. include the shorter ending followed by 16:9–20, including L, Ψ, 099, 0112, Syr[HarMg], and some Sah and Boh mss.

35. The addition to 16:14 is found only in Codex W (fourth-fifth century). Apparently Jerome was aware of it as well.

pearances.[36] My own view is that Mark originally ended at 16:8. I have argued for the authenticity of this ending on internal grounds in the previous chapter.[37] The early date of the manuscripts supporting this reading contrasts with the late support for 16:9–20. The non-Markan style and vocabulary, secondary character,[38] and theological aberrations (16:18ab) of 16:9–20 all render it unlikely as the original ending of Mark.

Another option? If Mark did not originally end with 16:8, either it was left unfinished or the original ending was lost before copies were made.[39] A number of scholars argue for the second option. As Metzger put it, "As seems most probable . . . the Gospel accidentally lost its last leaf before it was multiplied by transcription."[40] Scholars who take this view point out that the existence of 16:9–20 is evidence of early dissatisfaction with the ending at 16:8. They sometimes argue that the original ending of Mark can be detected and at least partially reconstructed by collating the agreements in the endings of Matthew (28:8–20) and Luke (24:8–50).[41] But even on the assumption that Matthew and Luke directly used Mark, it is unlikely that the agreements in their respective endings simply reproduced Mark's ending. It seems plausible that their editorial work would have omitted some Markan material and modified the material retained from Mark according to their own theological interests. The influence of Q would also need to be factored into this discussion.[42]

---

36. Supporters of 16:9–20 as the original ending of Mark include William Farmer, *The Last Twelve Verses of Mark* (Cambridge: University Press, 1974); Maurice A. Robinson, "The Long Ending of Mark as Canonical Verity," in *Perspectives on the Ending of Mark: Four Views*, ed. David Alan Black (Nashville: B&H, 2008), 40–80.

37. See also Daniel B. Wallace, "Mark 16:8 as the Original Conclusion to Mark's Gospel," in *Perspectives on the Ending of Mark*, 33–39.

38. Mark 16:9–11 could be based on Matt. 28:9–10; John 20:11–18. Mark 16:12–13 apparently summarizes Luke 24:13–35. Mark 16:14–18 could have been drawn from Matt. 28:16–20; Luke 24:36–49; John 20:19–23; Acts 1:6–8. Mark 16:19–20 reproduces the gist of Luke 24:50–53; Acts 1:9–11.

39. For the record, David Alan Black proposes yet another option by arguing that 16:9–20 was written by Mark as a supplemental public ending to his previous ending, one that recorded additional tradition from the apostle Peter. See Black, "Mark 16:9–20 as Markan Supplement," in *Perspectives on the Ending of Mark*, 103–23.

40. Metzger, *Textual Commentary*, 105.

41. Robert H. Gundry, *Mark: A Commentary on His Apology for the Cross* (Grand Rapids: Eerdmans, 1993), 1009–21; Robert H. Stein, *Mark* (Grand Rapids: Baker, 2008), 733–37; Stein, "The Ending of Mark," *BBR* 18 (2008): 79–98.

42. For concise discussions of the endings of Mark see Metzger, *Textual Commentary*, 102–7; Roger L. Omanson, *A Textual Guide to the Greek New Testament* (Stuttgart: Deutsche Bibelgesellschaft, 2006), 103–7. More detailed discussions of the numerous complexities related to this problem are found in D. A. Black, ed., *Perspectives on the Ending of Mark: Four Views*; N. Clayton Croy, *The Mutilation of Mark's Gospel* (Nashville: Abingdon, 2003); Bridget G. Upton, *Hearing Mark's Endings* (Leiden: Brill, 2006).

The Adulteress in John 7:53–8:11

John 7:53–8:11 is another major textual problem in the Gospels. The familiar story features the religious leaders who exploit a tawdry situation and twist the Torah[43] to test Jesus. Jesus's response, "Go and sin no more" (John 8:11), appears to authentically model God's holy and gracious character in dealing with sin in a merciful yet firm manner. There are, however, many issues that raise considerable doubt as to the place of John 7:53–8:11 in the original text of the Fourth Gospel.

External evidence. There are quite a few early manuscripts that omit the *Pericope Adulterae* entirely.[44] Other manuscripts include the passage but locate it in other places (after Luke 21:38; 24:53; John 7:36, 44; 21:25).[45] Still others have the passage in its location as John 7:53–8:11, but with various notations or markings such as asterisks or obeli that indicate doubt as to its authenticity.[46] Of course, the great majority of manuscripts locate the passage between John 7:52 and 8:12; the earliest is Codex D (Bezae, fifth century).[47] The earliest patristic citation is by Didymus the Blind (late fourth century). The ancient versions are split, with some having the passage and others omitting it. Patristic citations are rather few and late.

Internal evidence. Internal evidence such as style, vocabulary, and content, confirms the external testimony—John 7:53–8:11 differs from the rest of the Fourth Gospel. Although the word γραμματεύς occurs twenty-two times in Matthew, twenty-one times in Mark, and

---

43. Exodus 20:14 forbids adultery, and other texts prohibit men from coveting or having intercourse with married women (Exod. 20:17; Lev. 18:20). Leviticus 20:10 and Deuteronomy 22:22 command *both* parties in an adulterous relationship to be stoned. The leaders wish to apply this law selectively, and unjustly.

44. The papyri 𝔓[66, 75] (early third century), as well as the uncials ℵ, B, L, N, T, W, Δ, Θ, Ψ, 0141 (fourth–tenth centuries) omit the passage. Uncials A and C (fifth century) also probably omit it. Minuscules 33, 157, 565, 1241, 1333, 1424 (ninth–eleventh centuries) also omit it. It is also missing from some manuscripts of the Old Latin, Syriac, Coptic, Armenian, Georgian, and Slavonic versions. It is not found in Tatian's Diatessaron, or in the writings of Origen, Chrysostom, Cyril, Tertullian, or Cyprian (third–fifth centuries).

45. The grouping of minuscules known as *f*[13] (eleventh–fifteenth centuries) places the pericope after Luke 21:38. It comes after Luke 24:53 in 1333 (eleventh century). The minuscule 225 places it after John 7:36. Some Georgian mss. insert it after 7:44. It is placed after John 21:25 by 1, 565, 1076, 1570, 1582 (ninth–twelfth centuries).

46. Such manuscripts include E (eighth century; omits 7:53–8:1), Λ (ninth century; omits 7:53–8:2), S (tenth century), 28 (eleventh century), and the margin of 1424 (ninth–tenth century).

47. Greek manuscript support for the pericope standing as John 7:53–8:11 includes the codices D (fifth century), as well as E, (F), G, H, K, M, U, Γ, Π (sixth–tenth centuries and many later minuscules from the ninth to the fifteenth centuries. Among the versions, several Old Latin manuscripts from the fifth through the ninth centuries and the Vulgate (fourth–fifth century), along with a few Syriac (sixth century), Coptic (third century, and Slavonic (ninth century) manuscripts have it. Patristic testimony includes Ambrosiaster, Ambrose, Pacian, and Rufinus, Jerome, and Augustine (late fourth though late fifth centuries).

fourteen times in Luke, it is found in John only in 8:3. Fourteen other words, amounting to one of every six in the pericope, occur only here in John. The Jewish leaders' testing Jesus is a common synoptic theme,[48] but in John it occurs only in 8:6. Elsewhere in John testing is portrayed differently—Jesus tests his own disciple Philip (6:6). It also is difficult to understand how the pericope fits into the narrative flow of John 7–8. In terms of transcriptional probability, it is doubtful that the passage would have accidentally fallen out of John. The argument that the passage was intentionally omitted by ascetic scribes lacks evidence[49] and does not explain why 7:53–8:2 was omitted along with the allegedly offensive material about the adulteress in 8:3–11.

Conclusion. As with the ending of Mark, one's view of this question will largely be determined by one's view of manuscript value, whether one favors the testimony of relatively few more ancient manuscripts or that of relatively many more recent manuscripts.[50] From the standpoint of prioritizing the more ancient manuscripts, it is unlikely that the Fourth Gospel originally included John 7:53–8:11.[51] The external evidence against the pericope is early and relatively widespread. Although the majority of the later manuscripts contain the pericope, some of them contain notations about it and others place it in other NT locations. This evidence shows that there was doubt and confusion about the pericope as late as medieval times.

It is striking that many scholars who take the view that the passage is inauthentic in John quickly add that it does seem historically plausible, given what is known about Jesus from the Gospels.[52] In this view, John 7:53–8:11 was a traditional vignette that circulated orally. It was incorporated into various places in Luke and John where it seemed unobtrusive, and eventually found a home, so to speak, as John 7:53–8:11. This view provides an intellectual basis for teaching the passage as representing the real Jesus.[53]

---

48. See Matt. 16:1/Mark 8:11; Matt 19:3/Mark 10:2; Matt 22:15/Mark 12:15; Matt. 22:18, 35; Luke 10:25; 11:16.

49. Although see Augustine, *Incomp. Nupt.* 2.6.

50. For an argument that one should prefer the majority of manuscripts that contain the pericope, see Zane C. Hodges, "Problem Passages in the Gospel of John Part 8: The Woman Taken in Adultery (John 7:53–8:11): The Text," *BSac* 136 (1979): 318–32. See also the extended apparatus in Hodges and Farstad, *Greek NT according to the Majority Text*, xxiii–xxxii.

51. See the convenient summary of the issues in Andreas J. Köstenberger, *John* (Grand Rapids: Baker, 2004), 245–49.

52. Frederick Dale Bruner, *John: A Commentary* (Grand Rapids: Eerdmans, 2012), 507–11; Craig L. Keener, *The Gospel of John: A Commentary,* 2 vols. (Peabody, MA: Hendrickson, 2003), 1.736; Metzger, *Textual Commentary*, 188; Omanson, *Textual Guide*, 183.

53. See further John Paul Heil, who argues for the authenticity of the passage in "The Story of Jesus and the Adulteress (John 7:53–8:11) Reconsidered," *Bib* 72.2 (1991): 183–91.

The Western Text of the Book of Acts

Another major NT textual problem relates to a unique feature of the textual history of Acts. As early as the late seventeenth century, when scholars canvassed the textual tradition of Acts, they discovered the same variant readings occurred regularly in certain manuscripts, leading to a considerably longer text of Acts. Craig Keener believes that this issue amounts to "perhaps the thorniest text-critical situation in the NT."[54] The manuscript tradition containing these readings is calculated variously to be roughly 5 to 10 percent longer than the Alexandrian text of the book. It is commonly known as the "Western Text," although not all of its manuscript witnesses originated in the Western church. It is represented in the fragmentary papyri $\mathfrak{P}^{29}$, $\mathfrak{P}^{38}$, and $\mathfrak{P}^{48}$ (third century), but it is chiefly derived from Codex Bezae (D, fifth century), an Old Latin manuscript (it[h]), marginal and asterisked readings in the Harclean Syriac, and patristic sources such as Irenaeus, Tertullian, Cyprian, and Augustine. Additional manuscripts that commonly reflect the Western text include additional Old Latin and Vulgate manuscripts, the Old Georgian version, and minuscules 383, 614, and 1739. Although the Western text of Acts is occasionally shorter than the Alexandrian,[55] its tendency to paraphrase makes it more detailed and picturesque than the Alexandrian text. Some notable examples involve:

- aligning a passage with a related passage (1:18 with Matt. 27:5; 9:5–6 with 22:10; 26:14, and 13:33 with Ps. 2:7–8)
- adding circumstantial details to the text (1:5; 4:31; 5:21, 39; 6:10–11; 8:24, 37; 10:25; 11:2, 25–26; 12:1, 20; 14:2–7; 15:1–5, 12, 20, 29; 16:30, 35; 18:25, 27; 19:1; 21:12–15; 23:23–24; 24:10; 27:1–2; 28:31)
- smoothing out difficult syntax (3:16; 4:25; 13:20; 19:14–15)
- amplifying references to Jesus (1:21; 2:38; 6:7–8; 7:55; 13:33; 14:10; 17:31; 18:4, 8; 19:5)
- fuller explanation of baptism (2:41; 8:37, 39; 10:48; 16:15; 18:8; 19:5–6, 14)

Daniel B. Wallace responds in "Reconsidering 'The Story of Jesus and the Adulteress Reconsidered,'" *NTS* 39 (1993): 290–96. See also Chris Keith, "Recent and Previous Research on the Pericope Adulterae," *CBR* 6 (2008): 377–404; Keith, "The Initial Location of the Pericope Adulterae in Fourfold Tradition," *NovT* 51 (2009): 209–31. Current research on the pericope is analyzed in David Alan Black and Jacob N. Cerone, eds., *The Pericope of the Adulteress in Current Research* (London: Bloomsbury, 2016).

54. Craig L. Keener, *Acts: An Exegetical Commentary*, 4 vols. (Grand Rapids: Baker, 2012–2015), 1. 7–8. Bruce M. Metzger devoted fully a third of his textual commentary (223 out of 691 pages) to the textual variants in the book of Acts. See his *Textual Commentary*, 222–445.

55. See further Metzger, *Textual Commentary*, 164–66.

- fuller explanation the Holy Spirit's ministry (8:18, 39; 11:16–17; 15:7, 9, 32; 19:1, 6; 20:3; 26:1)
- heightening the fault of Jews (3:13–14; 4:13–16; 5:35; 6:10–11; 8:1; 13:27–29, 45, 50; 18:12–13; 23:23–24; 24:27; 28:19)
- minimizing women (1:14; 17:12, 34; 18:3, 18, 21, 26; 24:27)
- using different or more words to say essentially the same thing as the Alexandrian text (2:37; 16:13; 19:14; 20:24)

The proposed solutions. The history of scholarly attempts to explain this phenomenon is complicated, even convoluted. Some scholars concluded that this family of manuscripts all came from a common early source, not from the typical circumstances that occur when an ancient text was copied and circulated. One theory is that the author himself issued two different editions of Acts, one at the end of Paul's two-year imprisonment in Rome (Acts 28), and another one at a later date. The original, longer edition came into the hands of the church of Rome, while the later, condensed version was circulated in the East.[56] More recent scholars who accept the single author view argue that the second edition expanded the first edition. In both of these views the Western text of Acts originated with the author, either as the original edition or as an early revision. Other views do not attribute both textual traditions of Acts to the same author. One such view is that the Western text of Acts is the work of an editor who expanded Luke's original manuscript after Luke died. Other researchers attribute the Western text either to frequent free interpolation of oral tradition or to a deliberate second-century literary revision in additional research. Today, most scholars seem to think that the Western text of Acts is the result of a complex series of circumstances rather than a single comprehensive redaction. It might be more accurate to speak of Western texts of Acts or of Western tendencies in the history of the transmission of the text of Acts.

Some scholars today favor any one of the three major text-types as most nearly representing the original text of Acts. The oft-cited principle of preferring the shorter reading would tend to weigh against the longer Western readings. At the very least, the detailed readings of the Western text provide insight into the early reception history of Acts. The debate continues.[57]

---

56. This view originated with Friedrich Blass, *Acta Apostolorum, sive Lucae ad Theophilum Liber Alter* (Götingen: VandenHoeck and Ruprecht, 1895).

57. See further F. F. Bruce, *The Acts of the Apostles: The Greek Text with Introduction and Commentary*, 3rd rev. ed. (Grand Rapids: Eerdmans, 1990), 69–76; Ernst Haenchen, *The Acts of the Apostles* (Philadelphia: Westminster, 1971), 50–60; Peter M. Head, "Acts and the Problem of Its Texts," in *The Book of Acts in its Ancient Literary Setting*, eds. Bruce W. Winter and A. D. Clarke (Grand Rapids: Eerdmans, 1993), 415–44; Metzger, *Textual Commentary*, 222–36; W. A. Strange, *The Problem of the Text of Acts* (Cambridge: Cambridge University Press, 1992).

Case study. The following table provides an example of the methodology suggested previously in this chapter. It takes Acts 8:37 as a case study in dealing with the Western text of Acts. There are three major traditions regarding Acts 8:37, one that omits it and two that contain it in slightly different forms.

The External Evidence for Acts 8:37				
Reading	**Alexandrian**	**Western**	**Byzantine**	**Comments**
Omit Acts 8:37	$\mathfrak{P}^{45}$ $\mathfrak{P}^{74}$ A B C Ψ 33^{vid} 81 Cop$^{sa, bo}$	614 vg^{ww,st} eth^{pp} Ambrose	181 614 1175 1409 2344 *Byz* [L P] *Lect.* syr^p Chrysostom	Acts 8:37 is omitted by early Alexandrian mss. and by the Byzantine text.
Include Acts 8:37 with minor variants: ειπεν δε αυτω · ει πιστευεις εξ ολης καρδιας σου εξεστιν. αποκριθεις δε ειπε· πιστευω τον υιον του θεου ειναι Ιησουν Χριστον	cop^{meg}	36 1739 it$^{ar, c, dem, gig, l, p, ph, ro, t, w}$ vg^{cl} syr$^{h\ with\ *}$ Irenaeus Cyprian Ambrosiaster Pacian Chromatius Augustine Speculum	307 453 610 945 1678 1891 *Textus Receptus* *l*592 *l*1178 *l*^{AD}	• Codex D (Bezae, 05) lacks this portion of Acts. • arm, ethTH are early versions that support the reading. Their text-type is unknown to me. • Irenaeus (*Haer.* 3.23.8) apparently cites the last clause of this reading, showing the currency of this tradition in the second century. • Although Acts 8:37 is not found in the Majority or Byzantine text, Erasmus found it in the relatively few minuscules available to him. It entered the *TR* and via the *TR* it became a part of the King James Bible.
Include Acts 8:37 with minor variants: ειπεν δε αυτω ο Φιλιππος · εαν πιστευεις εξ ολης της καρδιας σου, σωθησει. αποκριθεις δε ειπε· πιστευω εις τον Χριστον τον υιον του θεου		E(08) It^e Greek mss^{acctoBede}		• Cyprian, *Treatises* 12.3.43 apparently cites the clause εαν πιστευεις εξ ολης της καρδιας σου, which is found in both readings of Acts 8:37.

Although the authenticity of Acts 8:37 is supported by some,[58] most doubt its originality on the grounds of its limited external support in the Western text and the *Textus Receptus*. Manuscripts that omit the verse are early and geographically widespread. On internal grounds, Metzger doubts that it would be intentionally omitted,[59] but some who favor the *TR* believe pedobaptist scribes who did not like its stress on believer's baptism deleted it. Of course, this argument could be reversed—scribes who favored believer's baptism could have added it.[60] It would take a comprehensive analysis of the Western text's overall tendencies to arrive at a conclusion. In terms of the basic rule of eclecticism—prefer the reading that best explains the existence of the other readings—I lean toward Metzger's understanding. If Acts 8:37 was removed by over-zealous pedobaptist scribes, one wonders why they did not treat other passages (e.g., Acts 2:38, 41; 8:12; 16:14–15, 30–33; 22:16) in a similar fashion. Patristic sources that cite the verse were pedobaptists. The authenticity of Acts 8:37 might be argued by consistent eclectics and by those who are convinced for religious reasons of the divine authority of the *TR*, but reasoned eclectics, conservative eclectics, and consistent conservatives will likely take the opposite view.

TRANSLATING THE TEXT: THEORY AND PRACTICE

The English-speaking church is well supplied, perhaps even over-supplied, with reliable translations of the Bible. Pastors and worship leaders find that the people in their congregations are using many different translations, which leads to questions about why there are differences from one translation to another. Books are written to discuss translations and translation theory and to advise readers on which translation may be best for a given situation.[61] In what follows we explain

---

58. E.g., Cottrel R. Carson, "Acts 8:37: A Textual Reexamination," *USQR* 51 (1997): 57–78.

59. Metzger, *Textual Commentary*, 315.

60. Acts 8 does not contain a direct confession of faith on the part of the eunuch. Scribes may have inserted what was previously a marginal comment containing such a confession into the text. In this view Acts 8:37 is a significant text for the practice of the church in the second century. For this view see C. K. Barrett, *A Critical and Exegetical Commentary on the Acts of the Apostles*, 2 vols. (Edinburgh: Clark, 1994), 1.443; Darrell L. Bock, *Acts*, BECNT (Grand Rapids: Baker, 2007), 348; Metzger, *Textual Commentary*, 315–16.

61. David Dewey, *A User's Guide to Bible Translations* (Downers Grove, IL: InterVarsity, 2004); Gordon D. Fee and Mark L. Strauss, *How to Choose a Bible Translation for All Its Worth* (Grand Rapids: Zondervan, 2007); Andreas J. Köstenberger and David A. Croteau, eds., *Which Bible Translation Should I Use?* (Nashville: B&H, 2012); Leland Ryken, *Understanding English Bible Translation: The Case for an Essentially Literal Approach* (Wheaton, IL: Crossway, 2009); Glen Scorgie, et al. eds., *The Challenge of Bible Translation* (Grand Rapids: Zondervan, 2003). See also the comparison of twenty translations in the compact but helpful pamphlet *Bible Translations Comparison* (Peabody, MA: Rose, 2018).

how one's view of language influences one's view of which translation theory is to be preferred, and in turn, which of the currently available Bible translations may be preferred for a given situation.

Linguistics and Semantics

James Barr's critique of the linguistic method of Kittel's *Theological Dictionary of the New Testament* effectively brought linguistics to bear on biblical studies.[62] Since then, a number of scholars have produced helpful works on the implications of linguistics for biblical studies.[63] All translation and exegesis of the Bible is based on a view of its language, even when the translator/exegete view is not self-consciously implementing that view. Although linguistics is a broad and complex field, students of the Gospels should be aware of the rudiments of linguistics, especially its approaches to how language works to produce meaning.[64]

Semiotics and Meaning

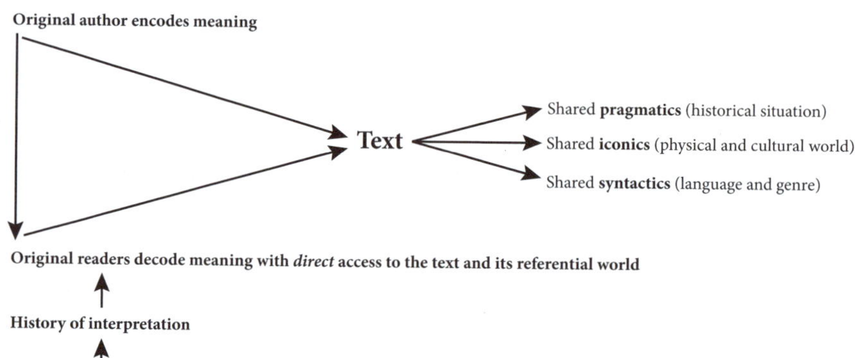

---

62.   James Barr, *The Semantics of Biblical Language* (London: Oxford University Press, 1961).

63.   E.g., David Alan Black, *Linguistics for Students of New Testament Greek* (Grand Rapids: Baker, 1988); G. B. Caird, *The Language and Imagery of the Bible* (Philadelphia: Westminster, 1980); Peter Cotterell and Max Turner, *Linguistics and Biblical Interpretation* (Downers Grove, IL: InterVarsity, 1989). Currently the Centre for Biblical Linguistics, Translation, and Exegesis promotes the specialized integration of linguistics and biblical studies in a series called Linguistic Biblical Studies, published by Brill. See further https://mcmasterdivinity.ca/cblte/publications/linguistic-biblical-studies.

64.   Vern S. Poythress points out that the quest for rigor and accuracy in determining the meaning of biblical texts should not lead to minimizing the complexity and richness of meaning that results from divine authorship. See "Truth and Fulness of Meaning: Fulness Versus Reductionist Semantics in Biblical Interpretation," *WTJ* 67 (2005): 211–27. Poythress's far-ranging essay canvasses key thinkers in linguistics and translation theory.

Linguistics. Basic aspects of language study of interest to students of the Gospels include *phonology* (the sound of language), *morphology* (patterns in the formation of words), *syntax* (structure in the formation of clauses), and *semantics* (the making of meaning). *Cognitive* linguistics addresses how the human mind functions in producing language structures, the reciprocal relationship between language and thinking.[65] When speaking of language structure, linguistics makes a basic distinction between *surface structure*, the syntactical relationships of words, and *deep structure*, the intentional mental activity behind the surface structure. Chomsky's transformational generative approach to grammar was built on the distinction between deep and surface structure. This approach helped scholars understand how the same meaning might be expressed through different structures.[66] One branch of linguistics, *semiotics*, understands any written text as a series of signs that encode an intended authorial referent. Semiotics is based on de Saussure's views of structural approach to language. De Saussure distinguished between *langue* (language as system) and *parole* (intentional speech–acts that implement *langue*). A conventional sign of *langue* such as a word or a phrase is both a signifier (*signifiant*) and what is signified (*signifié*).[67] In this approach to language, meaning is produced when readers who share the text's syntagmatic structure, pragmatic historical situation, and iconic physical world decode its sequential signs that were encoded by the author. Syntactical structure flows from shared linguistic conventions, pragmatics from the shared referential world. Entities of the shared physical world provide the icons from which metaphorical language is based.[68]

Semantics. Semantics, the study of how language produces meaning, is at the heart of the translation and exegesis of the Bible. Semantics takes note of the hierarchical structure of language, beginning with morphemes (meaningful components of words), and leading to lexemes (words), tagmemes (meaningful associations of words), syntagmemes (series of tagmemes), and discourses. Analysis of the dynamic, reciprocal relationship between the various parts of the discourse and the discourse as a whole leads to understanding meaning. At the level of words, meaning is not derived by isolating a word from its immediate associations and seeking its etymology or an illusory original meaning. Gaining awareness of a word's semantic range based on diachronic analysis is helpful in estab-

---

65. Bonnie Howe and Joel B. Green, eds., *Cognitive Linguistic Explorations in Biblical Studies* (Berlin: De Gruyter, 2014).

66. Noam Chomsky, *Aspects of the Theory of Syntax* (Boston: MIT Press, 1965).

67. Fernand de Saussure, *Course in General Linguistics*, trans. Wade Baskin, eds. Charles Bally and Albert Sechehaye (New York: Philosophical Library, 1959).

68. See further George Aichele, *Sign, Text, Scripture: Semiotics and the Bible* (Sheffield: Sheffield Academic, 1997).

lishing semantic parameters, but diachronics cannot pinpoint a word's contribution to meaning at any level of discourse. Rather, focus should be on synchronous elements, a word's immediate syntactical relations in any given discourse. At the level of tagmemes and syntagmemes (successive clauses), one should analyze whether a given clause is related to the previous clause by addition (parataxis, coordination) or by association (hypotaxis, subordination). At the level of discourse (generic segments, e.g., paragraphs, scenes, psalms), one should again analyze how a particular segment makes meaning in its relationship to its related discourses, to the metadiscourse (entire book) in which it occurs, and in relationship to the entire canonical metanarrative. The following figure displays this semantic inter-connectivity as an ongoing quest[69] for better analytic and synthetic understanding of the biblical message:

Semantics and Hierarchical Discourse Analysis
From analysis of the parts . . .

Morphemes
Lexemes (words)
Tagmemes (phrases and clauses)
Syntagmemes (segments)
Discourses (larger sections)
Books (fourfold Gospel including Acts)
Metanarrative (canonical biblical theology)

To synthesis of the whole
BIBLICAL CANON

Metanarrative (canonical biblical theology)
Books (fourfold Gospel including Acts)
Discourses (larger sections)
Syntagmemes (segments)
Tagmemes (phrases and clauses)
Lexemes (words)
Morphemes

To reanalysis of the parts

---

69. In terms of geometric metaphors, the process is not circular but spiral, as in Grant Osborne's hermeneutics textbook *The Hermeneutical Spiral*, rev. ed. (Downers Grove, IL: InterVarsity, 2006). Osborne's concept may be dependent upon J. I. Packer's description of hermeneutics as the ascending spiral of successive approximation. See "Biblical Authority, Hermeneutics, Inerrancy," in *Jerusalem and Athens*, ed. E. R. Geehan (Phillipsburg, NJ: Presbyterian and Reformed, 1971), 146. Accordingly, translation and exegesis can be described as successive approximation of textual meaning as depicted **Christo-telically** through the metanarrative of the canonical Scriptures.

Linguistics and Bible Translation

Speaking broadly, the linguistic insight that written texts have both surface structure and deep structure, syntactical constructions with intentional semantic referents, provides a helpful way to understand two major approaches to Bible translation. *Formal correspondence* is an approach to Bible translation that attempts as much as possible to reproduce the surface structure of the original language, resulting in a largely word-for-word rendering of the original language into the receptor language. When the receptor language's structures and idioms make a word–for–word translation awkward, adjustments are made in the direction of readability. *Functional equivalence* attempts to reproduce the deep structure of the original language, resulting in a largely thought-for-thought translation. When the receptor language's structures and idioms are equivalent to those of the original language, a word-for-word rendering might be found even in a functional equivalence translation. Typically, when a translation seeks functional equivalence rather than formal correspondence, more words are required in the receptor translation than in the original text.[70]

The difference between these two theories becomes clear when the matter of interpretive ambiguity is raised. Everyone acknowledges that ambiguities exist in the original language texts of the Bible. Such ambiguities result from many factors, including obscure literary genres, rare words, and unfamiliar ancient customs and metaphors. Faced with such ambiguities, *formal correspondence translations attempt to render accurately the surface structure of the author's text*, even when ambiguity remains for the reader. This approach is understood as being "transparent" to the original text's words, a desirable characteristic. Preachers and teachers who have gained facility in the original languages of the Bible might favor such "transparency" because it prompts their knowledge of the words and syntax and backgrounds of the original language texts, enabling them to resolve the ambiguities in their study, preparation, and delivery of sermons and lessons. Bible readers who lack such background might be confused by such ambiguities and view them as undesirable characteristics of a Bible translation. Yet advocates of formal correspondence might respond by saying that such confusion leads to deeper study and comprehension of the Bible. Such teachers might actually prefer their audience to be ambivalent about the Bible's meaning because that am-

---

70. For a fuller discussion of these two theories written from the formal correspondence perspective, see Ryken, *Understanding English Bible Translation*, 67–118. See also Ryken's previous work *The Word of God in English: Criteria for Excellence in Bible Translation* (Wheaton, IL: Crossway, 2002). Eugene A. Nida and Charles R. Taber present the classic case for dynamic or functional equivalence in *The Theory and Practice of Translation* (Leiden: Brill, 1969). See also Fee and Strauss, *How to Choose a Translation*, 25–34 and Jan de Waard and Eugene A. Nida, *From One Language to Another: Functional Equivalence in Bible Translating* (Nashville: Word, 1981).

biguity enables the professional teaching pastor to resolve it without interference from outside resources that might not be trustworthy.

On the other hand, when faced with ambiguity, *functional equivalence translations attempt to render clearly the deep structure of the text for the reader,* resolving the ambiguity. Since the orientation is toward the readers and their need to grasp the meaning of the text, clarity rather than ambiguity is desirable. Making the text's meaning transparent in the language of common people who do not have a formal biblical-theological education is the goal rather than making the original text's words transparent to educated readers. There is of course a greater degree of interpretation in functional equivalence translation than in formal correspondence translation, and the more interpretation, the more subjectivity, and the more subjectivity, the more disagreement.

Two Approaches to Bible Translation

Formal Correspondence
Surface structure
Words and syntactical constructions
Word-for-word "accuracy"
Orientation to author's words
Ambiguity
Caution

Functional Equivalence
Deep structure
Ideas and conceptual relationships
Thought-for-thought "readability"
Orientation to reader's understanding
Clarity
Freedom

The table below provides a selection of current versions with their approach to translation, whether word-based or idea-based.[71] The table

---

71. Versions represented in the Table are, from left-to-right, Eugene Peterson, *The Message* (Colorado Springs: NavPress, 2002); Kenneth N. Taylor, *The Living Bible* (Wheaton, IL: Tyndale House, 1971); *The New Living Translation.* 2nd ed. (Wheaton, IL: Tyndale House, 2004); *The Contemporary English Version* (New York: American Bible Society, 1995); *The Revised English Bible* (New York: Oxford, 1992); *The New American Bible*, rev. ed. (New York: Oxford, 2010); *The New International Version* (Grand Rapids: Zondervan, 2011); *The New Jerusalem Bible* (New York: Doubleday, 1985); *The New Revised Standard Version* (New York: Oxford, 1989); *Tanakh: The Holy Scriptures* (Philadelphia: Jewish Publication Society, 1985); *The Christian Standard Bible* (Nashville: Holman, 2017); *The New English Translation* (www.netbible.com; Richardson, TX: Biblical Studies, 2001); *The English Standard Version*

is selective, not exhaustive; omission of a version does not imply disapproval. Neither is the table precise; placement is somewhat subjective and relative. Several translations attempt to mediate between the two major approaches.

The Spectrum of Current Bible Translations

Paraphrase   Functional Equivalence   Mediating   Formal Correspondence   Interlinear

⟵————————————————————————————⟶

Message LB NLT CEV REB NAB NIV NJB NRSV JPS CSB NET ESV NASB KJV

Deep Structure/Semantics	Surface Structure/Syntax
Idea for Idea	**Word for Word**
"Readability"	**"Accuracy"**

Case Study

Although it seems that current Bible translations are typically marketed either as accurate (formal correspondence translations) or readable (functional equivalence translations), selective comparisons may lead one to think there is not as much difference between versions as expected. In the following case study we show why an exact word-for-word translation obscures the meaning of the original text. Then we evaluate multiple translations, ranging from formal to functional.

- Matt 5:12

χαίρετε καὶ ἀγαλλιᾶσθε, ὅτι ὁ μισθὸς ὑμῶν πολὺς ἐν τοῖς οὐρανοῖς·
Rejoice and be glad because the reward your great in the heavens
οὕτως γὰρ ἐδίωξαν τοὺς προφήτας τοὺς πρὸ ὑμῶν.
so for they persecuted the prophets the before you

An *exact* word-for-word translation runs amok because the word order, syntactical conventions, and idioms of Greek and English frequently do not align. English does not typically use an article to render an abstract head noun plus possessive pronoun construction (ὁ μισθὸς ὑμῶν). Greek regularly omits the linking verb "is," but English idiom typically inserts it. The expression ἐν τοῖς οὐρανοῖς reflects a Semitic view of multiple heavens that is typically rendered "in heaven" in English translations. English translations reverse the word order of

---

(Wheaton, IL: Crossway, 2001); *The New American Standard Bible* (La Habra, CA: Lockman Foundation, 1971; updated edition 1995); *The King James Version* (1611; public domain).

οὕτως γὰρ because English idiom does not match the postpositive nature of γὰρ in Greek. Finally, English idiom uses a relative pronoun clause to render τοὺς πρὸ ὑμῶν, a common Greek usage of an articular prepositional phrase as attributive adjective.

The following translations illustrate a more formal approach:

KJV: "Rejoice, and be exceeding glad: for great is your reward in heaven: for so persecuted they the prophets which were before you."

NASB: "Rejoice and be glad, for your reward in heaven is great; for in the same way they persecuted the prophets who were before you."

ESV: "Rejoice and be glad, for your reward is great in heaven, for so they persecuted the prophets who were before you."

NRSV: "Rejoice and be glad, for your reward is great in heaven, for in the same way they persecuted the prophets who were before you."

NIV: "Rejoice and be glad, because great is your reward in heaven, for in the same way they persecuted the prophets who were before you."

NAB: "Rejoice and be glad, for your reward will be great in heaven. Thus they persecuted the prophets who were before you."

All of the above translations render the *surface structure* of the Greek text into acceptable idiomatic English in a similar manner. There are only minor differences among them, but we will summarize the tedious details to illustrate the myriad choices translators face. KJV renders ἀγαλλιᾶσθε as "be exceedingly glad," which might be warranted lexically and by the parallelism with χαίρετε. Only NIV renders ὅτι, which begins the second clause, as "because" instead of "for." Perhaps the NIV translators did not wish to begin consecutive clauses with "for." KJV, followed by NIV, reverses the Greek word order in the second clause, putting the predicate nominative πολὺς before the subject μισθός. NASB reverses the Greek word order by placing the prepositional phrase ἐν τοῖς οὐρανοῖς before πολὺς. All the translations except NAB render the γὰρ which begins the third clause as "for." Only NAB omits the γὰρ and renders οὕτως with the semi-archaic "thus." The other translations render οὕτως as either "so" (KJV, ESV) or "in the same way" (NASB, NRSV, NIV). All in all, "in the same way" seems preferable in drawing out the continuity between Jesus's prophetic community and the biblical prophets. KJV alone has "persecuted they" instead of what the more idiomatic "they persecuted." Finally, NAB stands alone in supplying the future tense verb "will be" instead of the present "is." This move is likely related to the future tense verbs in the second through seventh of Jesus's eight beatitudes (Matt. 5:3–10).

We now move on to some thought-for-thought translations:

CEV: "Be happy and excited! You will have a great reward in heaven. People did these same things to the prophets who lived long ago."

NLT: "Be happy about it! Be very glad! For a great reward awaits you in heaven. And remember, the ancient prophets were persecuted in the same way."

LB: "Be *happy* about it! Be *very glad!* For a *tremendous reward* awaits you up in heaven. And remember, the ancient prophets were persecuted too."

Message: "You can be glad when that happens—give a cheer, even!—for though they don't like it, *I* do! And all heaven applauds. And know that you are in good company. My prophets and witnesses have always gotten into this kind of trouble."

The thought-for-thought translations above range from the relatively cautious CEV to the creative Message, which is actually more of a paraphrase than a translation. CEV uses only twenty-four English words to render the nineteen words of the Greek text, although it eliminates the conjunctions ὅτι and γάρ. CEV, NLT, and LB all use language that stresses that the disciples' reward is future, while The Message implies the disciples' reward is present, consisting in God's approval and all of heaven's applause. CEV's rendering of the third clause seems to understate the analogy between Jesus's disciples and the biblical prophets. The Message expresses this analogy most strongly, using twenty words to render the nine words of the Greek text. NLT renders the explanatory γάρ that introduces the third clause as "and remember"; The Message similarly has "and know." LB and The Message make liberal use of exclamation points and italics to stress key points. Perhaps the most debatable move in all of these renderings is The Message's rendering of the second clause ὁ μισθὸς ὑμῶν πολὺς ἐν τοῖς οὐρανοῖς with three clauses. The first clause, "for though they don't like it," refers to the persecutors' displeasure at the disciples' joy. Such displeasure would not be strange, but it is not implied contextually. Similarly, The Message's presentation of the disciples' reward as entailing all of heaven's applause seems to bring in the angels and/or the church triumphant, but there is nothing in the context that warrants this. It is fair to say that The Message is freer than an idea-for-idea translation. Accordingly, it should not be used as one's primary Bible translation but as an interpretive aid for Bible study.

Current Issues

Two additional issues related to Bible translation can be only briefly treated. The first links translation methodology to bibliology by arguing that only formal correspondence translations are consistent with the evangelical doctrine of the verbal plenary inspiration of the Bible.[72] This argument is well-meant but mistaken. A proper understanding of language does not diminish the importance of individual words in the quest for ideas—the ideas can be grasped only through the words in which they are couched. Yet texts convey meaning not by isolated individual words but by words that are associated with other words in phrases and clauses. Verbal plenary inspiration of the Bible means that every word is divinely inspired, and implies that every word must be taken into account when understanding the Bible's meaning. Such inspiration, however, does not require that each biblical word be translated in a one-for-one fashion into its receptor languages. Inspired biblical words in their syntactical relationships are the means by which *propositional* revelation is conveyed; the words taken *individually*, however inspired, do not constitute propositional revelation. Biblical revelation must be understood and translated conceptually, not atomistically. Accordingly, an idea-for-idea translation that flows from a careful study of grammar and syntax is consistent with a high view of biblical inspiration. Many evangelicals with unimpeachably high views of the Bible support functional equivalence translation.[73]

A second issue that requires comment is the place of gender in Bible translation.[74] The Gospels and Acts depict teachings of Jesus and the

---

72. See e.g., Wayne Grudem, "Are Only *Some* Words of Scripture Breathed-Out by God?" in *Translating Truth*, eds. Wayne Grudem, et al. (Wheaton, IL: Crossway, 2005), 19–56. Grudem summarizes his argument in two points, (1) every word of the Bible comes from God and is important, and (2) this strongly argues for "essentially literal" or word-for-word translation of the Bible (19). All evangelicals would accept Grudem's first point, but many find his second to be *non sequitur*. Some Muslims forbid any translation of the Arabic Qur'an on grounds similar to Grudem's first point. See further Fee and Strauss, *How to Choose a Translation*, 35–36.

73. See further Fee and Strauss, *How to Choose a Translation*, 35–36; Rodney J. Decker, "Verbal-Plenary Inspiration and Translation," *DBSJ* 11 (2006): 25–61, esp. 49–61.

74. This simmering issue came to a boiling point in evangelicalism with the publication of The New International Version Inclusive Language Edition in London in 1996 and Today's New International Version in the USA in 2005. For an anti-inclusive language discussion, see Vern S. Poythress and Wayne A. Grudem, *The Gender-Neutral Bible Controversy: Muting the Masculinity of God's Words* (Nashville: Broadman & Holman, 2000). More centrist views are argued by D. A. Carson in *The Inclusive Language Debate: A Plea for Realism* (Grand Rapids: Baker, 1998) and Mark L. Strauss, *Distorting Scripture? The Challenge of Bible Translation and Gender Accuracy* (Downers Grove, IL: InterVarsity, 1998).

apostles that were originally directed in most cases to groups of disciples made up of men and women alike. The original audiences that received the Gospels and Acts likewise typically contained men and women. In ancient times it was customary to refer to people in general with masculine language. Older Bible translations commonly used masculine pronouns to describe people in general. Recent cultural developments in the Western world have called this usage into question, and English usage is changing. How should Bible translators respond? One approach is to retain masculine language and point out that various lexicons and dictionaries acknowledge that terms like "man" or "brother" can in some contexts refer to people in general, human beings irrespective of gender.[75] While this approach is factual, it is not wise if the goal of the translation is making biblical meaning clear for readers who do not typically read the Bible with a dictionary nearby.

A specific example might add clarity to this discussion. In Mark 8:37 Jesus asks, τί γὰρ δοῖ ἄνθρωπος ἀντάλλαγμα τῆς ψυχῆς αὐτοῦ; Males are not exclusively in view here; Jesus has been speaking about *anyone* who wishes to follow him in 8:34 (εἴ τις θέλει ὀπίσω μου ἀκολουθεῖν) and 8:35 (ὃς γὰρ ἐὰν θέλῃ τὴν ψυχὴν αὐτοῦ σῶσαι). Translations whose goal is to mimic the underlying Greek text will render Mark 8:37 something like "For what shall a man give in exchange for his soul?" (KJV, NASB, ESV). Translations that are more oriented to making the meaning clear to readers render along the following lines, from more cautious to more free:

- "What can a person give in exchange for his life?" (NET)
- "What can anyone give in exchange for their soul?" (NIV)
- "What can they give in exchange for their life?" (NRSV)
- "What could you ever trade your soul for?" (Message)
- "Is anything worth more than your soul?" (NLT)

This example demonstrates the difficulties faced by translators and the differences that result the two major theories of translation are put into practice.

Conclusion

Individual Bible translations and the translation theories that are implemented in producing those translations have occasionally become controversial, even divisive issues among evangelicals. In order to make

---

75. BDAG, s.v. ἀδελφός. Compare meaning 1. (a male sibling) with meaning 2. (a close associate), 18–19; BDAG, s.v. ἄνθρωπος. Compare meaning 1. (a person of either sex) with meaning 3. (a male person), 81–82.

wise decisions about such matters, one must evaluate each Bible translation individually in terms of its theoretical basis, the competence of its translators, and its intended audience. The wide availability of multiple English Bible translations should increase interest in and study of the Bible. Translations that seek to render thought-for-thought while maintaining as much formal correspondence as idiomatic English allows should be primary. Translations that emphasize formal correspondence, even at the expense of English idiom, have a place for close Bible study, especially for people whose education enables them to resolve the inevitable ambiguities inherent in such translations. The more idiomatic translations also have their place, especially among untaught audiences and when general clarity is sought rather than precise detail.

STUDYING THE TEXT: CRITICAL METHODS

Having discussed establishing and translating the text of the Gospels and Acts, we turn now to focus on the methods used in studying the historical processes involved in the writing of these books. A cursory reading of the first three "Synoptic" Gospels reveals the fundamental difficulty known as the synoptic problem—why are these Gospels so similar in some respects and so different in others?[76] One possible solution would attribute the striking similarities and differences solely to the divine guidance of the authors, but reflection on Luke 1:1–4 shows that the origin of the Gospels and Acts in divine providence involved a historical process. Luke acknowledges that his Gospel is related to earlier accounts (διήγησις; Luke 1:1; cf. *Let. Aris.* 1, 8, 322; Josephus *A. J.* 11.68) and oral traditions emanating from eyewitnesses (αὐτόπτης; Luke 1:2; cf. Josephus *B. J.* 3.432; *A. J.* 18.342; 19:125; *C. Ap.* 1.55).

The historical process leading to the completion of the Gospels, including the complexities known today as the synoptic problem, involved both a preliterary history and a literary prehistory. In other words, oral traditions about Jesus arose from eyewitness accounts of his ministry. At some point early on, these traditions began to be written down. No doubt there was overlap between these two processes; it is, perhaps, simplistic to think of a preliterary oral stage abruptly transitioning into a stage when written accounts were the sole means of propagating traditions about Jesus. In modern biblical scholarship the study of putative *written* sources for the Gospels—their literary prehistory—came before

---

76. For surveys of the major views and issues, see D. A. Black and D. R. Beck, eds., *Rethinking the Synoptic Problem* (Grand Rapids: Baker, 2001); David L. Dungan, *A History of the Synoptic Problem* (New York: Doubleday, 1999); Stanley E. Porter and Bryan R. Dyer, eds., *The Synoptic Problem: Four Views* (Grand Rapids: Baker, 2016); and Robert L. Thomas, ed., *Three Views on the Origins of the Synoptic Gospels* (Grand Rapids: Kregel, 2002).

the study of the *oral* traditions—their pre-literary history that led to the written accounts. The historical process that gave rise to the Gospels themselves began with the oral transmission of memorized eyewitness testimony.

A great deal of the modern study of the Gospels is directed toward understanding the synoptic problem in light of three methods of studying the Gospels: form criticism, source criticism, and redaction criticism. These three approaches are sometimes called historical criticism because they seek to understand the historical development of traditions about Jesus tradition. Literary criticism seeks to understand the techniques used by the final authors of the Gospels to make their stories winsome and effective. Although literary criticism is often distinguished from historical criticism, we will discuss it here alongside historical criticism.

Form Criticism: Oral Traditions about Jesus

In ancient cultures, including the Near-Eastern culture of the NT, communication was more a matter of talking and listening than a matter of writing and reading. Literacy was not nearly as common then as it is in many current cultures. Jesus and the apostles were primarily teachers and preachers, not writers (Matt. 7:28–29; 13:53–54; Mark 1:22; 6:1–2; Luke 4:22). Jesus's teaching was carefully remembered and passed on orally by the earliest Christians (Luke 1:1–4). The Gospels and Acts narrate a great deal of the oral ministries of Jesus and the apostles. The "word of God" or "word of the Lord" in the New Testament is primarily a spoken message,[77] although at times the expression refers to the written Scriptures (Luke 3:4; Matt. 15:6/ Mark 7:13; Rev. 22:9, 18–19). The Pharisaic teachings occasionally opposed by Jesus were oral traditions, not written biblical commands (Matt. 15:2; Mark 7:3; cf. Gal. 1:14). Jesus affirmed that his words would be permanent, which implies they would be remembered and passed on (Matt. 24:35/Mark 13:31/Luke 21:33). Paul commended his churches for maintaining the teaching he passed on to them orally (1 Cor. 11:2; 2 Thess. 2:15, 3:6). Revelation 1:3 provides a window into this oral culture with its blessing for the one who reads the book (Rev. 1:11) aloud to the congregation (ὁ ἀναγινώσκων) and for those who hear (and obey) the prophetic word being read (οἱ ἀκούοντες

---

77. E.g., Matt. 4:4/Deut. 8:3; Mark 4:33; Luke 3:2; 5:1; 8:11, 21; 11:28; John 3:34; 8:47; 10:35; Acts 4:31; 6:2, 7; 8:14, 25; 11:16; 12:24; 13:7, 44, 46, 48; 14:3; 15:7, 35, 36; 16:32; 17:13; 18:11; 19:10, 20; 20:35; 1 Cor. 1:18; 14:36; 2 Cor. 2:17; Col. 4:3; 1 Thess. 1:8; 2:13; 4:15; 2 Thess. 3:1; 2 Tim. 2:9; Titus 1:3; 2:5; 6:3; Heb. 6:5; 13:7; 1 Peter 1:25; 1 John 2:14; Rev. 1:2, 9; 6:9; 19:9; 20:4.

τοὺς λόγους τῆς προφητείας).[78] According to Eusebius, writing in the fourth century A.D., the second-century bishop Papias did not think that information from books would help him as much as the personal recollections of a living person who had been in contact with Jesus's earliest followers (*Hist. eccl.* 3.39.3–4).

In the early twentieth century, form criticism arose as an attempt to get behind the written sources identified by source criticism to access earlier (and, in the view of many, more reliable) sources for the life of Jesus. The discipline began with the work of Hermann Gunkel, who attempted to understand Genesis as a collection of legends calculated to explain various things about Israel's history.[79] NT scholars soon applied to the Gospels Gunkel's way of reading of Genesis.[80] In general, scholars argued that early stories about Jesus circulated individually without a sequential framework. Most viewed the circulation of the passion narrative as an overall unit to be an exception to this rule. The approach identified several types of Jesus stories in the Gospels and viewed the geographical and chronological settings of such stories as later editorial additions by the Gospel authors as bridge material to frame the stories. By the time the stories received literary status in the Gospels they had been adapted and altered by communities to meet their own needs., Thus, the goal of the form critic was not simply to classify Jesus stories according to literary form but to write a history of tradition (*Traditionsgeschichte*) by distinguishing between the secondary accretions of the communities and the original pristine form of the story.

Most form critics were and are skeptical of the historical value of the oral traditions about Jesus. Units of tradition were preserved if they were viewed as relevant to a given community's needs, and the communities freely altered the units to fit their needs more closely.

---

78. See the discussion of orality and its implications for biblical studies and theology by John H. Walton and D. Brent Sandy, *The Lost World of Scripture* (Downers Grove, IL: InterVarsity, 2013), esp. 97–142, 244–47. See also Werner Kelber, *The Oral and Written Gospel* (Minneapolis: Fortress, 1983).

79. Hermann Gunkel, *The Legends of Genesis*, trans. W. Carruth (New York: Schocken, 1964). This book is a reprint of the introduction to Gunkel's larger work on Genesis, originally published in 1901.

80. K. L. Schmidt, *Der Rahmen der Geschichte Jesu* [The Framework of the History of Jesus] (Berlin: Trowitzsch und Sohn, 1919); Martin Dibelius, *Die Formgeschichte des Evangeliums* (Tübingen: Mohr, 1919). The second edition was translated into English by B. L. Woolf as *From Tradition to Gospel* (New York: Scribner's, 1934). Rudolf Bultmann, *Die Geschichte der synoptischen Tradition* (Tübingen: Vandenhoeck und Ruprecht, 1921). The third edition was translated into English by J. Marsh as *History of the Synoptic Tradition* (New York: Harper, 1963). Bultmann's work is the most comprehensive and influential. Vincent Taylor, *The Formation of the Gospel Tradition* (London: Macmillan, 1933). Taylor is relatively cautious and conservative in his use of the method.

Form critics tended to downplay or ignore the notion that faithful memorization and handing on of eyewitness testimony (Luke 1:1–4) exercised control over the content of the units. The British scholar Vincent Taylor, himself a cautious practitioner of form criticism, wrote, "It is on the question of eyewitnesses that form criticism presents a very vulnerable front. If the Form-Critics are right, the disciples must have been translated to heaven immediately after the resurrection."[81] Evangelicals will part company from the historical skepticism that influences form-critical writing of tradition history, but they should recognize the considerable exegetical value in identifying and understanding the literary forms identified by the form critics.[82]

The following elements are commonly viewed to be units of early oral traditions about Jesus that were later incorporated into our written Gospels.[83]

- *The passion narrative.* Most form critics believe that the various scenes of the passion narrative were not passed on individually, but as a unit. The passing on of this early tradition might have led to the passing on of other forms.
- *Stories about Jesus.* Sometimes called legends (to emphasize their transcendent content, not necessarily to deny their historicity), such stories are narratives that explain, reveal, or exalt Jesus without any stress on his teaching. For examples, see Mark 1:9–11; 11:1–10; Luke 2:41–52 and parallels where applicable.
- *Pronouncement stories.* Sometimes called paradigms or apothegms, such stories move without extraneous detail to a high point when Jesus concludes the story with an authoritative saying or pronouncement that resolves the debate. Sometimes such stories begin with controversy or opposition. For examples, see Mark 2:23–28, 10:17–31; 12:13–17 and parallels where applicable.
- *Miracle stories.* Sometimes called tales, or *novellen*, such stories involve rescues, exorcisms, healings, and epiphanies that resolve

---

81. Taylor, *Formation*, 41. Taylor went on to liken form criticism's strange separation of the early communities from the eyewitnesses to the separation of shipwrecked Robinson Crusoe from civilization.

82. Along these lines, see Craig Blomberg, *The Historical Reliability of the Gospels*, 2nd ed. (Downers Grove, IL: InterVarsity, 2007), 50–62; Darrell Bock, "Form Criticism," in *New Testament Criticism and Interpretation*, ed. D. A. Black and D. S. Dockery (Grand Rapids: Zondervan, 1991), 175–96; D. A. Carson and D. J. Moo, *An Introduction to the New Testament*, 2nd ed. (Grand Rapids: Zondervan, 2005), 79–85.

83. The terminology for the various forms or units of tradition tends to vary from one form critic to another. See the discussion of Edgar V. McKnight, *What is Form Criticism?* (Philadelphia: Fortress, 1969), 20–33.

    various difficulties by the power of Jesus. For examples, see Mark
    1:40–45; 4:35–41; 9:14–29 and parallels where applicable.
- *Conflict stories.* Sometimes called controversy stories, such stories
  involve Jesus entering into controversy with an opponent (usually the religious leaders) and engaging in polemics with them.
  At times such stories lead to a parable. For examples, see Mark
  3:1–6; 12:28–34 and parallels where applicable.
- *Sayings.* Sometimes called paraenesis, such stories involve teachings of Jesus not directly tied to a pronouncement story or an
  event, such as a conflict. Examples include aphorisms (Mark
  3:24–26), beatitudes (Matt. 5:3–12; Luke 6:20–23), I-sayings
  (Mark 2:17), and parables.

The Gospels and Acts contain other conventional forms or type-
scenes that are not typically emphasized by form critics. Such stories
about Jesus may echo similar stories from the OT. Among such conventional type-scenes are the following:

- *Genealogies* (Matt. 1:1–17; Luke 3:23–38; cf. Gen. 5:3–32; 10:1–
  32; 11:10–32; 25:12–20; 36:1–43)
- *Annunciation or birth stories* (Luke 1–2; Matt. 1:18–2:23; cf. Exod.
  1:15–2:10; 1 Sam. 1:1–2:21)
- *Calling stories* (Matt. 4:18–22/Mark 1:16–20/Luke 5:2–11; Matt.
  9:9/Mark 2:14/Luke 5:27–28; Acts 9:1–22; cf. Exod. 3:1–4:17;
  Josh. 1:1–9; Jer. 1:4–19)
- *Farewells* (John 13–17; Acts 20:17–38; cf. Genesis 48–49;
  Deuteronomy 31–34; Joshua 23–24)

Source Criticism: Written Stories about Jesus

Approaches to synoptic literary origins can be divided into two
main groups: those who posit the literary *independence* of each Gospel,
and those who affirm some sort of literary *interdependence* between the
Gospels. In other words, the debate revolves around whether or not the
authors of later Gospels directly utilized the earlier Gospels as source
documents when they composed their works.

Certain scholars argue from the prevalence of oral transmission of
memorized sacred tradition in the Ancient Near East that each Gospel
author could work from the available oral tradition without needing to
borrow from another Gospel.[84] In this view, sometimes called "the tra-

---

84. James Dunn, *Jesus Remembered* (Grand Rapids: Eerdmans, 2003); David Farnell, "The
    Case for the Independence View of Gospel Origins," in Thomas, *Three Views*, 226–309;
    Birger Gerhardsson, *Memory and Manuscript* [1964] and *Tradition and Transmission in Early*

dition hypothesis," the authors of the Gospels reflected on memorized oral tradition based on eyewitness testimony about Jesus's ministry as they composed their accounts. The oral memory approach plausibly accounts for the differences between the synoptics by positing the oral transmission of a central core of memorized tradition with some variation in supporting details. Many scholars, however, do not think this approach adequately accounts for the extensive verbatim agreements between the synoptic accounts (e.g., Matt. 3:7–9 with Luke 3:7–9; Matt. 9:14–17 and Mark 2:18–22).

Most scholars today conclude that some sort of literary interrelationship is necessary to explain the phenomena of the Gospels, especially their extensive verbal agreements. In the mid–second century Tatian sought to harmonize the four Gospels into one account in a fragmentarily preserved work known as the *Diatessaron* ("through four"). Origen, Augustine, and many others represented the consensus of the early view that the canonical order of the Gospels represented the historical order of their composition.[85] In the late eighteenth century the patristic approach to Matthean priority was revised by J. J. Griesbach, whose "Two-Gospel Hypothesis" posited (1) that Luke used Matthew, and (2) Mark used both Matthew and Luke.[86]

The Griesbach [Two-Gospel] Hypothesis: Matthean Priority

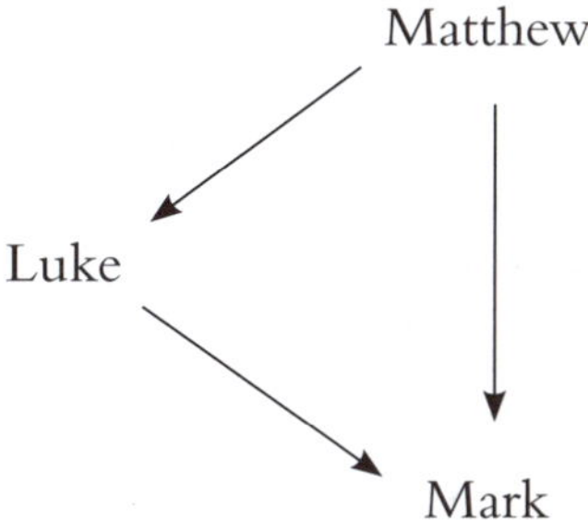

Christianity [1964] reprinted in one vol., trans. E. Sharp (Grand Rapids: Eerdmans, 1998); Rainer Riesner, "The Orality and Memory Hypothesis," in Porter and Dyer, *The Synoptic Problem*, 89–111; J. M. Rist, *On the Independence of Matthew and Mark* (Cambridge: Cambridge University Press, 1978); B. F. Westcott, *An Introduction to the Study of the Gospels* (London: MacMillan, 1895), 165–212.

85. Origen *Comm. Matt.* 1.1; Augustine, *Cons.* 1.1.1–4; 1.2.4; 1.3.6; 1.4.7; 4.10.11; Eusebius, *Hist. eccl.* 3.24.

86. J. J. Griesbach, *Commentario qua Marci Evangelium totum e Matthaei et Lucae commentariis decerptum esse monstratur*, 2 vols. (Jena, 1789–1790).

Although some scholars still hold to Matthean priority,[87] the scholarly consensus today favors Markan priority, with Matthew and Luke composing their Gospels in dependence on Mark and the hypothetical source Q,[88] which purportedly contained a collection of the sayings of Jesus. This view is known as the "two-source hypothesis" because it holds Mark and Q to be the sources of Matthew and Mark.[89] Major arguments for the view, based on close reading of **triple tradition** texts, include (1) a great deal of Mark's material also appears in Matthew and Luke, (2) Matthew and Luke commonly agree verbally with Mark and seldom agree against Mark, (3) Matthew and Luke typically agree with Mark's order of **pericopes**, and (4) Matthew and Luke arguably improve Mark's language and grammar.

The Two-Source Hypothesis: Markan Priority

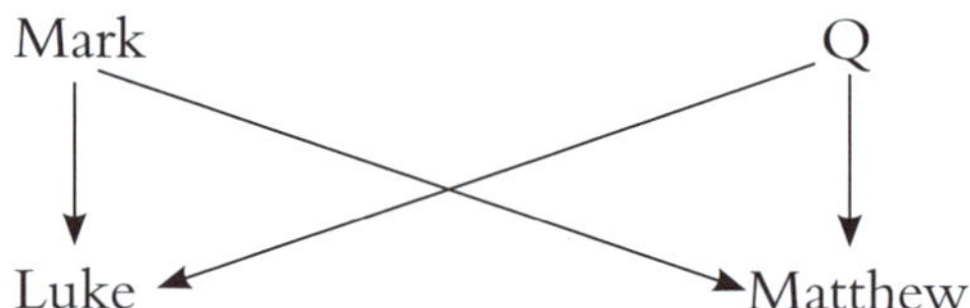

The two-source hypothesis as originally formulated accounted for material found in both Matthew and Luke but could not explain material that was unique to Matthew or Luke. For this reason, the theory was revised and expanded into the "four-source hypothesis," in which Mark and Q are supplemented by the additional hypothetical sources M for unique Matthean tradition (such as Matthew 1–2) and L for unique Lukan tradition (such as Luke 1–2).[90]

---

87. The patristic advocates of Matthean priority did not address what is today known as the synoptic problem. Modern advocates of the Augustinian hypothesis include B. C. Butler, *The Originality of St. Matthew* (Cambridge: Cambridge University Press, 1951), and John W. Wenham, *Redating Matthew, Mark, and Luke: A Fresh Assault on the Synoptic Problem* (London: Hodder, 1991). The Griesbach hypothesis is favored by William Farmer, *The Synoptic Problem: A Critical Analysis* (New York: Macmillan, 1964); David B. Peabody, "The Two Gospel Hypothesis," in Porter and Dyer, *The Synoptic* Problem, 67–88; C. M. Tuckett, *The Revival of the Griesbach Hypothesis* (Cambridge, Cambridge University Press, 1983).

88. Evidently Q is short for the German word *Quelle*, meaning "source."

89. Advocates include Craig A. Evans, "The Two Source Hypothesis," in Porter and Dyer, *The Synoptic Problem*, 27–45; Robert H. Stein, *Studying the Synoptic Gospels*, 2nd ed. (Grand Rapids: Baker, 2001), 29–169; B. H. Streeter, *The Four Gospels: A Study of Origins* (London: Macmillan, 1924), 150–95.

90. See Streeter's seminal diagram in *The Four Gospels*, 150.

The Four-Source Hypothesis: Markan Priority

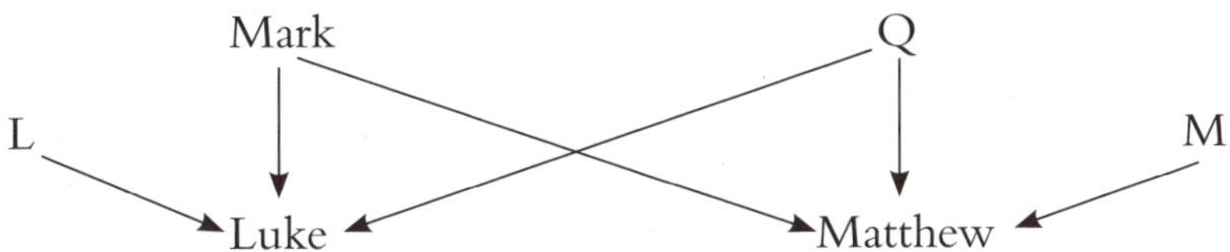

More recently, dissatisfaction with the Q-hypothesis has led some scholars, notably Austin Farrer, to posit Markan priority without Q. This hypothesis dispenses with the need for Q by explaining the common material in Matthew and Luke by Luke's use of Matthew as well as Mark. Farrer's hypothesis has been refined and advanced by such scholars as M. D. Goulder and Mark Goodacre.[91]

The Farrer Hypothesis: Markan Priority without Q

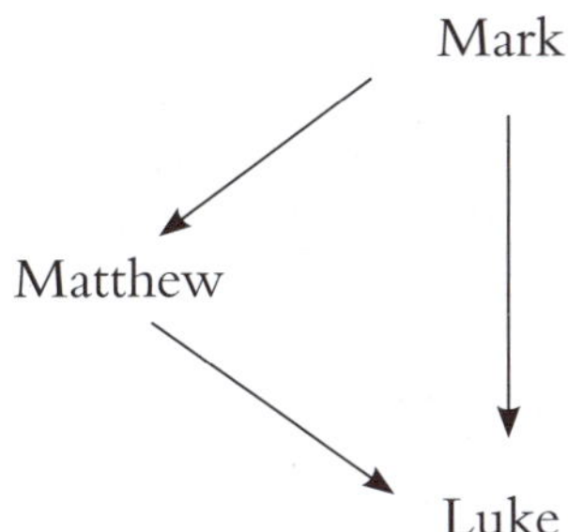

Scholarly opinion on Q varies widely. Scholars associated with the International Q Project have [re?]created it as a document, complete with its own tradition history, by compiling the material held in common by Matthew and Luke.[92] Others tend to use Q only as a convenient umbrella term for sources, either oral or written, used in the composition of Matthew and Luke. Those scholars who advocate the priority of Matthew join the followers of Farrer in dispensing with it altogether. One scholar poked fun at the nebulous results of the whole debate in an essay entitled "'Q' Is Only What You Make

---

91. Austin Farrer, "On Dispensing with Q," in *Studies in the Gospels: Essays in Memory of R. H. Lightfoot*, ed. D. E. Nineham (Oxford: Blackwell, 1955), 55–88; Mark Goodacre, "The Farrer Hypothesis," in Porter and Dyer, *The Synoptic Problem*, 47–66; M. D. Goulder, "Is Q a Juggernaut?" *JBL* 115 (1996): 667–81.

92. John S. Kloppenborg, *Q, the Earliest Gospel* (Louisville: Westminster John Knox, 2008); James M. Robinson, et al., eds., *The Critical Edition of Q* (Minneapolis: Fortress, 2000).

It"![93] However one evaluates the evidence for and against Q, those scholars who approach the Gospels not only as ancient tradition-based biographies but also as normative canonical Scriptures must assess the value of source criticism for the use of the Bible in the church. Understanding the historical process of Gospel origins in divine providence is a worthy scholarly endeavor, but the edification of the church is a matter of expounding the Gospel in its final canonical form. This consideration brings us to redaction criticism.

Redaction Criticism: Composing the Gospels

Form and source criticism tend to deconstruct the Gospels in their search for the earliest units of tradition that were ultimately used in composing the Gospels. Redaction criticism attempts to understand the history of Jesus tradition at this final stage by analyzing the editorial activity that led to the Gospels as we have them today. In seeking to understand the Gospels as literary wholes instead of conglomerates of various parts, redaction criticism's agenda is different from form and source criticisms. As Luke 1:1–4 alludes to historical processes leading to the composition of the Gospels, so John 20:30–31 provides a window into the sort of editorial activity that resulted in these four biographical narratives with all their similarities and differences:

> Now Jesus did many other signs in the presence of the disciples, which are not written in this book; but these are written so that you may believe that Jesus is the Christ, the Son of God, and that by believing you may have life in his name. (ESV)

The discussion of genre in chapter 1 noted the distinctive voices that make up the fourfold Gospel tradition. Redaction criticism seeks to understand each authorial voice individually.[94]

---

93. Stewart Petrie, "'Q' Is Only What You Make It," *NovT* 3 (1959): 28–33. What Petrie said almost sixty years ago is still true today: "There is something about the 'Q' hypothesis—a nebulosity, a capriciousness, an intractability—that is altogether baffling. 'Q' is confidently postulated and conveniently labeled; but the provision of an identity tag cannot of itself bring into existence a hypothetical source that that has yet to be tracked down and exhibited with really confident assurance" (28).

94. Helpful introductions to redaction criticism include Carson and Moo, *Introduction*, 103–12; Grant R. Osborne, "Redaction Criticism," in Black and Dockery, *NT Criticism and Interpretation*, 199–224. A brief, early, and sympathetic analysis is Norman Perrin, *What Is Redaction Criticism?* (Philadelphia: Fortress, 1974). From a similar perspective with more detail, see Joachim Rohde, *Rediscovering the Teaching of the Evangelists*, trans. D. Barton (Philadelphia: Westminster, 1968).

Redaction criticism arose as an alternative to form criticism just as form criticism arose as an alternative to source criticism. To some extent, the shift in methodology grew out of dissatisfaction with the previous method and the desire to explore questions that were not currently being addressed. Redaction critics, however, did not discard the previous methods. The "assured results" of the previous methods, ideas like the two-source hypothesis and the prior oral transmission of stories about Jesus, were accepted as the foundation of redactional activity. Influential early redaction critical essays include Gunther Bornkamm's essay on the calming of the storm in Matthew 8,[95] Hans Conzelmann's book on the theology of Luke,[96] and Willi Marxsen's book on Mark.[97] William Wrede's early-twentieth-century treatment of the messianic secret in Mark paved the way for such studies by treating Mark as a book with theological concerns.[98]

Perhaps the most basic assumption of redaction criticism is that the Gospels result from the redaction of received tradition. This redactional (editorial) activity involved selecting which traditions to include in their narratives and which to omit, organizing or arranging that material coherently, and wording the material in a way that fits the editorial/theological goals. At times the tradition is retained or conserved with little editorial activity. At other times, editorial activity is more obvious. Redaction critics also look for the seams or "glue" that hold the units of tradition together. Such seams provide pointers to why the material was arranged as it was and help the reader

---

95. Bornkamm's essay was originally published in 1948. It is included in G. Gornkamm, et al., eds., *Tradition and Interpretation in Matthew*, trans. P. Scott (Philadelphia: Westminster, 1963), 52–57. Bornkamm compared Matt. 8:18–27 to Mark 4:36–41. He commented that "Matthew is not only a hander-on of tradition but also its oldest exegete" (55), and that in Matthew's hands Mark's nature miracle "becomes a kerygmatic paradigm of the danger and glory of discipleship" (57).

96. Hans Conzelmann, *The Theology of St. Luke*, trans. G. Buswell (New York: Harper, 1960). This book was originally published in German in 1954. Conzelmann notably discussed Luke's theology of time as three segments, the time of Israel, the time of Jesus, and the time of the church.

97. Willi Marxsen, *Mark the Evangelist*, trans. J. Boyce, et al. (Nashville: Abingdon, 1960). This book was originally published in German in 1956. Among other things, Marxsen argued that, unlike Luke, Mark believed in the imminent appearance of Jesus, and against the backdrop of the Jewish revolt against Rome (c. A.D. 66) intended that Christians gather in Galilee in anticipation of that event.

98. William Wrede, *Das Messiasgeheimnis in den Evangelien* (Göttingen: Vandenhoeck & Ruprecht, 1901); English translation *The Messianic Secret in Mark*, trans. J. Grieg (Cambridge: Clarke, 1971). Other early works that anticipated what was to come were R. H. Lightfoot, *History and Interpretation in the Gospels* (London: Hodder, 1935) and Ned Stonehouse, *The Witness of the Synoptic Gospels to Christ* (Grand Rapids: Baker, 1979). This book contains material previously published in 1944 and 1951.

understand how the overall sequencing of the narrative reveals its editorial and theological interests.

Most redaction critics assume Markan priority and the existence of the hypothetical Q, M, and L sources. Accordingly, Matthew's received tradition is Mark, Q, and M; Luke's received tradition is Mark, Q, and L. Matthew and Luke proceed to handle their respective sources in a manner that implements their individual editorial perspectives and tendencies, resulting in two Gospels that take received tradition in two distinct directions to meet the needs of two distinct communities. Although the received tradition differs, Luke's editorial perspective and theological goals continue to be implemented in his second volume, Acts. From the perspective of editing received tradition, the editorial activity noted above in John 20:30 is evident in the Fourth Gospel, which shares only around ten percent of its content with the Synoptics. As to Mark, redactional activity is difficult to assess, in that Mark's traditional sources are unknown.

In contrast to form and source criticism's mutual goal of getting "behind" the Gospels to lay bare the history of the units of tradition, redaction criticism deals with how the Gospels as completed entities utilized received tradition to compose a narrative. In other words, form and source criticism deal with two aspects of the *process* that led to the Gospels, and redaction criticism with the Gospels as a *product* of that process. Accordingly, the methods are interrelated but distinct. They do not function in competition against but in combination with one another as complementary approaches to understanding the Gospels. Those scholars whose interests lie in the pretextual history of Gospel tradition will gravitate to form and source criticism, and those scholars who wish to exegete texts in the Gospels will find more value in redaction criticism.

On the typical assumption of the two-source view of Markan priority, redactional analysis of Matthew and Luke amounts to distinguishing between tradition and redaction by locating the respective sources (for Matthew, Mark, Q, and M; for Luke, Mark, Q, and L) and discerning Matthew's and Luke's respective editorial refinements as an indication of their unique theological interests. On the Farrer hypothesis, since Q is out of the picture, redactional analysis of Matthew is simpler. The analysis of Luke, however, must deal with his use of Matthew as well as Mark. As noted above, redactional analysis of Mark, John, and Acts cannot proceed on these assumptions.

Although many scholars assume that Markan-priority-based redactional process results in historically less reliable material in Matthew and Luke, this conclusion does not necessarily follow. Redaction need not amount to the creation of new material without historical foundation. Many evangelical scholars utilize redaction criticism in their work with the Gospels. Early on, evangelicals published redactional studies of the theology of the Synoptics,[99] and numerous conservative evangelical commentaries utilize the approach,[100] but there is a lingering question. If one accepts the traditional view of the apostolic authorship of Matthew, one may wonder why an eyewitness of Jesus's ministry would base his Gospel on the account of Mark, who was not an eyewitness. Since patristic tradition places Peter's recollections and authority behind the Gospel of Mark (Eusebius. *Hist. Eccl.* 3.39.15), Matthew would essentially be collaborating with another eyewitness, Peter.[101] Matthew would have added new material on the teaching of Jesus in five major discourses while condensing Mark's more vivid narratives of Jesus's deeds., If one takes Luke's preface seriously, Mark could very well be one of the accounts Luke consulted as he produced his Gospel.

On the view of Matthean priority, or the two-Gospel hypothesis, the redactional direction is reversed. Broadly speaking, Mark has omitted much of Matthew's material on Jesus's teaching but has added a great deal of detail to Matthew's compact narrative of Jesus's deeds., Matthew may well have been one of the accounts used by Luke. Ultimately, whether Mark abbreviated Matthew's discourses and expanded Matthew's narratives (the minority view), or whether Matthew adapted Mark's narrative to his discourses derived from Q (consensus view), what matters most to the church is the meaning of the Gospels as literary and theological wholes. Redaction criticism's emphasis on the Gospels as carefully edited documents leads us in a direction away from form and source criticism and brings us to literary or narrative criticism.

Narrative Criticism: The Gospels as Literature

The impossibility of arriving at certainty in solving the synoptic problem and the atomizing tendencies of form and source-critical studies have led some scholars to focus on the literary aspects of the Gospels and Acts. Literary criticism is a huge discipline with numerous theories and approaches. Narrative criticism is a way of

---

99. R. T. France, *Matthew: Evangelist and Theologian* (Grand Rapids: Zondervan, 1989); Ralph Martin, *Mark: Evangelist and Theologian* (Grand Rapids: Zondervan, 1972); I. Howard Marshall, *Luke: Historian and Theologian* (Grand Rapids: Zondervan, 1970; enlarged ed., 1989).

100. E.g., Craig Blomberg, *Matthew* (Nashville: Broadman, 1992); D. A. Carson, *Matthew*, The Expositors Bible Commentary Revised Edition, 2 vols. (Grand Rapids; Zondervan, 2010); Darrell Bock, *Luke*, 2 vols. (Grand Rapids: Baker, 1994, 96).

101. On this question see Robert H. Gundry, *Matthew*, 2nd ed. (Grand Rapids: Eerdmans, 1994), 621–22.

doing literary analysis of the Gospels and Acts that has appealed to many scholars. Broadly considered, narrative criticism begins with genre analysis (see chapter 1) and develops a method that is consistent with the phenomena of the Gospels and Acts as narratives that are historically based, pastorally motivated, and skillfully written. Narrative criticism draws conclusions about meaning and theology by comparing the parts of a narrative to the entire narrative rather than to its putative sources. According Powell, in order to read the Gospels as narratives "it is necessary to know everything that the text assumes the reader knows and to 'forget' everything that the text does not assume the reader knows."[102] In other words, narrative criticism implies a sort of world that the reader inhabits. The reader seeks to know everything about that world, and pays no attention to other worlds.[103]

If the Gospels are viewed as theologically interpreted history, written for the edification of Christian communities, narrative criticism is an appropriate way to study them. The Gospels functioned as living wholes within those communities, not as cadavers to be dissected or as layers of wallpaper to be peeled off or spread over previous layers. The preoccupation of modern scholars with uncovering the history of the traditions they find in the Synoptics is understandable and commendable, but such an approach was hardly that of ancient Christian communities. It is unlikely that such communities read one Gospel as an overlay of a previous Gospel, and it is difficult today to utilize source critical methodology for Gospel studies in the context of church ministry.

Ryken comments that "the most basic of all artistic principles is unity. The literary approach to the Bible accordingly looks for literary patterns and wholeness of effect."[104] Accordingly, narrative criticism focuses on the overall unity of the Gospels and Acts and how that unity is achieved individually by the features of each book. Segmenting the narrative into its individual scenes and noting the transitional seams between the scenes is essential, as is analyzing the ordering of the scenes as chronological or thematic. Such "narrative patterns" involve a number of structures, such as repetition of simi-

---

102. Mark Alan Powell, *What Is Narrative Criticism?* (Minneapolis: Fortress, 1990), 20.

103. Among many studies of biblical narrative and narrative criticism, see especially Robert Alter, *The Art of Biblical Narrative* (New York: Basic, 1981); Ada Berlin, *The Poetics of Biblical Narrative* (Sheffield: Almond, 1983); J. P. Fokkelman, *Reading Biblical Narrative* (Louisville: Westminster, 1999); James L. Resseguie, *Narrative Criticism of the New Testament* (Grand Rapids: Baker, 2005); Leland Ryken, *Words of Delight* (Grand Rapids: Baker, 1987), 35–156; Ryken, *Words of Life* (Grand Rapids: Baker, 1987), 29–87.

104. Leland Ryken, *How to Read the Bible as Literature* (Grand Rapids: Zondervan, 1984), 29.

lar stories, contrast between opposite stories, comparisons of similar stories, pivotal stories, climactic stories, inclusions, and chiasms.[105] Familiarity with subgenres, forms, and figures of speech embedded in stories further enhances the method's effectiveness.

Basic principles of how stories work—setting, characterization, plot, and point of view—are key to the method. These principles have been discussed at least as far back as Aristotle's *Poetics*. Setting involves the place, time, and culture of the various locales in the ancient Mediterranean world. Students will do well to understand that world from the standpoint of historical geography because such information is essential not only for historical and cultural insight but also reveals the world from which metaphors and other figures of speech are drawn. Characterization has to do with protagonists and antagonists, as well as with characters who are prominent and those who simply support and provide texture for the main characters. Plot is a feature not only of each book as a whole, but also of sections of the books, and even of each pericope taken individually. Plots are described as tragedies if an original serendipitous situation goes bad (often due to an antagonist) or as comedic if a problem is resolved and "they all live happily ever after" (often due to a protagonist). Point of view has to do with the author's worldview and ethic, and how that perspective informs the narrative. That perspective may or may not be immediately obvious to the intuitive reader. At times point of view is supplied by subtle features of the story or by explicit comments of the author inserted at strategic points in the story.

Pennington has written about such matters, and his use of "Freytag's Pyramid" is helpful in analyzing and communicating how individual stories work in the Bible.[106] According to Freytag (based to a degree on Aristotle's *Poetics*), stories typically introduce tension, bring it to a head, and then resolve it.[107] This sequence seems to be true of both tragedic and comedic plot movements. The model is applicable not only to individual narrative pericopes, but also to larger sections of narrative books. In God's providence, the model may even be applied to the metanarrative of the Bible as a whole.

---

105. Powell (*What Is Narrative Criticism?* 32–34) cites the work of David Bauer and others in identifying fifteen different organizational or compositional patterns in relating narrative pericopae.

106. Jonathan T. Pennington, *Reading the Gospels Wisely* (Grand Rapids: Baker, 2012), 172–75.

107. Gustav Freytag lived from 1816–1896. His *Die Technik des Dramas* was originally published in 1863. A recent English translation is *Freytag's Technique of the Drama*, trans. Elias MacEwan (Charleston SC: Biblio Bazaar, 2008).

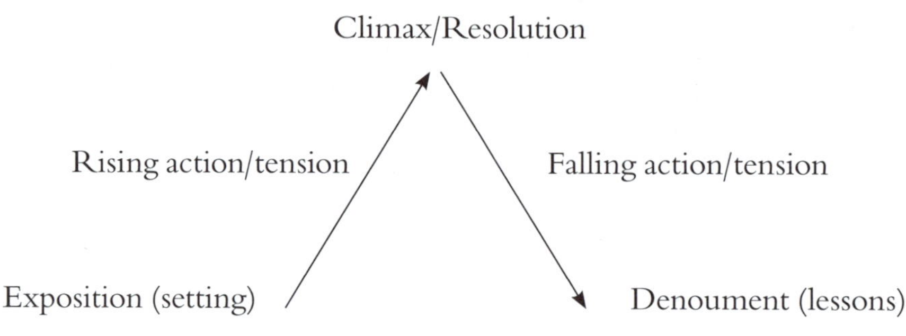

In narrative criticism, the attitude or mindset of the reader should come into alignment with the point of view of the author by seeking the author's answers to the author's questions based on the narrative world the author has provided, nothing more and nothing less. This hermeneutic is one of sympathy, not suspicion. As shown in the table below, the creative presentation of the story of Jesus and the apostles in the Gospels and Acts should engage the empathy of readers, drawing them into the story as active participants who share in both the foibles and victories of the protagonists, leading to character transformation, wisdom for life, and greater anticipation of God's ultimate *shalom*.

Interpreting the Gospels as Chronicles or Narratives[108]	
Historical Chronicle	**Literary Narrative**
Fidelity	Creativity
Detached objectivity	Engaged empathy
What happened	How it happened
Knowing facts	Sharing an experience
Passive spectators	Active participants
Information	Transformation

Given the genre of the Gospels and Acts as theologically interpreted biography/history and their canonical function as Holy Scripture, narrative criticism is more useful than form or source criticism for the study and teaching of the Gospels in a church context. If one is convinced of a theory of literary interdependence between the Gospels, redaction criticism can go hand in hand with narrative criticism. Both seek to understand the Gospels as wholes. Even if one is not convinced of the literary interdependence of the Gospels, one may still compare and contrast the narratives to determine what each emphasizes. A weakness of literary criticism in general and of narrative criticism in particular is the potential diminishing or even neglecting of historical referents and matters. The historicity of the literature is viewed as beside the point of literary studies. When Holy Scripture is engaged from an evangelical theological viewpoint, however, the historical events interpreted by the literary sources retain high value for theological teaching and pastoral ministry.

Just as no key unlocks every door, no single method answers every question posed in Gospel studies. Students of the Gospels and Acts should strive for methodological eclecticism. The exegesis and teaching of biblical narrative is both a science and an art in that one must know how to study the Gospels methodologically as well as when to use the art of applying the appropriate method to the text. Chapter 7 will provide examples of how to apply various methods to texts.

Chapter in Review

Because the text of the Gospels and Acts must be established before it can be studied, this chapter began with an overview of the transmission of the text, an explanation of different approaches to textual criticism, and two examples. Since translating the text is the next step, the chapter discussed the two major theories of Bible translation and provided examples of the results that are achieved when they are implemented. Finally, the chapter provided overviews of methods used in studying how the Gospels and Acts came into existence and how they function as literature.

---

108. This table is based on ideas gleaned from Ryken, *How to Read*, 33–34. Clearly the table's distinction between chronicle and narrative is facile, yet it raises important questions about genre as well as interpretation of biblical narrative. Conservative evangelicals may need to bring more of the right column of the table into their thinking about biblical narrative.

5

INTERPRETING PASSAGES IN THE GOSPELS AND ACTS

The Chapter at a Glance

An ideal comprehensive exegetical method begins with establishing the text to be exegeted, grasping its genre, and understanding its social-cultural-historical setting. These aspects of exegesis have already been discussed. This chapter focuses on the linguistic aspects of exegesis, which include translating the text from its original language into that of the exegete and analyzing the original language in terms of its structure, syntax, and key words. Interpreting passages in the Gospels and Acts begins with a wise approach to translation. Displaying the text visually might also be helpful in grasping the overall flow and understanding difficult syntactical constructions. Once the text has been initially translated, additional study of how its key words, phrases, and clauses coalesce to create meaning is needed. What remains is relating the text's meaning to other biblical texts (biblical theology) with awareness of one's own theological allegiances (historical theology) and ministry setting (pastoral theology and homiletics).[1]

---

1. Commendable summaries of exegetical method include Craig L. Blomberg with Jennifer Foutz Markley, *Handbook of New Testament Exegesis* (Grand Rapids: Baker, 2010); Richard J. Erickson, *A Beginner's Guide to New Testament Exegesis* (Downers Grove, IL: InterVarsity, 2005; Gordon D. Fee, *New Testament Exegesis: A Handbook for Students and Pastors*, 3rd ed. (Louisville: Westminster/Knox, 2002); George H. Guthrie and J. Scott Duvall, *Biblical Greek Exegesis* (Grand Rapids: Zondervan, 1998); Stanley E. Porter, ed. *Handbook to the Exegesis of the New Testament* (Leiden: Brill, 1997).

TRANSLATING THE TEXT

Segmenting the Text

ONCE THE TEXT HAS BEEN ESTABLISHED, the first step in translation
is determining the limits of the text to be translated. The choice of a
text for translation, study, and teaching should not be a random decision
based only on a momentary impression of a text's power or relevance.
Momentary impressions should be complemented by effort to understand
a memorable text's context. The narratives found in the Gospels and Acts
tell the story of Jesus and the early church in *pericopes*. The term pericope
refers to an individual narrative unit, scene, or episode. The author ar-
ranges such units sequentially or serially in chronological or topical/the-
matic order. One may choose to work through an entire pericope or a
discrete portion of a pericope. If only a portion of the pericope is chosen,
one should be aware of the need to understand that portion's relationship
to the pericope as a whole, and the role of that pericope in the entire book.

For example, if one were studying Luke-Acts and wanted to do translation work in Acts 2, one would note that the larger pericope of Acts
2:1–47 describes the coming of the Spirit promised by John the Baptist
(Luke 3:16) and Jesus (Luke 11:13; 12:12; 24:49; Acts 1:4–8; 2:33), a
coming understood by Peter as the fulfillment of Joel 2:28–32 (Acts
2:17–21). Tracing the flow of the pericope indicates that the sound accompanying the coming of the Spirit (2:1–4) drew the attention of a
large crowd of pilgrims and residents of Jerusalem who did not understand the significance of the disciples' speaking in tongues (2:5–13).
Peter's responding "sermon" (2:14–36) asserted that God was fulfilling
Joel 2:28–32 by raising Jesus from the dead and exalting him to his
right hand, effectively reversing the sinful crucifixion of Jesus. Peter
then commanded repentance and baptism for those who were convicted by his message as the means by which they would also receive the
Spirit (2:37–40). Around 3,000 people welcomed Peter's message and
were added to the dynamic community of Jesus's disciples (2:37–47).
The choice to translate, study, and teach from a text like Acts 2 should
keep the text's flow in mind, making sure not to compromise the point
of the whole story by focusing randomly on a part of it.

Translation

General Procedure. First, work toward a formal correspondence-type
translation,[2] but make sure your translation makes sense in idiomatic

---

2. We are now applying the major approaches to translation theory previously discussed in
chapter 4.

English. When you have finished your own work, compare it to word-based translations such as ESV, NASB, and KJV. Note any significant differences and check your work for errors. Next, compose a functional equivalence translation by considering how better to render ideas that are unclear when individual words are rendered formally. Think about obscure words, ancient metaphors that are not clear to your current audience, and other details that would likely be unclear to someone without academic biblical training. Compare your finished work to idea-based translations like NIV and NLT. Finally, from your functional equivalence translation, compose an expanded paraphrase that expounds the big ideas of the passage. Compare your paraphrase to LB and The Message.

Specific Steps. The following steps are advised for the initial formal correspondence translation of a passage:

- Segment the text, looking for each clause (a complete thought with noun and verb implied if not explicitly stated). Spotting conjunctions and noting the punctuation supplied by the editors of current editions of the NT are necessary for this step.
- Find, identify, parse, and provide a preliminary translation of the finite verbs.
- Find, identify, parse, and provide a preliminary translation of any associated verbal forms (participles, infinitives).
- Working from form to function, look for the primary nouns and pronouns that are directly related to the verbs in subject and predicate constructions.
    - nominative case: subjects and (when the verb is εἰμί or ὑπάρχω) predicates
    - genitive case: descriptors of various head nouns
    - dative case: indirect objects, means, adverbial constructions
    - accusative case: direct objects, adverbial constructions
- Note other supporting components in the clauses, such as adjectival structures, relative pronoun clauses, prepositional phrases, and adverbs.
- Provide a preliminary translation of each clause based on the preceding steps.
- Note the conjunctions that link the clauses and show the logical flow of the text. Make sure your translation of the individual clauses has accurately linked the clauses to one another.
- Distinguish between the coordinate and subordinate clause relationships (addition/*parataxis* and association/*hypotaxis*). Keep in mind the next step in exegesis, the visual display of the text clause by clause.

Useful Tools for Translation. Students who are looking to improve their translation skills will find help in various "readers" of biblical Greek.[3] These large-format workbooks aid students in working through selected texts by providing instructions on the translation process as well as notes on difficult words and syntax encountered in the selected texts. Similar although less comprehensive help may be found for the entire NT in grammatical aids books.[4] Thorough treatments of individual NT books designed to help translators are most helpful.[5]

Although parsing verbs is sometimes viewed as the bane of Greek studies, the task may be simplified by an overall grasp of basic tense-forms or principal parts of Greek verbs. Most basic Greek grammars provide an overview of the formulas or components of each tense-form. Irregular verbs often occur frequently and are recognizable by sheer repetition.[6] Recognition of unknown vocabulary words is another difficulty encountered in translation. Various sources are available to help with vocabulary knowledge by focusing on word frequency and cognates.[7] Use of BDAG for initial glossing of Greek words is rather cumbersome; shorter lexicons are more useful for this task.[8] Translators will also be helped by "readers' lexicons," which provide glosses of uncommon Greek words in a verse-by-verse rather than alphabetical format.[9] Similar help may be obtained

---

3. E.g., Rodney J. Decker, *Koine Greek Reader* (Grand Rapids: Kregel, 2007); William Mounce, *A Graded Reader of Biblical Greek* (Grand Rapids: Zondervan, 1996). Mounce's book also includes discussion and examples of phrasing and a helpful synthesis of Dan Wallace's *Greek Grammar beyond the Basics.*

4. E.g., Cleon L. Rogers Jr. and Cleon L. Rogers III, *The New Linguistic and Exegetical Key to the Greek New Testament; A Grammatical Analysis of the Greek New Testament.*

5. E.g., the Baylor University Press Handbook on the Greek New Testament series. Currently eight volumes are available, including one on Acts. See further http://www.baylorpress.com/en/Series/3/Baylor%20Handbook%20on%20the%20Greek%20New%20Testament. Kregel has begun the similar Big Greek Idea series with the publication of Herb W. Bateman and Aaron C. Peer, *John's Letters: An Exegetical Guide for Preaching and Teaching* (Grand Rapids: Kregel, 2018). See also the United Bible Societies' Handbook series, published with the needs of translators in mind. Handbooks are available for all four Gospels and Acts. See further http://www.ubs-translations.org/publications/ubs_handbook_series.

6. Jon C. Laansma and Randall K. Gauthier provide help with such verbs in *The Handy Guide to Difficult and Irregular Greek Verbs* (Grand Rapids: Kregel, 2017).

7. Bruce M. Metzger, *Lexical Aids for Students of New Testament Greek*, 3rd ed. (Grand Rapids: Baker, 1997); Warren C. Trenchard, *The Complete Vocabulary Guide to the Greek New Testament*, rev. ed. (Grand Rapids: Zondervan, 1998); Robert E. Van Voorst, *Building Your New Testament Greek Vocabulary* (Grand Rapids: Eerdmans, 1990).

8. E.g., Barclay M. Newman, *A Concise Greek-English Dictionary of the New Testament*, rev. ed. (Stuttgart: Deutsche Bibelgesellschaft, 2010). Certain editions of the UBS[5rev] and NA[28] Greek NT's include this lexicon. One of its helpful features is listing many irregular verb stems in alphabetical order along with the other words.

9. E.g., Michael H. Burer and Jeffrey E. Miller, *A New Reader's Lexicon of the Greek New Testament* (Grand Rapids: Kregel, 2008). This resource appears to be an improvement on Sakae Kubo,

by using "readers' editions" of the Greek NT, which provide glosses for uncommon words at the bottom of each page.[10]

Of course, software resources such as Accordance provide immediate access to data related to parsing and glossing Greek words. Having this information instantly available "at the click of the mouse" is a great time-saver. Such resources, however, supply only raw data, not the knowledge and skill that are required to understand and apply the data to translation, exegesis, and teaching. When students lack personal time and experience with the text, they cannot wisely utilize and apply the information. When students are developing their own knowledge of Greek grammar and syntax, software applications are very useful. Software is not a substitute for personal knowledge of Greek; it is helpful only to those whose hard work with the original biblical languages enables them to utilize

Case Study. Acts 2:37 describes the immediate response of some who heard Peter's sermon:

Ἀκούσαντες δὲ κατενύγησαν τὴν καρδίαν εἶπόν τε πρὸς τὸν Πέτρον καὶ τοὺς λοιποὺς ἀποστόλους· τί ποιήσωμεν, ἄνδρες ἀδελφοί;

The following comments implement the specific translation steps suggested above:

- Noting conjunctions and punctuation first, the postpositive δὲ expresses sequential transition from the sermon to the response. The next clause is linked to the first by the postpositive sequential particle τε.[11] This second clause contains the conjuction καὶ, which links the two objects of the verb εἶπόν. The end of this second clause is signaled by the editors' insertion of ·, equivalent to a colon or semicolon in conventional English punctuation. This insertion leads to a short question and a comma before the vocative construction indicating to whom the question is intended. Taking note of the above leads to the following clause divisions:

A Reader's Greek-English Lexicon of the New Testament (Grand Rapids: Zondervan, 2015), originally published in 1971.

10. E.g., Richard J. Goodrich and Albert L. Lukaszewski, *A Reader's Greek New Testament*, 3rd ed. (Grand Rapids: Zondervan, 2015). This edition footnotes and glosses words that occur less than thirty times in the NT. See also Barclay M. Newman and Florian Voss, *The Greek New Testament: A Reader's Edition* (Stuttgart: German Bible Society, 2014). This edition is based on the UBS[5] Greek NT. It footnotes and glosses NT words occurring less than thirty times and parses certain difficult words.

11. τε occurs 215 times in the NT, most frequently (around 150 times) in Acts. Its use is often the occasion of textual variants that have δέ. Cf. BDAG, s.v. τε (993).

(1) Ἀκούσαντες δὲ
(2) κατενύγησαν τὴν καρδίαν
(3) εἶπόν τε πρὸς τὸν Πέτρον καὶ τοὺς λοιποὺς ἀποστόλους·
(4) τί ποιήσωμεν, ἄνδρες ἀδελφοί;

- In terms of verb forms, clause (1) transitions from Peter's sermon with the circumstantial/temporal participle Ἀκούσαντες into clause (2) where the finite indicative verb κατενύγησαν speaks of the hearers' conviction. Clause (3) uses the common verb εἶπόν to lead into the response/question of the convicted hearers. Clause (4) uses the subjunctive ποιήσωμεν in a real, deliberative question directed to Peter and his apostolic colleagues.
- In terms of supporting constructions, τὴν καρδίαν in clause (2) is apparently an adverbial accusative of reference/respect that describes the nature of the conviction of Peter's hearers. In clause (3) there is a long prepositional phrase (πρὸς . . .) with a compound object. The second element of that object is an attributive adjective construction (τοὺς λοιποὺς ἀποστόλους). Clause (4) begins with the interrogative pronoun τί, signaling its function of the clause. This clause ends with the double vocative ἄνδρες ἀδελφοί, which appears to emphasize the earnestness of the question.
- In terms of clause relations, clause (1) with the participle Ἀκούσαντες is a subordinate clause describing the occasion of clause (2), the main clause, which states that hearing led to conviction. In clause (3) the main verb has as its object the subordinate clause (4) that expresses the hearers' question. The movement is from *hearing* to *conviction* that prompted the *interrogative* about what *to do*.

A strictly word-based or *formal correspondence* translation of Acts 2:37 would be "Having heard, they were pierced in heart and they said to Peter and the remaining apostles, 'What should we do, men, brothers?'" A somewhat less-stilted, more idea-based or *functional equivalence* translation would be "When they heard, they felt deep remorse. So they said to Peter and the rest of the apostles, 'Brothers, what should we do?'" Moving further from the words to the gist of the text's meaning would result in an *expanded paraphrase* such as "Hearing Peter's sermon left them heartbroken with deep, gut-wrenching guilt. It was like they had been stabbed in the heart. They could only cry out to Peter, 'What can we do now?'"

One question that arises in moving from a strict verbal correspondence toward an expanded paraphrase of the ideas of the verse is whether to render κατενύγησαν metaphorically in terms of its etymology or to render the word-picture of stabbing more prosaically. The following spectrum of translations moves from the first five that utilize the etymology of the verb to the second five that abandon the implied word-picture and focus on the abstract concept of remorse:

- "they were pricked in their heart" (KJV, ASV 1901)
- "they were pierced to the heart" (NASB, CSB)
- "they were cut to the heart" (ESV, NAB, NIV, NKJV, NRSV)
- "Peter's words pierced their hearts" (NLT)
- "Cut to the quick, they . . ." (Message)
- "they felt guilty" (NCV)
- "they had compunction in their heart" (Douay-Rheims 1899)
- "these words of Peter's moved them deeply" (LB)
- "they were acutely distressed" (NET)

Deciding how to render words like κατενύγησαν will put one's view of translation theory to the test. Translating this word as "they were pricked" seems almost as understated and bland as translating it as "they felt guilty." "They were cut to the heart" is accurate and idiomatic, and it has been adopted by many translations, including ESV and NIV. NLT's "Peter's words pierced their hearts" may best capture the deep conviction and remorse that resulted from Peter's sermon. We will revisit this expression as a case study for word study methodology below.

EXEGETING THE TEXT

The translation process itself is the beginning of the exegetical process, yet understanding the biblical text *begins* with the work of the Spirit in one's life, as we have just seen in Acts 2:37. The early teaching one receives as a Christian is instrumental in shaping provisional personal understandings of biblical texts, including their language, genre, meaning, and setting. Subsequent personal study of the Bible leads to varying degrees of revision to one's previous understandings as all the elements of the text are reciprocally understood in a more accurate fashion. Texts can be approached "from the outside in," that is, from the larger components to the smaller, as in the three applications below of the Freytag's pyramid model, to successively smaller units of text. Texts can also be understood "from the inside out," that is, from the smaller components to the larger. Both approaches are valid as long as students maintain the ongoing dialogue between their understanding of the text as a whole and their understanding of its parts. The following discussion of exegetical method will proceed "from the outside in," that is, from the larger components to the smaller, from the *structure* of the pericope as a whole and its component paragraphs to the *syntax* of its sentences, clauses, and phrases to its individual *words*. Three methods of visualizing the structure and syntax of the text will also be explained and illustrated.

Structure and Syntax

The history of analysis of Greek grammar and the theories spawned in that endeavor spans thousands of years and shows no signs of ending.[12] Analysis of Greek syntax (how words are put together into larger semantic units) is a key skill for those who wish to read the Greek NT closely. Traditionally, intermediate and advanced Greek grammars provide detailed taxonomies of the various nuances of Greek article and the various cases of its nouns, along with the tenses, voices, and moods of its verbs and the relationships of its clauses. There are many respected comprehensive grammars,[13] as well as specialized studies of individual issues.[14] Various handbooks provide step-by-step instructions for syntactical analysis.[15] There are helpful sources that show the relevance of theoretical linguistics for NT Greek studies.[16] Recent studies of Greek syntax have integrated linguistic insights into the traditional approach.[17]

---

12.   David Alan Black, "The Study of New Testament Greek in the Light of Ancient and Modern Linguistics," in D. A. Black and D. S. Dockery, eds. *New Testament Criticism and Interpretation* (Grand Rapids: Zondervan, 1991), 379–406; Campbell, *Advances*, 29–50.

13.   Presently the work that deserves top billing is Daniel B. Wallace, *Greek Grammar Beyond the Basics: An Exegetical Syntax of New Testament Greek* (Grand Rapids: Zondervan, 1996). Among other traditional treatments, see especially BDF: F. Blass and A. DeBrunner, *A Greek Grammar of the New Testament and Other Early Christian Literature*, trans. and rev. R. W. Runk (Chicago: University of Chicago Press, 1979); C. F. D. Moule, *An Idiom Book of New Testament Greek*, 2nd ed. (Cambridge: Cambridge University Press, 1959); A. T. Robertson, *A Grammar of the Greek New Testament in the Light of Historical Research*, 4th ed. (New York: Hodder, 1923); Nigel Turner, *Syntax*, vol 3 of *A Grammar of New Testament Greek*, ed. J. H. Moulton, 4 vols. (Edinburgh: Clark, 1908–76; vol. 3, 1963); G. B. Winer, *A Treatise on the Grammar of New Testament Greek*, 3rd ed., trans. and rev. W. F. Moulton (Edinburgh: Clark, 1882); M. Zerwick, *Biblical Greek Illustrated by Examples* (Rome: Pontifical Biblical Institute, 1963). Works that are more indebted to linguistics and recent research include David L. Mathewson and Elodie Ballantine Emig, *Intermediate Greek Grammar* (Grand Rapids: Baker, 2016), and Richard A. Young, *Intermediate New Testament Greek: A Linguistic and Exegetical Approach* (Nashville: B&H, 1994).

14.   E.g., Murray J. Harris, *Prepositions and Theology in the Greek New Testament* (Grand Rapids: Zondervan, 2012).

15.   E.g., Blomberg and Markley, *Handbook*, 143–65; Darrell Bock and Buist Fanning, *Interpreting the New Testament* (Wheaton, IL: Crossway, 2006), 57–72; Fee, *NT Exegesis*, 92–99; Scot McKnight, *Introducing New Testament Interpretation* (Grand Rapids: Baker, 1990), 75–95.

16.   Campbell's chapter "Linguistic Theories" (*Advances*, 51–71) helpfully summarizes relevant aspects of current linguistic thought. See also John Beekman and John Callow, *Translating the Word of God* (Grand Rapids: Zondervan, 1974); David Alan Black, *Linguistics for Students of New Testament Greek* (Grand Rapids: Baker, 1988); Peter Cotterell and Max Turner, *Linguistics and Biblical Interpretation* (Downers Grove, IL: InterVarsity, 1989); Moisés Silva, *God, Language, and Scripture* (Grand Rapids: Zondervan, 1990).

17.   E.g., Stanley A. Porter, *Idioms of the Greek New Testament*, 2nd ed. (London: Continuum, 1999); Matthewson and Emig, *Intermediate Greek Grammar*; Steven E. Runge, *Discourse*

Basics. The word "structure" commonly appears in discussions of biblical exegesis, but it means different things to different people. In the ensuing discussion the term simply denotes features of the text intended by the author to mark its narrative flow.

Syntactical analysis can take many forms and utilize many terms. Perhaps the most basic is the recognition that sentences have basic *content* words and variable structure or *function* words.[18] Content and function words may be compared to the bricks of a building (nouns and verbs) that are held together by the mortar (articles, adjectives, adverbs, prepositions, conjunctions). The function words' varied interrelationships with the content words lead to the many syntactical patterns that form the sentences, paragraphs, pericopes, and books of biblical narrative. These syntactical patterns or constructs—not the individual word-bricks from which they are built—are the locus of meaning. Meaning is a property of structure, not of a random pile of bricks or a bag of cement.

Sequential propositions in a discourse either *add* a new proposition to the previous one or *associate* a subproposition with the previous one. Added clauses are called coordinated independent clauses (*parataxis*), and associated clauses are called subordinated dependent clauses (*hypotaxis*). This basic structural distinction plays out several different basic or *kernel* sentence patterns. Black has six such patterns,[19] based on the nature of the verb:

- intransitive verbs: noun^{nom} + verb
  noun^{nom} + verb + adverb

- transitive verbs: noun^{nom} + verb + noun^{acc}
  noun^{nom} + verb + noun^{dat} + noun^{acc}

- linking verbs (e.g., εἰμί): noun^{nom} + verb + adjective^{nom}
  noun^{nom} + verb + noun^{nom}

The nouns and verbs in these six basic kernel sentence-types may expanded by the association of any number of function structures,

---

Grammar of the Greek New Testament (Peabody, MA: Hendrickson, 2010); Young, *Intermediate New Testament Greek.*

18. Black, *Linguistics,* 97–100; Rodney Decker, *Reading Koine Greek: An Introduction and Integrated Workbook* (Grand Rapids: Baker, 2014), 146–51.

19. Black, *Linguistics,* 102–6. In the above schematic, any of the nouns may be determined or modified with articles or adjectives. Decker provides a similar approach with NT examples in *Reading Koine Greek,* 146–51. See also the more detailed discussion of R. W. Funk in *A Beginning-Intermediate Grammar of Hellenistic Greek,* 3 vols. (Missoula, MT: Scholars, 1973), 2.377–91.

such as genitive constructions, prepositional phrases, adverbial participles, and relative pronouns clauses.[20] These expansions lead to the complex, dense syntax noted at times by anyone who attempts to translate and exegete the Greek NT. Such complexity will be much less problematic to the student who is developing the skills to distinguish between content words and function words and to discern the basic patterns summarized above.

Recent Developments. Campbell has provided a summary of recent developments in the study of NT Greek, including lexical semantics, deponency and the middle voice, verbal aspect, and discourse analysis.[21] Of these items, verbal aspect may be most significant for NT exegesis. Speaking very broadly, the discussion is over whether tense-forms mark or grammaticalize time. Traditional discussions of the Greek tenses tend to affirm that both time and type of action is conveyed by the indicative mood, but that the other moods convey only aspect or type of action. Problems with this understanding include the occasional use of the aorist for present or future events (e.g., John 13:31; Rom. 8:30)[22] and the common use of the present tense in narratives of past events.[23] Current discussion centers on whether any Greek tense form, including indicative mood forms, convey time of action. Some scholars argue that the time element is never morphologically marked by a feature like the verbal augment but is rather to be determined solely from deictic (contextual) factors.[24] Others take a more mediating position on the matter.[25]

---

20.   Black, *Linguistics*, 108–14.

21.   Campbell, *Advances*, 72–191. Lexical semantics will be discussed below in the word-studies section.

22.   Such aorists have been called proleptic or futuristic and understood to describe future events as certain (as good as already accomplished) due to the plan or promise of God. See Wallace, *Greek Grammar*, 563–64. See D. A. Carson, *Exegetical Fallacies*, 2nd ed. (Grand Rapids: Baker, 1996), 68–73, for further discussion of dubious interpretations of the aorist.

23.   Such uses of the present tense are typically called historical or dramatic, and are understood to add occasional vividness to the narrative or to mark spots of special emphasis. See Wallace, *Greek Grammar*, 526–30. Runge thinks that such uses of the present tense mark what follows for special emphasis. See *Discourse Grammar*, 125–43.

24.   Rodney J. Decker, *Temporal Deixis of the Greek Verb in the Gospel of Mark with Reference to Verbal Aspect* (New York: Peter Lang, 2001).

25.   See further Constantine R. Campbell, *Verbal Aspect, the Indicative Mood, and Narrative* (New York: Peter Lang, 2007); Buist Fanning, *Verbal Aspect in New Testament Greek* (Oxford: Clarendon, 1990); Stanley D. Porter, *Verbal Aspect in the Greek of the New Testament with Reference to Tense and Mood* (New York: Peter Lang, 1989). Fanning's view is more cautious, while Campbell and Porter tend to agree with Decker that time is not a property of the indicative mood but is deduced from pragmataic or contextual factors.

Visual Display

During the process of translation and exegesis, educated guesses are made as to the logical flow of the various clauses and their status as coordinate or subordinate to the previous clause. These relationships can be visually plotted in various ways, leading to an analysis of the "shape" of the text. Three ways of visualizing texts will be discussed here: Freytag's pyramid, phrasing, and line diagramming.

Freytag's Pyramid. Freytag's pyramid[26] provides visualized literary analysis of narratives by displaying the rise and fall of dramatic tension as characters interact in various situations as the plot of a story unfolds. The pyramid can be applied to individual pericopes, thematic groups of pericopes, and even to entire books. Freytag's pyramid orientation seems to recognize the same literary phenomenon as that pictured by analyses of *inclusio* and *chiasmus*—stories tend to come full circle with a decisive pivotal point in the middle. Many scholars have proposed analyses of the Bible with the cross as the central pivotal point between Genesis and Revelation. It is clear that several themes from Genesis 1–2 are recapitulated in Revelation 21–22. Luke-Acts as a whole can be analyzed with this model. The story of Luke's Gospel begins in Jerusalem, mentions Jerusalem frequently as Jesus travels there, and culminates in Jerusalem with the passion of Jesus. The epochal passion of Jesus resolves the tensions featured in Luke as the gospel goes out from Jerusalem all the way to Rome in fulfillment of Jesus's promise.

Jerusalem at the Center of Luke-Acts

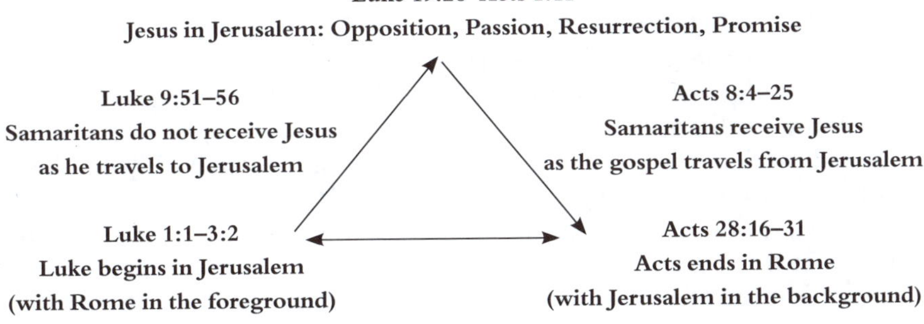

When one applies Freytag's pyramid to Acts 1–2, the promised coming of the Spirit (1:4–14) culminates in the phenomena of the Day of Pentecost (2:1–4), leading to the communal fellowship of the

---

26. Freytag's pyramid was explained in more detail in chapter 4.

disciples in Jerusalem (2:42–47). Peter speaks to the disciples in the days leading up to the anticipated coming of the Spirit, resulting in Matthias replacing Judas. Peter speaks to the crowd in the moments following the Spirit's coming, resulting in 3,000 people being baptized and uniting with the disciples. The disciples devoted themselves to united prayer in anticipation of the Spirit's coming (1:14), and they devoted themselves to prayer and other united activities after the realization of the Spirit's coming.[27] Jesus commanded that witness beginning at Jerusalem would follow the Spirit's coming, and Peter began to witness for Jesus in Jerusalem immediately after the Spirit's coming. The dual tension of an incomplete apostolate and an unfulfilled promise have been fulfilled, and the nascent church is experiencing daily conversions.

Acts 1–2: Pentecostal Promise and Fulfillment

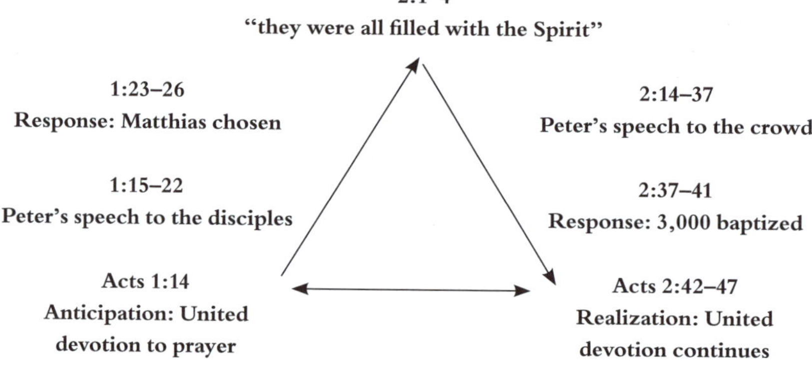

Acts 2:14–47 depicts Peter's sermon to the scoffers, a sermon that boldly accuses the Jews of crucifying their Messiah (2:22–23) before it confidently affirms that God raised him from the dead (2:24, 31–33). God dramatically reversed Jesus's apparent defeat in crucifixion; the resurrection demonstrates that Jesus is Lord and Messiah (2:36). There was mocking as Peter began to preach (2:13), and no doubt tension arose during the sermon, leading to deep conviction when Peter concluded (2:37). Peter's answer to his hearers' heartfelt question is the culmination of the sermon and the tension it caused (2:38–40). Peter's faith in the universal promise of God (2:39; cf. Joel 2:32/Acts 2:21) is

---

27. Compare 1:14 (οὗτοι πάντες ἦσαν προσκαρτεροῦντες ὁμοθυμαδὸν τῇ προσευχῇ) with 2:42 (Ἦσαν δὲ προσκαρτεροῦντες τῇ διδαχῇ τῶν ἀποστόλων καὶ τῇ κοινωνίᾳ, τῇ κλάσει τοῦ ἄρτου καὶ ταῖς προσευχαῖς) and 2:46 (καθ' ἡμέραν τε προσκαρτεροῦντες ὁμοθυμαδὸν ἐν τῷ ἱερῷ). Cf. Acts 6:4.

the basis of his answer to his convicted audience. The tension is resolved when 3,000 people respond to Peter's appeal by being baptized and joining the followers of Jesus. Their devotion to apostolic teaching, fellowship around the Lord's table, and prayer amounts to the resolution of their poignant question, "What shall we do?"

Acts 2:14–47: Believing God's Promise Brings Peace

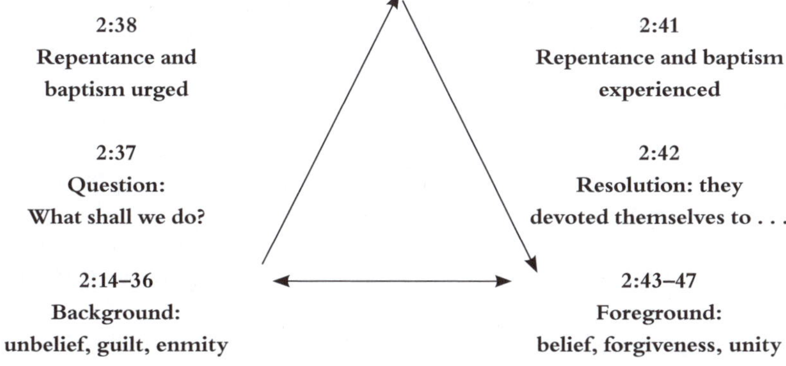

Phrasing. Another way of visually displaying a text is laying it out clause by clause. This approach is sometimes called phrasing.[28] The genius of phrasing is its visual implementation of the linguistic insight that successive clauses are either added to/coordinated with (*parataxis*) or associated with/subordinated to (*hypotaxis*) the previous clause. Starting with the left margin, a coordinate clause is arranged directly underneath the previous clause as if it were the parallel point in an outline. Subordinate clauses are indented under the previous clause. Phrasing can be done with a rough handwritten worksheet or with

---

28. E.g., Bock and Fanning, *Interpreting the NT*, 73–134; Blomberg with Markley, *Handbook*, 195–207; Fee, *New Testament Exegesis*, 41–58; Guthrie and Duvall, *Biblical Greek Exegesis*, 27–37; Scot McKnight, "New Testament Greek Grammatical Analysis," in *Introducing New Testament Interpretation*, ed. Scot McKnight (Grand Rapids: Baker, 1989), 75–95, esp. 89–95; Mounce, *A Graded Reader of Biblical Greek*, xv–xxiii, 10, 183–206. Mounce thinks that phrasing is not very effective for narrative because the flow of narrative is more obvious, and that phrasing "works best with theological passages" (xxiii). The distinction between narrative and "theological passages" is facile and dubious. Some may think that phrasing is tedious for longer narrative pericopes, but the effort expended will be rewarded with a clear grasp of the flow of the main plot of the passage as well as various asides, digressions, and subordinate clauses that support the main plot.

word processing software applications.[29] Depending on the complexity of the text and its levels of subordination, it may be best to use the landscape page format rather than the portrait format. Once the clauses have been laid out in this manner, the resulting display can be used as a worksheet for various types of additional observations, including:

- Adding comments on line-by-line logical flow in the right margin
- Using fonts (e.g., bold, italic, underline) to note various things
- Using color-coding for main verbs, repeated words
- Marking larger units of the text with double spacing
- Showing various connections with arrows and/or brackets

Phrasing is a simple method that is adaptable to each student's goals with each passage. Sometimes it will be helpful to distinguish only main clauses. At other times, subordinate clauses, prepositional phrases, and even parallel words may be placed on their own lines. The display below visualizes the flow of Acts 2:37–42, depicting the audience's question in 2:37 as the transition between Peter's sermon to the larger crowd (2:14–36) and his counsel to those from the crowd who were convicted by the sermon (2:38–40). The immediate outcome is portrayed in 2:41–42 as involving the baptism of 3,000 people and their ongoing attention to apostolic teaching, sharing around a common meal, and prayer. The larger pericope continues as 2:43–47 further describes the daily activities of the early church in Jerusalem. The basic technique of the diagram is simply indenting subordinate clauses. Additional techniques for visualization are as follows:

- Conjunctions are in bold font.
- Direct discourse is distinguished by italics.
- Interpretive comments are in parentheses to the right of the text itself.
- Syntactical and other exegetical observations are in footnotes.
- Double spacing has been used between 2:37 and 2:38 and between 2:40 and 2:41 to show the main units of the text. Along these lines, possibly there should also be double spacing added between 2:39 and 2:40.

---

29. I am a longtime user and advocate of Accordance Bible software. Downloadable text of the Greek NT is available from various websites. I regularly utilize the German Bible Society's site (http://www.academic-bible.com/en/online-bibles/about-the-online-bibles), where the texts of both UBS[5] and NA[28] are available, along with the Hebrew Bible, LXX, and Vulgate. The ESV and NET Bible are also available there.

Acts 2:37–42: Phrased Visual Display with Exegetical Notes

37   Ἀκούσαντες **δὲ**   (Transition from Peter's sermon)

        κατενύγησαν τὴν καρδίαν[30]   (Hearing Peter's words brought conviction)

        εἶπόν τε πρὸς τὸν Πέτρον **καὶ** τοὺς λοιποὺς ἀποστόλους·

        τί ποιήσωμεν,[31] ἄνδρες ἀδελφοί;   (Conviction led to a question)

38   Πέτρος **δὲ** πρὸς αὐτούς·   (Peter answered the question)

        μετανοήσατε, [φησίν,][32]   (Command 1)

        καὶ βαπτισθήτω ἕκαστος ὑμῶν   (Command 2)

              ἐπὶ τῷ ὀνόματι Ἰησοῦ Χριστοῦ[33]

              εἰς ἄφεσιν τῶν ἁμαρτιῶν[34] ὑμῶν

        καὶ λήμψεσθε[35] τὴν δωρεὰν τοῦ ἁγίου πνεύματος.[36]   (Promise)

39   ὑμῖν[37] **γάρ**[38] ἐστιν ἡ ἐπαγγελία   (Explanation of the promise)

           καὶ τοῖς τέκνοις ὑμῶν

           καὶ πᾶσιν τοῖς εἰς μακράν,

           ὅσους ἂν προσκαλέσηται κύριος ὁ θεὸς ἡμῶν.

40   ἑτέροις **τε** λόγοις πλείοσιν διεμαρτύρατο   (Editorial summary)

     καὶ παρεκάλει αὐτοὺς λέγων·

        σώθητε ἀπὸ τῆς γενεᾶς τῆς σκολιᾶς ταύτης.[39]

---

30.   The accusative with the passive verb is adverbial, likely expressing the reference or respect of the action.

31.   Aorist subjunctive in a deliberative question (one which sincerely seeks an answer).

32.   The textual tradition of Acts 2:38 has several variants. The editors of the NA and UBS texts place φησίν in brackets because of its presence in several early mss., but the word order is strange. Metzger's comment that the ellipsis of the verb of speech explains the rise of the other readings has merit (Bruce M. Metzger, *A Textual Commentary on the Greek New Testament*, 2nd ed. [Stuttgart: Deutsche Bibelgesellschaft, 1994], 261; cf. Acts 25:22; 26:28).

33.   The efficacy of the name of Jesus (τὸ ὄνομα Ἰησοῦ) is the basis of ministry in Acts (2:21; 3:6, 16; 4:7, 10, 12, 17, 30; 5:28, 40; 8:12, 16; 9:14–15, 21, 27–28; 10:48; 15:26; 16:18; 19:5, 13, 17; 21:13; 22:16; 26:9; cf. Luke 9:49; 10:17; 21:8, 12, 17; 24:47). Cf. BDAG, s.v. ὄνομα (711–14).

34.   The genitive is objective: God forgives the sins of those who repent and and are baptized.

35.   The predictive future indicative after two imperatives is equivalent to a protasis/apodosis. If Peter's hearers repent and are baptized, they will receive the Holy Spirit.

36.   The genitive is likely appositional. The gift *is* the Holy Spirit (Joel 2:28; Acts 1:5, 8; 2:17; 8:15, 17, 19; 10:47; 11:17; 19:2).

37.   ὑμῖν is the first of three datives of advantage that describe the intended recipients of the promise, leading into the indefinite relative clause ὅσους ἂν . . . (cf. Acts 2:21/Joel 2:32). All of this incrementally expresses the universal relevance of Peter's message for all humanity (Joel 2:28/Acts 2:17; cf. Isa. 57:19).

38.   As is typical, the γάρ clause explains the basis of Peter's answer, the promise in Acts 2:21/Joel 2:32.

39.   Luke's final excerpt from Peter's words (cf. Deut. 32:5; Ps. 78:8; Luke 9:41; 11:29; Phil. 2:15).

41   οἱ **μὲν οὖν**[40] ἀποδεξάμενοι τὸν λόγον αὐτοῦ ἐβαπτίσθησαν[41] (Response to Peter's answer)
καὶ προσετέθησαν ἐν τῇ ἡμέρᾳ ἐκείνῃ ψυχαὶ[42] ὡσεὶ τρισχίλιαι.   (Immediate)
42   Ἦσαν **δὲ** προσκαρτεροῦντες[43] τῇ διδαχῇ τῶν ἀποστόλων[44]   (Ongoing)
καὶ τῇ κοινωνίᾳ, τῇ κλάσει τοῦ ἄρτου[45]
καὶ ταῖς προσευχαῖς.

Line Diagramming. Traditionally, grade-school English teachers have used line diagrams to teach the parts of speech, the parts of sentences, and the relationships of clauses in a paragraph.[46] Some Greek teachers have adapted such diagramming for the analysis of NT syntax. The method is based on typical English word order: subject-verb-object.[47] According to a set scheme, each part of phrases, clauses, and sentences is placed in its own specific location on horizontal lines. Various intersecting vertical lines separate the parts of the sentence. Adjectival and adverbial modifiers are placed under their head nouns. Clauses are linked with dotted lines; with coordinate clauses the dotted lines are on the left margin, and with dependent clauses the dotted lines are in the middle of the page.

I have found the method to be useful in conceptually dense texts that have complex syntax, but line diagramming becomes tedious and atomistic when one applies it to lengthy segments of narrative that primarily contain a series of sequential coordinate (paratactic) clauses. In such passages I would recommend its use in the sections of a narrative that are didactic, sermonic, or editorial comments. Otherwise one is likely to lose the forest for the trees.

---

40.   As is typical, οὖν introduces a conclusion to what precedes or an inference based on it. Here, the outcome of Peter's appeal to his hearers was that 3,000 of them began to follow Jesus.

41.   Luke simply mentions the baptism of those who received Peter's message. Baptism presumes their prior repentance and leads to their reception of the promised Spirit.

42.   ψυχαὶ refers to people, not their "souls," as in the common LXX rendering of נֶפֶשׁ (cf. 2:43; 3:23; 7:14; 27:37). Cf. BDAG, s.v. ψυχή 3 (1098–1100).

43.   The periphrastic imperfect (cf. 1:14) describes the lifestyle of the early Jerusalem church.

44.   The genitive is subjective: the early believers were devoted to what the apostles taught. Cf. *Did.*

45.   The absence of the conjunction καὶ before τῇ κλάσει τοῦ ἄρτου may indicate that the fellowship spoken of here was specifically around the Lord's Table, or that the fellowship consisted in the table and prayer.

46.   Apparently this approach to analyzing English grammar may be traced back to the book *Higher Lessons in English*, published by Alonzo Reed and Brainerd Kellogg in 1877.

47.   This leads to a weakness of the method—Greek word order varies according to an author's style and emphasis. Line diagramming rearranges this original word order, removing the subtleties of the text as a text in order to display an analysis of the sentence-parts that are contained in the text.

A typical approach to line diagramming would look something like this:

Typical Approach to Line Diagramming[48]

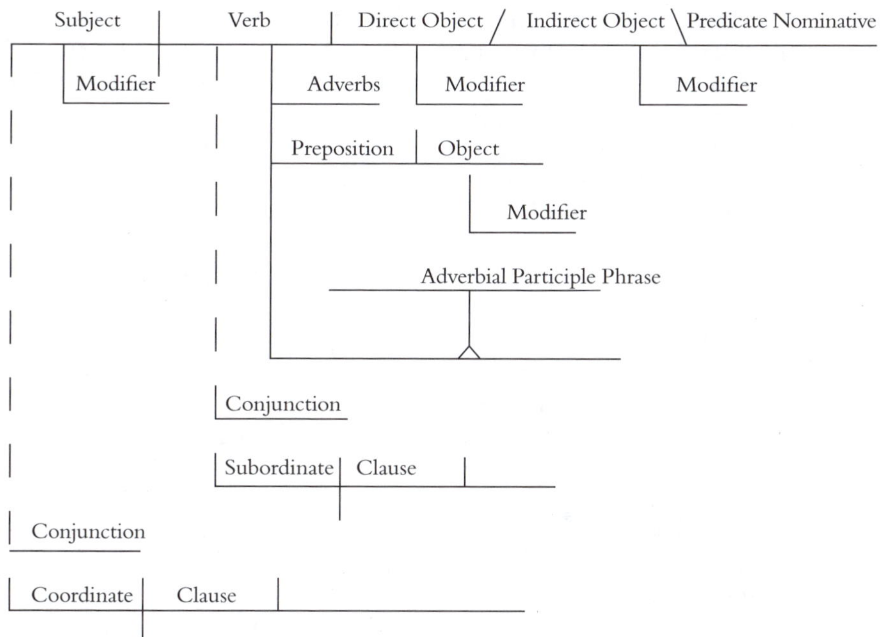

The part of Acts 2:37–42 that would most likely be illumined by a line diagram is Peter's reply to his questioners in 2:38–39. This text's syntactical complexity and theological importance makes it the sort of text within a larger narrative pericope that is most appropriate for a line diagram. Note the following about the line diagram that follows:

---

48. Detailed discussions and illustrations of line diagramming will be found in various books, including Lee L. Kantenwein, *Diagrammatical Analysis*, rev. ed. (Winona Lake, IN: BMH, 2005). Rodney J. Decker incrementally illustrates diagramming throughout *Reading Koine Greek: An Introduction and Integrated Workbook* (Grand Rapids: Baker, 2014). Software packages such as Accordance and Logos also provide aids for diagramming. Online resources include Lexel Software's "An Intermediate Guide to Greek Diagramming" (https://www. inthebeginning.org/ediagrams/documents/intermediategreektodiagramming.pdf).

- The real deliberative question[49] of 2:37 flows from the anguish of deep conviction. It leads to Peter's answer in 2:38–39. It is placed in the upper left section of the page.
- The main clause on which the bulk of 2:38–39 depends grammatically is Πέτρος δὲ πρὸς αὐτούς. It is placed in the left-middle of the page. The textually dubious φησίν adds a verb to this clause, one that was probably elided originally. The rest of 2:38–39, the content of Peter's reply to his listeners, amounts to the direct object of the elided verb.
- The main points of Peter's reply are expressed by two aorist imperatives and a predictive future indicative, μετανοήσατε . . . βαπτισθήτω . . . λήμψεσθε. These elements occupy the top right half of the page. It is likely that the two imperatives should be viewed as providing the conditional protasis for the future indicative apodosis.[50]
- An explanatory γάρ clause adds support to Peter's reply. The triple dative of advantage[51] construction (ὑμῖν . . . τέκνοις . . . πᾶσιν) gradually enlarges the intended recipients of the promise. This construction is placed on the bottom right half of the page.
- Finally, an indefinite relative clause[52] (ὅσους ἂν . . .) shows that the breadth of the γάρ clause (you, your children, all who are distant) is related to God's intent to call many to himself, as would be deduced from the key base-text of Peter's sermon, Joel 2:28–32 (Acts 2:17–21). Those who call upon the Lord's name (πᾶς ὃς ἂν ἐπικαλέσηται τὸ ὄνομα κυρίου; Acts 2:21/Joel 2:32) are those whom the Lord has called (ὅσους ἂν προσκαλέσηται κύριος ὁ θεὸς ἡμῶν; Acts 2:39).
- At first glance, line diagrams such as this one are imposing, even confusing. They can be useful, however, because they require every grammatical construction to be interpreted and displayed. This analytical process is probably more valuable than the resulting diagram, although the diagram's visual display itself should help with dense syntax. Line diagrams have their place in passages whose genre and content require close exegesis.

---

49. Wallace, *Greek Grammar beyond the Basics*, 465–67.

50. Wallace, *Greek Grammar beyond the Basics*, 489–92.

51. Wallace, *Greek Grammar beyond the Basics*, 142–44.

52. Wallace, *Greek Grammar beyond the Basics*, 478–79.

Line Diagram of Acts 2:38–39

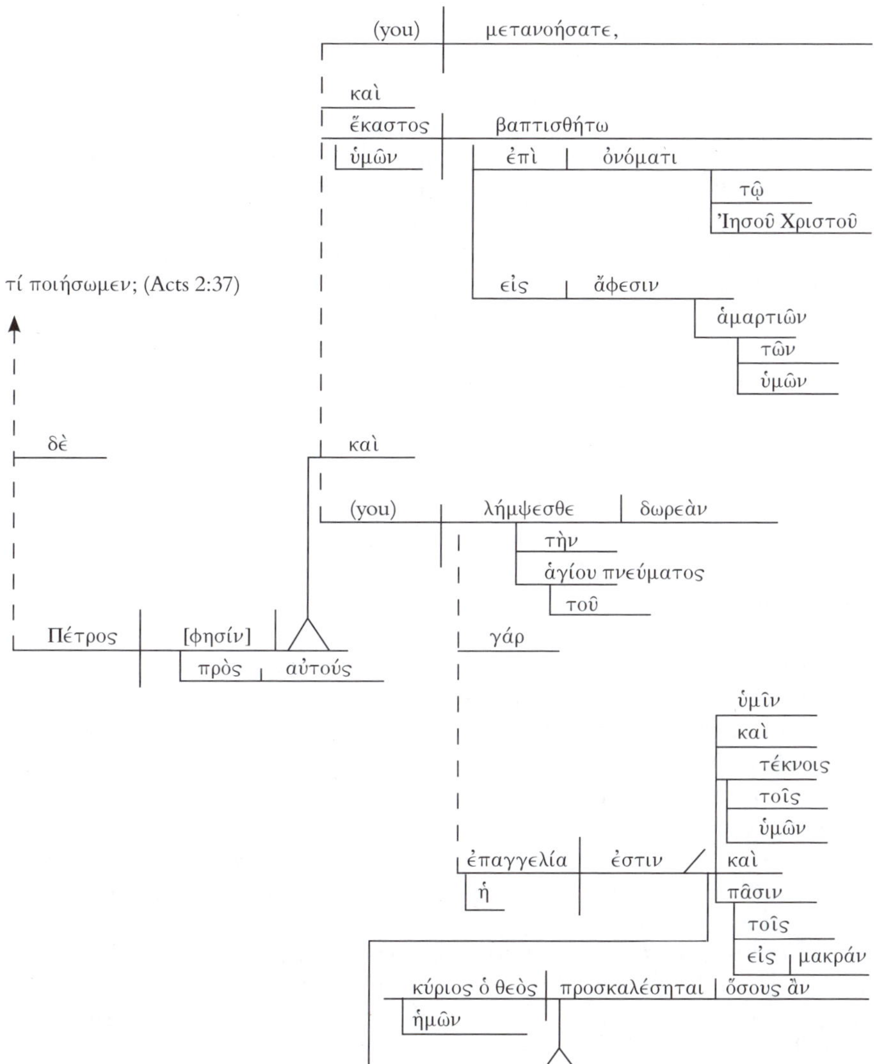

Words

Etymology. Although a word's **etymology** occasionally coincides with its actual meaning in context (e.g., "blackbird"), there are many words like "ladybird" and "butterfly" that show that etymology and meaning are not equivalent terms. Even so, one occasionally hears well-meaning Bible teachers expound the Gospel in terms of dynamite (δύναμις; Rom.

1:16), and speak of Christian giving as a hilarious activity (ἱλαρός; 2 Cor. 9:7). Along similar lines, the Holy Spirit is purported to have thrown Jesus out into the desert (ἐκβάλλω; Mark 1:12). Word studies must be better than these examples.[53] It is clear that the meaning of a word cannot be accurately understood solely from its etymology or by combining its components.[54] The "Ogden-Richards triangle" is frequently cited in sources that discuss an accurate understand of how words are used in oral or written discourse.[55] This figure displays the view that a word (symbol) is directly related to the content or image it suggests to those who hear or read it (sense), yet is only indirectly related to an actual entity or object in the real world (referent). Words signify the meanings conventionally associated with them by contemporary language users, not the meanings supposed to be originally or innately tied to them.

The Ogden-Richards Triangle

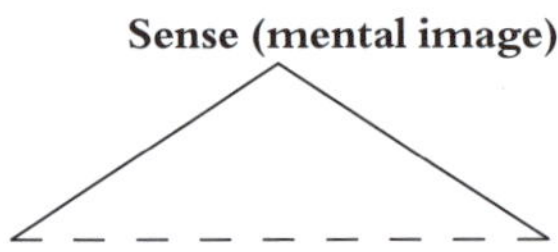

The principle of semantic change and the reality displayed in the Ogden-Richards triangle combine to show the limited value of etymology in understanding word meanings. Etymology may have some value when an extremely rare word is encountered, such as ἐπιούσιος in the familiar phrase "our daily bread" (τὸν ἄρτον ἡμῶν τὸν ἐπιούσιον δὸς ἡμῖν σήμερον; Matt. 6:11; cf. Luke 11:3). Two contextual factors combine with a suggested etymology for ἐπιούσιος to yield plausible meaning. Bread apparently should be understood as **synechdoche** for the staples that sustain life. This factor and the emphasis on the day (σήμερον in Matthew and καθ᾽ ἡμέραν in Luke) are consistent with an etymological understanding of ἐπιούσιος as combining the preposition ἐπί and the morpheme -ούσιος, understood as related to the participle of εἰμί. This would yield glosses like "for existence" or "necessary for living."[56]

---

53. It is fitting that D. A. Carson's book *Exegetical Fallacies* (2nd ed. Grand Rapids: Baker, 1996) begins with a discussion of word-study fallacies (27–64).

54. See especially Moisés Silva, *Biblical Words and Their Meaning* (Grand Rapids: Zondervan, 1983), 35–51.

55. C. K. Ogden and I. A. Richards, *The Meaning of Meaning* (New York: Harcourt, 1945), 11; Constantine R. Campbell, *Advances in the Study of Greek* (Grand Rapids: Zondervan, 2015), 73–74; Silva, *Biblical Words*, 102–3.

56. See the discussion of various etymologically derived glosses in BDAG, s.v. ἐπιούσιος (376–77).

Basic Linguistic Insights for Word Studies. Linguists commonly distinguish between denotative and connotative meaning. The former term describes meaning understood by most or all who hear or read a word, and the latter term describes meaning understood by a smaller group or even an individual. When the usage of a word is studied over a period of time, the phenomenon of semantic change becomes clear.[57] Authors typically use words with their present associations in mind, not their history. It was evidently proper for the translators of the KJV to gloss ἀγάπη in 1 Corinthians 13 with the English word "charity" in 1611, but 400 years later this gloss obscures Paul's meaning. Semantic anachronism occurs when a supposed original "root meaning" of a word is read into a later use of the word. This mistaken approach is known as the root-fallacy. The principle of semantic change also indicates that it would be wrong to read the meaning of a word in patristic Greek back into earlier NT texts. A related problem is studying the historical nuances of a word and attempting to funnel all of them into the exposition of a single passage. Barr called this approach "illegitimate totality transfer."[58] Another linguistic insight cautions those who study biblical words not to equate any single word with a theological idea or concept, which will be typically be expressed by any number of words.

Diachronic and Synchronic Approaches. The study of biblical words can take two tracks, diachronic and synchronic. The following table summarizes these contrasting approaches.

Two Approaches to Word Studies	
Diachronic Analysis	**Synchronic Analysis**
Traces a word's usage through time	Focuses on a word's immediate context
Traditional lexicography	Modern linguistics
Semantic range	Semantic field
Potential meanings in various texts	Actual meaning in a given text
The meanings of a word	The wordings of meaning

Diachronic analysis of a given word searches uses of the word in other texts and yields information on the word's meaning in those *other*

---

57. Silva, *Biblical Words*, 53–97.

58. James Barr, *The Semantics of Biblical Language* (Oxford: Oxford University Press, 1961), 218.

contexts.[59] This approach provides general guidance on parameters of meaning that may be *plausible* in the specific context of the text one is studying, not the *actual* meaning in that context. Synchronic analysis is typically more useful for exegesis given the reality of semantic change or development over time. When a word occurs in other contexts there will be more or less significant differences in such factors as author, genre, historical setting, literary context, and subject matter. The more such factors come into play, the less relevant the use of the word in the other context is.

Synchronic analysis looks to the immediate context of a word, examining its syntactical relations to other words. Text linguistics or discourse analysis insists that word choice itself implies meaning.[60] An author's use of a particular word instead of a synonym with overlapping meaning, a hyponym with a more specific meaning, or a negated antonym, is a choice that implies meaning. This choice involves an individual author's intent, style, idioms, and metaphors. J. P. Louw's approach to semantic domains is useful in analyzing word choice in a synchronic study.[61]

As shown in the circular figure below, in the case of an unusual NT word whose meaning is not clear in its immediate context, one should begin with NT uses that are contextually similar to the use being studied, and then look at more dissimilar uses.[62] Moving away from the NT toward more remote contexts should be in keeping with the concentric circle figure below. One would typically check usage in the

---

59. See Silva's discussion of circles of context in the process of determining meaning in *Biblical Words*, 137–69.

60. Runge, *Discourse Grammar of the Greek New Testament*, 5–7.

61. J. P. Louw, *Greek-English Lexicon of the New Testament based on Semantic Domains*, 2nd ed., 2 vols. (New York: United Bible Societies, 1999). Andrew W. Pitts has a helpful discussion of the theoretical basis of this work and its use at http://www.opentext.org/resources/articles/a10.html.

62. Use an exhaustive Greek concordance to find all of the NT uses of a word. Two such concordances are commonly used. The classic work is W. F. Moulton and A. S. Geden, *Concordance to the Greek Testament*, 5th ed. (Edinburgh: Clark, 1897, 1977). A more recent source is H. Bachmann and H. Slaby, *Computer Concordance to Novum Testamentum Graece* (Berlin: De Gruyter, 1985). This concordance uses a more current Greek text, provides a larger sample of the context of each usage, and lists how many times the word occurs in the NT. An even more advanced concordance is K. Aland, ed., *Vollständige Konkordanz zum griechischen Neuen Testament*, 2 vols. (Berlin: DeGruyter, 1978, 1983). Software such as Accordance and Logos will support concordance-type searches for individual words as well as inflected words and words in syntactical constructions. Consideration of the various contextual nuances of the word should be done in consultation with the detailed taxonomies supplied in BDAG. Using the BDAG lexicon is rewarding but it can be intimidating to beginners. Rod Decker's excellent introduction to BDAG is very helpful (http://ntresources.com/blog/documents/UsingBDAG.pdf), as is his list of errata (http://ntresources.com/blog/?page_id=2828).

LXX,[63] noting not only the semantic range of the Greek word being studied but also the Hebrew (and possibly Aramaic) words that the Greek word glossed. The use of the word in Hellenistic Jewish sources such as Josephus,[64] Philo,[65] and apocryphal/pseudepigraphical literature should be canvassed. Uses of the word in classical Greek sources which antedate the Greek of the Hellenistic period might also be significant if proper care is taken in noting the distance between the NT context and the classical context.[66] Uses of the word in Greek inscriptions and papy-

---

63. An indispensable book for beginning LXX study is Karen H. Jobes and Moisés Silva, *Invitation to the Septuagint* (Grand Rapids: Baker, 2000). The standard complete critical edition of the LXX is Alfred Rahlf, ed., *Septuaginta*, 2 vols. (Stuttgart: Deutsche Bibelgesellschaft, 1935; 1 vol. ed. 1979). Many scholars have contributed to yet incomplete ongoing multivolume Göttingen LXX, *Septuaginta: Vetus Testamentum Graecum* (Göttingen: Vandenhoeck&Ruprecht, various dates). The standard LXX concordance is E. Hatch and H. A. Redpath, *A Concordance to the Septuagint and Other Greek Versions of the Old Testament (Including the Apocryphal Books)*, 2 vols. (1897, reprinted, Grand Rapids: Baker, 1983; one vol. ed. with a new introduction 1998). Software programs such as Accordance enable concordance studies of words and grammatical constructions. A standard lexicon for the LXX is Johan Lust, et al., eds., *A Greek-English Lexicon of the Septuagint,* 2 vols. (Stuttgart: Deutsche Bibelgesellschaft, 1992, 1996). Standard grammars of LXX Greek are F. C. Conybeare and St. George Stock, *Grammar of Septuagint Greek* (1905, reprinted Peabody, MA: Hendrickson, 1995); H. St. John Thackeray, *A Grammar of the Old Testament in Greek according to the Septuagint. Introduction, Orthography, and Accidence* (Cambridge: University Press, 1909).

64. There are many works that introduce Josephus to NT students. Accessible introductions include Steve Mason, *Josephus and the New Testament* (Peabody, MA: Hendrickson, 1992); Tessa Rajak, *Josephus: The Historian and His Society* (Philadelphia: Fortress, 1984); Cleon Rogers Jr., *The Topical Josephus* (Grand Rapids: Zondervan, 1992). The most accessible critical text is H. St. John Thackeray et al. *Josephus, with an English Translation,* 13 vols., Loeb Classical Library (Cambridge: Harvard University Press, 1926–65). The Brill Josephus project is an ongoing series that provides a fresh translation and commentary on Josephus's works (http://www.brill.com/publications/flavius-josephus-translation-and-commentary). The standard concordance of Josephus is K. H. Rengstorff, *A Complete Concordance to Flavius Josephus: Study Edition,* 2 vols. (Leiden: Brill, 2002). Among lexicons, both LSJ and BDAG are useful for Josephus. Software resources such as Accordance provide searchable texts. Additional resources and links to downloadable texts will be found at http://www.josephus.org.

65. A helpful introductory guide to Philo is Torrey Seland, ed., *Reading Philo: A Handbook to Philo of Alexandria* (Grand Rapids: Eerdmans, 2014). The most accessible critical text is F. H. Colson and G. H. Whitaker, *Philo, with an English Translation,* 10 vols. Loeb Classical Library (Cambridge: Harvard University Press, 1929–53). The classic critical edition is Siegfried Reiter, et al., eds., *Philonis Alexandrini Opera quae Supersunt,* 7 vols. (1896–1930, reprinted, Berlin: DeGruyter, 1962–63). Among lexicons, both LSJ and BDAG are useful for Philo. Word studies in Philo will be aided by Peder Borgen, *The Philo Index: A Complete Greek Word Index to the Writings of Philo of Alexandria* (Grand Rapids: Eerdmans, 2000). See also Roald Skarsten, *The Complete Works of Philo of Alexandria: A Key-Word-in-Context Concordance* (Piscataway, NJ: Gorgias, 2005). Software resources such as Accordance provide searchable texts.

66. The standard lexicon for classical Greek is LSJ: H. G. Liddell and R. Scott, *A Greek-English Lexicon: A New Edition Revised and Augmented Throughout with Supplement,* rev. H. S. Jones and R. McKenzie, 9th ed. (Oxford: Oxford University Press, 1968). Shorter intermediate and abbreviated editions are also available.

ri could also be significant.[67] Early church authors may provide insight into how the word was understood by its earliest known interpreters.[68]

Comprehensive "theological dictionaries" are also helpful for word studies. Although Kittel's *Theological Dictionary*[69] received valid criticism for linguistic mistakes such as the equation of individual words and theological concepts, it contains a wealth of diachronic information on most NT words. Used with appropriate caution, it can be very helpful, especially with more obscure words. *The New International Dictionary of New Testament Theology and Exegesis*[70] is less detailed, but it improves upon Kittel's linguistics and is more up to date and theologically sound.

The Concentric Circles of a Word Study

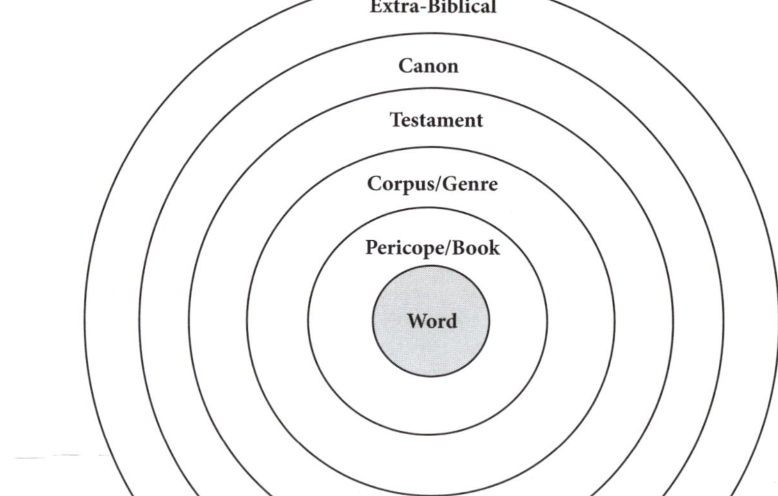

---

67. J. H. Moulton and G. Milligan, *The Vocabulary of the Greek New Testament Illustrated from the Papyri and Other Non-Literary Sources* (reprinted, Grand Rapids: Eerdmans, 1976). BDAG also includes citations of this material.

68. The standard lexicon for early Christian writers is G. W. H. Lampe, *A Patristic Greek Lexicon* (Oxford: Clarendon, 1961). Software resources such as Accordance provide searchable texts of patristic authors. BDAG also includes citations of this material.

69. Gerhard Kittel, ed., *Theological Dictionary of the New Testament*, trans. G. W. Gromiley, 10 vols. (Grand Rapids: Eerdmans, 1964–72).

70. Moisés Silva, ed., *The New International Dictionary of New Testament Theology and Exegesis*, 5 vols. (Grand Rapids: Zondervan, 2014).

- Word: Study the word in relationship to other words that might have been chosen (synonyms) and their antonyms. Note the word's syntactical relations, and possible metaphorical or idiomatic use.
- Pericope/book: Analyze the word's use in the immediate context of its pericope and in other pericopes in the book in which it occurs.
- Corpus/genre: Analyze the word's use in other books by the same author and in other books of the same genre (such as synoptic parallels) or in the same embedded genre.
- Testament: Analyze the word's use in the rest of the NT, especially in passages that are related thematically to your text. Note similarities and differences of usage and how the word's semantic range is affected.
- Canon: Analyze how the word is used in the LXX, and what Hebrew words it glosses. Note whether there are any intertextual relationships, and whether there is conceptual biblical theology in play.
- Extrabiblical: Analyze how the word is used in Hellenistic Jewish authors such as Josephus and Philo. Note also its use in more ancient classical sources and how it is understood and used later in patristic sources.

Case Study. Peter's message on the day of Pentecost clarified the significance of the **glossolalia** that confused some observers and led others to mock the followers of Jesus (Acts 2:6–13). His preaching of Jesus's resurrection and exaltation to God's right hand, supported by his citation of Joel along with Psalms 16 and 110 (Acts 2:14–36), convicted many of his hearers and led them to ask what their response should be (Acts 2:37). Their conviction is expressed by the phrase κατενύγησαν τὴν καρδίαν. The verb κατενύγησαν is a second aorist passive third person plural of κατανύσσω/ομαι. This word is an instance of *hapax legomena* (it occurs only here) in the NT. The cognate noun κατάνυξις occurs in Romans 11:8 (ἔδωκεν αὐτοῖς ὁ θεὸς πνεῦμα κατανύξεως) in a citation of Isaiah 29:10 (LXX: ὅτι πεπότικεν ὑμᾶς κύριος πνεύματι κατανύξεως), which describes a state of spiritual *stupor*. Anyone who needs further evidence that etymology is no guide to word meaning should consider that in Romans 11:8/Isaiah 29:10 κατάνυξις describes profound spiritual insensitivity, but in Acts 2:37 κατανύσσομαι describes deep spiritual brokenness. The simplex verb νύσσω occurs in the NT in John 19:34, describing the violent action of the Roman soldier in piercing Jesus's side (cf. Matt. 27:49 *v.l.*). It also occurs in Codex D of Acts 12:7 to describe the angel of the Lord nudging or poking Peter to awaken him. This range of meaning, ranging from relatively mild poking to forceful penetrating stabbing with a sharp instrument, is cited by BDAG in classical sources, Josephus, Philo, the LXX, and biblical apocrypha/pseudepigrapha.[71]

The word κατανύσσω/ομαι occurs sixteen times in the LXX, where it is used metaphorically to describe extreme anxiety, remorse, or stunned silence rather than physical poking or stabbing.[72] A particularly interesting usage is Psalm 108:16 (ET 109:16), where the Psalmist wishes that God would judge his enemy who persecuted a man who was "brokenhearted" (NIV, ESV). The LXX expression is κατανενυγμένον τῇ καρδίᾳ. A similar range of metaphorical meaning is found in Hellenistic Jewish literature.[73] Of special interest are *Testament of Job* 24:8 and *Joseph and Aseneth* 6:1. In the former text the expression κατανύγησα ἐν τῇ καρδίᾳ μου describes Job's wife's acute embarrassment at having to beg for bread in the marketplace. In the latter text the expression κατενύγη ἰσχυρῶς τῇ ψυχῇ describes Aseneth's shattered psyche upon seeing Joseph. Early Christian authors used the word in describing the process of conversion, especially of the compunction that led to repentance.[74] Hesychius of Jerusalem (the presbyter, c. A.D. 450) also spoke of one habitually possessing the Christian virtue of repentance as κατανενυγμένον τῇ καρδίᾳ (*de titulis Psalmorum* 108).

Looking at κατανύσσω/ομαι in terms of synchronic analysis begins with considering the choice of this word as opposed to others available to the author Luke. Louw's *Greek-English Lexicon of the New Testament based on Semantic Domains* is useful for such analysis. This two-volume lexicon contains an introduction to its approach and its listing of Greek words according to semantic domains in volume one. Volume 2 contains an index of Greek words and NT passages; the second volume is necessary to access the first. The word κατανύσσω/ομαι appears in domain 25, which contains 296 words and expressions that denote attitudes and emotions. These words are arranged into twenty-four subdomains. The subdomain dealing with sorrow and regret contains twenty-eight words and expressions, including κατανύσσω τὴν καρδίαν, described as "(an idiom, literally "to pierce the heart")" to experience acute emotion-

---

71.   For νύσσω as stabbing or pricking with a sharp instrument, see e.g., *Diog. L.* 2, 109; Plutarch, *Cleom.* 37, 16; *Gos. Pet.* 3:9; *Sib. Or.* 8, 296 Josephus, *B. J.* 3.335. The milder action of nudging or poking is found in *Od.* 14, 485; *Diog. L.* 6, 53; 3 Macc. 5:14; *Acts Paul* 7, 28. Particularly interesting is the use in Sir. 22:19, where pricking the heart is mentioned, evidently in a metaphorical sense. In *Ps. Sol.* 16:4 Solomon describes divine discipline in terms of a horse being goaded.

72.   LXX Gen. 27:38; 34:7; Lev. 10:3; 1 Kgs. 20:27, 29 (ET 21:27, 29); Ps. 4:5; 29:13 (ET 30:12); 34:15 (ET 35:15); 108:16 (ET 109:16); Isa. 6:5; 47:5. If space permitted, we would continue here by analyzing the various Hebrew verbs rendered by κατανύσσω/ομαι.

73.   E.g., *Sir.* 12:12; 14;1; 20:21; 47:20; *Sus.* 10; *Test. Job* 21:3; 24:8; *Test. Sol.* 20:3; *Jos. Asen.* 6:1.

74.   Lampe, *A Patristic Greek Lexicon*, s.v. κατανύσσω (713).

al distress, implying both concern and regret—'to be greatly troubled, to be acutely distressed.'" The description goes on to list Acts 2:37 and suggest a translation of the verse.[75] Perusal of subdomain 25 reveals relatively colorless terms for sorrow like μεταμέλομαι and λυπέω, along with more vivid ways of describing this emotion, such as the idioms τὴν ψυχὴν διελεύσεται ῥομφαία ("a sword piercing the soul," Luke 2:35), συνθρύπτοντές μου τὴν καρδίαν ("breaking my heart in pieces," Acts 21:13), and λύπη καταποθῇ ὁ τοιοῦτος ("such a person being swallowed up by grief," 2 Cor. 2:7). These last three expressions as well as the one used in Acts 2:37 speak very strongly, even hyperbolically, about people being absolutely crushed by grief. Luke's choice of terminology in Acts 2:37 shows his intent to describe remorse in the strongest possible way.

As Louw notes, the use of κατανύσσω/ομαι in Acts 2:37 requires attention to its syntactical connection with τὴν καρδίαν, likely to be analyzed as an adverbial accusative of respect, explaining the reference or sphere of the action of the passive form κατενύγησαν. Semantically, this construction would be roughly equivalent to αἱ καρδίαι αὐτῶν κατενύγησαν. Accordingly the meaning of κατανύσσω/ομαι cannot be ascertained without an understanding the meaning of καρδία. Καρδία, -ας is a well-known word in the NT,[76] and there is no doubt that it connotes the entire inner human person, encompassing the mind, the will, and the emotions.[77] As Luke-Acts unfolds, there are many descriptions of the impact of the message of Christ on the human heart, involving

- parents turning to their children (Luke 1:17/Mal. 4:6)
- proud people being humbled (Luke 1:51)
- thoughts being revealed (Luke 2:35)
- questions and disputes (Luke 5:22; 9:47)
- opposition by Satan (Luke 8:12; Acts 5:3)
- authentic, fruitful faith (Luke 8:15)
- hesitant faith (Luke 24:25, 38)
- excited enthusiasm (Luke 24:32)
- **deep remorse for sin** (Acts 2:37; cf. Luke 7:36–50)
- sincere joy (Acts 2:46)
- community of resources (Acts 4:32)
- resistance to God's Spirit (Acts 7:51)
- fury against God's messenger (Acts 7:54)

---

75. Louw, *Lexicon*, 1.319.

76. The word occurs 156 times in the NT, including twenty-one times in Luke and twenty times in Acts.

77. E.g., Luke 1:66; 2:19, 35, 51; 3:15; 6:45; 10:27/Deut. 6:4; Luke 12:34, 45; 16:1; 21:14, 34; Acts 2:26/Ps. 16:9; Acts 5:4; 7:23, 39; 13:22; 14:17; 21:13; Cf. BDAG, s.v. καρδία (508).

- lack of uprightness needing forgiveness (Acts 8:21–22)
- resolute, persevering faith (Acts 11:23)
- spiritual cleansing (Acts 15:9)
- spiritual openness (Acts 16:14)
- spiritual callousness (Acts 28:27/Isa. 6:10)

Diachronic and synchronic analysis of κατανύσσω/ομαι and a study of καρδία in Luke-Acts combine to show that the expression κατενύγησαν τὴν καρδίαν in Acts 2:37 describes deep personal remorse over the implications of Christ's crucifixion and resurrection. This visceral, gut-wrenching grief prompted an urgent question, "What should we do?" Peter's ensuing instructions regarding repentance and baptism lead to the assimilation of those who welcomed Peter's instructions into the nascent Christian community, where their formerly pierced hearts would experience messianic renewal, edification, awe, joy, and openness to the grace of God (Acts 2:46).

DOING THEOLOGY WITH THE TEXT

We have already looked into theological method and the theological emphases of the Gospels and Acts in chapter 3, so our discussion here will be brief. Theological analysis of the Bible can be understood in terms of describing the main themes of a biblical book or author, or of an author's entire literary corpus. More broadly, it can describe how an innate theme is presented in the OT or NT or even in the entire canonical metanarrative, resulting in a symphonic harmony of distinct voices in united testimony to a biblical theme.[78] Our understanding of the "biblical" theology that arises from this process should be related to the theological traditions we have received from our various denominational backgrounds, and how those traditions fit into the historical flow of the church's thought about the Bible. The ongoing interplay between our developing understanding of biblical themes and our received theological tradition provides a healthy basis for a theology of ministry in all its various forms. In other words, exegetical and theological development should happen in reciprocity as we shepherd God's flock. Moving from a study of Acts 2:37 to the broader matter of varying responses to the gospel of Jesus the Messiah in Luke-Acts and beyond brings us to the last stage of exegesis. In what follows we will

---

78. Evangelical studies of biblical theology include G. K. Beale, *A New Testament Biblical Theology* (Grand Rapids: Baker, 2011); G. E. Ladd, *A Theology of the New Testament*, 2nd ed. (Grand Rapids: Eerdmans, 1993); Thomas R. Schreiner, *New Testament Theology: Magnifying God in Christ* (Grand Rapids: Baker, 2008); and Frank Thielman, *Theology of the New Testament* (Grand Rapids: Zondervan, 2005).

briefly reflect on the matter of response to the gospel from the perspectives of biblical, systematic, and ministry theology.

Biblical Theology

Acts 2:37–47 is an account of response to proclamation of Jesus crucified yet now exalted, a response that begins with remorse and repentance and concludes with faithful participation in the church. Theological reflection on Acts 2 ought to note the text's urgent eschatological tone. What God promised in Joel 2 has begun to happen. By raising Jesus, God has dramatically turned Jesus's rejection into his exaltation, an exaltation that has led to the pouring out of the Spirit on God's renewed people. This divine irony of weak-crucified Jesus becoming powerful-exalted Jesus who empowers his community through the Spirit is at the heart of the powerful gospel message that broke the hearts of Peter's audience on the day of Pentecost, leading to the conversion of 3,000 people.

The overall narrative of Luke-Acts presents a wide spectrum of positive and negative responses to the gospel as it expands from a Jewish audience in Jerusalem to Jews and Gentiles in Syria, Asia, and Rome. In this process many come to faith in Jesus, but many more do not. In Luke's Gospel, Jesus's parable of the sower encapsulates the spectrum of responses. When Jesus interpreted the parable for the disciples he cited Isaiah 6 to the effect that the mysterious sovereignty of God was behind the varying responses (Luke 8:10/Isa. 6:9). Some heard the message, understood it, and became faithful followers of Jesus, yet others heard the same message to no effect except unbelief and ultimate ruin. It is noteworthy that in Acts, Paul cites the same Isaianic text when he receives a mixed response to his preaching in Rome (Acts 28:26–27/Isa. 6:9–10).

This mixed response to the gospel is vividly illustrated when one compares Acts 2:37–47 to Acts 7:54–60. In Acts 2 the preaching of the gospel resulted in the profound remorse of Peter's hearers, their ensuing repentance, and their assimilation into heartfelt Christian community. This is, to say the least, in stark contrast to the murderous fury of Stephen's hearers in Acts 7. Yet the visceral imagery of these antithetical responses is rather similar:

- Acts 2:37 Ἀκούσαντες δὲ κατενύγησαν τὴν καρδίαν . . .
- Acts 7:54 Ἀκούοντες δὲ ταῦτα διεπρίοντο ταῖς καρδίαις αὐτῶν . . .

In Acts 2:37, "Peter's words pierced their hearts" (NLT). In Acts 7:54 Stephen's words have the opposite effect—his hearers are cut to the heart,[79] gnash their teeth, rush upon him, drive him out of the city, and stone him to death. In both cases the gospel penetrates to the depths of the human heart (cf. Heb. 4:12–13), but with opposite outcomes. Peter's hearers welcomed[80] the message; Stephen's decidedly did not. Jesus promised his disciples that they would be received by some hearers (Luke 9:4; 10:5–9; cf. Acts 2:47; 4:21; 5:13; 16:15) and rejected by others (Luke 9:5; 10:10–11; 21:12–19; cf. Acts 13:50–51). Their fate was and is the same as his (Luke 6:22; 10:16; Acts 5:41).[81] The narrative of Paul's ministry in Acts shows the same range of responses to the gospel. Paul once violently opposed the gospel he later came to preach (Acts 7:58–8:3; 9:1–2, 13–14, 21, 26; Gal. 1:13). Paul himself experienced extremely negative responses to his own preaching of the gospel.[82] Paul's writings speak of the gospel as God's powerful means of salvation: Faith comes by hearing the word of God (Rom. 10:17).[83] Paul has a great deal to say about preaching the gospel and how people respond to it.[84]

Looking beyond Luke-Acts and Paul to John, it is clear that response to the gospel is at the heart of the Fourth Gospel. The purpose of this Gospel is explained near its end: It was written to bring people to life-giving faith (John 20:30–31). The individuals who interact with Jesus in John provide examples of belief and unbelief in God's saving message personified and taught by Jesus as the word of God who reveals the Father (John 1:1–2, 12–14). Peter and James also speak of the gospel message as the means by which believers are brought to new life in Christ (Jas. 1:18, 21; 1 Peter 1:22–2:3, cf. Isa 40:6). Hebrews repeatedly

---

79. διεπρίοντο is an imperfect passive of διαπρίω, a word that denotes vivisection by sawing in some contexts (e.g., LXX 1 Chron. 20:3; cf. πρίζω in LXX Amos 1:3; Heb. 11:37), leading to translations like "they were cut to the heart" (KJV, 1901 ASV, MEV) and "they were cut to the quick" (NASB). Most versions (e.g., ESV, NIV, NLT) abandon the etymologically based metaphor and render the verb in terms of fury and rage, as in Acts 5:33.

80. The word in Acts 2:42 is ἀπεδέξατο. Ἀποδέχομαι is used only eight times in the NT, exclusively by Luke. It is used to describe the crowd welcoming Jesus in Luke (Luke 8:40; 9:11). In Acts it also describes the welcome recommended for Apollos in Achaia (18:27), the welcome received by Paul's entourage in Jerusalem (21:17), and Paul's freedom to welcome visitors in Rome (28:30). In a somewhat different nuance, it is used by the lawyer Tertullus to welcome or acknowledge the benefits of Felix's government (Acts 24:3).

81. The theme could be expanded by thinking through relevant texts in the rest of the NT, such as 1 Cor. 1:18–31; 2 Cor. 2:14–16; 4:1–18; 6:1–10; 1 Peter 4:14, 16.

82. Acts 13:50; 14:5–6, 19; 16:19–24, 35–40; 17:5–10, 13–14, 32; 18:6, 12–17; 19:9, 23–41; 21:27–36; 22:22–29; 23:12–22; 24:1–9.

83. Rom. 1:16; 10:9–15; 15:16–21; 16:25; 1 Cor. 1:18, 24; 4:15; Gal. 1:6–9; Eph. 1:13; 3:6; Col. 1:5, 23; 1 Thess. 2:13; 2 Thess. 2:14; 2 Tim. 2:9. Conversely, rejection of the gospel has ominous implications in texts like Acts 17:31; 2 Thess. 1:8–9; 1 Peter 4:17.

84. Rom. 1:5; 10:8–15; 11:28; 1 Cor. 1:18–31; 15:1–2; 2 Cor. 3:12–17; 4:3–6; Col. 1:25; 1 Thess. 2:13.

speaks of the reception of God's word and the consequences of rejecting it (4:2; 6:4–8; 10:26–31; 12:25). Overall the NT speaks in a united voice that holds up the gospel of Christ—the message about his life, death, resurrection, session, and return (1 Cor. 15)—as the powerful and sufficient means by which God is forming his people.

Systematic Theology

Systematic theology speaks biblical truth, enriched by centuries of ecclesial reflection and tradition, to contemporary cultures.[85] When it comes to theological reflection on the proclamation of God's word and responses to it, three theologians are especially relevant: Luther, Calvin, and Barth. Martin Luther (1483–1546) has been characterized as a theologian of the word due to his stress on the power of the gospel.[86] One passage from a sermon by Luther encapsulates his view of the power of the word of God to reform the church:

> In short, I will preach it [the word], teach it, write it, but I will constrain no man by force, for faith must come freely without compulsion. Take myself as an example. I opposed indulgences and all the papists, but never with force. *I simply taught, preached, wrote God's Word; otherwise I did nothing. And while I slept, or drank Wittenberg beer with my friends Philip and Amsdorf, the Word so greatly weakened the papacy that no prince or emperor ever inflicted such losses upon it. I did nothing; the Word did everything. . . .* I did nothing; **I let the Word do its work**.[87]

For Luther the word of God—whether incarnate in Jesus Christ, written in the canonical Scriptures, or preached by Jesus's followers—was first and foremost the word of the cross.[88] John Calvin (1509–1564) also emphasized the power of the gospel message to elicit faith. His discussion of how the grace of Christ is received heavily stresses that faith rests upon the word of God. Calvin likens the inseparable relationship

---

85. Evangelical systematic theologies include Millard J. Erickson, *Christian Theology*, 3rd ed. (Grand Rapids: Baker, 2013); John M. Frame, *Systematic Theology: An Introduction to Christian Belief* (Phillipsburg, NJ: P&R, 2013); Wayne A. Grudem, *Systematic Theology: An Introduction to Biblical Doctrine* (Grand Rapids: Zondervan, 1994).

86. See e.g., Robert Kolb and Charles P. Arand, *The Genius of Luther's Theology* (Grand Rapids: Baker, 2008), 129–220.

87. Martin Luther, "Second sermon Monday after invocavit, Mar 10, 1522," in *Luther's Works*, eds. Jaroslav Pelikan, et al. (Philadelphia: Fortress, 1959), 51.76–78. Bracketed text added.

88. Robert Kolb, *Martin Luther and the Enduring Word of God* (Grand Rapids: Baker, 2016), 112–16; John T. Pless, "Martin Luther: Preacher of the Cross," *CTQ* 51 (1987): 83–102.

of faith to the word of God to the relationship of the rays of the sun to the sun itself. Further, the word of God is like a mirror in which people of faith may contemplate God himself.[89]

Karl Barth (1886–1968) viewed the word of God as analogous to the Trinity in having three unified forms, revelation, Scripture, and preaching. God's revelation in Christ is the most basic form of the word. Scripture attests to this revelatory word, and proclamation attests to Scripture.[90] Evangelicals may differ with Barth's understanding of Scripture and revelation, but Barth's emphasis on the transcendent power of the message of the cross was a strong corrective to mainstream Protestantism's "social gospel" emphasis during the twentieth century.[91]

Ministry Theology

The implications of Acts 2:37–47 for ministry are many and profound. Preachers will find much to emulate in the biblical content, directness, and fervor of Peter's sermon. The way in which the sermon led many who heard it to remorse, repentance, and committed participation in the church is an ideal result for Christian communication. At the same time, the book of Acts contains several narratives that feature very negative responses to the gospel. These positive and negative responses combine to teach a hopeful realism in ministry. The gospel message is sufficient to engender faith and conversion, but its proclamation may also elicit negative responses, including the persecution of the preachers. Jesus had somewhat cryptically warned Peter of this very thing (John 21:15–19).

Scot McKnight's little book *The King Jesus Gospel* speaks in a very helpful way about the ministry implications of the NT's teaching about the gospel, its preaching, and the various responses to it.[92] His central point is so unremarkable that it seems almost **tautologous** to mention it—the gospel is about the life, death, resurrection, session, and return of Jesus Christ as the fulfillment of Israel's story that began in Genesis 12. But this point merits frequent repetition in a time when the church's preoccupation with matters like cultural contextualiza-

---

89. John Calvin, ed. *Calvin: Institutes of the Christian Religion*, ed. John T. McNeill, trans. F. L. Battles, 2 vols. (Philadelphia: Westminster, 1960), 1.548–49 (3.2.6).

90. Karl Barth, *Church Dogmatics*, eds. G. W. Bromiley and T. F. Torrance (Edinburgh: Clark, 1957), 1/1.120–21.

91. See e.g., David M. Whitford, "*Deus Dixit*: The Power of the Word of God in Luther and Barth," *Perichoresis* 6 (2008): 69–83; Rosalene Bradbury, *Cross Theology: The Classical Theologia Crucis and Karl Barth's Modern Theology of the Cross* (Eugene, OR: Pickwick, 2011), 149–301.

92. Scot McKnight, *The King Jesus Gospel: The Original Good News Revisited* (Grand Rapids: Zondervan, 2011).

tion, persuasive sermon techniques, and encapsulated gospel sound bites tends to eclipse the gospel itself. Methodological wisdom and relevance is a good thing, but ultimate wisdom is found in reflecting on and speaking clearly about the transformative power of the cross. The transcendent revelatory content of the cruciform gospel message is sufficient to achieve the response God intends.[93]

Chapter in Review

This chapter focused on the linguistic aspects of exegesis, which include translating the text from its original language into that of the exegete and analyzing the original language in terms of its structure, syntax, key words, and theological teaching. Word-based (formal correspondence) and idea-based (dynamic equivalence) approaches to translation were both introduced and modeled. The chapter also discussed how narrative texts are structured, Greek syntax, and the study of key words. Various approaches to visually displaying the text were also introduced and modeled. The chapter concluded with a brief treatment of how the exegetical process relates the text's meaning to other biblical passages in the discipline of biblical theology, and how biblical theology informs systematic theology and ministry.

---

93. Sources that espouse a theologically informed rather than a pragmatic utilitarian approach to preaching include Richard Lischer, *A Theology of Preaching: The Dynamics of the Gospel*, rev. ed. (Eugene, OR: Wipf and Stock, 2001); Jason C. Meyer, *Preaching: A Biblical Theology* (Wheaton, IL: Crossway, 2013); Michael Pasquarello III, *Christian Preaching: A Trinitarian Theology of Proclamation* (Eugene, OR: Wipf and Stock, 2006).

6

COMMUNICATING PASSAGES IN THE GOSPELS AND ACTS

The Chapter at a Glance

Augustine's *On Christian Doctrine* provides sound advice on Christian communication as wise biblical teaching that delights and motivates the hearers. The original point or points of biblical narrative must be understood in terms of its pericope-based genre and use of characters and test-motifs. The current point or points of biblical narrative can be determined by discerning use of current approaches, including the meaning/significance distinction, speech act theory, bridging the biblical and cultural worlds, and *lectio divina*. Students of the Gospels and Acts should be creative in choosing effective sermon structures that are appropriate for the text, its audience, and the intended application.

INTRODUCTION

Anyone who wishes to communicate the Gospels and Acts would do well to read Augustine's *De Doctrina Christiana*, which is not a treatise on Christian doctrine as such but a treatise on how to understand and communicate Christian doctrine. Following Cicero,[1] Augustine spoke

---

1. See *De Or.* 1.69; 2.159; *Brut.* 89, *Or. Brut.* 69. Marcus Tullius Cicero (106–43 B.C.) was an influential Roman senator, lawyer, and orator. Cicero and other orators in his day were strongly influenced by Aristotle's theory of rhetoric. Cicero stated that one must be intelligent

of the goals of communication as teaching, delighting, and moving.[2] The first goal has to do with accuracy in content, the second with beauty in expression, and the third with effectiveness in persuasion. Accordingly, the one who communicates the Gospels and Acts is at the same time an exegete, an artist, and an advocate. For Augustine, clarity or intelligibility was of utmost importance. Communicators must seek first to be understood in *what* they say, even if *how* they say it is not high quality rhetoric. If they wish to capture the attention of their hearers and motivate them to act, however, communicators must speak artfully and urgently. The priority of clarity over eloquence meant more than mechanically reading, memorizing, and repeating the words of Scripture. For Augustine, wisdom in communication resulted from understanding acquired by looking into the heart of Scripture with the eyes of one's own heart (*Doctr. chr.* 4.5). This informed wisdom could be acquired by learning the original languages of the Bible (2.11) and grasping the interpretation of metaphors and other ambiguities.

One must keep informed wisdom in mind when one moves from grammatical-historical exegesis, which tends to produce factual details, to application of the significance of those details for one's current audience. When Augustine spoke of looking into the heart of the Bible with the eyes of one's own heart, he was apparently speaking of exegesis that is not only informed and accurate but also prayerful and wise in seeking biblical meaning for communication. This understanding seems to be consistent with what we speak of today as "the point," the key truth wisely deduced from the passage that should be preached accurately, artfully, and urgently.[3]

Readers of this book will have likely already concluded that it is wrong to grab a striking biblical text and use it sermonically without attention to its genre, historical setting, and literary context. The text must inform and shape the sermon, not *vice versa*. Christ gave himself for the church, and those who have been called to teach the church must give themselves to the Scriptures written by Christ's proxies through the Spirit. The Reformation's emphasis on *Sola Scriptura* is about practice as well as faith, and that practice includes the manner in which the church is taught. *Sola Scriptura* also assumes the **epistemological**

(*acutus*) in order to teach, weighty (*gravis*) in order to delight, and animated (*argutus*) in order to move one's listeners. See *Opt. gen.* 4.

2. Augustine, *Doctr. chr.* 4.12. Augustine had no problem with borrowing ideas about speaking well from non-Christian authors. If non-Christians could speak well in promoting their causes, why shouldn't Christians speak well in promoting biblical truth? (*Doctr. chr.* 4.2). On the priority of clear content and wisdom over eloquent expression, see 4.5, 10–12.

3. Perhaps Augustine's notion of informed wisdom drawn from the words of the text is comparable to the deductive approach of Haddon Robinson in "What's the big idea?" See *Biblical Preaching*, 3rd ed. (Grand Rapids: Baker, 2014), 15–26.

stance that however inspirational our ideas may be, God's are infinitely better. We are to think God's thoughts after him; he is already aware of our thoughts. This epistemology leads us to avoid using biblical texts as springboards from which we launch homiletical high dives and warns us that when we preach about current issues, we must bring the real meaning of the biblical text to bear on those issues. We are to be about the exegesis and exposition of Christ's word, just as Christ the Word was about the exegesis and exposition of the Father.[4] *Christian* communicators can do no less.

THE ORIGINAL POINT OF THE PASSAGE

We cannot ascertain the original point of a *passage* until we properly determine what *kind* of passage we are dealing with, and what its *limits* are. In the narrative genre of the Gospels and Acts we are studying texts that address the church's needs by creatively recounting selected historical events. Such texts narrate the events in self-contained scenes or episodes, commonly called pericopes by scholars. Such pericopes are the units by which the overall story line or plot of the book develops. Internal to each pericope are smaller units, typically presented as paragraphs that unfold that pericope's story. Accordingly, to speak responsibly of the original point of a narrative passage requires us to identify individual pericopes and the units that make up those pericopes. Communicators can choose to focus on an entire pericope or one of its constituent units. As units within a pericope contribute to the point of the pericope as a whole, so pericopes contribute to the meaning of books as a whole. A valid "point" at any of these levels, whether of a unit, a pericope, or an entire book, will be coherent and consistent with the "points" of the other levels.

Narrative pericopes make their point by the way in which their characters respond to tests that come their way. The authorial point of view embedded implicitly or explicitly in a narrative shows the reader whether the characters' attitudes and actions are to be emulated or rejected. "Freytag's pyramid," discussed in a previous chapter, provides a helpful grid for analyzing the dramatic movement of the plot of each pericope in a narrative book, as well as the overall plot of the entire book. When it comes to the Gospels and Acts, the divine point of view is clear, and the characters are relatively easily identified by their words and actions as heroic or villainous, positive or negative role models.

---

4. In John 1:18 (cf. Sir. 43:31) Jesus is portrayed as the exposition or exegesis of the Father (μονογενὴς θεὸς ὁ ὢν εἰς τὸν κόλπον τοῦ πατρὸς ἐκεῖνος ἐξηγήσατο). As the one and only God incarnate who is oriented toward intimacy with the Father (cf. κόλπος in John 13:23; Luke 16:22–23), all that Jesus did and said was a narration of the Father (cf. John 14:9).

Some narrative pericopes make their points more clearly than others. The Gospels and Acts tell us what Jesus *did* and *taught* (Acts 1:1); texts focusing on what he did make their points less explicitly than texts which focus on what he taught. A given pericope might narrate an interaction of Jesus with his disciples or his opponents that leads to an authoritative pronouncement on his part. Another might simply describe such interaction without any stated "moral" of the story. In one parabolic pericope Jesus might append a generalizing conclusion or interpret the parable in detail. In another parabolic text such interpretive hints might not be found. Overall it is fair to say that narrative texts typically make their points less directly and explicitly than the NT letters do. One should not conclude, however, that narratives are merely *descriptive* rather than *prescriptive*, which implies that one should use them solely for historical information, not for ethical transformation.[5] NT texts commonly take OT narratives as instructive for doctrine as well as practice, and we should take NT narratives in the same way.[6]

The implicit manner in which narratives commonly teach means that we should compare what we think we see implied in them to what we know from texts that teach more directly and propositionally. One should capitalize on the largely implicit nature of narrative teaching rather than viewing it as a weakness or problem. Vogt observed that

> The power of narrative comes in *showing* rather than *telling*. . . . [T]he authors of biblical narratives don't always tell the listeners what they should think about a particular person, action, or episode. Rather, they expect the listeners to be able to engage with those ideas on their own. Communication of the biblical narratives should follow the same practice to some degree. That is, the speaker should not always draw conclusions for the listeners but rather should point toward the conclusion without specifically identifying it.[7]

---

5. The historically descriptive versus theologically prescriptive dichotomy is false. All biblical texts teach God's people in a transforming manner; no biblical texts present information for its own sake.

6. See e.g., Matt. 10:15; 11:13; 12:3–4, 42; 19:5; 23:32; Rom. 4:1–25; 5:12–21; 11:1–5; 15:4; 1 Cor. 10:6, 11; 2 Tim. 3:16–17. The fact that we lack the revelational authority and insight of the NT authors does not relieve us of the duty to follow their example and counsel in viewing the biblical narratives as the story of the people of God, which we are. Traditional dispensational theology's stress on the discontinuity of the OT and NT in terms of law and grace tended to weigh against the direct application of OT narratives to Christians. Some dispensationalists went so far as to extend this discontinuity as far as the Gospels and Acts. The NT use of the OT and the use of the teachings of Jesus in the NT epistles militate against this approach.

7. Peter Vogt, *Interpreting the Pentateuch: An Exegetical Handbook* (Grand Rapids: Kregel, 2009), 173.

As we will see below, Vogt's counsel that we should be less explicit in stating the point of narratives fits the model of preaching sometimes called inductive or narrative preaching.

THE CURRENT POINT OF THE PASSAGE

The Relationship of Exegesis and Application

The Bible is a covenantal book; in God's providence it has come into existence incrementally through the centuries to show people how to please and enjoy the God who loves them and redeems them from sin. When we read the Bible we are reading texts that God intends to transform us. In its original ancient Near-Eastern setting as well as in all the myriads of settings in which the Bible has been subsequently been read all over the world through the centuries, the Bible was never read well if it was read only for information. Although our understating of the Bible is greatly enhanced by grammatical, historical, and literary insights into ancient literature, we dare not leave the Bible as an ancient book. We have not really understood the Bible unless we read it as a book that guides our lives today. Our character, thoughts, and lifestyle show whether we have understood the Bible as God meant for it to be understood when he led its authors to write it. Exegesis that does not guide and form the exegete's character and behavior is not just incomplete, it is a travesty. The ultimate step in exegesis is performance.[8]

When we read Scripture as canon, a norming authority, the distinction between exegetical interpretation and practical application cannot be turned into a rigidly sequential enterprise. Determining the current point or application of a text is the primary task, not a secondary matter to be bracketed and avoided until we finish the exegetical task. Sound exegesis is absolutely essential for valid and wholesome application, but the task of expositors has only begun with a historically accurate understanding of an ancient biblical text. Historical understanding is the necessary foundation for application, but it is only the foundation. The goal of current biblical expositors is the same as that of the ancient biblical authors—to form the people of God by making the message of God clear and showing its relevance. The expositor's pragmatic ministry situation cannot be divorced from the exegetical process. Expositors

---

8. S. C. Bartman, "New Testament Interpretation as Performance," *SJT* 52 (1997): 178–208. Kevin Vanhoozer's *Is There a Meaning in This Text?* (Grand Rapids: Zondervan, 1998) presents a comprehensive approach to the Bible as divine communicative act, and to biblical hermeneutics as interpretive speech-action, culminating in the cruciform embodiment of the text. Expositors would do well to ponder Vanhoozer's presentation of hermeneutics as interpretive martyrdom which bears Christlike witness to the text (438–41).

should pray for true awareness of their own needs as well as the needs of their audience *during* the exegetical process. Prayerful self-conscious-ness is needed to avoid the tendency to find and preach one's personal favorite doctrines and issues, or the "party line" that might be expected by the audience. Awareness of such pitfalls is necessary for Scripture to function in the ongoing reformation and renewal of God's people.

Speech Act Theory

The theory of human communicative action that has come to be known as *speech act theory* is useful in determining the current point of a biblical passage.[9] Speech act theory views utterances not as passive objects that yield information when properly understood, but as active influencers of behavior. For our purposes the Gospels and Acts, texts that narrate and interpret communicative acts, may be understood in the same way. The authors of these texts not only *meant* things; they also meant that their readers *do* things, that their texts should influence performance. Just as there are different kinds of speech acts (e.g., affirmations, requests, commands, promises, apologies), these are three distinct levels of speech acts:

- *Locutionary*: the simple authorial act that results in the semantic content or meaning of an utterance or a text.
- *Illocutionary*: what the author wishes the meaning or locution of utterance or text to accomplish; the pragmatic goal of the communicative action.
- *Perlocutionary*: the actual response to the locutionary and illocutionary levels of the communicative action; what the readers of the text do.

This three-level taxonomy of speech acts is useful for our discussion of the "current point" of texts from the Gospels and Acts. It is clear that our study of biblical texts is incomplete if we are satisfied with merely understanding their locutionary aspects. Our goal must be to understand the intended illocutionary force of the text and persuade people to take appropriate perlocutionary action. Only then have we responded appropriately to the divine speech action of Holy Scripture.

For example, after his sermon on the day of Pentecost (Acts 2:14–36), Peter responded to his audience's question, "What should we do?" with the answer "Repent and be baptized" (Acts 2:37–38). Peter

---

9. Seminal works related to speech act theory include J. L. Austin, *How to Do Things with Words* (Cambridge, MA: Harvard University Press, 1962); John Searle, *Speech Acts* (Cambridge: Cambridge University Press, 1969). See the summary of these and other language philosophers in Vanhoozer, *Is There a Meaning?* 209–14.

intended his words to convey meaning (locution) that would lead to action (illocution). Some of Peter's audience performed the appropriate perlocutionary actions prescribed by Peter (Acts 2:41–47). As an author, Luke's overall literary agenda (Luke 1:1–4; Acts 1:1) shows that his narrative of Peter's sermon and its aftermath (locution) has illocutionary implications: Luke intends for his readers to be informed, taught, and inspired by this narrative. When some of Peter's audience responded favorably by accepting Peter's words in Acts 2:41 (οἱ μὲν οὖν ἀποδεξάμενοι τὸν λόγον αὐτοῦ . . .), receiving baptism, and joining the nascent Christian community, their perlocution matched up perfectly with Peter's illocution. As an author, Luke's literary illocution extends his character Peter's rhetorical illocution, and Luke's readers' perlocutionary response should extend that of Peter's listeners, turning to Jesus in Christian community just like Peter's original audience did. Acts 2:37–47 is properly applied when readers of Luke perform as did Peter's audience, in repentance, baptism, and participation in Christian community.

Peter's audience's "acceptance" of his exhortation to save themselves from their ethically twisted culture (2:40–41) is a fitting model for determining the current point or applying the Bible. Applying a biblical text presupposes that the Spirit has used the gospel message to open one's heart to the perlocutionary performances implied and enjoined by the text. The central perlocution of the Bible, loving God with all one's heart and loving one's neighbor as oneself, is radically countercultural. The current point of the text (its application) is *ethical* performance that extends the original point of the text. The original point of Acts 2:37–47 is appropriately extended to its current point when Peter's hearers and their actions serve as a positive role model for response to the message of Jesus today. Their response and ours can be summarized as hearing and responding to divine speech action with honesty, openness, attention, and obedience.[10]

Genre, Meaning, and Significance

It is a bit simplistic to speak of *the* current point of a biblical passage, especially when it comes to poetic and narrative passages whose didactic intent is implicit. On the other hand, to say a text has only *one* interpretation yet *many* applications is to utter a cliché that gives license to just about any sort of application. The challenge is determining which applications are valid and which are not, and the conclusion must be based on the relationship of a potential application to the interpretation of the passage. Early in chapter 1 of this book we

---

10. Vanhoozer, *Is There a Meaning?* 373–78.

alluded to the literary theory of E. D. Hirsch as it related to the role of heuristic genre hypotheses determining textual meaning. Now we return to Hirsch's literary theory as it relates to the original *meaning* and the subsequent *significance(s)* of texts. As Hirsch put it, we must honor the author's intent in determining the meaning of a text's words. To abandon the author is to abandon meaning altogether. Yet the author's meaning should not be understood in a shallow and simplistic manner but as a complex willed type of meaning with traits, values, affects, and their implications.[11] Hirsch touches only briefly on the additional complexity of the authorial intent of divinely inspired scriptural texts.[12] For Hirsch the determinacy of the original meaning of a text is necessarily assumed when one speaks its *significance.* Significance is limitless; it describes any evaluation of the relevance of a text's meaning for any situation. In general literary criticism, subservience to the author's will is necessary to construe meaning, but construing significance is independent of the author's will.[13] Although this approach might be useful in the literary criticism of poems and novels, it is not at all helpful for didactic revelatory texts like the Gospels and Acts. In such texts, any significance that is valid must be an extension of the text's meaning.

Kevin Vanhoozer's adaptation of Hirsch's literary theory speaks of biblical meaning as divine-human communicative action. Vanhoozer argues that the revelatory character and didactic purview of biblical texts lengthen their authorial attention span. In other words, biblical texts intentionally address times and contexts that transcend their author's original situation.[14] Additionally, Vanhoozer argues that the entire biblical canon is a unified divine-human communicative act, and that the Holy Spirit leads the church to the application or significance of biblical texts.[15] If we accept Vanhoozer's suggestions, the meaning of

---

11.   E. D. Hirsch, *Validity in Interpretation*, (New Haven, CT and London: Yale University Press, 1967) 51, 54–57, 61–67. See also Hirsch's *The Aims of Interpretation* (Chicago: University of Chicago Press, 1976), 8.

12.   Hirsch, *Validity*, 126 n. 37. Hirsch discards the notion of the *sensus plenior* of biblical texts. He notes that the human author's meaning includes both his immediate conscious intent as well as his implicit willed type of meaning. Any meaning beyond that of the willed type of the human author is attributed to the divine author.

13.   Hirsch, *Validity*, 142; cf. 8–10, 38–39, 140–44; Hirsch, *Aims*, 2–3, 79–81, 146.

14.   In the Gospels, futuristic texts (e.g., Matt. 10:16–23; 24:14; 26:13; 28:18–20) take on an age-long authorial attention span. Paul's letters commonly imply an authoritative purview that extends well beyond their immediate situation and audience (e.g., Rom. 16:4; 1 Cor. 7:17; 11:6; 14:33, 37–38; 16:1; Col. 4:16). Second Peter 3:14–18 extends to the Pauline corpus an open-ended authority tantamount to that of the OT.

15.   Vanhoozer, *Is There a Meaning?* 260–65. As Vanhoozer notes, Hirsch acknowledges the possibility of transhistorical authorial intent. See E. D. Hirsch, "Transhistorical Intentions and the Persistence of Allegory," *New Literary History* 25 (1994): 549–67.

biblical texts is deepened and enriched. Additionally, significance is no longer an evaluation of the text that is independent of the author's will. Instead, the significance of a text is shown in enactments that extend the text's original canonical communication act as successive performances of the original drama.

It is potentially misleading to speak of the *current* point of a biblical passage, since doing so implies discontinuity, if not disparity, between how God addressed the original audience of the text and how God addresses later audiences. The Bible as God's word describes God's nature as one. The continuity of the plan of God for the redemption of the people of God implies that there is a fundamental continuity between the original intended performance of a biblical text and its current performance. The relationship between the original and current performances might involve the specific application of a general biblical teaching, or it might involve extrapolating a principle from a specific biblical teaching to an analogous situation. Cultural factors come into play in many situations (e.g., Matt. 20:27; Luke 7:45; Rom. 16:16; Eph. 6:5–9).[16] In any event, the points drawn from biblical texts by current expositors must be theologically and ethically continuous with the original author's Spirit-led purview.

Guidelines for Applying the Gospels and Acts

Although there is no simple formula for determining *the current* point of a given passage, there are wise guidelines that can aid us in distinguishing valid, sound, edifying points that will be used by the Spirit to form God's people in the image of Christ and points that will ultimately prove to be unhelpful if not damaging for that purpose. No one would actually preach from 2 Kings 2:23–24 that making fun of bald people leads to getting mauled by bears, would they? Some sermons are not far removed from that sort of application. Many resources warn against mistaken and simplistic approaches to applying biblical narrative and provide wise and helpful approaches. Consider the following guidelines for deriving current points or performances from the Gospels and Acts:

- Any point that is derived from an individual pericope must be in harmony with the divine purpose of Scripture. St. Augustine concluded that the central purpose of Christian instruction is to encourage love for God and neighbor: "Whoever, then, thinks that he understands the Holy Scriptures, or any part of them, but

---

16. See the helpful introduction to cultural factors in application in Mark L. Strauss, *How to Read the Bible in Changing Times* (Grand Rapids: Baker, 2011), 207–44.

puts such an interpretation upon them as does not tend to build up this twofold love of God and our neighbor, does not yet understand them as he ought (*Doctr. chr.* 1.36; cf. 1.23–29).[17]

- Any point that is derived from an individual pericope must take narrative genre into account. Narrative genre contains a plot that present characters (both protagonists and antagonists) in various sorts of tests that reveal their character as either in harmony with or in opposition to the divine point of view that informs the narrative. Positive and negative points alike may be derived from the manner in which these characters respond to the tests they face, and the consequences that result from their responses.

- Any point that is derived from an individual pericope must be compatible with the teaching of the entire book that contains the pericope, with the rest of the NT, and with the biblical canon as a whole.[18] The promise-fulfillment motif of the canonical metanarrative provides the ultimate framework for judging the pastoral utility of any potential point we might take from a pericope found in the Gospels and Acts. This principle has been described as the hierarchical nature of biblical narrative.[19]

- Any point that is derived from an individual pericope should take into account the specific part of the pericope that is the source of the point. Pericopes contain affirmations and denials, commands and prohibitions, promises and warnings, heroes and villains. Specific points of theological truth or ethical instruction may be derived from specific features of the pericope such as these.[20] General "takeaway" points may be derived from the overall impression the pericope leaves with the reader.

---

17. Augustine follows Moses (Deut. 6:4–5; Lev. 19:18), Jesus (Matt. 22:34–40/Mark 12:28–31; Luke 10:25–37; John 13:34–35), Paul (Rom. 13:8–10; 1 Cor. 13:8; Gal. 5:14; 1 Tim. 1:5), and James (2:8, 19).

18. Topical approaches to application must be used with caution because they simply match a felt need to a word used in a biblical text with little if any regard to genre, original context, or metanarrative. An example is the A–Z ("abandon" to "zeal") arrangement of Neil S. Wilson, ed., *The Handbook of Biblical Application* (Wheaton, IL: Tyndale House, 2000). The material in this book is apparently taken from the Life Application Bible and does direct its readers to various passages.

19. Fee and Stuart speak of the three levels of OT narrative as (1) the overall metanarrative, including the NT, (2) the outworking of God's covenant with Israel in the OT as a whole, and (3) the individual narratives and pericopes which make up the OT and the canonical Scriptures as a whole. See *How to Read the Bible for All Its Worth*, 3rd ed. (Grand Rapids: Zondervan, 2003), 91–92.

20. Jack Kuhatshek provides helpful suggestions for applying biblical commands, examples, and promises in *Taking the Guesswork out of Applying the Bible* (Downers Grove, IL: InterVarsity, 1990), 87–154.

- Any point that is derived from an individual pericope should be taken with awareness of the history of the pericope's influence on the church, shown in the church's developing understanding of that pericope. This developing understanding of a pericope should, at the very least, caution us as to the wisdom of points that are entirely novel.[21]

Description and Prescription, Precedent and Norm

Before discussing approaches to sermonizing, we return to the question of description versus prescription in biblical narrative. Another way of putting the question is in terms of precedent and norm: How does a text which tells *what* happened yield a teaching on what *must* happen? Although the NT provides many examples of doctrinal and ethical teaching supported by OT narratives, it provides no explicit instructions on how to make the connection. Understanding how narratives teach is not a simple matter, especially when it comes to understanding Acts. Obeying Acts is not a transactional matter of mechanically repeating the church's practice in a single pericope and expecting God to respond in kind.[22]

Lectio Divina

A very different approach to discerning the current point of a passage is the contemplative approach known as *lectio divina*, divine or spiritual reading. This approach was advocated by Benedict in the sixth century, and some scholars trace it back to Augustine. A practice traditionally identified with monastic spirituality, it has become more widespread recently, even in evangelical protestant circles. The following four steps, associated with the twelfth-century Carthusian monk Guigo, are commonly used today.

---

21. More thorough discussion of current application of the Gospels and Acts may be found in Daniel M. Doriani, *Putting the Truth to Work: The Theory and Practice of Biblical Application* (Phillipsburg, NJ: P&R, 2001); William W. Klein, Craig L. Blomberg, and Robert L. Hubbard Jr., *Introduction to Biblical Interpretation* (Nashville: Nelson, 2004), 477–504; Andreas J. Köstenberger and Richard D. Patterson, *Invitation to Biblical Interpretation* (Grand Rapids: Eerdmans, 2011), 784–808; Abraham Kuruvilla, "Applicational Preaching," *BSac* 173 (2016): 387–400; Craig B. Larson, ed., *Interpretation and Application* (Peabody, MA: Hendrickson, 2012); Gary T. Meadors, ed., *Moving Beyond the Bible to Theology* (Grand Rapids: Zondervan, 2009); Grant R. Osborne, *The Hermeneutical Spiral*, rev. ed. (Downers Grove, IL: InterVarsity, 2006) 410–33; Jonathan Pennington, *Reading the Gospels Wisely* (Grand Rapids: Baker, 2012), 213–28; David Veerman, *How to Apply the Bible*, 2nd ed. (Wheaton, IL: Tyndale, 1993).

22. On the matter of historical precedent and normative teaching in Acts, see Gordon D. Fee, *Gospel and Spirit: Issues in New Testament Hermeneutics* (Peabody, MA: Hendrickson, 1991), 83–104; Fee and Stuart, *How to Read the Bible*, 107–25.

- *Lectio*: attentive, reflective, and repeated *reading* of a selected biblical passage
- *Meditatio*: letting the text sink into the heart by open hearted *reflection* rather than rational analysis
- *Oratio*: dialogical spoken *response* to God based on reflection
- *Contemplatio*: silencing one's own thoughts while *listening* for the transforming voice of God

The emphasis of *lectio divina* on an attitude of worshipful reflection is certainly appropriate for anyone who wishes to study and communicate the Bible. Many biblical texts speak glowingly of the awe and joy that ought to accompany our prayerful reflection on God's revealed truth (e.g., Ps. 119; Eph. 1:17–19; 3:10, 16–19; Col. 1:9–12; 1 Peter 1:8). There are, however, potentially troubling aspects to this practice.[23] The notion of a totally "open" contemplative state where one's own thoughts are silenced so that only the still small voice of God is heard has affinities with the meditative practices of Eastern religions. Some advocates of *lectio divina* advocate the repetition of a biblical word or phrase as a means to shut out everything but the voice of God. This somewhat troubling practice calls to mind the repeated use of a mantra (sacred utterance) in Eastern spirituality as a means of altering the consciousness. These concerns aside, others use the term *lectio divina* to describe biblical reading that is done with an intentionally devotional focus that expectantly waits for God to show the reader how the text applies to his or her life. Such reading which focuses the meaning of a biblical text on the life of the reader is appropriate, and should accompany the academic practices stressed here. Let our study be prayer.

HOMILETICAL PACKAGING

Defining Expository Preaching

The eminent preacher and preacher-teacher Haddon Robinson defined expository preaching as follows:

> Expository preaching is the communication of a biblical concept, derived from and transmitted through a historical, grammatical, and literary study of a passage in its context, which the Holy Spirit first applies

---

23. See further David G. Benner, *Opening to God: Lectio Divina and Life as Prayer* (Downers Grove, IL: InterVarsity, 2010). Benner speaks of the four stages of the *lectio* as attending, pondering, responding, and being.

to the personality and experience of the preacher, then through the preacher, applies to the hearers.[24]

Robinson's definition of an appropriate homiletic counsels that our exegesis arrives at a key idea or concept that is synthesized from our chosen text, and that this idea should affect the expositor before it can effectively affect the congregation. David Helm goes a step beyond Robinson by asserting that the biblical text should influence not only the content but also the structure of the sermon: "Expositional preaching is empowered preaching that rightfully submits the shape and emphasis of the sermon to the shape and emphasis of a biblical text."[25] Helm's concern is that the preacher's concern for contextualization, communicating the Bible in ways that are appropriate for contemporary culture, will outweigh the preacher's concern for communicating the original meaning of the Bible accurately. He thinks that many preachers spend more time on creative, artistic packaging of the Bible than on accurately understanding the Bible to begin with:

> Some preachers spend more time reading and meditating on our cultural setting than we do on God's Word. We get caught up in sermonizing about our world or city in an effort to be relevant. As a result, we settle for giving shallow impressions of the text. We forget that the biblical text is the relevant word. It deserves our greatest powers of meditation and explanation.[26]

Helm is no doubt correct that content should take priority over context. When preachers miss the content of the biblical text, it matters little whether they are skillful in contextualizing their ideas. When preachers communicate the text accurately, the power of the biblical message can overcome their lack of cultural savvy. Ideally, preachers will value the revelational content of the biblical text so highly that they will work to communicate that text in a contextually relevant manner.

---

24. Robinson, *Biblical Preaching*, 4. Robinson acknowledges that this is an elaborate and dry definition.

25. David R. Helm, *Expositional Preaching: How We Speak God's Word Today* (Wheaton, IL: Crossway, 2014), 13.

26. Helm, *Expositional Preaching*, 17. Helm's view of the priority of content over context appears to be similar to that of Augustine, which was discussed above. Helm does speak to appropriate contextualization on 87–110.

The Tension in Homiletics: Which Comes First?	
Contextual Relevance >>>>>>	**<<<<<< Revelational Content**
Currency	Accuracy
Postmodern cultures	Ancient Near Eastern cultures
Contemporary slang	Hebrew, Aramaic, and Greek
Facebook, Twitter, Instagram	Biblical genres such as narrative and parable
Internet acronyms and emojis	Biblical tropes such as parallelisms and chiasmus

Deductive and Inductive Preaching

It stands to reason that every sermon should be expository. However the sermon is packaged, its substance must explain and herald the biblical text rather than the preacher's views. Today there is a debate in homiletics theory over deductive and inductive approaches to exposition. Much of this discussion arises from the thought of Fred Craddock, who spoke of preachers who wonder "whether it is best to continue to serve up monologue in a dialogical world."[27] Craddock's analysis of the culture that informed his congregation led him to write sermons that attempted to draw his audience into sharing his own process of discovery. Traditional homiletical theory is commonly described as deductive because the sermon begins with a thesis or proposition that is demonstrated logically by subsequent points and a concluding illustration. Such is the oft-caricatured "three points and a poem" sermon. The "new homiletic" often traced back to Craddock uses a more inductive approach, one in which the preacher leads the congregation in a shared process of gradual discovery of the sermon's thesis.

---

27. Fred Craddock, *As One Without Authority*, rev. ed. (St. Louis: Chalice, 2001), 15. Craddock's book was first published in 1971. Before Craddock, Grady Davis pointed in the direction of inductive preaching in his book *Design for Preaching* (Philadelphia: Muhlenberg, 1958).

Two Approaches to Biblical Communication

Deductive Preaching	Inductive Preaching
Thesis is stated at the beginning	Thesis becomes clear at the end
Preacher argues to support the thesis	Congregation listens to discover the thesis
Logical development of propositions	Skillful presentation of a narrative
Didactic monologue	Existential dialogue
Proclamation by an authoritative preacher	Reflection by a responsive audience
Accurate and orthodox	Interesting and suspenseful
Clarity is essential	A degree of ambiguity is embraced
A passive congregation accepts the preacher's views?	An active congregation is free to reach their own conclusions?

Neither of these two approaches to preaching—nor any other approach, for that matter—is explicitly mandated or modeled in the NT. When preparing to preach, we first form an idea that is legitimately derived from the author's willed type of meaning. There is no room for creativity or imagination in this first exegetical step; we are describing what we find in the text, no more, no less. Many homileticians suggest that this exegetical content—variously called the thesis, the proposition, or the big idea—should be distilled and expressed in one simple sentence. Once the basic content or "what?" of the sermon is clear, it is time to consider the method or "how" of the sermon. This step is a matter of packaging the exegetical content to the audience in a manner that is clear, culturally appropriate, winsome, and persuasive. It is the preacher's responsibility to choose wisely and prayerfully a sermonic model that is most appropriate for the content to be communicated and for the recipients of the communication. Throughout this process preachers should cultivate variety in their homiletical repertoire rather than settling into a single approach to pulpit discourse.[28]

---

28. Faris D. Whitesell and Lloyd M. Perry, *Variety in Your Preaching* (Westwood, NJ: Revell, 1954). The central idea of this dated textbook is valid and some of its ideas are still helpful.

Genre-based Preaching

Thomas G. Long has argued that the literary genre of a text should influence the creation of sermons on the text. Ignoring this principle leads to preachers viewing texts as inert containers of theological concepts and approaching sermonizing as throwing the containers into the exegetical winepress to extract the concepts. The containers are discarded and the concepts are turned into sermons. As Long points out, however, texts are not containers with literary decorations; their literary form and their conceptual content are linked, and homiletics should honor that linkage by the form and content of the sermon.[29] When it comes to the Gospels and Acts, sermons ought to do justice to the narratival genre of the pericopes. Sermons on biblical narratives ought to focus on the rise and resolution of dramatic tension as the characters respond to tests that demonstrate values in harmony with or in opposition to the divine point of view. Biblical stories should be illustrated and applied by using comparable stories. Resolution of the drama and suspense should usually come only at the end, when (or if) "the moral of the story" is explained in the text. At this point deductive logic and propositional truths can summarize the values of the story and explain how the characters provide positive and negative role models for current life.

Other Sermonic Approaches

Andy Stanley suggests another way of achieving homiletical clarity and effectiveness. He believes that communication strategy should focus on two questions:

(1)   What is the one thing I want my audience to know?
(2)   What do I want them to do about it?[30]

Stanley's two questions seem to address biblical truth and life application respectively. Haddon Robinson's suggestion that every sermon should have a big idea also included two related questions:

(1)   What is the author talking about? (homiletical subject)
(2)   What is the author saying about what he is talking about? (homiletical complement)[31]

---

29.   Thomas G. Long, *Preaching and the Literary Forms of the Bible* (Philadelphia: Fortress, 1988), 12–13. Long applies this insight to biblical narrative and the parables of Jesus on 66–106.

30.   Andy Stanley and Lane Jones, *Communicating for Change* (Colorado Springs: Multnomah, 2006), 103.

31.   Robinson, *Biblical Preaching*, 31–48.

Robinson's two questions both seem to relate to exegesis, moving from a general subject to a specific aspect of it. Stanley's two questions relate to both exegesis and application. Abraham Kuruvilla's writings emphasize a single question: "What is the author doing with what he is saying?"[32] This approach seems to be compatible with speech act theory's distinction between the locutional and illocutional levels of discourse. Kuruvilla seems to frame homiletics as perlocution, implying the question, "What is the preacher doing with what he or she is saying about what the author is doing with what he is saying?" In other words, what is the preacher's point? What does the preacher want the congregation to do about the sermon?

Bryan Chapell believes that every text focuses in some way on the fallen human condition (FC) and on Christ as the redemptive solution (RS).[33] Jonathan Pennington adds a focus on virtue formation (VF) to Chapell's approach, yielding the following homiletical rubric:[34]

The Framing Questions for a Sermon on the Gospels

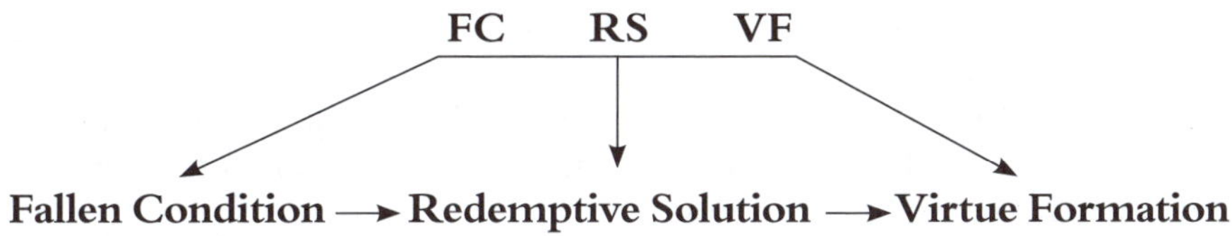

Pennington suggests that every narrative pericope contains these three elements, and that every sermon should integrate this pattern, both implicitly as the sermon develops and explicitly in the sermon's conclusion. Although the individual elements of this rubric are thoroughly biblical, it seems overly rigid to expect every pericope to deliver these elements, and overly predictable to structure each sermon along these lines. It is debatable that the current point or applicational performance of every pericope should be construed as virtue formation. Such an approach could result in an unintended anthropocentricity. Using the rubric to structure a sermon or its conclusion might also get in the way of the pericope's story dynamics, spoil its drama, and reduce its appeal. Despite these concerns, Pennington's adapta-

---

32. E.g., Abraham Kuruvilla, "The Naked Runaway and the Enrobed Reporter of Mark 14 and 16: What Is the Author Doing with What He Is Saying?" *JETS* 54 (2011): 527–45.

33. Bryan Chapell, *Christ-Centered Preaching: Redeeming the Expository Sermon*, 2nd ed. (Grand Rapids: Baker, 2005).

34. Pennington, *Reading the Gospels Wisely*, 219–25.

tion of Chapell's approach provides a serviceable sermonic structure, albeit not one to be overused.[35]

BRIDGING THE WORLD OF THE PASSAGE AND WORLD OF THE READER

The heading for this section amounts to a conflation of popular language about the application of the Bible. For instance, the deservedly well-known NIV Application Commentary series has a triadic structure: original meaning, bridging the gap, and contemporary significance.[36] As John Stott put it, there is a sense in which Christian communicators stand between the world of the Bible and the world of their audience.[37] Yet this business about bridging gaps between two worlds can be problematic. It is not as though the expositor stands between two worlds trying as a mediator to bridge a labor dispute by eliciting a compromise between the company and the union. Also, the two "worlds" are not on different planets, one inhabited by human beings and the other by extraterrestrials. Both of these "worlds" are rooted in God's creative power and providential wisdom. Both of these worlds are inhabited by human beings who are no less images of God today than in biblical times. God's redeeming love for humanity shown in the power of the gospel of a crucified and risen Lord has not diminished. The word of God is still sufficient to form the people of God when it is communicated accurately and wisely in dependence on the Spirit of God.[38]

What Stott meant by the title of his classic book *Between Two Worlds* is related to how he later described biblical preaching. He spoke of the

---

35. Additional resources on preaching biblical narrative include Bryan D. Anderson, *Big Idea in Biblical Narrative* (Maitland, FL: Xulon, 2012); Joel Green and Michael Pasquarello, eds., *Narrative Reading, Narrative Preaching: Reuniting New Testament Interpretation and Proclamation* (Grand Rapids: Baker, 2003); Haddon Robinson and Craig Brian Larson, eds., *Biblical Preaching: A Comprehensive Resource for Today's Communicators* (Grand Rapids: Zondervan, 2005), 66–106; Leland Ryken and Todd Wilson, *Preach the Word: Essays on Expository Preaching in Honor of R. Kent Hughes* (Wheaton, IL: Crossway, 2007).

36. E.g., see the editors' "Series Introduction" in Gary M. Burge, *John*, The NIV Application Commentary (Grand Rapids: Zondervan, 2000), 9–12. In this introduction the editors speak helpfully of Scripture as both timely in its original setting and timeless in its ultimate relevance.

37. John R. W. Stott, *Between Two Worlds: The Art of Preaching in the Twentieth Century* (Grand Rapids: Eerdmans, 1982).

38. Hirsch's critique of "faulty perspectives" in hermeneutics raises questions about theories of application that over-emphasize differences between individual interpreters or eras of interpretation. See *The Aims of Interpretation*, 36–49. Mark Strauss also expresses concern for this language in *How to Read the Bible in Changing Times*, 211–13. See also Joel Green's concerns from the perspective of theological exegesis in *Seized by Truth: Reading the Bible as Scripture* (Nashville: Abingdon, 2007), 56–61.

two main obligations of a biblical expositor as *faithfulness* to the unchanging ancient biblical text and *sensitivity* to the changing modern culture.[39] This helpful mandate calls expositors to commit themselves to biblical and cultural literacy. In the Gospels, Jesus speaks about the kingdom of God in the language and idiom of his Jewish audience, using literary genres and illustrations from the world they inhabited. In Acts, Paul communicates to a wide range of audiences, from synagogue attenders to the Sanhedrin, from rustic and intellectual pagans to Roman governors. When all of Paul's speeches are compared and contrasted, it is clear that he spoke with awareness of and sensitivity toward the varied backgrounds of his audiences in mind, and that in doing so he remained faithful to God's word.[40] Today's expositors likewise must exegete both the people in their audiences and the Bible, just as bilingual translators who are fluent in the language of the speaker they translate as well as the language of those who are listening to the speaker. We can extend the analogy of bilingual translation to include not only our responsibility to translate the divine speaker's language accurately but also the mysterious power of that language to persuade even the most recalcitrant listener.

Case Study: Acts 2:37–47

Acts 2:37–47 narrates the response of the audience to Peter's sermon on the day of Pentecost. This text is one of many biblical texts that describe the proclamation of God's message and its results.[41] Response to the gospel message is a matter of central importance in Luke-Acts, which portrays the spread of messianic salvation from Jerusalem to Rome, from the Jews to all the nations. The narration of the spread of messianic salvation in Luke-Acts contains both positive and negative responses.[42] Preachers may be confident that these narratives provide

---

39. John R. W. Stott, "A Definition of Biblical Preaching," in Robinson and Larson, eds., *Biblical Preaching: A Comprehensive Resource*, 3–5.

40. E.g., compare Paul's speech to the synagogue audience in Pisidian Antioch (Acts 13:16–43) to his hasty comments to the rural gentiles in Lystra (Acts 14:8–18) and his Areopagus address to the educated Gentiles in Athens (Acts 17:22–33).

41. The Bible describes both authentic and inauthentic proclamation as well as faithful and faithless hearing of the message. This can be seen from the very outset of the biblical metanarrative, where Adam and Eve listen and respond to both God and Satan. See also the many accounts of authentic and inauthentic prophetic utterance, e.g., Deut. 13:1–18; 14–22; 2 Chron. 24:19; Jer. 5:31; 23:13–40; Ezek. 2:1–3:11; 33:30–33; Matt. 7:15–27; Matt 13:1–23/Mark 4:1–20/Luke 8:4–15; 1 Thess. 2:13; James 1:21–27; 2 Peter 2:1.

42. Luke's account of Jesus's parable of the sower and its interpretation (8:4–15) sets the scene for mixed responses to the kingdom in Luke-Acts. Individual pericopes often include instances of belief and unbelief alike. Positive responses to the message of Jesus and his kingdom in

examples that challenge people today by encouraging obedient responses and warning of the consequences of disobedience.

A *deductive* exposition of Acts 2:37–47 could be based on the proposition "Responding to the gospel of Jesus Christ requires your heart and your life." This exposition would, of course, be built upon a clear presentation of the gospel, such as Peter's in Acts 2:14–36. One would simply follow the sequential flow of the narrative to discover that people in Peter's audience experienced remorse and were told to repent (2:37–38). They accepted Peter's counsel, were baptized, and identified with the church and its activities (2:41–42). Reflecting on the text leads to the conclusion that the successive responses were initially internal, attitudinal and negative, involving admission of sin and resolve to turn from it, and subsequently external, behavioral and positive, involving initial identification with Christ and ensuing activities in concert with the community of Christ's followers. The following structure could be used to summarize this response:

How to Respond to the Gospel of Jesus

> I.   Respond from your heart by turning from sin (Acts 2:37–40).
>   A. Remorse (acknowledging sin)
>   B. Repentance (turning away from sin)
> II. Respond with your life by identifying with Christ and the church (Acts 2:41–47).
>   A. New identity (baptism as the first step of faith)
>   B. New community (participation in Christ with like-minded people)

The application of this sermon would be to urge nonbelievers to turn to Christ, and to provide those who believe themselves to be Christians with clear marks of what the Christian life ought to involve. The sermon could be part of a series that expounds the book of Acts, or a series that explores passages that portray various responses to the gospel, both positive and negative.

A more *inductive* approach to the passage might begin with a question rather than a proposition, something like "How do we respond to the gospel of Jesus Christ?" or "What does real response to the gospel of Jesus

Luke-Acts include Luke 3:7–13; 19:1–10, 48; 21:38; 24:32; Acts 2:37–47; 4:4; 8:4–8, 26–40; 10:17–48; 13:4–12, 42–43, 46–49; 14:1, 21; 16:11–15, 27–34; 17:1–4, 10–12, 34; 18:7–11; 19:17–19; 28:24. For negative responses, see Luke 4:16–30; 6:6–11; 15:1–16:14; 18:18–23; 19:47; Acts 4:1–3, 13–18; 5:17–18, 33–42; 6:8–7:60; 9:20–25; 13:44–45, 50; 14:2, 4–7, 19; 16:19–24; 17:5–9, 13, 32; 18:6, 12–17; 19:8–9, 23–41; 21:27–22:23; 23:1–16; 24:24–27; 26:24–29; 28:24.

Christ look like?" The sermon could begin by exploring how people have responded and might be expected to respond to the gospel. Perhaps the sermon could recount noteworthy experiences of well-known believers, as well as notorious nonbelievers. Perhaps people in the congregation could be asked to recount their own experience when they were first confronted with the Christian message. Then the passage could be examined in such a way that the congregation comes to discover Peter's audience's angst over sin, their plea for relief from the acute guilt they were feeling, and the life change they experienced when repentance led to baptism and participation in the church as a community of Christ-followers. The application would be to urge the congregation to identify with Peter's audience's response rather than other possible responses.

Another way to preach texts like Acts 2:37–47 is *thematically*.[43] As noted above, response to the gospel is a keynote of Luke-Acts, and readers of Acts encounter notable examples of belief and unbelief. A series of sermons could begin with an exposition of Jesus's parable of the sower in Luke 8:4–13, noting key factors that hinder saving faith. Subsequent sermons could examine key instances of belief and unbelief in Luke-Acts, linking these texts to the themes discovered in the parable of the sower. The congregation could be encouraged to ponder the gravity of response to the gospel, to share it more faithfully, and to be aware of the volatile results that may come. When Acts 2:37–47 is viewed as a key instance of proper response to the gospel, many subthemes arise as elements of proper response to the gospel. As would be expected, Luke emphasizes these subthemes throughout Luke-Acts, and they are essential to his narrative of the spread of the gospel. Each of these subthemes could serve as the focus for a sermon or even a series of sermons. Sermonic structure for thematic sermons based on these narrative texts should not transform the narratives into deductive theological discourses. Among such themes are:

- Conviction of sin (2:37; cf. Luke 5:8; 18:9–14; Acts 16:30)
- Repentance (2:38, 41; cf. Luke 3:3, 8; 5:32; 13:1–5; 15:7, 10, 17–19; 24:47; Acts 3:19; 17:30; 19:18–19; 26:18–20)
- Baptism (2:28, 41; cf. Luke 3:3; 7:29; Acts 8:12, 36; 9:18; 10:47; 16:15, 33; 18:8; 19:3; 22:16)
- Forgiveness of sins (2:38; cf. Luke 1:77; 3:3; 5:20–23; 7:36–50; 24:47; Acts 3:19; 5:31; 10:43; 13:38; 26:18)

---

43. For additional insight into preaching on Luke-Acts, see Ronald L. Allen, *Preaching Luke-Acts* (St. Louis: Chalice, 2000). Allen wisely recommends preaching on recurrent themes in Luke-Acts rather than on isolated pericopes. He has in mind topics like the character and work of the Holy Spirit, the kingdom of God, the participation of women in the Gospel, and the stewardship of material resources (1–2).

- The Holy Spirit (2:38; cf. e.g., Luke 3:16, 22; 10:38; 11:13; 12:12; 24:49; Acts 1:5, 8; 2:4, 17, 33; 5:32; 9:17; 11:15–18; 20:28)
- The apostles' teaching (2:42; cf. Luke 1:4; 4:15, 32; 5:21, 25, 28, 42; 10:39; 13:22; 20:1; 23:5; Acts 1:1; 4:2, 18; 5:28; 6:4; 11:26; 15:35; 18:11; 20:20)
- Christian fellowship and common meals (2:42, 46; cf. Luke 22:19; 24:35; Acts 20:7; 27:35)
- Prayer (2:42; cf. Luke 1:13; 2:37; 5:16; 6:12; 9:28; 10:2; 11:1–13; 18:1–8; 22:39–46; Acts 1:14, 24; 4:23–31; 6:4, 6; 12:5, 12; 13:3; 14:23; 16:25; 20:36)
- Reverence and praise (2:43, 47; cf. Luke 1:50; 2:13, 20; 5:26; 17:18; 18:43; 19:37; Acts 3:8; 4:21; 9:31; 10:35)
- Signs and wonders (2:43; cf. Luke 11:16, 29–30; 21:7, 11, 25; 23:8; Acts 2:19, 22; 4:16, 22, 30; 5:12; 6:8; 7:36; 8:6; 14:3; 15:12)
- Stewardship of material resources (2:44–45; cf. Luke 8:3; 12:13–34; 18:22–30; 21:1–4; Acts 4:32–5:11; 6:1; 11:27–30; 16:15; 20:35; 24:17)
- Favorable reputation (2:47; cf. Luke 2:52; Acts 5:13)
- Ongoing conversions (2:47; cf. 6:1, 7; 9:31; 12:24; 19:10, 20)

Chapter in Review

This chapter began with an introduction to communicating the Gospels and Acts. We examined Augustine's teaching in *On Christian Doctrine* about the threefold purpose of Christian communication (to teach, to delight, and to move). Then, we discussed the matter of determining the original point of passages in the Gospels and Acts, focusing on narrative genre and pericope structure. Discussion of determining the current point of a passage ensued, with emphasis on the meaning/significance distinction and speech act theory. Varying approaches to sermonizing were summarized in the next section on homiletical packaging. Finally, John Stott's ideas about the necessity of fidelity to the text and sensitivity to the audience were discussed in the last section on bridging the ancient world of the passage and the current world of the reader. The chapter concluded with an exploration of various ways to preach a case study text, Acts 2:37–47.

7

FROM TEXT TO SERMON: TWO EXAMPLES

The Chapter at a Glance

Studying a biblical text with a view to its proclamation involves two interwoven tasks: exegesis and exposition. Exegetical method starts with establishing and translating the text, which leads to analyzing its genre, syntax, and key words. Exegetical method addresses the text's referential world, including its history, geography, and culture. Exegetical method engages the thought of the text, how its teaching is related to that of the Bible as a whole, as well as how the church's ongoing reflection has understood and applied the text. Communicating the text brings all this exegetical insight to bear on the church's situational need for instruction, correction, and edification. The study of Mark 4:1–20 models how to work with the synoptic triple tradition in a challenging passage which includes an embedded genre (parable), intertextual depth (Isa. 6:9), theological mystery, and pastoral relevance. The study of John 1:1–18 models how to work with the Fourth Gospel and the Johannine corpus as a whole. This passage serves not only as the prologue to John's Gospel but also as a seedbed for Johannine biblical theology.

INTRODUCTION

ADVOCATES OF HISTORICAL-CRITICAL METHODOLOGY tend to view exegesis as a purely descriptive task that must be kept separate from the pragmatic concerns that influence prescriptive application and communication of the Bible. The idea is that one must not think of the text's current application during exegesis in order to maintain interpretive neutrality and objectivity. It is impossible, however, for humans to function in such a mechanical manner. Inner biblical exegesis—the use of earlier OT texts in later OT texts as well as the use of the OT in the NT—does not model such bifurcation of exegesis and exposition. The theological interpretation of the Bible movement correctly opposes rigid separation of exegesis and exposition, arguing that exegetes should acknowledge the text's pastoral interests as well as their own and should engage the church's prior reflection on and teaching of the text during the exegetical process. At the same time exegetes should beware of what has come to be known as confirmation bias, the tendency to find what one is looking for. It is true that people tend to believe what they want to believe, but exegetes must seek the mind of the Spirit. As exegetes work to understand the text, they open themselves to better self-understanding and pastoral insight under the guidance of the Spirit.

The process of exegesis and exposition has been discussed at great length in preceding chapters. In what follows here I present the method in five steps:

- Establishing and translating the text: textual criticism and translation
- Analyzing the text: genre, syntax, literary structure, key words
- Setting the text: social, cultural, and historical features
- Thinking with the text: biblical, historical, and systematic theology
- Teaching the text: pastoral communication

In what follows we provide a case study of expositional exegesis (or exegetical exposition) in the synoptic tradition from Mark 4:1–20.

MARK 4:1–20

Establishing and Translating the Text

Textual Criticism

The apparatus of NA[28] cites numerous variant readings in Mark 4:1–20, but most are of little or no consequence for translation and meaning. UBS[5] only cites variants in 4:8, 15, and 20, and they have very little impact on meaning. There are multiple issues in 4:8 (cf. 4:20), leading the UBS editors to acknowledge the difficulties in determining the original reading with a {C} rating. The neuter plural ἄλλα (supported by א*, B, C, L) is read as the neuter singular ἄλλο in some manuscripts (א^c, A, D, Δ), but the plural explains the origin of the singular better than *vice versa* (cf. 4:5, 7). Related to this problem, the neuter plural participle αὐξανόμενα (א, B, 1071) is read as masculine αὐξανόμενον (A, D, L, W, Δ) or αὐξανόντα (C, Θ, *f*¹, *f*¹³) and is understood to agree with καρπòν instead of ἄλλα. The difficulty in resolving these variants is not equivalent to their exegetical importance since it matters little whether the growth is understood to be that of the planted seed or the resulting fruit. The text as it stands in NA²⁸ and UBS⁵ better explains the origin of the variants than *vice versa*.

Also in 4:8 (cf. 4:20), some manuscripts (א, C*^vid, Δ, 28, 700) have the masculine εἰς. . . εἰς. . . εἰς instead of the neuter ἓν . . . ἓν . . . ἓν. This reading is complicated further by the ambiguity of the triple εν here and in 4:20. This word is understood as ἓν in NA²⁸ and UBS⁵ (with *f*¹³ and most early versions), but other manuscripts have it as ἐν (*f*¹, 33, 157, *Byz*). An Aramaic idiom in which the number one (חד) functions as a multiplication sign ("times") may stand behind the reading. If ἓν is read, a sort of ascending ratio is implied.[1] Either way, it is clear that the word ἐν introduces a series of clauses that describe the extent of the fruit borne by the good ground.

A variant at the end of 4:15 should also be mentioned. Here NA²⁸ and UBS⁵ read εἰς αὐτούς (supported by B, W, *f*¹, *f*¹³, 28, 205). The reading ἐν αὐτοῖς (א, C, L, Δ, 579) is smoother and easier and thus less likely. The reading ἐν ταῖς καρδίαις αὐτῶν (D, 33, Θ, *Byz*) apparently resulted from assimilation to Matthew 13:19. In any event, the meaning of the text is not altered to a great degree by any of the variants.[2]

Translation

The following discussion of translation refers to the phrased analysis in the following section. The more difficult morphological and syntactical constructions will be highlighted.

In the third clause of 4:1 (ὥστε αὐτòν εἰς πλοῖον ἐμβάντα καθῆσθαι ἐν τῇ θαλάσσῃ), ὥστε is followed by the aorist infinitive καθῆσθαι in a result clause. The accusative αὐτòν refers to Jesus and functions as the subject of the infinitive. The participle ἐμβάντα (second aorist active from ἐμβαίνω) functions adverbially (temporally or as attendant circumstance). The clause indicates the result of the crowd pressing Jesus

---

1. Roger L. Omanson, *A Textual Guide to the Greek New Testament* (Stuttgart: Deutsche Bibelgesellschaft, 2006), 68.

2. Discussion of textual variants in Mark 4:1–20 may be found in the exegetical commentaries. See also Bruce M. Metzger, *A Textual Commentary on the Greek New Testament*, 2nd ed. (Stuttgart: Deutsche Bibelgesellschaft, 1994), 71; Omanson, *Textual Guide*, 68–69.

along the shore, and should be translated along these lines: "so that he got into a boat and sat in it on the sea."

In 4:3 (ἐξῆλθεν ὁ σπείρων σπεῖραι), σπεῖραι (aorist active infinitive of the liquid verb σπείρω) indicates the purpose of ἐξῆλθεν: the sower went out in order to sow seed.

In the first clause of 4:4, the prepositional phrase ἐν τῷ σπείρειν with the present infinitive as object amounts to a temporal clause describing the sowing process. It could be translated "during the sowing," "while he was sowing," or "as he sowed."

In the second clause of 4:4, ὃ μὲν ἔπεσεν signals the beginning of a series[3] that continues with καὶ ἄλλο ἔπεσεν . . . in 4:5 and 4:7, and by καὶ ἄλλα ἔπεσεν . . . in 4:8. The first three expressions are singular and the fourth (4:8) is plural. The question is whether one should translate the series as individual seeds[4] or groups of seeds[5] that fell on the four types of soil. Most interpreters take the second option, which answers to the plurals in Jesus's interpretation (4:15–19) and results in translations like the following: "Part (or 'some') of the seed fell . . ."

As noted in the textual discussion above, it seems best to take the three ἐν constructions in 4:8 and 4:20 with the numerical terms as equivalent to thirty fold, sixty fold, and hundred fold. With the verb ἔφερεν, this reading would result in a translation along the lines of "some produced (or 'bore, yielded') thirty fold, others . . ."

The citation of Isaiah 6:9 in Mark 4:12 raises several translation questions. The first is whether to render ἵνα as a marker of purpose. Although some scholars are reluctant to do so for theological reasons, it seems clear that Mark 4:12 cites Isaiah to explain Jesus's intention that at least some of the parables conceal.[6] The first two lines of the passage reflect a sort of Hebrew parallelism that is sometimes called synonymous, and the third line is a negated purpose clause. As translation Greek,[7] the participle plus subjunctive constructions (βλέποντες . . . βλέπωσιν and ἀκούοντες . . . ἀκούωσιν) reflect the use of the Hebrew infinitive absolute to intensify the imperative.[8] These emphatic constructions under-

---

3. One might expect a δέ clause to follow, but it is not unusual to find anacolouthetic constructions after μέν. See BDAG, s.v. μέν, 2 (630).

4. As argued by Robert H. Gundry, *Mark: A Commentary on His Apology for the Cross* (Grand Rapids: Eerdmans, 1993), 192–93, who takes the singular seeds to indicate nonintentional or chance results of the sowing process.

5. As argued by Robert H. Stein, *Mark*, BECNT (Grand Rapids: Baker, 2008), 197–98, and reflected in most English translations.

6. Robert H. Stein, *An Introduction to the Parables of Jesus* (Philadelphia: Westminster, 1981), 27–35.

7. BDF §4.

8. B. K. Waltke and M. O'Connor, *An Introduction to Biblical Hebrew Syntax* (Winona Lake, IN: Eisenbrauns, 1990), 584–88.

line the surprising and anomalous result in each case—the seeing and hearing do not lead to perception and understanding.[9] English translations need to reflect this irony. A formal correspondence approach would lead to a translation like "in order that seeing they might see but not perceive." A functionally equivalent translation would be "in order that they really might see, and yet not perceive." Possibly the first clause could be taken as concession, resulting in the translation "in order that, although they really do see, they might not perceive."

Translating 4:13 requires a decision about how to punctuate the first clause. If the first clause is understood as a question, the verse implies that understanding this parable is a key to understanding parables as a whole: "Don't you understand this parable? How then will you understand all the parables?" If the first clause is understood as a simple statement of fact, it might be understood as an exclamation: "You don't understand this parable! How then will you understand all the parables?" Another option would be to take the first clause as an implied conditional protasis: "If you don't understand *this* parable, how then will you understand *any* of the parables?"

Translating Jesus's interpretive comments on the four groups of seeds in 4:14–20 recalls the difficulty of translating the initial series of four groups of seeds in the parable proper in 4:4–8. Demonstrative pronouns (οὗτοι[10] δέ εἰσιν . . . καὶ οὗτοι εἰσιν . . .; 4:15, 16) introduce the first two groups. The expression καὶ ἄλλοι εἰσὶν . . . (4:18) introduces the third group, and expression καὶ ἐκεῖνοί εἰσιν . . . (4:20) introduces the fourth group. Formal correspondence translations of this phraseology would be something like "These are the ones (sown) along the path . . ." (4:15). A functional equivalence approach would be more along the lines of "Some people are like the seeds sown along the path . . ." or "The seeds sown along the path represent people who . . ."

Translating the three fruitful results in the good soil in 4:20 should be consistent with the translation of 4:8 as discussed above.

Analyzing the Text

The discussion here proceeds from genre to syntactical and literary structure, and then on to key words. Most attention is given to structure, with focus on a phrased worksheet, discourse analysis, vertical reading, and horizontal reading.

---

9. In keeping with the versatile Hebrew וְ, the conjunction καὶ that links the two halves of each clause should be translated adversatively as "and yet" or "but." See BDAG, s.v. καί (1 b η), 495.

10. The interpretation of the four results of sowing seed (4:3–8) is unfolded by οὗτοι δέ εἰσιν . . . (4:15), καὶ οὗτοι εἰσιν . . . (16), καὶ ἄλλοι εἰσὶν . . . (4:18), and καὶ ἐκεῖνοί εἰσιν . . . (4:20).

Genre

The analysis of any text should begin with a consideration of its genre. In a previous chapter we discussed the importance of genre assumptions for interpretation, the narrative genre of the four Gospels and Acts, and the embedded genres that commonly occur in these narratives. Mark 4:1–20 is a section of the narration of Jesus's words and deeds during the Galilean ministry. This passage speaks of Jesus teaching by the Sea of Galilee in parables, and it embeds the parable of the sower (4:3–9) as a key to understanding all of Jesus's parables (4:13).[11] The aftermath of the parable involves the disciples asking Jesus about the parables. His reply embeds the intertext Isaiah 6:9 (4:11–12) and provides a detailed interpretation of the sower (4:14–20).

We have discussed the general interpretation of parables as an embedded genre in the Gospels in a previous chapter. Since the parable of the sower pericope also includes a detailed interpretation of the parable, it is important to note that some scholars view the interpretations of the parables as later ecclesiastical allegories that are not in keeping with the simple original "moral of the story." Such scholars typically try to distinguish between a possible core of authentic Jesus tradition and the accretions of later ecclesiastical traditions. There are good reasons to discard this approach; among them its inherent subjectivity and the impossibility of reliably distinguishing between Jesus and the later church. Following other evangelical scholars, we will view both the parable and its interpretation as rooted in authentic Jesus tradition.[12]

It is helpful to compare the parable of the sower to other ancient texts that speak metaphorically about sowing seed. Biblical texts will be discussed later, but for now it should be mentioned that several texts from 4 Ezra (late first century A.D.) are relevant. Fourth Ezra 4:28–32 reflects on eschatological judgment under the image of a great threshing floor. The evil seed first sown in the beginning in the heart of Adam (cf. 4 Ezra 3:20–21) has multiplied into heads of grain without number. In 4 Ezra 8:41–45 an angel compares humans and their ultimate salvation to seeds sown in a field. Many seeds do not come up, and many that come up are ruined by too much or too little rain. Ezra protests that humans made in God's image should not be compared to mere seeds. Fourth

---

11.   We have addressed the interpretation of parables in a previous chapter.

12.   E.g., see Craig Blomberg, *Interpreting the Parables* (Downers Grove, IL: InterVarsity, 1990), 13–22, 226–29; Phillip B. Payne, "The Authenticity of the Parable of the Sower and Its Interpretation," in *Gospel Perspectives*, eds. R. T. France and David Wenham (Sheffield: JSOT, 1980), 1.181–86; Klyne R. Snodgrass, *Stories with Intent: A Comprehensive Guide to the Parables of Jesus* (Grand Rapids: Eerdmans, 2008), 15–17, 24–35, 145–77; Stein, *Introduction to the Parables*, 53–81.

Ezra 9:30–35 speaks of the Torah being sown in Israel, although Israel has not kept it. Fourth Ezra 9:14–35 uses several images, including field and seed, to state that more people will be lost than will be saved. The mid-late second-century gnostic *Gospel of Thomas* 8 contains a simple version of the parable of the sower. In this text a worms eats the seed of the thorn-choked plants. The late rabbinic text *Avot of Rabbi Nathan* (8:2) contains a parable that is similar to that of the sower.

Syntax and Literary Structure

Phrased Worksheet. During the translation process, it is helpful to distinguish between main and subordinate clauses and display them on a worksheet. The use of such a phrased worksheet has been explained in a previous chapter. The following analysis of Mark 4:1–20 models this method, which enables exegetes to grasp a passage's syntactical and literary structure and to discover matters that deserve further study. Footnotes address salient exegetical matters that can be pursued more fully in grammars and commentaries. The words of Jesus are placed in italics. Double spacing distinguishes the segments of the pericope. The central intertext, Isaiah 6:9 in Mark 4:12, is presented in bold font for emphasis.

Phrased Worksheet on Mark 4:1–20

1   Καὶ[13] πάλιν[14] ἤρξατο διδάσκειν[15] παρὰ τὴν θάλασσαν·
        καὶ συνάγεται[16] πρὸς αὐτὸν ὄχλος πλεῖστος,
            ὥστε[17] αὐτὸν εἰς πλοῖον ἐμβάντα[18] καθῆσθαι
            ἐν τῇ θαλάσσῃ,
            καὶ πᾶς ὁ ὄχλος πρὸς τὴν θάλασσαν ἐπὶ τῆς
            γῆς ἦσαν.

---

13.   Note how the passage develops sequentially through the repeated use of καὶ. At times (e.g., 6:6, 12) καὶ may express contrast rather than continuation.

14.   Apparently πάλιν links this teaching of Jesus to previous occasions when he taught (cf. Mark 1:21; 2:13 and thirteen subsequent uses of διδάσκω).

15.   Complementary infinitives are commonly encountered in the NT.

16.   The "historical present" is traditionally understood to add vividness to the narrative. Recent research understands it to draw attention to what follows its use. Cf. 4:13.

17.   ὥστε + the infinitive καθῆσθαι expresses the result of the crowd pressing Jesus. See additional uses of the infinitive in 4:3 (purpose), 4:4 (temporal), 4:5, 6 (causal), 4:9 (epexegetical).

18.   The participle ἐμβάντα may be the most difficult word in the passage to parse. Daniel B. Wallace, *Greek Grammar beyond the Basics: An Exegetical Syntax of New Testament Greek* (Grand Rapids: Zondervan, 1996), 640–45, would likely view it as expressing circumstances attending the infinitive καθῆσθαι. Note other uses of infinitives in 4:3, 4, 5, 6, 9.

2   καὶ ἐδίδασκεν[19] αὐτοὺς ἐν παραβολαῖς πολλὰ
        καὶ ἔλεγεν αὐτοῖς ἐν τῇ διδαχῇ αὐτοῦ·

3   Ἀκούετε.[20]
        ἰδοὺ ἐξῆλθεν ὁ σπείρων σπεῖραι.
4   καὶ ἐγένετο ἐν τῷ σπείρειν
                ὃ[21] μὲν ἔπεσεν παρὰ τὴν ὁδόν,
                καὶ ἦλθεν τὰ πετεινὰ καὶ κατέφαγεν αὐτό.
5   καὶ ἄλλο ἔπεσεν ἐπὶ τὸ πετρῶδες
                ὅπου οὐκ εἶχεν γῆν πολλήν,
                καὶ εὐθὺς ἐξανέτειλεν διὰ τὸ μὴ ἔχειν βάθος
        γῆς·
6   καὶ ὅτε[22] ἀνέτειλεν ὁ ἥλιος ἐκαυματίσθη καὶ
        διὰ τὸ μὴ ἔχειν ῥίζαν ἐξηράνθη.
7   καὶ ἄλλο ἔπεσεν εἰς τὰς ἀκάνθας,
        καὶ ἀνέβησαν αἱ ἄκανθαι
        καὶ συνέπνιξαν αὐτό,
        καὶ καρπὸν οὐκ ἔδωκεν.
8   καὶ ἄλλα ἔπεσεν εἰς τὴν γῆν τὴν καλὴν
        καὶ ἐδίδου καρπὸν ἀναβαίνοντα καὶ
        αὐξανόμενα
        καὶ ἔφερεν ἓν τριάκοντα καὶ ἓν ἑξήκοντα καὶ
        ἓν ἑκατόν.
9   καὶ ἔλεγεν·
        ὃς ἔχει ὦτα ἀκούειν ἀκουέτω.[23]

---

19.   The imperfect verbs ἐδίδασκεν and ἔλεγεν introduce the parable in 4:3–8 as the words of
      Jesus. See also 2:27; 3:23; 4:9, 11, 13, 21, 24, 26, 30, 35 and note how the structure of the
      narrative turns on these expressions.

20.   The imperative Ἀκούετε introduces the parable proper in 4:3–8. Hearing God's message is
      obviously at the heart of this pericope, its Isaianic intertext (Isa. 6:9, cited in 4:12 and 8:18),
      and Mark as a whole. See 3:8; 4:3, 10, 12, 15, 18, 20; 5:27; 6:2, 11, 20; 7:14, 25, 37; 8:18;
      9:7; 10:47; 11:14, 18; 12:28–29, 37; 14:58, 64; 15:35.

21.   Note how the four different results of the sowing are expressed by ὃ μὲν ἔπεσεν . . . in 4:4,
      καὶ ἄλλο ἔπεσεν . . . in 4:5 and 4:7, and by καὶ ἄλλα ἔπεσεν . . . in 4:8. The first three
      expressions are singular, describing three seeds or groups of seeds. The fourth expression
      (4:8) is plural, encompassing the three seeds (or groups of seeds) that fell on good soil and
      bore fruit.

22.   ὅτε introduces a temporal clause using the indicative mood. In 4:15–16 temporal clauses
      with ὅταν and the subjunctive occur.

23.   The parable concludes as it began in 4:3, with an imperative stressing the importance of
      hearing (ἀκουέτω; cf. 4:23).

10   Καὶ ὅτε ἐγένετο κατὰ μόνας,[24]
        ἠρώτων αὐτὸν οἱ περὶ αὐτὸν σὺν τοῖς δώδεκα τὰς
        παραβολάς.
11   καὶ ἔλεγεν αὐτοῖς·
        ὑμῖν τὸ μυστήριον δέδοται[25] τῆς βασιλείας τοῦ θεοῦ·
        ἐκείνοις δὲ τοῖς ἔξω ἐν παραβολαῖς τὰ πάντα γίνεται,
12   **ἵνα[26] βλέποντες βλέπωσιν καὶ μὴ ἴδωσιν,**
        καὶ ἀκούοντες ἀκούωσιν καὶ μὴ συνιῶσιν,
        μήποτε[27] ἐπιστρέψωσιν καὶ ἀφεθῇ αὐτοῖς.

13   Καὶ λέγει αὐτοῖς·
        οὐκ οἴδατε τὴν παραβολὴν ταύτην,[28]
        καὶ πῶς πάσας τὰς παραβολὰς γνώσεσθε;[29]
14   ὁ σπείρων τὸν λόγον σπείρει.[30]
15   οὗτοι[31] δέ εἰσιν οἱ παρὰ τὴν ὁδόν·
        ὅπου σπείρεται ὁ λόγος
        καὶ ὅταν ἀκούσωσιν,
        εὐθὺς ἔρχεται ὁ σατανᾶς
        καὶ αἴρει τὸν λόγον τὸν ἐσπαρμένον εἰς
        αὐτούς.

---

24. κατὰ μόνας is an idiom describing Jesus being alone with the disciples in the absence of the crowd. This marks a transition in the pericope from the public parable to the private explanation of the purpose of parables in general (4:10–12) and the details of the sower in particular (4:13–20).

25. δέδοται is an instance of the "divine passive," an understated way of expressing God's agency. Cf. ἀφεθῇ in 4:12.

26. Mark's use of ἵνα to introduce Isaiah 6:9 is controversial because it apparently portrays the purpose of parables as negative judicial hardening of unbelievers. See Gundry (*Mark*, 202–3) for discussion and advocacy of the telic view of ἵνα.

27. μήποτε apparently introduces a negated purpose clause, lending credence to a telic view of the previous ἵνα.

28. As punctuated here, this clause is apparently an implied conditional protasis for the following rhetorical question. Alternatively, both clauses of 4:13 are questions, with the first assuming a negative answer.

29. The rhetorical question answers the disciples' question of 4:10. It underlines the importance of the parable of the sower for understanding parables in general and transitions from general comments about parables to the specific interpretation of the sower (4:14–20).

30. The general statement of 4:14 effectively unlocks the parable as an extended metaphor of the proclamation and reception of the kingdom message (τὸν λόγον; cf. 1:45; 2:2; 4:15–20, 33; 7:13; 8:32, 38; 10:22, 24; 13:31 [16:20]). The interpretive details that follow in 4:15–20 parallel the parabolic details of 4:3–8.

31. The interpretation of the four results of sowing seed (4:3–8) is unfolded by οὗτοι δέ εἰσιν . . . (4:15), καὶ οὗτοί εἰσιν . . . (4:16), καὶ ἄλλοι εἰσὶν . . . (4:18), and καὶ ἐκεῖνοί εἰσιν . . . (4:20).

16   καὶ οὗτοί εἰσιν οἱ ἐπὶ τὰ πετρώδη σπειρόμενοι,
          οἳ ὅταν ἀκούσωσιν τὸν λόγον
          εὐθὺς μετὰ χαρᾶς λαμβάνουσιν αὐτόν,
17   καὶ οὐκ ἔχουσιν ῥίζαν ἐν ἑαυτοῖς
          ἀλλὰ πρόσκαιροί εἰσιν,
          εἶτα γενομένης[32] θλίψεως ἢ διωγμοῦ διὰ τὸν
          λόγον εὐθὺς σκανδαλίζονται.

18   καὶ ἄλλοι εἰσὶν οἱ εἰς τὰς ἀκάνθας σπειρόμενοι·
          οὗτοί εἰσιν οἱ τὸν λόγον ἀκούσαντες,
19   καὶ αἱ μέριμναι τοῦ αἰῶνος
          καὶ ἡ ἀπάτη τοῦ πλούτου
          καὶ αἱ περὶ τὰ λοιπὰ ἐπιθυμίαι
          εἰσπορευόμεναι συμπνίγουσιν τὸν λόγον καὶ
          ἄκαρπος γίνεται.
20   καὶ ἐκεῖνοί εἰσιν οἱ ἐπὶ τὴν γῆν τὴν καλὴν σπαρέντες,
          οἵτινες ἀκούουσιν τὸν λόγον
          καὶ παραδέχονται
          καὶ καρποφοροῦσιν ἓν τριάκοντα καὶ ἓν
          ἑξήκοντα καὶ ἓν ἑκατόν.

Discourse analysis.[33] A phrased worksheet can become the basis of a descriptive analysis of a pericope's structure. The previous worksheet leads to the following analysis:

---

32. γενομένης is part of a genitive absolute clause describing events that lead to apostasy.

33. "Discourse analysis" as used here refers to a structural analysis of the logical flow of the pericope in its narrative setting. The more technical sense of the term in text linguistics is helpfully explained and its key features discussed in David L. Mathewson and Elodie Ballantine Emig, *Intermediate Greek Grammar* (Grand Rapids: Baker, 2016), 270–90.

Discourse Analysis of Mark 4:1–34

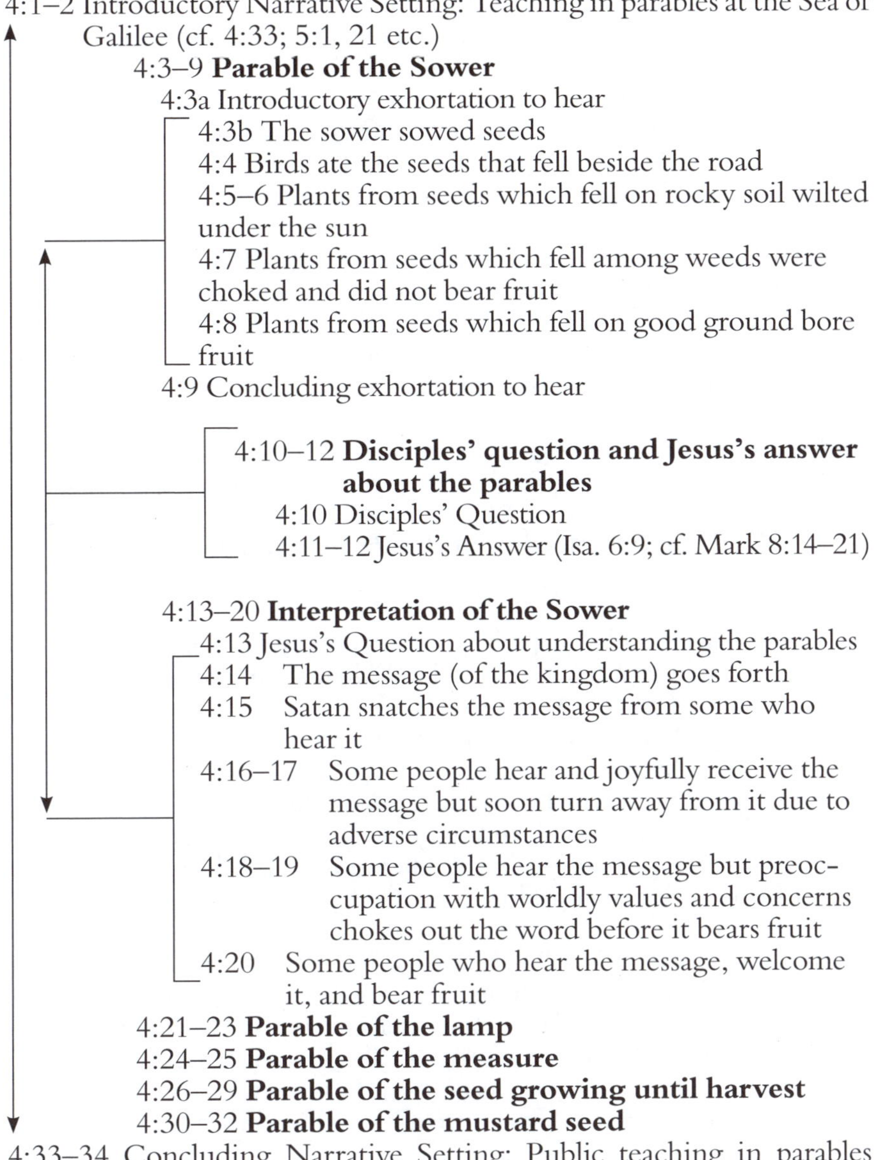

4:33–34 Concluding Narrative Setting: Public teaching in parables with private explanation (cf. 4:33; 5:1, 21 etc.)

A detailed discourse analysis may be simplified to show the basic structure of a passage. The resulting structural outline may be useful in the transition from exegesis to communication.

Structural Outline of Mark 4:1–20

- the public phase (4:1–9)
    - narrative setting of the parable (4:1–2, leading to 4:33–34)
    - the parable proper (4:3–9)
- the private phase (4:10–20)
    - intertextual explanation of the general role of parables (4:10–12 with Isa. 6:9)
    - interpretation of this specific parable (4:13–20)

Scholars note that there is a symmetry to the parable of the sower in that there are both negative and positive triads. The three types of unproductive soil are balanced by the good soil's three levels of production. Additionally, within each triad there is a progression from worst to best. Reasons for the lack of production are explained in 4:4–7, but the good soil's production is simply affirmed in 4:8. Overall, the parable (and its interpretation) progress from the least to the greatest amount of growth, from one extreme to the other, as the following figure shows:

Chiastic Progression in the Parable of the Sower

"Hear!" (4:3)

Seed sown beside the path but immediately eaten by birds (4:4)

Seed sown in shallow soil but plant soon withered by the sun (4:5–6)

Seed sown among thorns but plant gradually choked by thorns (4:7)

Seed which produced thirtyfold in the good soil (4:8)

Seed which produced sixtyfold in the good soil (4:8)

Seed which produced a hundredfold in the good soil (4:8)

"Let the one with ears hear!" (4:9)

Another feature of Mark 4:1–20 that seems significant for communication is the placement of Jesus's intertextual explanation of the purpose of parables between the parable itself and Jesus's explanation of the parable. The central position of Mark 4:10–12 in the pericope's flow argues for its centrality in communication. Homiletical structure should be influenced by and may even mimic literary structure.

Vertical Reading

Reading the text vertically in its literary context leads to an understanding of its narrative logic and plot flow, revealing themes that come from preceding pericopes and lead into subsequent pericopes. As is well known, Mark moves rapidly from the ministry of John to that of Jesus in 1:14. News of Jesus's authoritative teaching and amazing miracles (1:22, 27) in Capernaum soon spreads throughout all Galilee (1:28), and Jesus begins to travel throughout that region to preach in the synagogues and cast out demons (1:39). The cleansing of a leper leads to the Markan "messianic secret" theme (1:44–45), and Jesus returns to Capernaum (2:1). His ministry there leads to controversy as the scribes object to Jesus forgiving the sins of a paralyzed man (2:6), but many people glorify God for Jesus's ministry (2:12). The theme of controversy continues as the scribes and Pharisees object to Jesus's associating with tax gatherers and his Sabbath practices (2:16, 24), and John's disciples ask about fasting (2:18).

Sabbath controversy intensifies in Mark 3:1–6, with the Pharisees and Herodians plotting to do away with Jesus. Additional ministry at the Sea of Galilee leads to crowds pressing Jesus and his telling them not to make him known (3:13). Jesus appoints the Twelve for ministry (3:13–19), and returns to Capernaum. His popularity does not extend to his own family, who doubt his sanity (3:21), or to the Pharisees, who accuse him of consorting with Satan (3:22). As Mark 3 ends, Jesus redefines his family as those who do God's will (3:35).

Several themes emerge from Mark 1–3 that are relevant for Mark 4:1–20. Jesus's (and to a lesser extent, his disciples') authoritative kingdom teaching and kingdom action informs the imagery of the sower (4:3, 14). Satan's activity (1:13; cf. 4:4, 15), the opposition of various leaders to Jesus's ministry, and even his own family's lack of understanding provide a context for understanding the unfruitful aspects of the parable (4:4–7, 15–19). Most clearly, Jesus began to use parables in Mark 3:23 in response to the Jerusalem scribes' slander that his power over demons came from the ruler of the demons. Apparently, the guilt of these scribes (3:28–29) anticipates the teaching of 4:11–12/Isaiah 6:9 on outsiders getting everything in parables so that they might not understand. Perhaps they are the ones from whom Satan snatches the message (4:4, 15). In this case, ironically, those who accuse Jesus of collaboration with Satan are themselves Satan's victims.

Reading further into Mark beyond 4:1–20 leads through four additional parables (4:21–32) to a narrative conclusion in 4:33–34 that answers to 4:1–2. This conclusion underlines the theme of public parables and private explanations modeled in 4:1–20. Accordingly, 4:1–20 should be understood as the central parable-pericope of Mark's Gospel, one that deals with foundational teachings related to the proclamation and reception of the kingdom message. As Jesus's Galilean ministry continues, the focus is on Jesus's miracles until he arrives in his hometown, evidently Nazareth (6:1). Sadly, unbelief ruled in that place (6:6). As the narrative proceeds, Jesus's disciples (cf. 1:16–20; 3:13–19) take on additional kingdom ministry responsibilities (6:7–12). Their performance and understanding, however, have significant weaknesses (6:30, 35–37, 45–46, 49–52; 7:17–23; 8:1–4, 14–21). Their lack of understanding of Jesus's parabolic statements echoes Mark 4:10 and leads Jesus to raise doubt about the authenticity of their faith (7:17–18; 8:14–21; cf. 6:52). As in 4:14–20, fruitful faith in the kingdom message is not widespread.

Jesus's Galilean ministry continues until he heads south to Judea, where his teaching once again is immediately opposed by the Pharisees (10:1–2). This opposition is not surprising, since scribes from Jerusalem have already accused Jesus of consorting with Satan (3:22; cf. 7:1–23; 8:11–12), and Jesus has already predicted the outcome of his ministry (8:31–32; 9:31). On the final leg of his travel to Jerusalem, he again predicts his impending death (10:32–34), and once he arrives in the city, opposition continues (11:18, 27–33). His cursing the fruitless fig tree is a sort of acted parable against Jerusalem's leaders (11:11–14, 20–25), and the ensuing vineyard imagery of the parable of the tenants similarly styles those who oppose Jesus as those who do not bear fruit (12:2; cf. 4:7, 19). It is perhaps subtly ironic that, after finding no fruit in Jerusalem, at the last supper Jesus anticipates drinking the fruit of the vine in the future kingdom of God (14:23–25).

Horizontal Reading

Reading the text horizontally by comparing it with its synoptic parallels (when these exist) helps one understand its distinctive emphases and implications. Mark 4:1–20 is a triple tradition text with parallels in Matthew 13 and Luke 8. The following comments simply note differences without assuming a view of direct literary interdependence. Perusal of a synopsis or harmony of the Gospels[34] reveals that Mark 4:1–20 is "paralleled" by Matthew 13:1–23 and Luke 8:4–15. Looking further, one notes that the Greek texts of the three accounts are not similar in length: Matthew's account is most extensive, with about 415 words, and Luke's is least extensive, with around 235. Mark is in the middle with around 350 words. These differing lengths are immediately clear when one looks at the amount of space taken up on the page by the respective accounts. As the following table shows, however, simplistic statements such as "Matthew's account is more extensive than Mark's" are incorrect. The individual segments of the pericope present a more complicated picture:

---

34. Students are encouraged to construct their own Greek synopses by using personal computer software or accessing Greek NT texts online. Standard resources include K. Aland, ed., *Synopsis Quattuor Evangeliorum* (Stuttgart: Deutsche Bibelstiftung, 1976); J. B. Orchard, ed., *A Synopsis of the Four Gospels in Greek* (Edinburgh: Clark, 1983). See also R. L. Thomas and S. N. Gundry, *The NIV Harmony of the Gospels* (San Francisco: Harper, 1988).

The Parable of the Sower in the Synoptic Tradition

	Matthew 13 *414 words*		Mark 4 *348 words*		Luke 8 *235 words*	
Setting	1–3a	*40 words*	1–2	*46 words*	4	*14 words*
Parable Proper	3b–9	*91 words*	3–9	*105 words*	5–8	*76 words*
Explanation of Parables	10–17	*155 words*	10–12	*52 words*	9–10	*36 words*
Interpretation of the Sower	18–23	*128 words*	13–20	*145 words*	11–15	*109 words*

Luke's account is by far the most compact in each segment of the pericope. Although overall shorter than Matthew's account, Mark's account is more detailed than Matthew's in three of the four segments. Matthew's account gets its overall length from its much more detailed portrayal of Jesus's explanation of the role of parables (13:10–17), which includes a more lengthy citation of Isaiah 6:9–10 and a statement of how the disciples are blessed to be able to understand the kingdom portrayed by the parables (cf. Luke 10:23–24). As is often the case, Mark presents a more detailed and vivid picture of what Jesus *did* and Matthew presents a more thorough picture of what Jesus *taught*. From the standpoint of Markan priority, Matthew's unique material in 13:12, 14–17 would be viewed either as Q material omitted by Luke or as M material. In this view, Matthew has expanded Mark's material on the reason for and role of parables in Jesus's teaching. From the standpoint of Matthean priority, Mark has condensed Matthew's material on the reason for and role of parables but has added a few details to Matthew's account.

One need not be convinced of literary interdependence to read Mark 4:10–20 horizontally. In any approach, the following unique features of Mark's account are worthy of further study in light of the overall teaching of this Gospel:

- Mark's language in 4:2 stresses Jesus's parables as a means of teaching (ἐδίδασκεν . . . ἐν τῇ διδαχῇ αὐτοῦ).
- Mark's Ἀκούετε in 4:3 is not found in Matthew or Luke.
- Mark's final clause of 4:7 (καὶ καρπὸν οὐκ ἔδωκεν) is not found in Matthew or Luke.

- In 4:8 Mark vividly describes the growth process of the seed that fell on good soil and describes its fruitfulness in ascending order (ἀναβαίνοντα καὶ αὐξανόμενα καὶ ἔφερεν ἐν τριάκοντα καὶ ἐν ἑξήκοντα καὶ ἐν ἑκατόν). Cf. 4:20.
- Mark's καὶ ἔλεγεν (4:9, 21, 24, 26, 30) regularly signals transitions within the larger narrative (note also Καὶ λέγει in 4:13).
- In 4:10 Mark mentions that others with the Twelve (οἱ περὶ αὐτὸν σὺν τοῖς δώδεκα) ask Jesus about the parables, and they do so when he is alone (Καὶ ὅτε ἐγένετο κατὰ μόνας). Cf. 4:34.
- In 4:11 those who receive teaching only in parables and do not understand the mystery of the kingdom are described as outsiders (ἐκείνοις δὲ τοῖς ἔξω . . .).
- Mark's citation of Isaiah 6:9–10 in 4:12 is condensed yet complete (see further below).
- In 4:13 Jesus turns the disciples' question (4:10) back on them, implying that understanding this parable is key to understanding the rest of the parables.
- In 4:15 Mark describes Satan's snatching of the seed as something done immediately (εὐθύς).
- In 4:19 Mark adds a third reason why the kingdom message is unfruitful in the weedy soil: καὶ αἱ περὶ τὰ λοιπὰ ἐπιθυμίαι.[35]

Key Words

Analysis of the overall syntax and structure of a passage enables exegetes to make wise decisions about the interpretation of individual words in their contexts. In Mark 4:1–20, the following words appear to be key for interpreting the passage, and warrant further study of their semantic domains:

- Jesus as "teacher" (Mark 4:1; cf. 1:21–22, 27; 2:13; 4:1–2; 4:38; 5:35; 6:2, 6, 30, 34; 7:7; 8:31; 9:17, 31, 38; 10:1, 17, 35; 11:17–18; 12:14, 19, 32, 35, 38; 13:1; 14:14, 49). In Mark only Jesus is addressed as "teacher." There is one reference to Jesus's commissioned apostles' teaching (6:30) and one reference to the empty traditional teachings of the scribes and Pharisees when Jesus cites Isaiah 29:13 in Mark 7:7.
- Teaching by "parables" (4:2, 10, 13; cf. 3:23; 4:30, 33; 7:17; 12:1, 12). Parables are the most prominent method of teaching employed by Jesus.

---

35. For a helpful comparison of the synoptic accounts, see Snodgrass, *Stories with Intent*, 150–54.

- "Hearing" the kingdom "word" (4:3, 9, 12, 15–16, 18, 20; cf. 3:8, 21; 4:23; 5:27; 6:2, 11, 14, 16, 20; 7:14, 25, 37; 8:18; 9:7; 11:14, 18; 12:28, 37; 14:58, 64; 15:35; [16:11]). Response to the message about the kingdom is a major emphasis of Mark.
- "Mystery" (4:11) occurs only in this pericope in the synoptic tradition (cf. Matt. 13:11; Luke 8:10).
- "Kingdom of God" (4:11; cf. 1:15; 3:24; 4:26, 30; 9:1, 47; 10:14, 23–25; 11:10/Ps. 118:25; 12:34; 14:25; 15:43). The many facets of this theological "umbrella" require careful study and nuancing.
- "Satan" (4:15; cf. 1:13; 3:23, 26; 8:33). The adversary's initial role in testing Jesus extends to hindering the impact of the kingdom message and testing Jesus's disciples. Ironically, the leaders accuse Jesus of collaborating with his greatest enemy.
- Temporary faith and "falling away" (4:17; cf. Mark 6:3; 9:42–47; 14:27, 29). Serious spiritual offense is an ominous issue during the ministry of Jesus.
- Producing "fruit" (4:7; cf. 4:26–29; 11:14; 12:2). This parabolic metaphor in Mark 4 returns in Mark 11–12 during Jesus's teaching in Jerusalem before the passion.

The word "mystery" (μυστήριον) is the most obscure of the above words. It is key to Jesus's answer to the disciples' question about his parables (4:11). Here it refers to God's selective disclosure of the kingdom to the disciples through Jesus's private teaching, while outsiders receive only parabolic teaching that they do not grasp. Moving beyond this immediate context to diachronic usage, μυστήριον occurs in descriptions of the teachings and rites and of Greco-Roman religions that were available only to their initiates. In Second Temple apocalyptic literature it describes God's secret plan for the future that is now being revealed.[36] In LXX Daniel 2:18–47 it occurs several times (translating the Aramaic רָזָה) in the narrative of Daniel's God-given ability to reveal and interpret the details of Nebuchadnezzar's dream.[37]

The word is likely more familiar to students of Paul than it is to students of the Gospels. In Paul's letters it often refers to the revelation Paul received about the inclusion of Gentiles in the people of God simply on the basis of faith in Jesus, leading to the reception of the Spirit (e.g., Eph. 3:1–11).[38] Other nuances related to divine secrets include

---

36. E.g., *1 En.* 16:3; 103:2; 104:10, 12; 106:19; *2 Bar.* 81:4; *4 Ezra* 12:36, 38.

37. In the LXX cf. Jdt. 2:2; Tob. 12:7, 11; 2 Macc. 13:21; Wisd. 2:22; 6:22; 14:15, 23; Sir. 22:22; 27:16, 21.

38. For Paul's use of μυστήριον, see Rom. 11:25; 16:25; 1 Cor. 2:1, 7; 4:1; 13:2; 14:2; 15:51; Eph. 1:9; 3:3, 9; 5:32; 6:19; Col. 1:26; 2:2; 4:3; 2 Thess. 2:7; 1 Tim. 3:9, 16.

(1) how Israel's majority unbelief plays into Gentile salvation (Rom. 11:25), (2) how Christians are transformed at Christ's return (1 Cor. 15:51), (3) revelations through specially gifted people (1 Cor. 14:2), (4) Christ himself as the agent of Gentile inclusion (Col. 1:27; 2:2; 1 Tim. 3:16), and (5) the progress of evil toward its eschatological end (2 Thess. 2:7). The various nuances found in the semantic range of the word relate to the concept of a secret that has finally been revealed. The Apocalypse uses μυστήριον to describe the interpretation of visionary details (Rev. 1:20; 17:5, 7). It also describes other puzzling features of God's plan (Rev. 10:7).

With the diachronic texture of μυστήριον in mind, it is all the more apparent that Mark 4:11 speaks of the kingdom of God as something grasped only by God's revelation. Although the sower parable may not seem all that esoteric when Mark 4:3–9 is read, the contextual denouement in 4:10–20 shows it to be an enigma grasped by relatively few, apparently only by those who heard Jesus's interpretation. In this context, the parable of the sower seems to take on the mysterious connotation of a riddle (Prov. 1:6), not unlike certain of the מְשָׁלִים of the Hebrew Bible. These proverbial sayings may sometimes be glossed as "byword," a prophetic warning designed to discourage people from following a negative example.[39] As Mark's narrative proceeds, even Jesus's disciples will later come perilously close to the unproductive soils (6:52; 8:14–21).

Setting the Text

Exegesis takes into account not only the narrative world of the text but also the real world in which the text "sets." Exegetes must understand or "set" biblical texts in the ancient world to which the texts refer, not impose the contemporary world of the exegetes upon them. The narratives contained in the Gospels and Acts are not fables but are rooted in the geography, social history, culture, and politics of the first-century eastern Mediterranean world, including Palestine, Syria, Asia Minor, Greece, and Rome. In Mark 4:1–20 and in other parables, Jesus uses imagery from this ancient referential world to make crucial points about receiving the message of kingdom of God. We will briefly look at the Sea of Galilee, the region of Galilee, and the process of sowing and harvesting grain.

The Sea of Galilee

The Sea of Galilee is near the northern end of the Jordan rift valley, with its surface nearly 700 feet below sea level. Mountains and

---

39. Gerald Wilson, *NIDOTTE*, s.v. מָשַׁל (2.1135).

hills surround the sea except at its southern end and northwest projection, where there are fertile plains. Some believe this topography leads easily to severe storms (Mark 4:35–41; 6:48). Roughly harp-shaped, the sea is over twelve miles long, nearly eight miles wide, and around 150 feet deep. The Jordan River (Mark 1:9; 3:8; 10:1) rises from sources roughly thirty miles to the north near Caesarea Philippi (Mark 8:27) and flows into the northern end of the sea. It exits at the south end of the sea and flows around sixty miles south to the Dead Sea. The area around the sea was probably the most densely populated region of Galilee because it produced fish and numerous crops (Josephus, *War* 3.43).

Much of Jesus's Galilean ministry occurred near the northern shore of the sea. The contextual references to Jesus coming home (3:20; cf. 1:21, 29; 2:1) and being by the sea (4:1; cf. 1:16; 2:13) likely point to the seaside region near Peter's house in Capernaum as the locus of Mark 4:1–20.[40] In Mark 4:1, pressed by the crowd, Jesus got into a boat[41] and taught the multitudes on shore from the sea.[42] If the land sloped down to the shore, the topography would have provided a natural theater and good acoustics.

The Region of Galilee

Galilee's natural boundaries are the Litani River on the north, the Plain of Esdraelon on the south (roughly sixty miles apart), the Jordan River and Sea of Galilee on the east, and the Mediterranean Sea on the west (roughly thirty miles apart). It is common to speak of the area roughly northwest of the Sea of Galilee as upper Galilee, and of the area west of the sea as lower Galilee. This region has the coolest climate in Israel. Its lush, well-watered terrain alternates between mountains and alluvial valleys. According to Josephus, Herod the Great subdued the bandits who had formerly plagued the region (*A. J.* 14.158–60). Major trade routes traversed Galilee, including the *Via Maris* that came north from Egypt along the coastal plain and entered the Plain of Esdraelon by a pass through the Carmel mountain range at Megiddo. From there one branch went northwest through Tyre

---

40. Stein (*Mark*, 179–80) understands the expression in 3:20 (Καὶ ἔρχεται εἰς οἶκον) as a reference to an unknown house.

41. In 1986 during a drought, Jewish fishermen discovered an ancient boat near the NW shore of the Sea. The boat has been reliably dated to the latter first century B.C. or early first century A.D. It is twenty-seven feet long and may be viewed at Kibbutz Ginnosar.

42. The expression Sea of Galilee occurs in Mark 1:16; 7:31; cf. "the sea" in Mark 2:13; 3:7; 4:1, 39, 41; 5:1, 13, 21; 6:47–49. Texts like Mark 9:42; 11:23 would likely have evoked thoughts of the Sea of Galilee.

to Turkey, another branch went northeast to the upper Jordan valley on its way to Damascus, and a third branch went east through Beth Shean (Scythopolis) into the northern Decapolis region east of the Sea of Galilee. The population of Galilee varied from one area to another with Jews and various Gentile groups living in relative peace with one another.

The majority of Jesus's miracles and parables that are narrated in the Gospels occurred in Galilee. Mark 4:1–20 evokes the agrarian lifestyle of commoners who lived in Galilee[43] in villages like Nazareth (1:9, 24; 10:47; 16:6; cf. Mark 6:1–6), which overlooked the Jezreel plain, and Capernaum (1:21; 2:1; 9:33), about forty miles northeast of Nazareth on the northern shore of the Sea of Galilee. Bethsaida (Mark 6:45; 8:22) was another village at or near the northeastern shore of the sea. Mary Magdalene (Mark 15:40, 47; 16:1, [9]) was apparently from the village of Magdala, on the northwestern shore of the sea.[44] A key governmental administrative city for Galilee was Tiberias on the west side of the sea (John 6:1, 23; 21:1). Herod Antipas ruled from Tiberias during the life of Jesus, but the Gospels do not mention Jesus ever frequenting this city. Another important Hellenized city in Galilee not mentioned in the Gospels is Sepphoris, which is only several miles northwest of Nazareth.

Farming,[45] shepherding (Mark 6:34; 14:27), and fishing (1:16–20; 6:38, 41, 43; 8:7) sustained life in Galilee. Josephus commented on the fertility of the region for growing grapes and figs (*B.J.* 3.518–19). Others worked in a trade (Mark 6:3) or did manual labor (Mark 1:20). Roman forces occupied the territory (Mark 15:39, 44), and collecting taxes for the Romans was an unpopular occupation (2:14–16).[46] Various illnesses afflicted the people (1:32, 34; 2:17; 6:5, 13, 55–56; [16:18]), and physicians tried to heal them (2:17). Synagogues were centers of worship, teaching, and settling civil disputes (1:21, 23, 29; 3:1; 5:22, 36, 38; 6:2). Sabbath observance was a way of life (Mark 1:21; 2:23, 27; 3:2, 4; 6:2; 15:42; 16:1). Although the Jerusalem temple[47] was roughly seventy-five miles away, a walk of several days, its presence was felt in

---

43. Mark 1:9, 14, 28, 39; 3:7; 6:21; 9:30; 14:26; 15:41; 16:7).

44. Early reports on current excavations at Migdol speak of a large first-century synagogue, and a stone that was found there with carved images, including a menorah.

45. Farmers grew grains (Mark 2:23; 4:4–8, 26–29, 31–32; 13:16), grapes (Mark 12:1–2, 8–9; cf. wine in Mark 2:22; 14:25; 15:23, 36), olives (Mark 11:1; 13:3; 14:26), and figs (Mark 11:13, 20, 13:28).

46. Opinion is divided over the nature of Levi's duties in 2:14. Some believe his tax office or toll booth was a sort of checkpoint for goods being brought through the region on overland or sea trade routes. Others view him as a collector of taxes from the residents of the area.

47. Mark 11:11, 15, 27; 12:35; 13:1, 3; 14:49, 58; 15:29, 38; cf. 2:25–26.

Galilee (1:44). Torah experts were found in the region (1:22; 2:6, 16; 3:22; 7:1, 5; 9:11, 14).[48]

Sowing and Harvesting

References to sowing seed and harvesting grain are common in the Bible, both as a means of sustenance and as a metaphor of life and judgment to come.[49] The basic premise of Jesus's parable of a sower sowing seeds (cf. Mark 4:26–29) would have been clear to his Galilean audience. The features of the parable would seem to be a commonplace of life in first-century Galilee. Both exegetes who are only aware of modern mechanized farming techniques in wide, flat fields as well as urban exegetes who have no acquaintance with farming at all will need to look carefully at this parable. Backyard gardeners may have the best intuitive grasp of the parable. The sower scatters seed with his hand, not with an implement of any sort. The "road" (NASB) along which the seed falls (παρὰ τὴν ὁδόν, 4:4) is in reality a narrow footpath or right of way across what was likely a relatively small area that was level enough for planting. The situation is like that mentioned in Mark 2:23 (cf. Deut. 23:25). The omnivorous predation of birds is a common biblical theme and a result of divine judgment.[50] Jubilees 11:10–13 speaks of the evil angel Mastema sending birds to eat the seed planted by Terah (Gen. 11:24–32), and the Apocalypse of Abraham similarly interprets Genesis 15:10–11. The "rocky soil" (τὸ πετρῶδες, 4:5) is problematic not because it has pebbles and rocks in it but because it has little depth (διὰ τὸ μὴ ἔχειν βάθος γῆς, 4:5) over outcrops of the underlying bedrock. The plants' roots have nowhere to go for moisture. The aggressive growth of thorns (ἀνέβησαν αἱ ἄκανθαι, 4:7; cf. Jer. 4:3) is especially problematic when there are no herbicides or mechanical cultivators to protect the crop.

Although not a part of the parable, the agricultural cycle was completed when the crop was harvested. Harvesting was a rigorous task that began with using a sickle to cut the stalks of grain, which were bound into sheaves. The sheaves were taken to a threshing floor, typically a location where the wind was strong. Larger grains were threshed (sepa-

---

48. See further S. Freyne, *Galilee, Jesus, and the Gospels* (Minneapolis: Fortress, 1988); J. L. Reed, *Archaeology and the Galilean Jesus* (Harrisburg, PA: Trinity, 2000); Mark A. Chancey, *Greco-Roman Culture and the Galilee of Jesus* (Cambridge: Cambridge University, 2005).

49. E.g., Gen. 8:22; 45:6; 47:23; Exod. 23:10, 16; Lev. 19:19; 25:3, 11, 20, 22, 26; Deut. 24:19; 26:2; 2 Kgs. 19:29; Ruth 1:22; Prov. 10:5; Eccl. 11:1–6; Isa. 28:23–29; 55:10; Jer. 50:16. For sowing and reaping as metaphor, see Job 4:8; Ps. 126:5–6; Isa. 17:4–11; Jer. 2:3; 31:27; Hos. 2:23; 8:7; Matt. 9:37; John 4:36; 1 Cor. 9:10; 2 Cor. 9:10; Rev. 14:15, 19.

50. E.g., Gen. 15:10–11 (cf. *Apoc. Abr.* 13); 40:17; Deut. 28:26; 1 Sam. 17:44, 46; 1 Kgs. 16:4; Ps. 79:2; Jer. 17:33; Ezek. 39:4; Matt. 6:26; Rev. 19:17, 21.

rated from the stalks and husks) by being trampled by animals pulling a heavy sledge.[51] When the wind was adequate, the trampled matter would be winnowed (tossed into the air with a winnowing fork), and the wind would separate the grain from the chaff.[52] The biblical references to harvest often serve as metaphors of divine judgment.

There is debate over at least two features of the parable. The first is whether the ground was plowed before or after the sowing. Ancient texts attest to both techniques.[53] Plowing in ancient times would stir or harrow the soil, not turn it completely over as modern turnplows or moldboard plows do. This technique would either prepare soil to receive seed by softening it and tearing out unwanted vegetation, or it would bury seed that had already been sown so that it would receive moisture and sprout quickly. It is also possible that in some cases the soil was plowed both before and after planting. Jesus's parable of the sower does not clearly reflect either technique, and its interpretation does not depend on this question.

The second debate concerns whether the thirtyfold, sixtyfold, and hundredfold yields are realistic or exaggerated. It is difficult to answer this question with confidence. Some ancient sources speak of a tenfold yield as customary, but others speak of much higher yields, up to a hundredfold.[54] Certain of Jesus's parables may have hyperbolic features (e.g., Matt. 18:24),[55] but such an interpretation is unnecessary here. It seems better to conclude that certain soils produce marginal crops and others

---

51.   There are around fifty references to threshing in the Bible, including Lev. 26:5; Num. 15:20; Deut. 15:14; 25:4/1 Cor. 9:9–10; Judg. 6:37; 1 Chron. 21:20–23; Isa. 21:10; 27:12; 28:27–28; 41:15; Dan. 2:35; Hos. 10:11; Joel 2:24; Amos 1:3; Mic. 4:13; Hab. 3:12.

52.   Ruth 3:2; Ps. 1:4; Prov. 20:8, 26; Isa. 30:24; 41:16; Jer. 4:11; 15:7; 51:2; Matt. 4:12/Luke 3:17.

53.   Texts that speak of plowing to prepare the soil before sowing seed include Isa. 28:24–26; Jer. 4:3; Ezek. 36:9; *Gos. Thom.* 20; Pliny the Elder, *Nat.* 18.176, 180–81; *t. Ber.* 7.2. Texts that speak of plowing to embed seed already sown include *Jub.* 11:11, 24; *m. Shabb.* 4.12; *t. Shabb.* 4.12.; *t. Neg.* 6.2.

54.   Genesis 26:12 describes God's blessing on Isaac as including his receiving a hundredfold yield in Gerar, a valley in the northwest Negev. Among ancient sources, Varro (second century B.C.) spoke of some areas receiving hundredfold yields (*Rust.* 1.44.2). See also *Sib. Or.* 3.263–64, Theophrastus, *Hist. plant.* 8.7.4; Strabo, *Geogr.* 15.3.11; Pliny the Elder, *Nat.* 18.21.94–95. In Mark 10:30 Jesus speaks of his followers receiving a hundredfold reward in this life. See further the exegetical commentaries and R. K. McIver, "One Hundred-fold Yield—Miraculous or Mundane?" *NTS* 40 (1994): 606–8.

55.   Truly hyperbolic yields are sometimes found in eschatological texts such as Amos 9:13. All the more so, *1 Enoch* 10:18–19 speaks of a thousandfold yield, and *2 Baruch* 29:5 of a ten-thousandfold yield. Irenaeus spoke negatively of Papias's alleged view that a single grain of wheat would produce ten thousand heads of wheat, and each head would have ten thousand grains (*Haer.* 5.33.3–4). The Talmud speaks of a ship carrying only one grape in the world to come (*b. Ketub.* 111b–112a).

produce bumper crops, depending on variables such as when the crop was planted, the amount and timing of rainfall received, and the temperature during the growing season. A hundredfold yield would be exceptional but not necessarily miraculous or even hyperbolic. In any event, the interpretation of the parable does not turn on the answer to this question.

Thinking with the Text

In thinking with the text we engage its inherent concepts, its background in antecedent biblical texts, and its foreground in the history of the interpretation of the text's meaning and effects. This process entails the text's implicit and explicit intertexts, biblical theology, historical theology, and systematic theology. The following brief discussion merely suggests key ideas rather than providing a comprehensive overview.

Intertextuality

The parable of the sower draws from agrarian imagery commonly found in the OT, but it is arguable whether this imagery is derived from specific biblical texts or more likely from the biblical world. Mark does not directly mention Psalm 78:2, which is cited in Matthew 13:35 in connection with the use of parables in a context of involving revelation of hidden things. One suspects that there is an echo of the שְׁמַע (Deut. 6:4) behind Mark's stress on truly hearing the words of Jesus about the kingdom of God. The citation of Isaiah 6:9–10 in Mark 4:12 is the major matter to be noted here. The particulars of the citation may be gleaned from the table below, which uses bold font for LXX words that are implicated, whether Mark uses the same words or synonyms. Overall, it is clear that Mark (unlike Matthew 13:14–15) presents a condensed sample of this text. Mark gets right to the heart of Isaiah 6:9, and then omits the first part of 6:10. He cites the conjunction that introduces the five negated purpose clauses (μήποτε . . .) of 6:10 and then omits the first three clauses, and includes the last two. The following details are noteworthy:

- Mark begins with Isaiah's commission but omits its setting.
- Mark diverges from both the Hebrew Bible and the LXX by reversing the order of the hearing and seeing in Isaiah 6:9.
- Mark's rendering of the Hebrew construction in 6:9 differs syntactically from the LXX.
- Mark omits the first three clauses of Isaiah 6:10. These imperatives tell Isaiah to harden the heart of his audience. LXX renders them as a γὰρ clause that explains the situation in 6:9.

Mark 4:11–12 in Intertextual Perspective		
Isaiah 6:9–10 HMT	**Isaiah 6:9–10 LXX**	**Mark 4:11–12**
		καὶ ἔλεγεν αὐτοῖς· ὑμῖν τὸ μυστήριον δέδοται τῆς βασιλείας τοῦ θεοῦ· ἐκείνοις δὲ τοῖς ἔξω ἐν παραβολαῖς τὰ πάντα γίνεται, ἵνα
וַיֹּאמֶר	καὶ εἶπεν	
לֵךְ וְאָמַרְתָּ לָעָם הַזֶּה	Πορεύθητι καὶ εἰπὸν τῷ λαῷ τούτῳ	
שִׁמְעוּ שָׁמוֹעַ וְאַל־תָּבִינוּ	**Ἀκοῇ ἀκούσετε καὶ οὐ μὴ συνῆτε**	βλέποντες βλέπωσιν καὶ μὴ ἴδωσιν,
וּרְאוּ רָאוֹ וְאַל־תֵּדָעוּ׃	καὶ **βλέποντες βλέψετε καὶ οὐ μὴ ἴδητε·**	καὶ ἀκούοντες ἀκούωσιν καὶ μὴ συνιῶσιν,
הַשְׁמֵן לֵב־הָעָם הַזֶּה	ἐπαχύνθη γὰρ ἡ καρδία τοῦ λαοῦ τούτου,	
וְאָזְנָיו הַכְבֵּד	καὶ τοῖς ὠσὶν αὐτῶν βαρέως ἤκουσαν	
וְעֵינָיו הָשַׁע	καὶ τοὺς ὀφθαλμοὺς αὐτῶν ἐκάμμυσαν,	
פֶּן־יִרְאֶה בְעֵינָיו	**μήποτε** ἴδωσιν τοῖς ὀφθαλμοῖς	μήποτε
וּבְאָזְנָיו יִשְׁמָע	καὶ τοῖς ὠσὶν ἀκούσωσιν	
וּלְבָבוֹ יָבִין	καὶ τῇ καρδίᾳ συνῶσιν	
וָשָׁב וְרָפָא לוֹ	καὶ **ἐπιστρέψωσιν καὶ** ἰάσομαι αὐτούς.	ἐπιστρέψωσιν καὶ ἀφεθῇ αὐτοῖς.

The use of Isaiah 6:9–10 in Mark 4:12 is intended to warn Jesus's audience (and Mark's later readers) that Israel's response to Jesus as the agent of God's kingdom can be understood in light of Israel's response to God's rule in the days of Isaiah. Israel's hardness of heart in that day serves as a warning in Jesus's day. Jesus's own family is concerned that he has lost his mind. They want to take charge of him (Mark 3:21). Scribes from Jerusalem have just accused Jesus of collusion with Satan (Mark 3:22–30). This leads to his use of parables and his redefinition of family as those who truly hear his teaching (Mark

3:31–35). The citation of Isaiah 6:9–10 underlines the consequences of not hearing him.

Much more could be said about Isaiah 6:9–10 and about similar texts such as Jeremiah 5:21 and Ezekiel 12:2 (cited in Mark 8:18). Exegetical commentaries and sources that address the NT use of the OT should be consulted for further discussion.[56]

Biblical Theology

The sower sows the word. A biblical theology of the word of God begins at creation, when God simply speaks the world and all its creatures into existence (Gen. 1:1, 3, 6, 9; Ps. 33:6–9; 148:1–6; Heb. 11:3; 2 Peter 3:5). By that same word Adam and Eve were instructed on how to be stewards of God's creation. When our first parents rejected that word of creation and stewardship, a long process punctuated by words of redemption began. God instructed Adam and Eve despite their sin on how to renew their relationship with him. He later spoke to Noah, Abraham, and the biblical patriarchs. Through Moses he spoke a covenant with Abraham's descendants at Sinai, and later reminded his people through Moses that they would truly thrive when they received sustenance that transcended their physical needs: *people do not live by bread alone but by every word that comes from God's mouth* (Deut. 8:3; Matt. 4:4/Luke 4:4). God regularly sent Israel prophets who spoke God's word to the nation, despite their tendency to neglect those reminders and occasionally even kill those who reminded them (2 Chron. 36:16). Nevertheless, God's word remains powerful and sufficient to accomplish the redemptive purpose he intends for it (Isa. 55:6–13, especially 10–11). Jesus is the ultimate agent of that word, and those who have ears must hear him.

The kingdom of God is at hand! Jesus's words and deeds in Mark expound and embody the kingdom or reign of God.[57] Biblical texts on the kingdom are commonly understood as relating to both God's universal and providential reign over the world and to his special reign through mediators, beginning with Adam and Eve, and including such figures as the OT judges and the Davidic dynasty. Any pretense of God's mediatorial rule ended with the just demise of the remnants of the Davidic kings at the hands of Nebuchadnezzar king of Babylon, but Israel's return to their promised land at the behest

---

56. See especially Craig Evans, *To See and Not Perceive: Isaiah 6:9–10 in Early Jewish and Christian Interpretation* (Sheffield: Sheffield Academic, 1989) and Rikk E. Watts, "Mark" in G. K. Beale and D. A. Carson, eds. *Commentary on the New Testament Use of the Old Testament* (Grand Rapids: Baker, 2007), 150–55.

57. Understanding Jesus's teaching about the kingdom in Mark should begin with the study of Mark 1:15; 3:34; 4:11, 26, 30; 9:1, 47; 10:14–15, 23–25; 11:10; 12:34; 14:25; 15:43.

of Cyrus king of Persia renewed hopes for a Jewish state that would manifest God's reign on earth. The Hasmoneans were inadequate at best in fulfilling these hopes. The coming of Roman rule led some to abandon hope for a Jewish state, but some harbored hope for a political Messiah who would throw off the Roman yoke and return Israel to its former glories. As Mark 1:15 indicates, Jesus came to inaugurate a different sort of kingdom, one that first required the renewal of Israel, not a political revolt against Rome. This ethical renewal is the basis of the kingdom's political implications. It is not that the kingdom is either God's present rule in believer's hearts, or his eventual political rule over the world—both are true. In Mark the kingdom is inaugurated with both present and future implications. Jesus's parables are foremost parables of the kingdom in their portrayal of God's rule encroaching on that of Satan (Mark 3:23, 27; 4:26, 30). Jesus's kingdom may be entered now (Mark 10:14), and it eventually will be manifested in all its glory (Mark 10:23; 14:25). Followers of Jesus who truly hear his word learn of this revealed secret (Mark 4:10–12), and their fruitbearing will be acknowledged at the final judgment (4:20), when the kingdom comes in all its fullness.

To you has been given the mystery. The revealed secret of the kingdom is not available to everyone. A wide audience hears the parables, but relatively few hear Jesus's explanation (4:11, 34). For these "outsiders" (Mark 3:31; 4:11) it seems the parables are opaque glass that keeps out the light, not windows through which kingdom truth shines. To those who are "with Jesus" (Mark 3:14; 5:18, 24; 9:2; 14:33; 15:41; [16:10]), God graciously discloses the secret, namely the kingdom of God (cf. Luke 12:32). The term "outsiders" most obviously implicates the scribes from Jerusalem who have just slandered Jesus by accusing him of being possessed by Satan and of casting out demons by Satan's power.[58] Jesus's own family at this point doubt his sanity (3:21) and are also in a sense "on the outside looking in" (3:32), instead of being with those who are sitting around Jesus to hear him teach (3:32, 34), whom he describes as those who "do the will of God" (3:35). Among the crowd of others who follow Jesus due to his miracles would be many other "outsiders" who do not understand his teachings (2:4, 13; 3:9, 20, 32; 4:1). None of these outsiders—whether the slandering scribes, the concerned family, or the thrill-seeking crowd—have yet received the secret disclosure about the kingdom. Isaiah 6:9–10 applies to these people in that their perception of Jesus through his parables is superficial. He does not disclose the kingdom to them. As in the days of Isaiah, his ministry in parables only confirms their lack of perception.

---

58.   On the scribes, see Mark 3:22; cf. 2:6, 16. See also the Pharisees in 2:16, 24, 3:6.

As noted above, Mark 4:12 omits Isaiah 6:10a on hardness of heart. Yet Mark does speak of hardness of heart in 3:5; 6:52; and 8:17–21. Although 3:5 seems to be describing the Pharisees, 6:52 and 8:17–21 are about the disciples. Only a thin line of grace separates the enemies of Jesus from his own disciples in Mark. The teaching of Jesus in Mark 4:10 is much like his teaching in Matthew 11:25: God hides himself and his grace from those who deem themselves too wise to receive it, but God reveals himself to babes, those who humbly acknowledge their need of him. It is not that the "wise" or "outsiders" lack opportunity. Only after they squander their opportunity does everything come to them in parables. It is not that the "babes" are more worthy. Grace is all they can rely on.

Historical Theology

In Mark 4:13–20 Jesus gave a detailed interpretation of the parable of the sower. It goes without saying that many of his parables are not interpreted in such a fashion. Yet, in the early church, Jesus's detailed interpretation was viewed as support for allegorizing all the parables. In particular, Clement of Alexandria understood Mark 4:11 to teach that parables, when rightly interpreted, disclosed mystical secrets about Jesus (*Strom.* 5.12). Augustine expounded the parable of the sower in his homilies on Matthew. He treated the parable of the sower and the parable of the wheat and tares together, and linked the bad ground to the tares. He exhorted his hearers to repent and become good ground so that they would be gathered into the barn at the harvest (*Serm.* 23; 38.3).

Chrysostom's view of this parable is also found in his homilies on Matthew. Chrysostom took the various soils as human souls, into whom Jesus sowed his teachings without respecting persons. He exhorted his hearers that the good ground implied there was hope for those who had deep roots in Jesus and who cleansed themselves from the world (*Hom. Matt.* 44.1). Among later interpreters, Luther's disdain for allegory is well known, and the reformation by and large understood the parables less mystically. Calvin took the parable of the sower simply to teach that the preaching of the gospel is not uniformly productive, but stated that the four types of soil should not be viewed as numerical percentages of the varied responses. His final comment takes Jerome to task for relating the thirty-, sixty-, and hundredfold fruit respectively to the married, the widows, and the celibate, as if married people were less godly than the celibate.[59]

---

59. John Calvin, *A Harmony of the Gospels Matthew, Mark, and Luke,* 3 vols., Calvin's Commentaries, D. W. and T. F. Torrance eds., A. W. Morrison, trans. (Grand Rapids: Eerdmans, 1972), 2.270–73.

Systematic Theology

Theologians today seem to view the parable of the sower as providing a summary of the mixed response to the preaching of the gospel. Those who lean toward Arminianism tend to explain the mixed response as a function of human responsibility (they would likely call it "free will"). Those who are more Calvinistic in their leanings would not deny the responsibility of those who consciously reject the message but would also speak more freely about the mysterious counsel of God and sovereign election. Isaiah 6:10a (omitted in Mark 4:12) speaks of Isaiah's ministry as hardening the hearts of the people, lest they turn and be forgiven. This text, along with others like Exodus 9:16; 33:19; and Romans 9:6–18, is used in the discussion of gracious election, just preterition, and *praedestinatio duplex*.[60] Earnest followers of Christ have come to different conclusions on how to best articulate these matters that pertain to God's prerogatives in redeeming his people.

Another theological issue that poses a pressing pastoral problem is dealing with the matter of temporary faith (Mark 4:16–19). Pastors are commonly asked whether the rocky soil and the thorny soil represent Christians who have "lost their salvation." Others speak of these two soils as representing carnal or inconsistent Christians. The imagery of the unfruitful branches of the vine in John 15:6 raises the same question. Arminians and historic Calvinists alike characteristically stress perseverance as a distinguishing mark of genuine faith and differ primarily over whether a genuinely regenerate person can exhibit temporary faith. The "grace movement" in evangelicalism tends to resist a necessary connection between saving faith and perseverance. However one resolves the problem of temporary faith theoretically, it is a heartbreaking reality of Christian ministry.[61]

Teaching the Text

In the previous chapter we summarized Augustine's view of Christian communication as teaching, delighting, and moving. The three aspects of this insightful approach call us to communicate accurately, creatively, and urgently. Following the approach of the previous chapter, we engage Mark 4:1–20 in terms of its main point, both to its original and current audiences. Then we approach potential homiletical structures for teaching the text deductively, inductively, and topically or thematically.

---

60. E.g., John Calvin, *Institutes of the Christian Religion*, 3.24, especially 3.24.13–14.

61. A somewhat controversial argument that genuine faith is persevering faith is John McArthur's *The Gospel according to Jesus*, rev. ed. (Grand Rapids: Zondervan, 2008).

The Point of the Passage

Although some speak helpfully of distinguishing between the original and current points of a passage, and of bridging the gap between the ancient and current audiences of the Bible, such language runs the risk of implying that the message of God changes from one generation to the next, or that the Bible is so removed from current audiences that it is unintelligible. It is better to speak in terms of how, in the wisdom of God and through the power of the Spirit, the biblical message transcends its original historical setting and is relevant for any and all human cultures. The God who spoke to Israel through their prophets in ancient times still speaks in power today to all humanity through the message centered on his son, Jesus Christ. It is desirable and profitable as a practical matter that we communicate the point of the text in an artful manner that is fresh and contemporary, but it is essential as a matter of faithfulness to God that we communicate the text accurately. Since parables are metaphorical narratives, not prosaic linear arguments, accuracy is not always a simple matter. Parables invite us to imagine, not just analyze; a degree of polyvalence is built into them. It is easier to exclude interpretations that are contextually or theologically suspect than it is to isolate *the* correct interpretation.[62]

It seems clear that the parable of the sower could have three central points.[63] It speaks of (1) a sower who (2) sows his seed on (3) four types of soil. Accordingly, expositors could focus on the sower (apparently Jesus, his apostles, and perhaps later preachers), or on the process of sowing seed (apparently preaching the kingdom of God), or on how the four soils received the seed (apparently three ways the kingdom message is heard). The parable is primarily about either *messengers* of the kingdom, the *message* about the kingdom, or the *reception* of the message about the kingdom, and application can therefore be made primarily about those who proclaim the kingdom, the nature of the kingdom that is proclaimed, or responding to the proclamation of the kingdom.[64]

---

62. See the helpful comments of Snodgrass on "adapting the parable" (*Stories with Intent*, 175–76).

63. Blomberg (*Interpreting the Parables*, 226) understands the three points to be related to the sower, the unproductive seeds, and the productive seeds.

64. Snodgrass (*Stories with Intent*, 155–56) lists eight possible points (which he calls options for interpretation), but emphasizes the parable's intertextual dimensions. The remnant of Israel is being sown in the land (Isa. 60:21; Jer. 23:8; 24:5–7; 31:27–28; Ezek. 36:8–10; Hos. 2:22–23), yet Israel must take Isaiah 6:9–10 to heart and hear the kingdom message: "[T]here is no need to drive a wedge between God sowing his people and God sowing his word. It is by sowing the word that the end-time people of God is planted" (169).

<table>
<tr><th colspan="3" style="text-align:center">The Point of the Parable of the Sower</th></tr>
<tr><th>The Parable Proper</th><th>The Interpretation of the Parable</th><th>The Application of the Parable</th></tr>
<tr>
<td>The Sower as messenger</td>
<td>Jesus and his apostles (and current preachers)</td>
<td>
<ul>
<li>Be realistic about the mixed reception you will receive.</li>
<li>Be confident that your preaching will have positive results.[65]</li>
<li>Trust that there will be an eventual glorious harvest.</li>
</ul>
</td>
</tr>
<tr>
<td>Sowing the seed as the message</td>
<td>The nature of the kingdom that is preached</td>
<td>
<ul>
<li>Many people do not welcome the kingdom.</li>
<li>The kingdom is present through all circumstances, whether it is rejected or received.</li>
<li>Despite setbacks, the kingdom will take root in the present and will eventually come in its fullness.</li>
</ul>
</td>
</tr>
<tr>
<td>The Four Soils as reception of the message</td>
<td>People respond to the message in different ways</td>
<td>
<ul>
<li>Take care how you hear the message of the kingdom.</li>
<li>Pray for Satan's opposition to the gospel to be bound.</li>
<li>Don't allow Satan to use external things such as adverse circumstances (persecution) to ruin the work of the gospel in your life.</li>
<li>Don't allow Satan to deceive you with internal attitudes such as materialistic values, to ruin the work of the gospel in your life.</li>
<li>Seek to be as productive as possible for the kingdom.</li>
</ul>
</td>
</tr>
</table>

Athough all three of the above approaches to the parable present insights that are theologically sound and pastorally useful, it is clear that the third approach is most consistent with the parable's interpretation and its context. The description of the result of the sowing in the four

---

65. Justin Martyr seems to be take this interpretation in *Dialogue* 125:1–2.

soils takes up the bulk of the parable itself in Mark 4:3b–8 and the ensuing interpretation of the parable in Mark 4:14–20. The parable proper is bracketed by exhortations to hear (4:3a; 4:9). Jesus's reply to the disciples' question about the parables (4:10–12) alludes to Isaiah 6:9–10 to the effect that, as a matter of divine sovereignty, hearing the message does not necessarily lead to understanding it. Also, Jesus's interpretation of the parable overlooks the sower entirely and only briefly identifies the seed as the kingdom message (Mark 4:14). The bulk of his interpretation is given over to explaining how the message is received, and each soil is said to have heard the message. Accordingly, the parable of the sower is really, as many have noted, the parable of the soils, and it is about how the gospel is received. Craig Blomberg is right—this parable is primarily about "How do you hear?"[66]

By an extended use of the familiar biblical imagery of sowing seed and harvesting grain, Jesus teaches his disciples that their capacity to understand the kingdom message is a matter of God's gracious revelation. At the same time, he warns them of Satan's opposition to people receiving the kingdom message. Satan can quickly remove the message from people's hearts before it takes root. Satan can bring adverse circumstances to bear on those who have recently received the message, and he can deceive them with worries and desires based on materialistic values. Yet God is able to embed the kingdom message permanently in some hearts, and by his grace he reveals it to them, augmenting the public parabolic teaching with private instruction (4:33–34). With these realities in mind, Jesus's followers should humbly respond to his double exhortation. They have ears, so they should cultivate their capacity to hear with humility, eagerness, and perseverance throughout their lives until the time of eschatological harvest.[67] "To be a disciple of the kingdom means hearing and remaining focused on the message of the kingdom in such a way that one is defined by it."[68]

A Homiletical Paraphrase

Make no mistake, Mark 4:1–20—not unlike the rest of Mark—is deceptively difficult to understand and preach. The text's literary structure is relatively easy to grasp, and its pastoral imagery of seeds being scattered by hand is quaint and interesting. The story, however, creates

---

66. Craig L. Blomberg, *Preaching the Parables* (Grand Rapids: Baker, 2004), 105–17. Blomberg is speaking of Matthew's version of the parable, but the point still stands.

67. Hearing the words *of* Jesus and the words of others *about* Jesus are both stressed in Mark. See 4:3, 9, 12, 15–16, 18, 20; cf. 3:8, 21; 4:23; 5:27; 6:2, 11, 14, 16, 20; 7:14, 25, 37; 8:18; 9:7; 11:14, 18; 12:28, 37; 14:58, 64; 15:35; [16:11].

68. Snodgrass, *Stories with Intent*, 175.

a rollercoaster of emotions. Is it a comedy or a tragedy? Anyone who has ever planted and tended a garden can relate to it.

- The calm serenity of a farmer scattering seeds by hand on a beautiful sunny day is *interrupted by a flock of ravenous birds that arrive to gulp down anything they can find.*
- But soon some of the remaining seed sprout and plants spring up rapidly *only to wilt away seemingly overnight because their soil was warmed so soon by the sun only because it was so shallow and contained insufficient moisture to sustain growth.*
- But some seeds have enough depth of soil to produce promising plants *only to be eventually choked out by faster-growing plants which produce only sharp thorns.*
- But some seeds survive the birds, the uneven soil depth, and the thorns! They produce a bumper crop, with yields varying from thirtyfold to sixtyfold to a hundredfold.

As the story ends, it appears that despite the problems, the farmer's family "all lived happily ever after." Well, at least their labors have produced enough of a crop to sustain them until the next growing season. *But why was Jesus telling all these stories to begin with?*

Jesus's stark answer to the disciples' question about the parables is unnerving because it bluntly affirms that whether or not people truly hear the message of God's kingdom and come to faith is ultimately a matter of God's choice, not ours. God is God and we are not. It is by his grace that we have been given insight into his kingdom, but lots of others who have heard the same message we have heard have no clue about its importance for their lives and no interest in paying further attention to it. If we do not get the reason for the story of the sower, there is little hope we will get any of Jesus's stories about the kingdom. So, Jesus explains it to us.

As we scatter kingdom-seeds,

- Some folks stop what they are doing to listen to us, *but as soon as they hear a little of the message, they are off to other pursuits. Our adversary has distracted them.*
- Other folks joyfully accept our message and seem to be on fire for God, *but it is not long until someone turns up the heat on them because of their faith, and they are gone.*
- Other folks listen to our message and begin to respond to it in promising ways, *but the desire for stuff, and all the worries about getting it and keeping it, crowd out the values of Jesus, and these folks never follow him faithfully.*
- Other folks take the time to really listen to the message. They get it and despite opposition they welcome it into every area of their

lives. It has a deep impact on their values. They follow Jesus faithfully and produce fruit for him. *Just when we are about to give up, we find out the story is a comedy after all. They all live happily ever after.*

Homiletical Packaging

In the previous chapter we discussed three basic approaches to homiletics: deductive, inductive, and topical. The first two approaches explain and apply a specific text, while the third selects a specific feature of a text for explanation and application, often in conjunction with other texts. In what follows we provide example of how each approach might be applied to Mark 4:1–20.

Deductive. Assuming the thrust of the previous section, a thesis or proposition statement for a sermon on Mark 4:1–20 should focus on the fruitful reception of the kingdom message. Adapting the previous analyses to a more homiletical motif, a verse-by-verse exposition of the passage as it stands could look like this:

Paying Attention to Jesus (Mark 4:1–20)

Three Moments in Jesus's Teaching about Hearing the Message about His Kingdom

1. A moment of ambiguity (Mark 4:3–9) [*Huh?*]
   - Jesus began teaching by means of a parable to get people's attention and make them wonder what he was talking about.
   - *Are you interested in what Jesus is talking about?*

2. A moment of humility (Mark 4:10–12) [*Woe is me!*]
   - Jesus brought in Isaiah's ominous commission to make people realize that God is not obligated to reveal himself to them.
   - *Are you grateful that God has given you an opportunity to understand and commit yourself to Jesus and his kingdom?*

3. A moment of clarity (Mark 4:13–20) [*God is good!*]
   - Jesus explained the details of the parable so that people would not be discouraged by the puzzling parable and the humbling reference to Isaiah.
   - Jesus wanted the people to ponder whether they really heard and were committed to his teaching, or whether they were distracted by Satan, by adversity, or by wealth from following Jesus faithfully and productively.

- *God helping you, will you commit yourself to the grace of God and follow Jesus faithfully?*
- *God helping you, will you resist Satan's attempts to snatch Jesus's word from your heart?*
- *God helping you, will you weather the storms of persecution that come your way because of your allegiance to Jesus and his kingdom?*
- *God helping you, will you resist the lure of materialism and live by the values of Jesus's kingdom?*

The three sections of Mark 4:1–20 could be handled in many other ways. At the center of the passage, centered by the parable itself and Jesus's interpretation of it, is Jesus's central teaching about the kingdom in Mark 4:10–12. The allusion to Isaiah 6:10–11 found here ought to function as a stern warning against the anthropocentric assumption that humans are free to take Jesus or leave him, whenever they see fit. Rather, God is free to graciously reveal himself to them, or not, as he sees fit. The opportunity to hear the message of the kingdom, understand it, and live productively for its values is a gift of God's amazing grace, an opportunity not to be squandered. An exposition of Mark 4:1–20 that begins with this central teaching on humbling oneself under the free grace of God may create greater openness and interest in what it means to hear the gospel message well.

Inductive. Inductive sermons on Mark 4:1–20 should subtly yet clearly lead the audience to conclusions about what genuine response to the kingdom message entails. Lowry suggests that inductive sermons on the parables should reflect the plot or narrative the parable presents.[69] In other words, instead of deducing principles or morals from the parable, preachers should allow it to speak for itself. Typical narrative plots find characters in situations that lead to complications or tensions. Decisions made by the characters resolve the situations in some fashion. The question is then one of application: how does the author intend his character's conflict resolution to impact the reader? Perhaps the sermon could drive toward the three "moments" suggested above.

- Mark 4:1–9: Do you understand the parable? We can all relate to having difficulties with *ambiguity* in the Bible.
- Mark 4:10–12: Would you like to ask Jesus what the parable means? What is even more important is that we realize who God

---

69. Eugene L. Lowry, *How to Preach the Parables* (Nashville: Abingdon, 1989). Jeffrey Arthurs also advocates sensitivity to parabolic genre in *Preaching with Variety* (Grand Rapids: Kregel, 2007), 102–28.

is. Sometimes God reminds us that we are not God and that we need *humility*.

- Mark 4:13–20: Once we have acknowledged our lack of insight, not only into this parable, but also into our total need for grace, God has our attention and leads us to *clarity* on the parable and on our need to follow Jesus faithfully and fruitfully.

An inductive sermon could focus on all of Mark 4:1–20 or any of its three sections in any order. The first three soils as warnings about inadequate responses might be sermonically styled as fake faith. Points like these could be made:

- Fake faith is clueless about the enemy (the birds/Satan in 4:4c, 15b).
- Fake faith is passionate but short-lived. It cannot take the heat (shallow soil/persecution, 4:5–6, 16–17).
- Fake faith values stuff more than Jesus (thorns/worries/riches, 4:7, 18–19).
- Fake faith does not lack information; it lacks insight (seeing and hearing without revealed perception, understanding, repentance, and forgiveness, 4:8–10).
- Real faith hears about Jesus, welcomes him, follows him, and reaps an eternal harvest (4:8, 20).

Topical. Several topics or themes in Mark 4:1–20 could be "spun off" into a sermon or series of sermons on Mark specifically or on the teaching of Jesus in the Synoptic Gospels. The two most obvious topics would be the parables as Jesus's most common teaching method and the kingdom of God as the central content taught by the parables. The parables and the kingdom they illumine are both major topics in studies of Jesus and the Gospels. So, anyone undertaking their exposition had better count the cost in terms of hours needed for preparation and occasions needed for presentation. Other likely topics for a sermon or series from Mark or the Synoptics would include:

- Hearing the word of the kingdom. Christians tend to talk about how well the pastor preached, but seldom do we consider how well we listen. Mark has a great deal to say about hearing or listening to God's word, and what hinders such listening.
- Satan, the adversary of Jesus and his kingdom. Satan appears in Mark as the tempter of Jesus before he is mentioned in this parable. It is high irony that Jesus's human opponents accused him of being in collusion with Satan in his exorcisms.
- Isaiah 6:9–10, alluded to by Jesus in Mark 4:12, is worthy of a sermon in its own right. One also finds it cited in John 12:39–41

and Acts 28:26–27, so it is an important text in the NT. One might also preach a series on the Bible of Jesus, the OT texts he cited during his ministry.

- Hindrances to hearing. This parable mentions persecution and materialism as hindrances to productive hearing of the gospel. Are there others in Mark?
- This parable says much about how farmers planted grain in biblical times, and how that process illustrates preaching and hearing the gospel, as well as about what God will expect from us at the final judgment. A series of sermons on biblical customs and how they are used in the Bible to teach about following Jesus could be an interesting change of pace.

JOHN 1:1–18

Establishing and Translating the Text

NA[28] and UBS[5] note relatively minor variants in John 1:3, 4, 6, 13, 15, 16, and 17.[70] Critical commentaries and Metzger's *Textual Commentary* discuss some of these variants. None are likely to be original, and none significantly alter the meaning of their respective verses. The following discussion addresses three more significant textual matters.

Textual Criticism

Segmenting the "Prologue." P. J. Williams has argued, based on the segmentation of John 1 found in early manuscripts, versions, and commentators, that the earliest segmentation of John 1 involved a paragraph break at 1:5. Accordingly, 1:1–5 amounts to a preface, and the main body of the Gospel begins with 1:6.[71] The argument in effect is that early segmentation shows the early church did not view John 1:1–18 as a discrete prologue, but that John 1 is mainly a series of John the Baptist's testimonies to Jesus. Evaluation of this view is ongoing. Opponents raise questions about its minimizing the arguable chiastic structure of John 1:1–18, the parallel emphasis of John 1:1, 14 on the λόγος, and the inclusio stressing Christ's deity in 1:1, 18. These structural matters will be discussed below.

------

70. A few mss. have ἐστιν instead of ἦν in the first clause of verse 4. The textual tradition of John 1:13 is a bit complicated, but the meaning is not substantially altered by the various readings. A few mss. have the singular construction ὅς οὐκ . . . ἐγενήθη instead of the plural οἱ οὐκ . . . ἐγεννήθησαν. A few mss. have ἐγενήθησαν instead of ἐγεννήθησαν.

71. P. J. Williams, "Not the Prologue of John," *JSNT* 33 (2011): 375–86. See also the discussion at http://evangelicaltextualcriticism.blogspot.com/2011/06/not-prologue-of-john.html.

Segmenting 1:3–4. Two alternatives for segmentation arise near the end of 1:3. The question is whether a punctuation break should be read between οὐδὲ ἕν and ὃ γέγονεν at the end of 1:3.[72] If a break is read,[73] verse 3 concludes with the statement that nothing was made apart from the Word (χωρὶς αὐτοῦ ἐγένετο οὐδὲ ἕν), and verse 4 begins with the statement that what happened through the Word was the life which enlightened humans (ὃ γέγονεν ἐν αὐτῷ ζωὴ ἦν, καὶ ἡ ζωὴ ἦν τὸ φῶς τῶν ἀνθρώπων). If no break is read between οὐδὲ ἕν and ὃ γέγονεν,[74] verse 3 concludes with the statement that nothing that happened apart from the word (χωρὶς αὐτοῦ ἐγένετο οὐδὲ ἕν ὃ γέγονεν), and verse 4 begins with the statement that in the Word was the life that enlightened humans (ἐν αὐτῷ ζωὴ ἦν, καὶ ἡ ζωὴ ἦν τὸ φῶς τῶν ἀνθρώπων). The alternative segmentations are as follows:

Alternative Segmentation of John 1:3–4

πάντα δι' αὐτοῦ ἐγένετο,	πάντα δι' αὐτοῦ ἐγένετο,
καὶ χωρὶς αὐτοῦ ἐγένετο οὐδὲ ἕν.	καὶ χωρὶς αὐτοῦ ἐγένετο οὐδὲ ἕν ὃ γέγονεν.
ὃ γέγονεν ἐν αὐτῷ ζωὴ ἦν,	ἐν αὐτῷ ζωὴ ἦν,
καὶ ἡ ζωὴ ἦν τὸ φῶς τῶν ἀνθρώπων·	καὶ ἡ ζωὴ ἦν τὸ φῶς τῶν ἀνθρώπων·

Metzger's discussion of this matter[75] indicates that the editors of the UBS[4rev] Greek NT could not arrive at unanimity on this question after considering external evidence, Johannine style, and the history of the passage's interpretation. The two approaches to segmentation make only a subtle difference in the teaching of the passage. If one reads χωρὶς αὐτοῦ ἐγένετο οὐδὲ ἕν ὃ γέγονεν with the majority of manuscripts, there is emphasis on the exclusive agency of the Word in creating anything and everything that was ever created. If one reads χωρὶς αὐτοῦ ἐγένετο οὐδὲ ἕν. ὃ γέγονεν ἐν αὐτῷ ζωὴ ἦν, with the older manuscripts, the Word's agency in creating everything is still affirmed, but there is added emphasis on the Word as the creator of light which enlightens humanity. This second option follows the more ancient testimony to the passage. It is also consistent with John's ethical dualism of life and death, symbolized by light and darkness (cf. John 1:7, 9; 3:19–21; 5:35; 8:12; 9:5; 11:9–10; 12:35–36, 46), and hints that the

---

72. An additional complication is the curious double punctuation οὐδὲ ἕν· ὃ γέγονεν· ἐν . . . found in 28 205 1241 and a few other mss.

73. p^{75c} C L W 050* 0141*[vid], a few versions, and several early church writers have a period.

74. The great majority of manuscripts including Q Y 050[c] 33 180 *Byz Lect*, many versions, and many early church writers place a period after ὃ γέγονεν.

75. Metzger, *Textual Commentary*, 167–68.

allusion to Genesis 1:1–3 is the basis for a theology of creation renewal through the Word.

The one and only in 1:18. John 1:18 is a key christological text, and the varying ancient readings of this text have received a extensive scrutiny. The discussion chiefly concerns whether the adjective μονογενὴς describes the noun θεός or the noun υἱός in the second clause of the verse. Relatively few yet more ancient manuscripts read either μονογενὴς θεός[76] or ὁ μονογενὴς θεός.[77] More numerous yet more recent ancient witnesses have μονογενὴς υἱός.[78] In light of the use of μονογενὴς υἱός elsewhere in the Johannine corpus (John 3:16, 18; 1 John 4:9), μονογενὴς θεός is clearly the harder reading. In other words, it is unlikely that a scribe would *intentionally* alter the text from μονογενὴς υἱός to μονογενὴς θεός. But in ancient manuscripts, *nomina sacra* (sacred names)[79] were often abbreviated by using the first and last letters of a word under a horizontal line, so the reading in question would be either $\overline{\Theta\Sigma}$ or $\overline{\Upsilon\Sigma}$ Accordingly, it would be relatively easy for the alteration to occur *unintentionally*.[80]

Both of the above readings are compatible with the high Christology of the Fourth Gospel,[81] as seen in this prologue and other passages, such as John 3:13; 8:58; 14:9; 17:5; 20:28.[82] As noted above, the μονογενὴς υἱός reading is more typical of John's thought, but the striking μονογενὴς θεός reading could be intended to stress Jesus's uniqueness as God-in-flesh.

---

76. $\mathfrak{P}^{66}$ ℵ⋆ B C⋆ L Syr. Among the early versions, the Syriac tradition supports the reading (Peshitta and Harklean[mg]), as does some of the Georgian. Early Christian witnesses supporting the reading include two of four allusions in Origen, Didymus, and one of four allusions in Cyril.

77. $\mathfrak{P}^{75}$ ℵ² 33. Among the early versions, the Bohairic Coptic supports this reading. Supporting early Christian witnesses include two of three allusions in Clement of Alexandria, some of the allusions in Eusebius, two of four allusions in Greek versions of Origen, and Gregory of Nyssa.

78. A C³ W[supp] Δ Θ Ψ 0141 *f*¹ *f*¹³ 28 157 180 205 *Byz* ($\mathfrak{M}$) and many other minuscules, as well as most lectionaries. The reading is also supported by many ancient versions, including the Old Latin, the Vulgate, some of the Syriac tradition, the Armenian, the Ethiopic, some of the Georgian, and the Slavonic. The many ancient Christian witnesses include Irenaeus, one of three allusions in Clement of Alexandria, Hippolytus, one of two allusions in Latin versions of Origen, some of the allusions in Eusebius, Athanasius, Chrysostom, and Tertullian.

79. See further Larry W. Hurtado, "The Origin of the *Nomina Sacra*: A Proposal," *JBL* 117 (1998): 655–73.

80. This is argued by Alan Wikgren in a dissenting opinion in Metzger, *Textual Commentary*, 170.

81. Rodderbos's comment (Herman Ridderbos, *The Gospel according to John: A Theological Commentary*, trans. John Vriend [Grand Rapids: Eerdmans, 1997], 59) to the effect that μονογενὴς θεός is not impossible but difficult on material grounds is puzzling. Keener's discussion (Craig L. Keener, *The Gospel of John: A Commentary*, 2 vols. [Peabody, MA: Hendrickson, 2003], 1.425–26) explains why μονογενὴς θεός is not only plausible but also the more likely reading.

82. On the deity of Jesus and textual criticism, see Brian J. Wright, "Jesus as Θεος: A Textual Examination," in *Revisiting the Corruption of the New Testament*, ed. Daniel B. Wallace (Grand Rapids: Kregel, 2011), 229–65.

Other texts in John speak in a similarly striking way of Jesus's preexistence and deity (e.g., John 8:58; 14:9; 20:28). The existence of **anarthrous** and articular μονογενὴς θεὸς readings is noteworthy, with the former likely giving rise to the latter. The anarthrous reading coheres with John 1:1. The distinction in 1:18 between God (θεὸν οὐδεὶς ἑώρακεν πώποτε) and Jesus as μονογενὴς θεὸς may be intended as a sort of conceptual inclusion with 1:1, where the Word who was with God is God. The expression μονογενὴς θεὸς is likely another striking way of putting the Word's intimate relationship with God, one that is the basis of the enfleshed Word being the unique[83] and ultimate revelator of God (ἐκεῖνος ἐξηγήσατο). It is possible that we are to read John 1:18 appositionally: "No one has ever seen God—the unique one, God himself, the One who is closest to the Father—he has revealed him."

Translation

At one level, the mostly short, **paratactic** clauses of John 1:1–18 (see the discussion of syntax below) are not that difficult to translate, even for relatively new students of NT Greek. Yet interpreting and expounding the profound concepts expressed by the syntax is another matter, one that challenges seasoned scholars and teachers. As always, translators must choose between as word-oriented or concept-oriented approach to their work. See the footnotes in the phrased layout below for discussion of some key matters that affect translation. The following notes address some of the more challenging issues.

1:1—It is challenging to translators that the Word is presented here as both distinct from God (ὁ λόγος ἦν πρὸς τὸν θεόν, 1:1b) and as God (καὶ θεὸς ἦν ὁ λόγος, 1:1c).[84] Possibly καί should be rendered as a mild adversative, "and yet." Rendering πρὸς as "with" seems adequate for the Word's orientation toward God; the expression εἰς τὸν κόλπον τοῦ πατρὸς in 1:18 expounds the relationship expressed here by πρὸς. If the ubiquitous "the Word was God" seems inadequate, one might render with NET "the Word was fully God." NEB, followed by REB, translate a bit more freely: "what God was, the Word was."

1:2—The demonstrative οὗτος here and in 1:7 is apparently equivalent to αὐτός and should be rendered "he." See also the note on 1:8.

---

83. "Only begotten" is not the best gloss for μονογενής, a term whose usage (Luke 7:12; 8:42; 9:38; John 1:14, 18; 3:16, 18; Heb. 11:17; 1 John 4:9) confirms its etymology as a marker of uniqueness, leading to current translations like the NIV's "one and only." See BDAG, s.v. μονογενής (658). The word is semantically related to another term prominent in christological controversies, πρωτότοκος (Luke 2:7; Rom. 8:29; Col. 1:15, 18; Heb. 1:6; 11:28; 12:23; Rev 1:5).

84. On the heretical translation "the word was a god," found in the Watchtower's *New World Translation*, see Wallace, *Greek Grammar beyond the Basics*, 266–69.

1:3—The second aorist verb ἐγένετο may be translated "were made," or "happened," or even "came into existence." Compare the use of this verb to describe the creation of the world in LXX Genesis 1:3.

1:5—The second aorist verb κατέλαβεν [85] can be taken as marking mental or physical apprehension. The meaning is likely either "the darkness did not *suppress* the light" (ESV, NAB, NIV, NLT, NRSV) or "the darkness did not *comprehend* the light" (Douay, KJV, NASB; cf. 1:10). The ambiguity may be intentional, given John's penchant for double meanings. The English words "master" and "get" are similarly ambiguous. Given the imagery of light and darkness, perhaps the translations of "put out" or "extinguish" are warranted. This key metaphor expresses ethical dualism in John. The second καί in 1:5 should probably be translated as a mild adversative ("and yet") if κατέλαβεν is taken in the sense of "comprehend" (cf. 1:10c; 1:11b).

1:7—The preposition εἰς seems to mark intent here, and εἰς μαρτυρίαν may be translated "to be a witness" or "for a testimony." With the cognate verb μαρτυρήσῃ in the following ἵνα clause, ESV renders the phrase "he came *as a witness*, to bear witness." NIV is less repetitive: "he came as a witness to *testify*."

1:8—John is referred to as οὗτος in 1:6 and ἐκεῖνος in 1:8. Both of these demonstrative pronouns may be rendered as equivalent to the personal pronoun αὐτός, but it may be that ἐκεῖνος in 1:8 is intended to contrast John with Jesus, who is referred to as οὗτος in 1:2.[86] As noted in the phrased layout below, translators should supply a verb such as "he came" or "he arrived" for the elliptical ἀλλ᾽ ἵνα.

1:9—As noted in the phrased layout below, the participle ἐρχόμενον is ambiguous and may be taken with either τὸ φῶς . . . ὃ or ἄνθρωπον. In the former option, the participle is adverbial of time and describes the light's work "when it comes into the world" (NASB, similarly ESV, NIV, NLT and most translations). In the latter, the participle is adjectival: the light enlightens "every person who comes into the world" (KJV, LB).

1:10—The irony of this verse should be clarified by rendering the second καί as an adversative: "He was in the world, and the world was made by him, *and yet* the world did not recognize him." Given the relational/covenantal nuance commonly conveyed by γινώσκω (cf. ידע in the OT), it is better to render ἔγνω as did not "recognize" (LB, NET, NIV, NLT) than "did not know" (ESV, KJV, NASB).

1:11—As in 1:10c, the καί is adversative and should be rendered "and

---

85. BDAG, s.v. καταλαμβάνω (519) discusses the semantic range of the word and lists examples of its usage. It occurs fifteen times in the NT, seventeen if the references to the Pharisees *apprehending* the adulterous woman are included (John 8:3). More significantly, it is used in John 12:35, as Jesus warns the disciples to walk while there is light, before darkness comes upon them.

86. Mathewson and Emig, *Intermediate Greek Grammar*, 43–44.

yet" or similarly. Exegetical commentaries discuss reasons for the different genders of τὰ ἴδια (neuter plural accusative) and οἱ ἴδιοι (masculine plural nominative). Some take τὰ ἴδια (cf. John 4:44; 16:32; 19:27) as a reference to his own *land* and οἱ ἴδιοι as a reference to his own *people* (cf. 10:3–4, 12; 13:1; 15:19), but this distinction is far from clear.[87]

1:12—This verse is central to the prologue and to the message of the entire Fourth Gospel. See the syntactical notes in the layout below. The conjunction δέ contrasts those who receive Jesus with those who did not recognize him in 1:11 and might be rendered "nevertheless." It is difficult to convey the connotation of ὄνομα as a word that encodes someone's true identity, their *persona*. Believing in Jesus's name is having confidence in his person, who he really is.[88]

1:13—The repetitive nature of the verse, involving three negated phrases followed by a climactic positive conclusion, deserves careful attention. The difficult plural "bloods" in the first phrase (ἐξ αἱμάτων) likely refers to natural physical descent from two parents.[89] The NIV's functionally equivalent "natural descent" is preferable to the formal verbal correspondence of ESV's "blood." The second phrase (ἐκ θελήματος σαρκὸς) speaks in general of human desire or agency (cf. John 3:3–6).[90] The third phrase (ἐκ θελήματος ἀνδρὸς) focuses specifically on a husband's decision or male sexual impulse (cf. John 4:16–18).

1:14—Most translations render σάρξ as "flesh," but given the ambiguity of that word in English, one might prefer "became human" (NLT) or "became a human being" (CEV, LB). Another choice is presented by ἐσκήνωσεν, which is commonly rendered "dwelt." Some have "made his home" (NIV), "made his dwelling" (NLT), or even "took up residence" (NET), perhaps in view of the allusion to God's mobile presence with the Israelites in the OT Tabernacle (Exod. 25; Heb. 9; Rev. 7:15; 21:3). Rendering μονογενοῦς is another key question for translators. "Only" (ESV, LB) and "one and only" (CSB, NET, NIV, NLT) are preferable to "only begotten" (KJV, NASB).[91]

1:15—The use of both the (historical?) present μαρτυρεῖ and the perfect κέκραγεν together emphasizes the importance and perhaps the ongoing validity of John's testimony. Translators should note that κράζω marks loud and urgent communication. The participle λέγων (cf. לֵאמֹר in the OT) introduces the following direct quotation. In this context the participle is **pleonastic** and need not be translated.

---

87. ἴδιος occurs in John 1:11, 41; 4:44; 5:18, 43; 7:18; 8:44; 10:3, 12; 13:1; 15:19; 16:32; 19:27.

88. BDAG, s.v. ὄνομα 1. d. γ. ב. (713). Cf. John 2:23; 3:18; 1 John 5:13.

89. BDAG, s.v. αἷμα 1. a. (26).

90. Translating σάρξ is not an easy task. Although the term may mark fallen human nature (1 John 2:16), in this verse and in 1:14 it simply distinguishes humanity from deity.

91. See above the discussion of "the one and only in John 1:18."

1:16—The expression χάριν ἀντὶ χάριτος should receive careful attention in the translation/exegesis process. Apparently the quotation of John the Baptist ends with 1:15, and 1:16 should be taken as the author's comment, explaining (ὅτι) the significance of John's testimony about Jesus's superiority. Like John, all believers have experienced fullness of grace through Jesus. The relationship of "Jesus-grace" to "Moses-grace" is expressed by the preposition ἀντί here and by 1:17. A formal correspondence approach leads to translations like "grace for grace" (KJV), or "grace upon grace" (ESV, NRSV). A more functionally equivalent approach leads to translations like "grace in place of grace already given" (NIV), "one gracious gift after another" (NET; NLT is similar). LB has "blessing upon blessing heaped upon us."

1:17—One's translation of 1:16–17 flows from the biblical theology of Moses and Jesus; that is, the relationship between the two Testaments. The clauses of 1:17 are juxtaposed asyndetically (without a connective); translators seem to have either followed this pattern (ESV, NASB, NIV, NRSV), or interjected a conjunction that reflected their view that the law of Moses and the grace of Jesus should be contrasted. LB provides an extreme example with "For Moses gave us only the Law with its rigid demands and merciless justice, while Jesus Christ brought us loving forgiveness as well." In my view, even the conjunction "but" (KJV, NET, NLT) implies a theological contrast that is not warranted by the scriptural allusions of John 1:1–18 and the view of Moses found elsewhere in John.[92] Major translations do not explicitly reflect a view of theological continuum between Moses and Jesus in 1:17. I would suggest a translation commonly used with Hebrew parallelism: "The Law was given through Moses, *what's more*, grace and truth came through Jesus Christ." Perhaps something along the lines of the following is warranted as a paraphrase: "Although God did indeed give the law through Moses, God's covenant love and truth are fully realized through Jesus Christ."

1:18—The key word μονογενὴς has already been discussed in the note on 1:14. See also the discussion of 1:18 in the textual criticism section above. The word κόλπος (cf. John 13:23; Luke 6:38; 16:23; Acts 27:39) describes Jesus's unique and intimate relationship to the Father. In its semantic range, the word marks some sort of fold or indentation, whether of a person's bosom or chest (with no hint of female anatomy), of a blanket, or even a cove in the shoreline of a body of water. Formal correspondence translations include "bosom" (KJV, NASB, RSV). ESV's "at the Father's side" and LB's "the companion of the Father" seem to understate the intimacy often contextually connoted by the word. Notable attempts at functional equivalence such as NET's "in closest fellowship with the Father" and NIV's "in closest relationship with the Father"

---

92. See John 1:45; 5:39–47; 7:22–23, and the discussion of biblical theology below.

seem to miss the anatomical basis of the metaphor. NLT's "near to the Father's heart," and NRSV's "close to the Father's heart" seem better. Perhaps we could go so far as to speak of Jesus experiencing his Father's hug or embrace. The verb that expresses Jesus's crucial revelatory role is ἐξηγήσατο (cf. Luke 24:25; Acts 10:8; 15:12, 14; 21:19). The range of this word includes reporting, describing, interpreting, and explaining. All such glosses require human speech, but as the divine λόγος, not only Jesus's words but also his *persona* and works reveal the Father. In view of texts like John 1:14; 14:9; 20:28, Jesus is the quintessential embodiment of God whose very existence amounts to the exegesis of God. Any human description of this profound concept will be limited, but accurate glosses include "declared him" (KJV), "made God known" (NET, NIV, NRSV), "explained him" (NASB), and "revealed God" (NLT).

Analyzing the Text

Genre

Culpepper echoes many scholars when he says, "By any estimate the prologue to the Gospel of John is one of the most profound passages in the Bible."[93] John 1:1–18 is no exception to the rule that the opening of a literary work provides insight into its genre, content, and purpose.[94] The unique "Word-become-flesh" (John 1:14) Christology of the Fourth Gospel is given its impetus here. Most scholars view the prologue's language as a blending of heightened prose and poetry. Many take it as a reworking and expansion of an earlier hymn to wisdom (such as Prov. 8:22–25; Wis. 9:9–12; Sir. 24:5–27), now embedded in 1:1–5, 9–14, 16–18, with prose insertions (1:6–8, 15). Yet few agree on how the earlier material has been reworked, or on the seams between the earlier material and the evangelist's fresh composition. Preoccupation with such matters amounts to missing the forest for the trees.[95]

Martin Hengel described the prologue as a whole as "a hymn or psalm to the Logos, composed with great linguistic art and deep reflection" by the evangelist. He argued that the four memorable words of 1:14 (ὁ λόγος σὰρξ ἐγένετο) are "the one decisive point that is developed in the whole Gospel."[96] Culpepper argued that the prologue

---

93. R. Alan Culpepper, *The Gospel and Letters of John* (Nashville: Abingdon, 1998), 110.

94. The role of the openings of the Gospels in determining their genre and content has been discussed in chapter 1.

95. Keener (*John*, 1.334–37) provides a fair evaluation of such proposals.

96. Martin Hengel, "The Prologue of the Gospel of John as the Gateway to Theological Truth," in *The Gospel of John and Christian Theology*, eds. Richard Bauckham and Carl Mosser (Grand Rapids: Eerdmans, 2008), 268.

provides reliable exposition of Jesus's identity, preparing the reader to understand and interpret the numerous *anagnorisis* (recognition) type-scenes (Aristotle, *Poetics* 1452–55) that follow in the Gospel. In such scenes, characters recognize Jesus, recognize him only partially, or fail to recognize him at all.[97] Brodie argued that the interweaving of poetry and prose suggests a theological motif rather than a literary prehistory: "The interweaving is a way of expressing, through the very form of the language, one of the prologue's central ideas—the descent of the (soaring, poetic) Word into the (prosaic) reality of human life."[98]

The relationship of the prologue to the Fourth Gospel as a whole has been likened to the relationship of an overture to a symphony or to the relationship of an entrance or atrium to a fine building. The musical and architectural analogies both help the reader of John to understand how the Gospel profoundly develops the seminal ideas expressed briefly in the prologue.

Syntax

The interwoven poetry and elevated prose of John 1:1–18 mostly involves short clauses in **paratactic** relationship. Key words are often repeated in slightly different syntactic structures, and one notices parallelisms, whether introverted (**chiasmus**) or stepped. More complicated **hypotactic** structures are encountered in 1:7–9 and 12–13, where purpose clauses and relative clauses introduce theologically dense concepts. The following phrased layout analytically displays the passage, with footnotes dealing with many of the more obvious syntactical issues.

PHRASED LAYOUT OF KATA IΩANNHN 1:1–18

1   Ἐν ἀρχῇ ἦν ὁ λόγος,[99]
        καὶ[100] ὁ λόγος ἦν πρὸς[101] τὸν θεόν,
        καὶ θεὸς[102] ἦν ὁ λόγος.
2   οὗτος ἦν ἐν ἀρχῇ πρὸς τὸν θεόν.[103]

---

97. Culpepper, *The Gospel and Letters of John*, 72–78.

98. Thomas L. Brodie, *The Gospel according to John* (Oxford: Oxford University, 1993), 134.

99. Note the allusion to Genesis 1:1; on λόγος see BDAG, 601 3.

100. καὶ occurs sixteen times in John 1:1–18. Typically it functions to coordinate clauses or words, but occasionally it marks an adversative relationship between clauses (1:5b, 10b, 11b).

101. On πρὸς here and in 1:2 see BDAG, 875 3. g. and Murray J. Harris, *Prepositions and Theology in the Greek New Testament* (Grand Rapids: Zondervan, 2012), 190–92.

102. On anarthrous θεός and Colwell's Rule see Wallace, *Greek Grammar beyond the Basics*, 256–70.

103. The better exegetical commentaries discuss the chiastic structure of John 1:1–2 and of John 1:1–18 as a whole.

3 πάντα δι᾽[104] αὐτοῦ ἐγένετο,[105]
    καὶ χωρὶς αὐτοῦ ἐγένετο οὐδὲ ἕν.
4 ὃ γέγονεν[106] ἐν αὐτῷ ζωὴ ἦν,
    καὶ ἡ ζωὴ ἦν τὸ φῶς τῶν ἀνθρώπων·[107]
5 καὶ τὸ φῶς ἐν τῇ σκοτίᾳ φαίνει,[108]
    καὶ ἡ σκοτία αὐτὸ οὐ κατέλαβεν.[109]
6 Ἐγένετο ἄνθρωπος,
        ἀπεσταλμένος[110] παρὰ θεοῦ,
        ὄνομα αὐτῷ[111] Ἰωάννης·
7 οὗτος[112] ἦλθεν εἰς[113] μαρτυρίαν
        ἵνα μαρτυρήσῃ περὶ τοῦ φωτός,
            ἵνα πάντες πιστεύσωσιν δι᾽ αὐτοῦ.
8 οὐκ ἦν ἐκεῖνος τὸ φῶς,
        ἀλλ᾽ ἵνα[114] μαρτυρήσῃ περὶ τοῦ φωτός.
9   Ἦν τὸ φῶς τὸ ἀληθινόν,[115]
            ὃ φωτίζει πάντα[116] ἄνθρωπον,
                ἐρχόμενον[117] εἰς τὸν κόσμον.

---

104. On δι᾽ αὐτοῦ here and in 1:10 expressing personal agency, see BDAG, 225 A. 4 and διὰ Μωϋσέως in 1:17.

105. Note the prevalence of γίνομαι in John 1:3–4, 6, 10, 14, 17 and in Genesis 1 for היה, describing the result of God's creative activity.

106. Note the punctuation question here. See the UBS⁵ apparatus and the exegetical commentaries.

107. The expression τὸ φῶς τῶν ἀνθρώπων apparently should be understood as verbal head noun with an objective genitive (Wallace, *Greek Grammar beyond the Basics*, 116–19). Cf. 1:9.

108. The present tense verb φαίνει stands out (*BNTS* 224 5.? or 226 7.?) Cf. φωτίζει in 1:9 and μαρτυρεῖ in 1:15. Note the allusion to Genesis 1:2–5 and the implicit creation renewal motif. Cf. the use of σκοτία in 1:5 and other texts in John such as 8:12.

109. The meaning of κατέλαβεν is somewhat ambiguous, perhaps intentionally so. See BDAG, 519 and John 1:11–12.

110. The anarthrous participle can be taken adverbially as an explanation of John's arrival or adjectivally as a description of John.

111. The dative αὐτῷ seems to mark reference and is similar to a genitive marking possession (Wallace, *Greek Grammar beyond the Basics*, 149–51; Mathewson and Emig, *Intermediate Greek Grammar*, 23–24). Cf. Nicodemus in 3:1.

112. On the use of the demonstrative for a personal pronoun see Wallace, *Greek Grammar beyond the Basics*, 328–29. Cf. 1:8, 15, 18.

113. Note the telic sense of εἰς in BDAG, 290 4. d. e. f. Cf. 1:19, 32, 34. With the three following ἵνα-clauses, purpose is expressed in a cascading manner.

114. There is apparently an ellipsis of a main verb such as ἦλθεν or ἐγένετο with ἀλλ᾽ ἵνα. See BDAG, 476 2. f.

115. This is a key word in John, subtly contrasting the authenticity of Jesus versus various pretenders. Cf. 4:23, 37; 6:32; 7:28; 8:16; 15:1; 17:3; 19:35.

116. Note the implicit universality here and in 1:7.

117. The participle ἐρχόμενον can be understood as in grammatical agreement with either φῶς or ἄνθρωπον. Accordingly, translations could speak of the light that enlightens every person

10   ἐν τῷ κόσμῳ ἦν,
          καὶ ὁ κόσμος δι᾽ αὐτοῦ ἐγένετο,[118]
          καὶ[119] ὁ κόσμος αὐτὸν οὐκ ἔγνω.[120]

11   εἰς τὰ ἴδια[121] ἦλθεν,
          καὶ οἱ ἴδιοι αὐτὸν οὐ παρέλαβον.

12   ὅσοι[122] δὲ[123] ἔλαβον αὐτόν,
          ἔδωκεν αὐτοῖς ἐξουσίαν τέκνα θεοῦ γενέσθαι,[124]
                    τοῖς πιστεύουσιν[125] εἰς τὸ ὄνομα αὐτοῦ,

13   οἳ[126] . . . ἐγεννήθησαν.
                                  οὐκ ἐξ[127] αἱμάτων[128]
                                  οὐδὲ ἐκ θελήματος σαρκὸς[129]
                                  οὐδὲ ἐκ θελήματος ἀνδρὸς
                                  ἀλλ᾽ ἐκ θεοῦ ἐγεννήθησαν.[130]

---

when it comes into the world of the light enlightening every person who comes into the world. Cf. 1:4b.

118. The first two clauses of 1:10 reprise the main emphases of 1:3–9, preparing the reader for the irony of 1:10c (cf. 1:5).

119. Note the adversative sense of καί (BDAG, 495 1. b. η.). Cf. 1:5b, 11b, and how 1:11 repeats the ideas of 1:10.

120. ἔγνω is interesting in terms of its morphology (second aorist, third person singular), *aktionsart* (constative or global) and relational lexis (meaning). See BDAG, 200 7. Cf. e.g. ידע in Exod. 1:8; Ps. 1:6; Amos 3:2.

121. The switch from the neuter accusative plural ἴδια to the masculine nominative plural ἴδιοι is difficult to explain (BDAG, 467 4. a. b.).

122. The nominative plural correlative pronoun ὅσοι introduces a pendent clause which "hangs" until it is picked up by αὐτοῖς in the following main clause. Cf. 1:18b–c. See Wallace, *Greek Grammar beyond the Basics*, 51–53; Mathewson and Emig, *Intermediate Greek Grammar*, 8–9.

123. This is the only time δὲ occurs in the prologue. It apparently marks contrast between those who received (ἔλαβον) Jesus in 1:12a and those who did not (οὐ παρέλαβον) in 1:11b (BDAG, 213 4.).

124. The infinitive γενέσθαι is adjectival or epexegetical, describing ἐξουσίαν (Wallace, *Greek Grammar beyond the Basics*, 607; Mathewson and Emig, *Intermediate Greek Grammar*, 203).

125. The participle πιστεύουσιν is appositional to αὐτοῖς.

126. This relative clause points back to a string of antecedents, starting with the believers (τοῖς πιστεύουσιν), who are those (αὐτοῖς) given authorization to become God's children, who are those (ὅσοι) who received Jesus.

127. The four consecutive ἐκ-phrases, the three of which are negated, emphatically describe the monergistic agency of God as the origin or cause of the authorization of children of God (BDAG, 296 3. a.). Cf. John 3:5, 6, 8; 8:41, 47; 1 John 2:29; 3:9; 4:7; 5:1, 4, 18.

128. On the plural αἱμάτων, see BDAG, 26 1. a.

129. The genitives σαρκὸς and ἀνδρὸς with the head noun θελήματος are apparently subjective, expressing the agency of the will. See BDAG, 447 2. a; Wallace, *Greek Grammar beyond the Basics*, 113–16; Mathewson and Emig, *Intermediate Greek Grammar*, 14–17.

130. On γεννάω, see also John 3:3–8; 1 John 2:29; 3:9; 4:7; 5:1, 4, 18.

14 Καὶ ὁ λόγος σὰρξ[131] ἐγένετο
καὶ ἐσκήνωσεν[132] ἐν ἡμῖν,
καὶ ἐθεασάμεθα τὴν δόξαν[133] αὐτοῦ,
  δόξαν ὡς μονογενοῦς[134] παρὰ πατρός,
  πλήρης χάριτος καὶ ἀληθείας.[135]
15 Ἰωάννης μαρτυρεῖ[136] περὶ αὐτοῦ καὶ κέκραγεν[137] λέγων:[138]
  Οὗτος ἦν ὃν[139] εἶπον:
    Ὁ ὀπίσω μου ἐρχόμενος[140] ἔμπροσθέν μου
    γέγονεν,
      ὅτι[141] πρῶτός μου[142] ἦν.

16 ὅτι ἐκ τοῦ πληρώματος[143] αὐτοῦ ἡμεῖς πάντες ἐλάβομεν
καὶ χάριν ἀντὶ χάριτος:[144]

---

131. On σάρξ, see BDAG, 915 3. b. Cf. John 6:51–56; 20:20, 24–27; 1 John 4:2; 2 John 7; Luke 24:39; Heb. 2:14; 5:7.

132. The biblical overtones of ἐσκήνωσεν are significant in light of the tabernacle (הַמִּשְׁכָּן/σκηνή) of Moses. Cf. BDAG, 929; Exod. 25:9; 26:1 ff.; 33:7–11; Rev. 7:15; 21:3.

133. The biblical overtones of δόξα (BDAG, 257 1. b.) are significant in light of כְּבוֹד יְהוָה in such texts as Exod. 29:43; 33:18, 22. The association of glory and light (cf. 1:4–5) in Isa. 60:1, 19; 2 Cor. 4:4, 6; Rev. 21:23 is also noteworthy.

134. On the exegetical and theological crux μονογενής, see BDAG, 658 2. and 1:18; 3:16; 1 John 4:9. Note Gen. 22:2: קַח־נָא אֶת־בִּנְךָ אֶת־יְחִידְךָ אֲשֶׁר־אָהַבְתָּ אֶת־יִצְחָק. Cf. Zech. 12:10.

135. On the two genitives following πλήρης, see Wallace, *Greek Grammar beyond the Basics*, 92–94. Cf. 1:16–17. Note the likely intertextuality with Exod. 34:6- רַב־חֶסֶד וֶאֱמֶת. Cf. Ps. 86:15 and Ps. 25:10; 61:7; 85:10; 89:14; 96:3.

136. The present tense-form μαρτυρεῖ is striking. Recent thinking about what has been called the "historical" present views it not so much as conveying vividness in itself (as in Wallace, *Greek Grammar beyond the Basics*, 526–32), but as an indicator of prominence that emphasizes what follows it. See Mathewson and Emig, *Intermediate Greek Grammar*, 115–16, 126–27.

137. The perfect tense-form focuses on John's completed witness in the past, not a present state of affairs. See Mathewson and Emig, *Intermediate Greek Grammar*, 133–36.

138. On the pleonastic or redundant participle that introduces a quotation, see Wallace, *Greek Grammar beyond the Basics*, 649–50.

139. The reader needs to supply the omitted antecedent of the relative pronoun. See Wallace, *Greek Grammar beyond the Basics*, 339–42.

140. The substantive participle phrase is the subject of the sentence.

141. The logical flow of the three consecutive ὅτι clauses in 1:15–17 is challenging.

142. The genitive construction πρῶτός μου is similar to a genitive of comparison. See BDAG, 893 2. a. b. Cf. 1:30. John's testimony to Jesus is expanded in 1:19–27, 29–35; 3:27–30.

143. On πλήρωμα, see BDAG, 829 3. b. Cf. πλήρης in 1:14.

144. The prepositional phrase χάριν ἀντὶ χάριτος is difficult. (BDAG, 87 2.: "God's favor comes in ever new streams.") The phrase with its explanation in the next clause is crucial for Johannine biblical theology of Jesus and Moses. Given the intertextual relationship with Exod. 33–34, continuity rather than discontinuity is in view. Recent English translations render it in various ways: ESV "grace upon grace"; NIV "grace in place of grace already given"; NLT: "one gracious blessing after another."

17   ὅτι ὁ νόμος διὰ[145] Μωϋσέως ἐδόθη,[146]
                      ἡ χάρις καὶ ἡ ἀλήθεια διὰ ᾽Ιησοῦ Χριστοῦ ἐγένετο.[147]
18   θεὸν οὐδεὶς ἑώρακεν πώποτε·
            μονογενὴς θεὸς[148] . . . ἐκεῖνος ἐξηγήσατο.
                      ◀ ὁ ὢν εἰς τὸν κόλπον[149] τοῦ πατρὸς

Structure

Those who think that John 1:1–18 was based on a hymn or poem look at the prologue as a blend of poetic strophes (e.g., 1:1–2, 3–5, 10–13, 16–18) and prose insertions (e.g., 1:6–8, 15).[150] Such approaches have merit in that they present a plausible redactional process that clarifies the distinctive theology of John, but their inconsistencies do not commend confidence. The approach here will focus on the canonical text of John 1:1–18 as a finished product rather than on theories about the text's literary prehistory.

More than one scholar has noticed that John 1:1–2 exhibits a chiastic or inverted structure with catchwords (below in bold) linking the clauses:

¹Ἐν ἀρχῇ
    ἦν
        ὁ **λόγος**, καὶ
        ὁ **λόγος**
            ἦν
                πρὸς τὸν **θεόν**, καὶ
                θεὸς
            ἦν
        ὁ **λόγος**.
        ²οὗτος
    ἦν
ἐν ἀρχῇ πρὸς τὸν θεόν.

---

145. Cf. 1:3, 10. On διά see BDAG, 224 4 and Harris, *Prepositions and Theology*, 70–71.

146. On the "divine passive" with διά as agent marker, see Wallace, *Greek Grammar beyond the Basics*, 433–34, 37–38; Mathewson and Emig, *Intermediate Greek Grammar*, 147–48; BDAG, 224 4.

147. The asyndetic relationship of the two clauses is noteworthy. John simply juxtaposes the clauses without a connective, leaving the reader to construe the relationship of Jesus and Moses from the immediate context and its intertextual background in Exodus 33–34. The use of ἐγένετο instead of ἐδόθη in the second line of 1:17 is significant, given the use of γίνομαι in 1:3–4, 10.

148. Note the significant textual variant υἱός and the evidence in UBS⁵ 307 n. 5 with discussion in Metzger's *Textual Commentary*², 169.

149. On εἰς τὸν κόλπον as an image of closest intimate association see BDAG, s.v. εἰς 1. a. d. (288) and s.v. κόλπος 1 (556). See also Harris, *Prepositions and Theology*, 86–88. This text expounds ὁ λόγος ἦν πρὸς τὸν θεόν in 1:1. Cf. 14:8–11.

150. Culpepper (*The Gospel and Letters of John*, 111–15) provides an accessible version of a typical approach. Urban C. von Wahlde (*The Gospel and Letters of John*, 3 vols. [Grand Rapids: Eerdmans, 2010], 2.17–32) goes into more detail.

Catchwords are not used in 1:2, although the **chiasmus** is completed with the repetition of ἐν ἀρχῇ. John 1:1–18 as a whole reflects a repetitive structure that focuses attention on its center, 1:10–13, where the irony of unbelief is contrasted with the gracious blessing of entering God's family through faith. Several scholars present different chiastic analyses of John 1:1–18 as a whole.[151] The following is a simplified version of a typical approach:

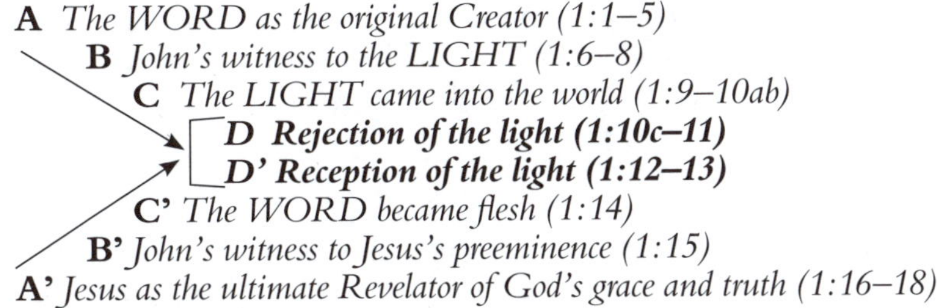

A CHIASTIC ANALYSIS OF JOHN 1:1–18

A *The WORD as the original Creator (1:1–5)*
 B *John's witness to the LIGHT (1:6–8)*
  C *The LIGHT came into the world (1:9–10ab)*
   D *Rejection of the light (1:10c–11)*
   D' *Reception of the light (1:12–13)*
  C' *The WORD became flesh (1:14)*
 B' *John's witness to Jesus's preeminence (1:15)*
A' *Jesus as the ultimate Revelator of God's grace and truth (1:16–18)*

When this structure is taken into account, the purpose of John's prologue is to call on its readers to "receive" Jesus as the divine Word (**D D'**) who took on flesh and came into the world (**C C'**) according to John's testimony (**B B'**) in order to shine renewing light on a benighted world by revealing God's grace and truth (**A A'**).

Another way to understand the repetitive flow of thought in John 1:1–18 is to key on the two statements where Jesus is described as "the Word." This leads to a step-parallel analysis of the prologue's structure that is somewhat similar to the above:

A STEP-PARALLEL ANALYSIS OF JOHN 1:1–18

A The Word as transcendent creator (1:1–3a)
 B The Word as giver of life and light to humans (1:3b–5)
  C John the Baptist's testimony to Jesus as the light (1:6–9)
   D Rejection and Reception: Contrasting responses to Jesus (1:10–13)

A' The Word as incarnate human (1:14a–b)
 B' The Word as glorious revealer of God's full grace and truth (1:14c)
  C' John the Baptist's testimony to Jesus's surpassing status (1:15)
   D' Moses and Jesus: Partial and complete revelations of God's grace and truth (1:16–18)

---

151. E.g., R. Alan Culpepper, "The Pivot of St. John's Gospel," *NTS* 27 (1980): 1–31.

This second analysis, based on the two statements about the Word, portrays 1:14–18 as an interpretive summary of the main ideas of 1:1–13. The Word is both transcendent and incarnate (**A A'**). The Word creates enlivening light and reveals God's glorious grace and truth (**B B'**). John's testimony (**C C'**) is foundational to both stages of the Word's activity. All of which implies that the reader's response to Jesus (**D**, rejection or reception, 1:10–13) is related to the reader's view of Moses (**D'**, 1:16–18). Moses's revelation of God's grace centered in the glorious giving of the law at Sinai, yet Moses longed for a fuller experience of the divine, one that can be realized only through faith in Jesus. John's ensuing narrative will show that the readers must not reject Jesus because they think Moses is God's ultimate prophet (John 9:24–29). Rather, correctly understanding Moses will lead them to faith in Jesus (5:38–47).

Key Words

Previous discussions of the translation and analysis of John 1:1–18 have identified key words and collocations that are crucial for the exegesis and communication of the text. The following are particularly important:

- 1:1: The referent of "beginning" is crucial, as is the meaning of "the Word" and the Word's relationship to God.
- 1:4: The full biblical connotations of "life" and its metaphor "light" should be explored, especially in the Johannine corpus.
- 1:6: John's status is one who was "sent from God."
- 1:7–8: John's ministry was as a "witness" so that all might "believe" (cf. 1:13, 15).
- 1:9: "World" is an important term here and elsewhere in the Fourth Gospel.
- 1:10–11: The parallel verbs "acknowledge" and "receive" (cf. 1:12) are reciprocally definitive.
- 1:12: The relationship of "authority" as it relates to becoming "children" of God should be explained.
- 1:14: "Flesh" is a crucial term that will be discussed below. Understanding God's "glory" here and in the intertext Exodus 33:18–19 is important. Jesus as the "only" (or the "only begotten," cf. 1:18) one from the Father is a theological watershed. The paired expression "grace and truth" (cf. 1:17) needs to be understood in light of its intertext Exodus 34:6.
- 1:16: The Word's "fullness" is an expression that needs further explanation.
- 1:18: "Seeing" God is evidently more a term for intimate experience than physical sight (Exod. 33:18–34:9). Jesus's ability to

"explain" God based on his being in "closest relationship" with God deserves further study.

The "high Christology" rightly associated with the Fourth Gospel is not always associated with John's clear teaching about Jesus's humanity,[152] which develops from the key word σάρξ here in the prologue. This word occurs thirteen times in John, 147 times in the NT, and around 200 times in the LXX, typically for בשׂר. As may be seen by perusing lexical sources,[153] the semantic range of σάρξ in the NT is extensive. We list several common glosses below with references in John and elsewhere that likely fit each gloss:

- "Flesh" as the material that covers the bones of a creature, whether human or animal
    (John 6:51–56; 1 Cor. 15:39)
- The "body" as the physical aspect of a living creature
    (John 3:6; 6:63; cf. 1 John 4:2; 2 John 7)
- Fallen physical existence characterized by sinful activities
    (1 John 2:16; Rom. 7:18; 8:4–6; 2 Peter 2:10)
- A "human being" consisting in a body (with no implications of sinfulness)
    (John 1:13–14; 17:2; cf. Matt. 24:22/Mark 13:20; Luke 3:6 [Isa. 40:5])
- One's ancestral connections or "descent"
    (Rom. 1:3; 4:1; 9:3, 8; 11:14; Heb. 5:7)
- The "external" or circumstantial side of human life
    (John 8:15; 1 Cor. 1:26; Eph. 6:5)

Related to the noun σάρξ are the adjectives σαρκικός (Rom. 15:27; 1 Cor. 3:3; 1 Peter 3:3) and σάρκινος (Rom. 7:14; 1 Cor. 3:1; Heb. 7:16). Other words related to the root σάρξ occur outside the NT.

A similar range of meanings for σάρξ is found in Hellenistic-Jewish Greek literature and in classical Greek. In the LXX, σάρξ often occurs as the gloss for בשׂר, describing the human body (Gen. 2:21; Exod. 30:32), human flesh (Gen. 40:22), human relatives (Gen. 37:27; 1 Chron. 11:1), animal meat as food for humans (Gen. 9:4; Dan. 10:3), and the frailty and finiteness of human existence (Gen. 6:3; Ps. 56:4; 78:39; Jer.

---

152. See further, briefly, Craig R. Koester, *The Word of Life* (Grand Rapids: Eerdmans, 2008), 84–86; and in detail, Marianne Meye Thompson, *The Humanity of Jesus in the Fourth Gospel* (Minneapolis: Augsburg Fortress, 1988), and *The Incarnate Word* (Peabody, MA: Hendrickson, 1993).

153. E.g., BDAG, s.v. σάρξ (914–16); *NIDNTTE,* s.v. σάρξ (4.251–52); *TDNT,* s.v. σάρξ (7.98–151).

17:5). Humanity as a whole is commonly described as "all flesh" (πᾶσα σάρξ, כָּל־בָּשָׂר; Gen. 6:12; Isa. 40:5–6; 66:23; Jer. 39:27=HB/ET 32:27; cf. John 17:2; Acts 2:17 [Joel 3:1=HB/ET 2:28]). Similarly, the collocation σάρξ καὶ αἷμα (Sir. 14:18; 17:31; cf. Matt. 16:17; Eph. 6:12; Heb. 2:14) describes human finiteness, not necessarily sinfulness, as opposed to God's transcendence.[154]

Some explain ὁ λόγος σάρξ ἐγένετο in John 1:14 as Jesus simply taking on a human *body*.[155] This understanding is true as far as it goes, but it does not go nearly far enough and actually amounts to a mild form of **Docetism**. John 1:14 simply states that the Word—the One who was with God in the beginning and who was God—became human for the purpose of renewing creation and revealing the Father. It is true that σάρξ (like בשר) at times refers only to the material part of the human being, but John 1:14, seen in the context of John's overall teaching about Jesus, not to mention the rest of the NT (e.g., Phil. 2:6–8; 1 Tim. 2:4; Heb. 2:14–18), is describing Jesus becoming fully human, taking on all that is essentially human. This concept is far more than more than a mere appearance of divinity in the form of a human body, something that would not have been out of the ordinary for those steeped in Greco-Roman mythology (Acts 14:11–12). Christian theology rightly speaks of Jesus as both *fully* God and *fully* human,[156] as will be discussed further below.

Setting the Text

Historical and Cultural Background

The setting of John. John's prologue is sophisticated, conceptually dense literature that makes little overt reference to its historical and cultural setting. According to ancient tradition, the impetus behind the Fourth Gospel was the desire for the beloved disciple to write a "spiritual" Gospel to complement the previous Gospels' emphasis on Jesus's humanity.[157] John's intended audience is vigorously debated. Most recently Bauckham and others have argued that all four Gospels were written for

---

154. J. Lust et al., *Greek-English Lexicon of the Septuagint,* s.v. σάρξ (422).

155. *NIDNTTE,* 4.259.

156. Expositions of John 1:14 that are both exegetically and theologically helpful on this point include D. A. Carson, *The Gospel according to John,* PNTC (Grand Rapids: Eerdmans, 1991), 126–30; Keener, *The Gospel of John,* 1.406–8; Ridderbos, *The Gospel of John,* 48–55.

157. According to Eusebius (*Hist. eccl.* 6.14.6–7; c. A.D. 320), Clement of Alexandria said that John, at the encouragement of his associates, composed a spiritual Gospel (πνευματικὸν ποιῆσαι εὐαγγέλιον) because he perceived that the previous Gospels had emphasized external matters (τὰ σωματικά).

the entire church, not for specific demographic or geographic segments of the church.[158] When it comes to John, Bauckham's thesis confronts the view of J. Louis Martyn[159] and others that the pericope of Jesus healing the blind man in John 9 reveals the setting and audience of the book—followers of Jesus were being thrown out of synagogues (cf. John 9:22) because of decisions made by a Rabbinic council at Jamnia (Jabneh) after the Temple was destroyed in A.D. 70. Today, it is widely doubted that such a council ever occurred, but this debate raises important questions about John's origins and purpose in relation to formative Judaism. Such questions may be addressed by engaging John's λόγος Christology.[160]

The Johannine λόγος. The various ways of explaining the Johannine λόγος are directly related to various views of John's intent and audience. Putting the matter simply, one may ask whether John uses λόγος to mediate Christian teaching to Gentiles steeped in Greek philosophy, or to relate Jesus to Hellenistic Jewish thought, or to link Jesus with the way the Hebrew Bible speaks of God's powerful, creative Word. We briefly consider each possibility below.[161]

Some interpreters believe John uses the term to connect with people who are aware that in Greek philosophy λόγος describes the unifying principle of all being.[162] In this view, John's strategy is similar to that of Paul in Athens, when he connects the "unknown God" worshipped by the Athenians with the God of the Bible who created all things and sent Jesus into the world (Acts 17:23–31). It is doubtful, however, that the Gospel of John's primary readers were Gentile adherents to Greek philosophy who would have been interested in a novel approach to λόγος.

Others think John uses the term λόγος to portray Jesus as the embodiment of God's wisdom in a way that is similar to Proverbs 8 (especially verses 22–31) and other Jewish literature of the period (e.g.,

---

158. Richard Bauckham, ed. *The Gospels for All Christians: Rethinking the Gospel Audiences* (Grand Rapids: Eerdmans, 1997), esp. 9–48, 147–71. This book's title may beg a crucial question. One wonders, in view of John 1:11–13 and 20:30–31, not to mention many of the vignettes found in the Fourth Gospel, whether the book was written *primarily* for Christians.

159. J. Louis Martyn, *History and Theology in the Fourth Gospel*, 3rd ed. (Louisville: Westminster Knox, 2003). A more satisfactory alternative to Martyn's thesis is provided by Edward W. Klink III, "Expulsion from the Synagogue: Rethinking a Johannine Anachronism," *TynBul* 59 (2008): 99–118.

160. See further Köstenberger's survey of the historical setting of the Johannine corpus in *Theology of John's Gospel*, 37–99. On the Jewish setting of John, see W. D. Davies, "Reflections on Aspects of the Jewish Background of the Gospel of John," in R. Alan Culpepper and C. Clifton Black, eds. *Exploring the Gospel of John* (Louisville: Westminster/Knox, 1996), 43–64.

161. See Keener, *John*, 1.339–63 for a detailed discussion. See also Daniel Boyarin, "The Gospel of the *Memra*: Jewish Binitarianism and the Prologue to John," *HTR* 94 (2001): 242–84 and John Ronning, *The Jewish Targums and John's Logos Theology* (Grand Rapids: Baker, 2010).

162. Relevant Hellenistic and Hellenistic-Jewish sources are cited in M. Eugene Boring, et al., eds. *Hellenistic Commentary on the New Testament* (Nashville: Abingdon, 1995), 238–43.

Sir. 1, 15, 24; Wis. 7:22–10:21; Bar. 3:9–4:4). In this view, John's Jewish audience would have already been thinking of God's wisdom as a creating force and associating it with the Law of Moses. John would be countering this understanding with his presentation of Jesus as God's wisdom and revelation. This approach is plausible, yet these texts portray wisdom as God's first *created* entity (Prov. 8:22–25; Sir. 24:8–9), not as the *Creator* (John 1:3, 10). Although John might have spoken in this way in order to build on his audience's preunderstanding of wisdom, his use of λόγος transcends the portrayal of wisdom in these texts.

Although these two views are plausible, it seems most likely that John uses the term λόγος, along with the phrase ἐν ἀρχῇ (1:1), primarily to portray Jesus as the one who originally gave voice to God's work of creation, as well as the one who reveals God's new beginning designed to transform that creation. Jesus was "the word" through which God spoke the world into existence (cf. Gen. 1:3, 6, 9, 11, 14, 20, 24, 26; Ps. 33:6, 9; 148:5; Isa. 40:8; 55:10–11). Just as the Word is God's agent through which the world was created, so Jesus is sent by the Father to be the ultimate embodiment of God's glorious creating, renewing, revealing voice (cf. Heb 1:1–2). This primary understanding of *logos* is perhaps complemented by the previous two views. John's λόγος Christology may well have been chosen because it would be meaningful to a wide audience.[163]

Thinking with the Text

Intertextuality

Although no OT texts are explicitly cited in John 1:1–18, analysis of its themes and details reveals its overall dependence on two major OT passages, Genesis 1 and Exodus 33–34. John 1:1–5 echoes the creation account in Genesis 1, using it as a backdrop for the renewal of creation and humanity through the life and light brought by the Word.[164] Similarly, John 1:14–18 echoes the giving of the law (Exod. 31:18; 34:28) and Moses's longing to see the glorious face of God in Exodus 33:7–34:9. The point of these allusions is to show that God's grace and truth, seen genuinely yet only partially by Moses, are now fully revealed through Jesus the ultimate Word or message from God (Exod.

---

163. See Köstenberger's summary of the voluminous literature on this topic (*Theology of John's Gospel*, 338–41).

164. Related OT texts on God's powerful word include Ps. 33:6; Isa. 40:8; 55:10–11.

34:6; John 1:14, 17).[165] Taking John's prologue as an implicit midrash[166] (commentary) on Genesis 1 and Exodus 33–34 exalts Jesus as the Word who originally created humanity and who ultimately renews humanity by revealing the glorious fullness of God's grace and truth. Jesus then is the unique son[167] who "has made God known" (1:18) as creator and governor of his people. Jesus is the exegesis of God.[168]

Biblical Theology

John's prologue has been compared to the entry or foyer of a mansion because from its vantage point one may see the grand plan of the Fourth Gospel to present Jesus as the one who reveals the Father's glory and calls people to receive him by faith. One can view it as a sort of seedbed for the rest of the Gospel because several of John's major themes are introduced here. The later development of Trinitarian doctrine owes much to reflection on the prologue's implications for the relation of the Father and the Son and the upper room teaching teaching on the coming advocate (John 13–17).[169] Among the many themes that could be mentioned, the following are particularly noteworthy:

- *Jesus's preexistent glory before he came to earth* (1:1–3; cf. 1:30; 3:13, 31; 6:38, 42, 62; 8:14, 23, 58; 10:36; 12:41; 13:3; 16:5, 27–30; 17:5, 24; cf. 1 John 1:1; Rev. 1:4, 8, 17; 3:14; 21:6; 22:13). Other NT texts that speak of Jesus's preexistence include Colossians 1:15–17 and Philippians 2:6. The several texts that speak of Jesus as creator also imply his preexistence.

- *Jesus as creator of the world and renewer of his creation* (John 1:3–4, 10–13). Additional texts that associate Jesus with the work of creation and new creation include Matthew 19:28; 1 Corinthians

---

165. Moses's desire for a more intimate experience of God's presence should be seen in the context of God's mobile presence in the Tabernacle (e.g., Exod. 25:1–9; 33:7; 40:1–38), likely alluded to by ἐσκήνωσεν in John 1:14.

166. Daniel Boyarin, "*Logos*, a Jewish Word: John's Prologue as Midrash," in *The Jewish New Testament*, eds. Amy-Jill Levine and Marc Zvi Brettler (New York: Oxford University, 2011), 546–49.

167. Jesus as in John 1:14, 18 also reminds the reader of "only sons" in such OT texts as Gen. 22:2 (בִּנְךָ אֶת־יְחִידְךָ אֲשֶׁר־אָהַבְתָּ).

168. See further the summary discussions in exegetical commentaries and Andreas Köstenberger, "John," in Beale and Carson, eds. *Commentary on the NT Use of the OT*, 421–23. A full treatment is found in C. A. Evans, *Word and Glory: On the Exegetical and Theological Background of John's Prologue* (Sheffield: Sheffield Academic, 1993).

169. Andreas J. Köstenberger and Scott R. Swain, *Father, Son, and Spirit: The Trinity and John's Gospel* (Downers Grove, IL: InterVarsity, 2008).

8:6; 2 Corinthians 5:17; Colossians 1:15–20; Hebrews 1:2–3, 10/Ps. 102:25–27; 2 Peter 3:10–13; Revelation 21:1–5. The OT basis for this truth is found in Genesis 1 and Isaiah 43:1–21; 65:17–23; 66:22–23.

- *Jesus as the light of the world* (1:4–5, 9; cf. 3:19–21; 8:12; 9:5; 11:9–10; 12:35–36, 46) who brings life (cf. 3:15–16; 4:14, 36; 5:21, 24, 26, 29, 39–40; 6:27, 33, 35, 40, 47–48, 51, 53–54, 63, 68; 8:12; 10:10, 28; 11:25; 12:50; 14:6; 17:2–3; 20:31). Jesus as light, and his people as reflectors of his light, is found elsewhere in the NT in Matthew 4:14–17/Isaiah 9:1–2; Matthew 5:14–16; Luke 1:79/Isaiah 9:2; Luke 2:32/Isaiah 42:6; Acts 13:47/Isaiah 49:6; Acts 26:18, 23; Romans 13:12; 2 Corinthians 4:4–6; Ephesians 5:8; 1 Peter 2:9; 1 John 1:7; 2:8–10; Revelation 21:23–24; 22:5. The imagery of salvation as light is especially prominent in OT texts like 2 Samuel 23:4; Psalms 27:1; 30:26; 36:9; 42:6; 43:3; 56:13/Luke 2:32, 49:6; 51:4; 59:10; 60:1, 3, 19–20. All of this imagery begins with Genesis 1:3–5, 15–18.

- *John the Baptist's testimony to Jesus* (1:6–8, 15; cf. 1:19–36; 3:22–30; 4:15:33–36; 10:40–42). John's testimony to Jesus is found repeatedly in the synoptic triple tradition that summarizes John's ministry, culminating with his baptism of Jesus (Matt. 3:1–17/ Mark 1:2–11/Luke 3:1–22), where it is tied back to Isaiah 40 and Malachi 3–4. See also Matthew 4:12 (cf. Mark 1:14; Luke 3:20); Matthew 11:2–19/Luke 7:18–35; Matthew 14:1–12/Mark 6:14–29/Luke 9:7–9; Matthew 16:14/Mark 8:28/Luke 9:19; Matthew 17:13; 21:23–32/Mark 11:27–33/Luke 20:1–8; Luke 1:13–17, 60–63; 11:1; 16:16. John's ministry is also remembered in Acts and included in the early preaching narrated there (Acts 1:5; 11:16; 13:24–25; 18:25).

- *The world loved by God, yet hostile to God* (1:9–10; cf. 1:29; 3:16–19; 4:42; 6:33, 51; 7:7; 8:12, 26; 9:5, 39; 11:9, 27; 12:31, 46–47; 13:1; 14:17, 27, 30–31; 15:18–19; 16:8–11, 20, 28, 33; 17:6, 9, 14–18, 21, 23, 25; 18:20, 36–37; cf. 1 John 2:2; 4:9, 14). God's faithful love and providential care for humans, including those who do not love him in return, is emphasized throughout the Bible (Ps. 9:8; 96:10; Prov. 8:31; Matt. 24:14; 26:13; Acts 14:15–17; 17:24–31; Rom. 1:8; 11:12, 15; 2 Cor. 5:19).

- *Belief in Jesus contrasted with the irony of unbelief* (1:10–13; cf. 1:37, 49; 2:11, 17–25; 3:12, 15–21, 36; 4:39–42, 45–53; 5:24–25; 30–47; 6:29–71; 7:5, 10–44, 47–48; 8:24–30, 45–59; 9:16, 22,

27–28, 35–41; 10:4–5, 9, 14, 24–27, 37–38, 41–42; 11:25–27, 37, 40, 42, 45–53, 57; 12:9–11, 36–50; 13:11, 19, 21–30; 14:1, 10–12, 29; 16:8–9, 30–33; 17:6–8, 20–23; 19:35, 38; 20:8, 24–31). Saving faith in God is one of the most pervasive themes of biblical theology. See e.g., Genesis 15:6/Romans 4:3, 6, 9–12, 22–25/Galatians 3:6/James 2:23; Habakkuk 2:4/Romans 1:17/Galatians 3:11/Hebrews 10:38–39; Acts 10:43; 11:14; 13:39, 48; 15:7; 16:31; Romans 3:21–28; 5:1; Ephesians 2:8–9; Hebrews 11.

- *The complex relationship of Jesus's signs (σημεῖα) to belief in Jesus* (2:11, 18, 23; 3:2; 4:48, 54; 6:2, 14, 26, 30; 7:31; 9:16; 10:41; 11:47; 12:18, 37; 20:30). Signs play a role in authenticating God's messengers in the OT (e.g., Exod. 4:9 ff.; 7:3; 10:1; Num. 14:11; Deut. 4:34; 34:11; Josh. 24:17; Neh. 9:10; Jer. 32:20; Dan. 6:27), in Acts (2:19, 22/Joel 2:30; Acts 2:43; 4:16, 22; 30; 5:12; 6:8; 7:36; 8:6, 13; 14:3; 15:12), and in Paul's letters (Rom. 15:19; 1 Cor. 1:22; 14:22; 2 Cor. 12:12; 2 Thess. 2:9). Opponents of God are also able to perform deceptive signs (Exod. 7:11–12, 22; 8:7; Matt. 24:24/Mark 13:2; 2 Thess. 2:9; Rev. 13:13; 16:14; 19:20).

- *Jesus's as God's one and only Son, the Word-become-flesh who reveals the Father* (1:1, 14, 18; cf. 2:16; 3:16–18, 34–35; 4:21–23, 34; 5:17–27, 30, 36–38, 43; 6:27, 29, 32, 37–40, 44–46, 57; 7:16–18, 28–29, 33; 8:16–19, 26–29, 38, 40, 42, 49, 54–55; 9:4; 10:15–18, 25, 29, 32, 36–38; 11:41–42; 12:26–28, 44–45, 49–50; 13:1, 3, 20, 31–32; 14:6–12, 16, 20–21, 23–24, 26, 28, 31; 15:1–2, 8–10, 15–16, 21, 23–24, 26; 16:3, 5, 10, 15, 23, 25–28, 32; 17:1–26; 18:11; 20:17, 21). The NT as a whole presupposes that Jesus is the ultimate revelator of God, and teaches this truth expressly in such texts as 1 Corinthians 1:21–25; 2 Corinthians 1:20; Colossians 1:19; 2:9; Hebrews 1:2; 2:1–3; 9:11–28.

- *Jesus anticipated by Moses* (cf. 1:45; 3:14; 5:45–47; 6:32; 7:19, 22–23; [8:5]; 9:28–29). The relationship of Jesus to Moses is important to the Gospels, especially Matthew (e.g., Matt. 5:17–48), and Paul (Galatians). Early Christian preaching spoke of the relationship of Jesus to Moses (Acts 3:22–26; 7:20–44; 26:22–23; 28:23). This preaching was distorted and made the basis of false accusations (Acts 6:11–15). With burgeoning Gentile conversions, the ongoing role of the Law of Moses in assimilating Gentile converts became a matter of great controversy (Acts 15; 21:20–26; Galatians). The role of Moses and the law in redemptive history is especially important for Paul's theology (Rom.

2:12–3:31; 4:9–16; 5:14–20; 9:4; 10:19; 1 Cor. 9:9; 10:2; 2 Cor. 3:7, 13, 15; 2 Tim. 3:8) and for the author of Hebrews (Heb. 3; 7:14; 8:5; 9:19; 10:28; 11:23–29; 12:21). See also Jude 9 and Revelation 15:3.

Historical Theology

Even a brief comprehensive discussion of the history of interpretation of John 1:1–18 is well beyond the scope of this book. The following summary selectively represents the crucial role played by this text in the church's early Christological controversies[170] and ensuing doctrinal developments, leading to orthodox Christology and trinitarianism.

Athanasius. Athanasius of Alexandria (c. A.D. 296–373) is known as "the father of orthodoxy" because of his effective statements and defense of orthodox Christology and trinitarianism. Much has been written on his crucial role in the church's theological controversies and development.[171] In contesting adoptionism, Athanasius stressed that the Word did not merely come into a man who was already alive, or change from a divine into a human being, but actually became human (*C. Ar.* 2.6–8; 3.30–31). Because the Word is the image of the Father, the Word can become human and restore humanity's capacity to image God (*C. Ar.* 6.20–21; *De incarnatione* 41, 80).

Creedal developments. The third line of the Trinitarian Apostles' Creed (late fourth century) describes Jesus as follows:

> [I believe] in Jesus Christ, God's **only** Son, our Lord . . .
> [Πιστεύω] εἰς Ἰησοῦν Χριστὸν, υἱὸν αὐτοῦ τὸν **μονογενῆ**, τὸν κύριον ἡμῶν . . .
> [*Credo*] *in Iesum Christum, Filium Eius **unicum**, Dominum nostrum* . . .

As the church faced the heresies of Arianism and Apollinarianism, among others, exegesis of John 1:1–18 played a key role in formulating successive creeds.

In the following excerpt from the Nicene Creed words in common with John 1:1–18 are in bold.

---

170. For an introduction and translation of relevant primary sources, see Richard A. Norris Jr., *The Christological Controversy* (Minneapolis: Fortress, 1980). For a summary of key issues, see Douglas W. Johnson, *The Great Jesus Debates: 4 Early Church Battles about the Person and Work of Jesus Christ* (St. Louis: Concordia, 2005).

171. E.g., Charles Kannengiesser, "Athanasius of Alexandria and the Foundations of Traditional Christology," *TheolSt* 34 (1973): 103–13; Thomas G. Weinandy, *Athanasius: A Theological Introduction* (Farnham: Ashgate, 2007).

Nicene Creed (A.D. 381, Council of Constantinople)[172]

Πιστεύομεν εἰς ἕνα **Θεὸν**
 Πατέρα παντοκράτορα
 ποιητὴν οὐρανοῦ καὶ γῆς
  ὁρατῶν τε πάντων καὶ ἀοράτων·
καὶ εἰς ἕνα Κύριον Ἰησοῦν Χριστὸν
 τὸν υἱὸν τοῦ Θεοῦ τὸν Μονογενῆ,
 τὸν ἐκ τοῦ Πατρὸς γεννηθέντα πρὸ πάντων
τῶν αἰώνων,
  Φῶς ἐκ Φωτός,
  Θεὸν ἀληθινὸν ἐκ Θεοῦ ἀληθινοῦ,
  γεννηθέντα οὐ ποιηθέντα,
  ὁμοούσιον τῷ **Πατρί**,
  δι' οὗ τὰ πάντα ἐγένετο·
 τὸν δι' ἡμᾶς τοὺς **ἀνθρώπους** καὶ διὰ τὴν
ἡμετέραν σωτηρίαν κατελθόντα ἐκ τῶν οὐρανῶν,
 καὶ **σαρκωθέντα** ἐκ Πνεύματος Ἁγίου καὶ
Μαρίας τῆς παρθένου,
  καὶ ἐνανθρωπήσαντα,

We **believe** in one **God,**
 the almighty Father,
 the maker of heaven and earth,
  of all things visible and invisible.
And in one Lord **Jesus Christ,**
 the one and only Son of God,
 the one begotten from the Father before all
ages,
  Light from Light,
  true **God** from true God,
  begotten, not made;
  of the same essence with the Father.
  through whom all things were made.
 the one who came down out of heaven for us
humans and for our salvation,
 and who became **flesh** by the Holy Spirit and
Mary the virgin,
  and took on human nature.

The Definition of Chalcedon further developed the implications of John 1:1–18. Key excerpts are in bold.

The Definition of Chalcedon (A.D. 451)

Ἑπόμενοι τοίνυν τοῖς ἁγίοις πατράσιν ἕνα
καὶ τὸν αὐτὸν ὁμολογεῖν υἱὸν τὸν κύριον
ἡμῶν Ἰησοῦν Χριστὸν συμφώνως ἅπαντες
ἐκδιδάσκομεν, **τέλειον τὸν αὐτὸν ἐν θεότητι
καὶ τέλειον τὸν αὐτὸν ἐν ἀνθρωπότητι, θεὸν
ἀληθῶς καὶ ἄνθρωπον ἀληθῶς τὸν αὐτὸν,**
ἐκ ψυχῆς λογικῆς καὶ σώματος, **ὁμοούσιον
τῷ πατρὶ κατὰ τὴν θεότητα, καὶ ὁμοούσιον
τὸν αὐτὸν ἡμῖν κατὰ τὴν ἀνθρωπότητα,**
κατὰ πάντα ὅμοιον ἡμῖν χωρὶς ἁμαρτίας· **πρὸ
αἰώνων μὲν ἐκ τοῦ πατρὸς γεννηθέντα κατὰ
τὴν θεότητα, ἐπ' ἐσχάτων δὲ τῶν ἡμερῶν
τὸν αὐτὸν δι' ἡμᾶς καὶ διὰ τὴν ἡμετέραν
σωτηρίαν ἐκ Μαρίας τῆς παρθένου τῆς
θεοτόκου κατὰ τὴν ἀνθρωπότητα,**

We, then, following the holy Fathers, with one consent, teach men to confess one and the same Son, our Lord Jesus Christ, **the same perfect in deity and also perfect in humanity; truly God and truly man**, of a reasonable [rational] soul and body; **of the same essence with the Father according his deity, and of the same essence with us according to his humanity;** in all things like unto us, without sin; **begotten before all ages by the Father according to his deity, and in these latter days, for us and for our salvation, born of the Virgin Mary, the Mother of God, according to his humanity;**

---

172. This creed, sometimes called the Constantinopolitan Creed or Creed of 150 Fathers, repeats the Creed of Nicaea, sometimes called the Creed of 318 Fathers (A.D. 325). It makes two additions to strengthen the A.D. 325 creed: (1) "before all ages (line 8 above) and (2) "by the Holy Spirit and Mary the virgin" (lines 18–19 above). See further John Leith, Creeds of the Churches, 3rd ed. (Atlanta: Knox, 1982), 28–36.

ἕνα καὶ τὸν αὐτὸν Χριστόν, υἱόν, κύριον, **μονογενῆ**, ἐκ δύο φύσεων [ἐν δύο φύσεσιν], ἀσυγχύτως, ἀτρέπτως, ἀδιαιρέτως, ἀχωρίστως γνωριζόμενον· οὐδαμοῦ τῆς τῶν φύσεων διαφορᾶς ἀνῃρημένης διὰ τὴν ἕνωσιν, σωζομένης δὲ μᾶλλον τῆς ἰδιότητος ἑκατέρας φύσεως καὶ εἰς ἓν πρόσωπον καὶ μίαν ὑπόστασιν συντρεχούσης, οὐκ εἰς δύο πρόσωπα μεριζόμενον ἢ διαιρούμενον, ἀλλ᾽ ἕνα καὶ τὸν αὐτὸν υἱὸν καὶ **μονογενῆ, θεὸν λόγον**, κύριον Ἰησοῦν Χριστόν· καθάπερ ἄνωθεν οἱ προφῆται περὶ αὐτοῦ καὶ αὐτὸς ἡμᾶς ὁ κύριος Ἰησοῦς Χριστὸς ἐξεπαίδευσε καὶ τὸ τῶν πατέρων ἡμῖν καραδέδωκε σύμβολον.

one and the same Christ, **Son**, the **one and only** Lord, to be acknowledged in two natures, without confusion, without change, without division, without separation; the distinction of natures being by no means taken away by the union, but rather the property of each nature being preserved, and concurring in one Person and one Subsistence, not parted or divided into two persons, but one and the same **Son**, and **one and only God the Word**, the Lord Jesus Christ, as the prophets from the beginning [have declared] concerning him, and the Lord Jesus Christ himself has taught us, and the Creed of the holy Fathers has handed down to us.

Memorable reflections. One finds many eloquent comments on the Johannine prologue in ancient Christian scources. The following are exemplary:

- "I will not endure to hear that Christ was born of Mary unless I also hear, 'in the beginning was the Word . . . and the Word was God," (Hilary of Poitiers, c. A.D. 350, *De synodis*, 27.70 on John 1:1)
- "From where do we get life, from where does he get death? . . . He had nothing where he could get death from; we had nothing where we could get life from. He accepted death from what was ours, in order to give us life from what was his. . . . He was life for us; we were death for him." (Augustine, *Serm.* 232.5 on John 1:4)
- "For he became Son of Man, who was God's own son, in order that he might make the sons of men to be children of God. For when the high associates itself with the low, it does not touch its own honor at all. Instead, it raises up the other from its excessive lowness. So it was with the Lord. By no means did he diminish his own nature by his condescension, but he raised us, who had always sat in disgrace and darkness to unspeakable glory." (Chrysostom, *Hom. Jo.* 11.1, on John 1:14)
- "He is Son by nature, we by grace; he is the 'only son,' we are many; because he is born, we are adopted. (Augustine, *Serm.* 348A.3, on John 1:14, 18)
- "For [in place of] the grace of the law, which has passed away, we have received the abiding grace of the gospel, and, instead of the shadows and figures of the ancient covenant, truth has come by Jesus Christ." (Jerome, *Epist.* 75, on John 1:16–17). One might challenge Jerome's view that the law has passed away, but at least he recognized that the law was a gracious gift of God.

Systematic Theology

Engagement with John 1:1–18 keeps the church on track in its doctrinal teaching about the person of Jesus and the Trinity. The two central affirmations about Jesus—that he created the world (1:1) and that he became human to reveal God (1:14)—lay the foundation for all of John's subsequent reflection on Jesus's person and relationship to the Father and the Holy Spirit.

One unfortunate departure from biblically sound teaching about the Word who became flesh, is that of the Watchtower Bible and Tract Society (Jehovah's Witnesses), whose New World Translation renders the last clause of John 1:1 as "the Word was a god," and the second clause of John 1:18 as "the only begotten god who was in the bosom [position] with the Father." Curiously, this translation renders Thomas's words to Jesus in 20:28 "My Lord and my God." The NWT rendering of John 1:18 affirms, as did ancient Arianism, that Jesus was not truly God, but was the first being created by God, a god or heavenly spirit creature who subsequently created everything else. This translation is contradicted by the immediate context— John 1:3 states that the Word created everything (not everything besides the Word) and that nothing was created apart from the Word. It is based on a mistaken approach to the Greek grammar of John 1:1, an approach refuted by many evangelical scholars.[173] After its positive confession of Jesus cited above, the Creed of Nicaea went on to condemn any teaching about Jesus that affirmed that once he did not exist, or that once he began to exist, or that he was in any sense a creature.

Another mistaken approach to John's Prologue is to take it as minimizing Jesus's humanity, stated so simply and powerfully in 1:14 by "the Word became flesh and made his dwelling among us." Both in ancient times and still today certain Bible teachers, often identified as gnostics, affirmed that Jesus was not truly human but only seemed to be so. This mistake was reinforced by a character in Dan Brown's novel *The Da Vinci Code*, a historian named Leigh Teabing, who claimed that the Emperor Constantine had destroyed some seventy "gospels" that affirmed Jesus's humanity, leaving only four that affirmed his deity. This suggestion badly garbles church history as well as Christian theology. The humanity of Jesus is resoundingly affirmed in John 1:14 and illustrated at points in the ensuing narrative (e.g., 4:6; 11:35–36; 19:26–27). The same Creed of Nicaea that in A.D. 325 confessed the deity of Jesus also spoke clearly of his humanity as the incarnation of the eternal Word. The Definition of Chalcedon (A.D. 451) expounded

---

173. See the discussions above on the translation and analysis of John 1:1.

these matters in greater detail, and Christ's church continues to stand on this firm foundation.[174]

Teaching the Text

Raymond Brown notes,

> If John has been described as the pearl of great price among the New Testament writings, then one may say that the Prologue is the pearl within this Gospel. In her comparison of Augustine's and Chrysostom's exegesis of the Prologue, M. A. Aucoin points out that both held that it is beyond the power of man to speak as John does in the Prologue. The choice of the eagle as the symbol of John the Evangelist was largely determined by the celestial flights of the opening lines of the Gospel.[175]

Communicating the *theological profundity* of John 1:1–18 is a daunting task, yet the *literary simplicity* of the passage implies that the task can be accomplished if we choose to speak about the text simply, with relatively few wisely chosen words, rather than attempting to demonstrate our own intellectual prowess pompously and verbosely. An old sermonic line typically tied to St. Augustine or Charles Haddon Spurgeon has it that the Gospel of John is deep enough for an elephant to swim in and shallow enough for a lamb to wade in.[176] This text's innate conceptual depth and communicative simplicity should be a model for those who would expound it.

The Point of the Passage

Based on our previous exegetical and theological reflections, we may describe the point of John 1:1–18 as follows: The Word became human in Jesus in order to renew the world he originally created by revealing God's grace and truth so that people might believe in him and share God's life. Subthemes deriving from this main point include:

- Jesus is the Word-become-flesh who originally created the world and who is now renewing the world.

---

174. See further Thompson, *The Humanity of Jesus in the Fourth Gospel* and *The Incarnate Word*. See also Oliver D. Crisp and Fred Sanders, eds., *Christology: Ancient and Modern* (Grand Rapids: Zondervan, 2013), and Gerald O'Collins, *Christology: A Biblical, Historic, and Systematic Study of Jesus*, 2nd ed. (Oxford: Oxford University, 2009).

175. Raymond Brown, *John*, 2 vols. (Garden City, NY: Doubleday, 1966, 1970), 1.18.

176. On this point see http://drdavidlturner.com/2018/08/john-the-spiritual-gospel-soaring-eagles-wading-lambs-and-swimming-elephants.

- John the Baptist testified to Jesus as his forerunner.
- Many did not believe in Jesus when he came into the world, but God authorizes those who receive him by faith to become his children.
- Jesus as God's unique Son fully reveals the glorious grace and truth that was only glimpsed by Moses.

Communicating John 1:18 accurately requires linking the story of Jesus Christ to three "chapters" in the overall story found in the biblical **metanarrative**. *Proximately*, the story of Jesus Christ revisits the recent story of John the Baptist, whose words pointed Israel to messianic renewal through Jesus. *Intermediately*, the story of Jesus Christ revisits the story of Moses and renews the gracious instruction Moses gave Israel through the law. *Ultimately*, the story of Jesus Christ revisits the ancient story of creation, when God spoke the world into existence, and renews the relationship of humans to God. The communicator's task, however, has only begun once Jesus has been linked to John the Baptist, Moses, and to God's creation of the world. The vital link that must be made clear is that of the audience to Jesus Christ (John 1:11–13). Communicators of John 1:1–18 must not fail to explain the need for faith in Jesus Christ as the key point of not only the prologue but also of the entire Gospel (John 20:30–31). Receiving Jesus Christ by faith authorizes people to become members of God's family, where they may bask in the full light of God's grace in Christ. Being a member of God's family means *entering* God's story instead of merely *watching* it from a distance. Receiving Jesus authorizes *participation* in God's life and light; rejecting Jesus means that even *observation* of God's life and light is impossible due to the darkness cast by sin.

Communicating the Metanarrative of John

Authorization to join God's family comes through **receiving** Jesus Christ,

who has made God's glorious **grace and truth** crystal clear by completing God's story.

God created the world through the Word.	God instructed his people through the law of Moses.	God called out a remnant through John the Baptist.
The Word brings renewing light and life to the world.	*The Word-become-flesh reveals God's glorious grace and truth.*	*The Word is the light to which the forerunner John testified.*

Homiletical Packaging

Homiletical packaging should be consistent with the literary structure and metanarratival linkages of the text. Andy Stanley's dictum that communicating the Bible involves what the speaker wants the audience to know and what the speaker wants the audience to do about what they know is useful here. The audience should know that Jesus as Word-become-flesh is (1) the original *creator* and ultimate *renewer* of the world and its people, (2) the ultimate *revealer* of God's grace, and (3) the ultimate *agent* of God's deliverance of his people. What the audience should do about this knowledge is clear from the center of the text's structure (1:12–13)—the audience must receive the Word in simple faith, realizing that their own efforts can never authorize them to join God's family and participate in God's story. These truths are non-negotiable in communicating John 1:1–18, but *how* these truths are to be communicated is a matter of Spirit-led creativity.

A deductive sermon. Deductive sermons state their thesis/proposition at the beginning and develop it for the audience by linear logic. One way to use this approach might be to focus attention on the two statements about the λόγος (1:1, 14) and to make the literary center of the prologue (1:12–13) the concluding point that climaxes a sermon on the absolute uniqueness (cf. μονογενής in John 1:14, 18) of Jesus:

John 1:1–18 portrays the absolute uniqueness of Jesus Christ in three ways.

Introduction: How is Jesus different from the founders of other world religions?

1. Jesus is absolutely unique because *he is the original Creator of the world* (1:1–5).
   - John tells us something amazing here. Jesus is God—he shares the divine nature. And yet Jesus is a person distinct from God the Father—he is at the Father's side. This is part of the Christian teaching known as the Trinity.
   - Jesus created the world by speaking light and life into existence at the very beginning.
   - Jesus also brings light and life into the world today by revealing God to people.
   - *Do you believe that Jesus originally created the world and that he still speaks light into people's lives today?*

2. Jesus is absolutely unique because *he is the ultimate Revealer of God* (1:14–18).
    - According to the Bible, how has God revealed himself?
    - In the Old Testament, God revealed himself through Moses and the prophets. This was a beautiful and gracious revelation, yet one that was incomplete and that anticipated the future ultimate revelation in Jesus.
    - In the New Testament, God revealed himself through Jesus, the one who originally created the world, and humankind in his image. He miraculously became human and perfectly revealed God's grace and truth to humankind.
    - *Do you believe that all of God's revelation culminates in Jesus, and that today he still shows people who God is?*

3. Jesus is absolutely unique because *he is the Savior of all who receive him* (1:6–13).
    - John the Baptist testified to the uniqueness of Jesus.
    - Amazingly, many did not receive Jesus when he came into the world he had created in order to reveal the Father.
    - Those who did receive Jesus were given a new birth from God into God's family. This was something they were absolutely unable to accomplish on their own.
    - *Do you believe that you are a child of God, a member of God's family? Why do you believe this?*

Conclusion: Is the absolutely unique Creator and Revealer your personal Savior?
    - If you have received Jesus and become a child of God, worship him, love him, obey him, and serve him.
    - If you have not received Jesus, understand that you are powerless to become a child of God apart from him. Receive him in faith today. If you are not yet willing to do so, please read further in this Gospel to learn more about him.

The outline above contains considerable content for a single sermon, perhaps too much for many audiences. Each of the three main sections of the outline could become one of a series of three sermons on John's prologue. Alternatively, the outline above could be the first sermon that introduces a series on John 1:1–18 based on the word πλήρωμα in John 1:16:

From Jesus's abundance we receive a full understanding of God's glorious grace and truth. Four sermons on John 1:1–18:

1. How did the world begin? (John 1:1–5)
   - Jesus is the creator and renewer of the world.
   - *Jesus spoke light into existence and he still enlightens people today.*

2. How can we know God? (John 1:14–18)
   - Jesus is the ultimate revealer of God.
   - *Jesus completes Moses's gracious revelation of God's truth.*

3. Why did John the Baptist come? (John 1:6–9, 15)
   - John the Baptist came to bear witness to Jesus as the light of the world.
   - *Jesus was before the forerunner who testified of his coming.*

4. How can we become the children of God? (John 1:10–13)
   - Many preferred their own flawed insight and will to God's revelation through Jesus.
   - *Jesus authorizes all who receive him to be born from God and join God's family.*

An inductive sermon. Inductive sermons gradually lead their audience to grasp the sermon's thesis by the end. Assuming the literary structure and theological emphasis reflected in the deductive structures above, one might proceed inductively with the following three questions. Again, an overview sermon might deal with all three questions, or each might be handled in more depth with a single sermon.

If Christ is the answer, what are the questions? John 1:1–18 and the answers to three questions all thinking people have:

1. How did we get here?
   - Gradually lead the audience through views of cosmogony and human origins. Perhaps include interactive discussion not only of academic theories but also of personal experiences. Include ancient and modern viewpoints, and conclude with the teaching of John 1:1–5, relating it to the ideas and experiences of others.

2. How does God communicate with us?
   - Gradually lead the audience through various views of divine revelation, moving from non-Christian to

Christian views. Consider how God spoke to people in the Old Testament, and conclude with John 1:14–18 by explaining how Jesus completes the revelation of God's grace and truth that is found in the Old Testament.

3. How can we have a relationship with God?
  - Gradually lead the audience through various views of experiencing God, moving from non-Christian to Christian views. Focus on the testimony of John to Jesus as the light of the world, and on the irony that many people preferred and their own fallen insights to the prophetic message of John and the incarnation of their creator, Jesus. Stress the mystery of faith today, urging the audience to surrender their own ideas and inclinations and submit to the power of God in Christ and the opportunity to join God's family through him.

Topical sermons. The literary role of John 1:1–18, as a seedbed where many of the key ideas of the Fourth Gospel are "sprouted," warrants topical sermons that show how the key figures and concepts of the prologue are developed in the remainder of the Gospel, and even in the rest of the NT. Review the previous discussion of key words in John 1:1–18, its intertextual allusions, and its use of key biblical theology themes. Consider the following possibilities for a topical sermon or series of sermons:

- Glory before the world began: the preexistence of Jesus in the Fourth Gospel
- The law of Moses and the gospel of Jesus: you can't have one without the other
- John the Baptist and Jesus: forerunner or "afterrunner"?
- Jesus, Phillip, and Thomas: Jesus as God in the Fourth Gospel
- Thirsty and weeping for his friend: Jesus as human in the Fourth Gospel
- Rejection and reception: how people respond to Jesus in the Fourth Gospel

Illustrating the text. John 1:1–18 is intensely conceptual. Its allusions to the larger referential world should be emphasized so that the audience can relate the abstract concepts to the biblical narrative and then to their own lives. The following ideas may be useful:

- The literary function of John 1:18 as it relates to the rest of the Gospel may be illustrated by architectural design in which an atrium or foyer functions aesthetically to open up the rest of a beautiful building to those who enter. A similar illustration comes from the world of music, where key motifs of classical symphonies are introduced at the outset in the overture. One may also draw from the use of a characteristic riff at the beginning of a rock song. This sort of illustration is enhanced if the communicator is able to utilize PowerPoint slides for relevant images and audio clips.

- John 1:1–18 refers to various events (e.g., creation), institutions (e.g., the tabernacle), and characters (e.g., Moses, John the Baptist, and Jesus) in the biblical metanarrative. Allusions to these concrete entities and the role they play in the biblical metanarrative will help the audience to understand the abstract concepts of the text.

- It might be helpful to allude to biblical figures (e.g., Moses, Isaiah, Ezekiel) who saw God (John 1:18; cf. Exod. 24:9–11; 33; Isa. 6:9–11; Ezek. 1–3; etc.) and how their experiences compare and contrast with God's revelation in Christ according to John. Another dimension would be to compare and contrast biblical experiences of seeing God with experiences of seeing God that are purported in current pop culture.

- It might be appropriate to include the traditional "Trinitarian triangle" as a visual illustration of the church's developed reflection on the implications John 1:1–18 regarding the Word who was with God (a distinct personality) and who was God (deity), the original creator and ultimate revealer of God as Father, Son, and Holy Spirit. Images of this triangle, many from stained glass and other architectural settings, are plentiful on the Internet. A rudimentary version is below.

Trinitarian Triangle

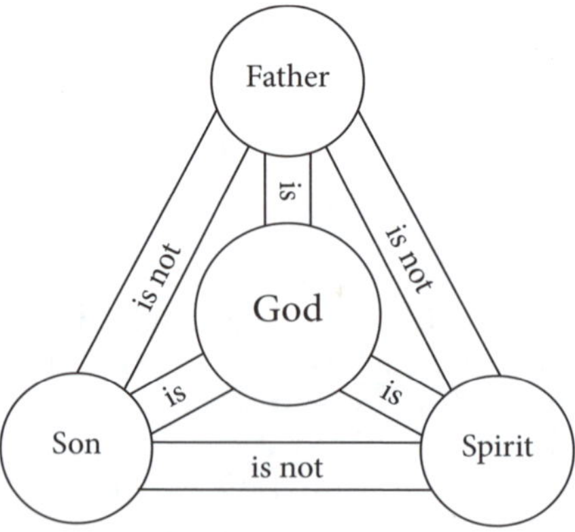

Chapter in Review

In this chapter, we used Mark 4:1–20 and John 1:1–18 as case studies in moving from studying a text in the Gospels and Acts to preparing a sermon on that text. We presented the tasks of textual exegesis and congregational exposition as interwoven, not separate and sequential. In both cases, we began with establishing and translating the text, and moved into analysis of a text's syntax, structure, key words, literary context (vertical reading)—and, in the case of Mark 4, distinctive emphases in the synoptic tradition (horizontal reading). Next we moved to understanding key features of the texts' referential world, including history, geography, and culture. The final step in exegesis with a view to exposition was thinking with the texts in their own right (intertextuality and biblical theology), as well as engaging their reception (historical theology) and current implications (systematic theology). Each case study concluded with ideas and examples of how to communicate the texts. These included suggestions on deductive, inductive, and topical sermonic packaging.

8

SELECTED RESOURCES

The Chapter at a Glance

In this chapter we provide a selection of resources that should prove to be valuable for students of the Gospels and Acts. The selection begins with other bibliographies and electronic resources. It then lists resources useful for establishing the Greek text, studying it, and understanding its historical setting. Useful encyclopedias and commentaries are then surveyed. Finally, after biblical and systematic theology, resources for communicating these books are listed.

INTRODUCTION

PRINTED BIBLIOGRAPHIES AGE QUICKLY. New resources and revisions of previous resources regularly appear. This bibliography is by necessity selective. In keeping with this book's intended audience, the selection tends to privilege more recent evangelical resources. No doubt the following list will inevitably omit many worthy works (Eccl. 12:12).

This bibliography does not include periodical articles on specific topics in the study of the Gospels and Acts. Students are advised to search the online database of the American Theological Library Association (ATLA) for current monographs and periodical articles.

Students will find additional focused resources in the footnotes of each preceding chapter. An asterisk (★) following an entry indicates that it was written at a more advanced level.

BIBLIOGRAPHIES

- David E. Aune, *Jesus & the Synoptic Gospels* (Downers Grove, IL: InterVarsity, 1980).

- J. K. Elliott, *A Bibliography of Greek New Testament Manuscripts*, 2nd ed. (Cambridge: Cambridge University, 2002).

- Craig A. Evans, *Jesus,* IBR Bibliographies (Grand Rapids: Baker, 1992).

- Craig A. Evans, *Life of Jesus Research: An Annotated Bibliography* (Leiden: Brill, 1996).

- Joel B. Green and Michael C. McKeever, *Luke-Acts and New Testament Historiography* (Grand Rapids: Baker, 1994).

- Scot McKnight and Matthew C. Williams, *The Synoptic Gospels: An Annotated Bibliography* (Grand Rapids: Baker, 2000).

- Watson Mills, *Bibliography of the Periodical Literature on the Acts of the Apostles 1962–1984* (Leiden: Brill, 1986).

- Watson Mills, *The Gospel of John* (Lewiston, NY: Mellen, 1995).

- Watson Mills, *The Gospel of Luke* (Lewiston, NY: Mellen, 1994).

- Watson Mills, *The Gospel of Matthew* (Lewiston, NY: Mellen, 2002).

- Séan Nealy, *Mark's Gospel: A History of Its Interpretation from the Beginning until 1979* (New York: Paulist, 1982).

- F. Neirynck, *The Gospel of Mark: A Cumulative Bibliography 1950–1990* (Leuven: University/Peeters, 1992).

- F. Neirynck, *The Gospel of Matthew: A Cumulative Bibliography 1950–1995* (Leuven: University/Peeters, 1998).

- Stephen F. Noll, *The Intertestamental Period: A Study Guide* (Downers Grove, IL: InterVarsity, 1985).

ELECTRONIC RESOURCES

It is difficult to keep pace with burgeoning new electronic aids for biblical studies. Websites with idiosyncratic, factually false, and heretical content earn the sarcasm of "If it's on the Internet, it must be true." The following vetted resources have earned a strong reputation for credibility and usefulness.

Software

- Accordance Bible Software (Oaktree Software) https://www.accordancebible.com

- Logos Bible Software (Bellingham, WA) www.logos.com

Web-based Resources

- http://www.academic-bible.com/en/online-bibles/about-the-online-bibles
  German Bible Society. Scholarly texts of the Hebrew Bible, LXX, Greek New Testament, and Latin Vulgate available in unicode fonts.

- https://bible.org
  Access to numerous Bible translations and original language texts. Additional resources including the NET Bible and a Bible study tool called Lumina.

- https://biblia.com
  Searchable access to many Bible translations, English and otherwise. Limited original language capability.

- https://www.blueletterbible.org
  Limited but helpful resources for biblical studies.

- http://www.ccel.org
  Resources and discussion groups for biblical and patristic studies.

- https://net.bible.org
  The NET Bible, with extensive translator's notes and other helps.

- http://www.oxfordbiblicalstudies.com/resource/
  InternetResources.xhtml
  Links to various websites on various aspects of biblical studies.

- http://www.perseus.tufts.edu/hopper
  Recources for reading and studying classical Greco-Roman texts, as well as many others, including Josephus, the Vulgate, the Liddell-Scott-Jones Greek Lexicon, and the Westcott-Hort Greek NT.

- http://sites.utoronto.ca/religion/synopsis/meta-5g.htm
  Resource for studying the canonical Gospels as well as the Gospel of Thomas synoptically.

- http://virtualreligion.net/primer
  Resource for studying the Gospels in the RSV synoptically.

ESTABLISHING THE TEXT

- Kurt and Barbara Aland, *The Text of the New Testament*, 2nd ed., trans. E. B. Rhodes (Grand Rapids: Eerdmans, 1989).

- David Alan Black, ed., *Perspectives on the Ending of Mark: Four Views* (Nashville: B&H, 2008).

- David Alan Black, ed., *Rethinking New Testament Textual Criticism* (Grand Rapids: Baker, 2002).

- David Alan Black and Jacob N. Cerone, eds., *The Pericope of the Adulteress in Current Research* (London: Bloomsbury, 2016).

- D. A. Carson, *The King James Version Debate: A Plea for Realism* (Grand Rapids: Baker, 1979).

- The Center for the Study of New Testament Manuscripts (http://www.csntm.org)

- N. Clayton Croy, *The Mutilation of Mark's Gospel* (Nashville: Abingdon, 2003).

- Bart D. Ehrman, *The Orthodox Corruption of Scripture*, updated ed. (New York: Oxford University, 2011).

- Bart D. Ehrman and Michael W. Holmes, eds., *The Text of the New Testament in Contemporary Research* (Leiden: Brill, 2013).★

- Eldon J. Epp and Gordon D. Fee, *Studies in the Theory and Method of New Testament Textual Criticism* (Grand Rapids: Eerdmans, 1993).★

- Evangelical Textual Criticism (http://evangelicaltextualcriticism.blogspot.com)

- Robert F. Hull, *The Story of the New Testament Text* (Atlanta: SBL, 2010).

- Institut für Neutestamentliche Textforschung/Institute for New Testament Textual Research (http://egora.uni-muenster.de/intf/index_en.shtml)★

- Thomas J. Kraus and Tobias Nicklas, eds., *New Testament Manuscripts: Their Texts and Their World* (Leiden: Brill, 2006).★

- Bruce M. Metzger, *Chapters in the History of New Testament Textual Criticism* (Leiden: Brill, 1963).

- Bruce M. Metzger, *A Textual Commentary on the Greek New Testament,* 2nd ed. (Stuttgart: Deutsche Bibelgesellschaft, 1994).

- Bruce M. Metzger and Bart D. Ehrman, *The Text of the New Testament*, 4th ed. (New York: Oxford University Press, 2005).

- Roger L. Omanson, *A Textual Guide to the Greek New Testament* (Stuttgart: Deutsche Bibelgesellschaft, 2006).

- D. C. Parker, *An Introduction to the New Testament Manuscripts and Their Texts* (Cambridge: Cambridge University Press, 2008).★

- Wilbur N. Pickering, *The Identity of the New Testament Text*, rev. ed. (Nashville: Nelson, 1980).

- Stanley M. Porter and Andrew W. Pitts, *Fundamentals of New Testament Textual Criticism* (Grand Rapids: Eerdmans, 2015).

- Robert B. Stewart, ed., *The Reliability of the New Testament: Bart D. Ehrman & Daniel B. Wallace in Dialogue* (Minneapolis: Fortress, 2011).

- W. A. Strange, *The Problem of the Text of Acts* (Cambridge: Cambridge University Press, 1992).★

- Harry Sturz, *The Byzantine Text-type and New Testament Textual Criticism* (Nashville: Nelson, 1984).

- David G. K. Taylor, ed., *Studies in the Early Text of the Gospels and Acts,* The Papers of the First Birmingham Colloquium on the Textual Criticism of the New Testament (Atlanta: Society of Biblical Literature, 1999).★

- Bridget G. Upton, *Hearing Mark's Endings* (Leiden: Brill, 2006).

- Daniel B. Wallace, ed., *Revisiting the Corruption of the New Testament* (Grand Rapids: Kregel, 2001).

- James R. White, *The King James Only Controversy* (Minneapolis: Bethany, 1995).

EDITIONS OF THE GREEK NEW TESTAMENT

- Barbara Aland, et al., eds., *The Greek New Testament*, 5th rev. ed. (Stuttgart: Deutsche Bibelgesellschaft, 2014). Read online at http://www.academic-bible.com/en/online-bibles/greek-new-testament-ubs5/read-the-bible-text.

- Barbara Aland, et al., eds., *The Greek New Testament. A Reader's Edition*, 5th rev. ed. (Stuttgart: Deutsche Bibelgesellschaft, 2015).

- Barbara and Kurt Aland, et al., eds., *Novum Testamentum Graece*, 28th rev. ed. (Stuttgart: Deutsche Bibelgesellschaft, 2012). Read online at http://www.academic-bible.com/en/online-bibles/novum-testamentum-graece-na-28/read-the-bible-text.

- Barbara and Kurt Aland, et al., eds., *Novum Testamentum Graece*: *Greek-English New Testament,* 28th rev. ed. (Stuttgart: Deutsche Bibelgesellschaft, 2012).

- Richard J. Goodrich and Albert L. Lukaszewski, *A Reader's Greek New Testament*, 3rd ed. (Grand Rapids: Zondervan, 2015).

- Zane C. Hodges and Arthur Farstad, *The Greek New Testament according to the Majority Text*, 2nd ed. (Nashville: Nelson, 1985).

- Michael W. Holmes, ed., *The Greek New Testament: SBL Edition* (Atlanta: SBL, 2010). Free download at http://sblgnt.com.

- Dirk Jongkind and Peter J. Williams, *The Greek New Testament* (Wheaton, IL/Cambridge: Crossway/Cambridge University Press, 2017).

- Η ΚΑΙΝΗ ΔΙΑΘΗΚΗ. *The New Testament. The Greek Text Underlying the English Authorized Version of 1611* (London: Trinitarian Bible Society, 1976).

- B. F. Westcott and F. J. A. Hort, *The New Testament in the Original Greek,* 2 vols. (Cambridge: Macmillan, 1881–82).

SYNOPSES OF THE GOSPELS

- Kurt Aland, *Synopsis of the Four Gospels, Greek-English Edition* (New York: United Bible Societies, 1982).

- Kurt Aland, *Synopsis Quattuor Evangeliorum*, 10th ed. (Stuttgart: Deutsche Bibelstiftung, 1976).

- F. W. Beare, *Earliest Records of Jesus: A Companion to the Synopsis of the First Three Gospels by Albert Huck* (Oxford: Blackwell, 1962).

- Albert Huck, ed., *Synopsis of the First Three Gospels*, rev. ed. (Oxford: Blackwell, 1972).

- Albert Huck, ed., *Synopsis of the First Three Gospels with the Addition of the Johannine Parallels*, 13th ed. (Grand Rapids: Eerdmans, 1982).

- John Bernard Orchard, *A Synopsis of the Four Gospels in Greek* (Macon, GA/Edinburgh: Mercer/Clark, 1983).

- Robert Thomas and Stanley Gundry, *The NIV Harmony of the Gospels* (San Francisco: Harper, 1988).

INTRODUCTORY WORKS

- Richard Bauckham, ed. *The Gospels for All Christians: Rethinking the Gospel Audiences* (Grand Rapids: Eerdmans, 1997).

- D. A. Black and D. R. Beck, eds., *Rethinking the Synoptic Problem* (Grand Rapids: Baker, 2001).

- D. A. Black and D. S. Dockery eds., *New Testament Criticism and Interpretation* (Grand Rapids: Zondervan, 1991).

- Craig L. Blomberg, *Jesus and the Gospels* (Nashville: B&H, 1997).

- Darrell Bock and Buist Fanning, *Interpreting the New Testament* (Wheaton, IL: Crossway, 2006).

- D. A. Carson and D. J. Moo, *An Introduction to the New Testament*, 2nd ed. (Grand Rapids: Zondervan, 2005).

- David L. Dungan, *A History of the Synoptic Problem* (New York: Doubleday, 1999).★

- Luke Timothy Johnson, *The Writings of the New Testament*, 3rd ed. (Minneapolis: Fortress, 2010).

- Werner Kelber, *The Oral and Written Gospel* (Minneapolis: Fortress, 1983).

- Jonathan T. Pennington, *Reading the Gospels Wisely* (Grand Rapids: Baker, 2012).

- Stanley E. Porter and Bryan R. Dyer, eds., *The Synoptic Problem: Four Views* (Grand Rapids: Baker, 2016).

- Robert H. Stein, *Studying the Synoptic Gospels*, 2nd ed. (Grand Rapids: Baker, 2001).

- Robert H. Stein, *The Synoptic Problem: An Introduction* (Grand Rapids: Baker, 1987).

- B. H. Streeter, *The Four Gospels: A Study of Origins* (London: Macmillan, 1924).

- Mark L. Strauss, *Four Portraits: One Jesus* (Grand Rapids: Zondervan, 2007).

- Robert L. Thomas, ed., *Three Views on the Origins of the Synoptic Gospels* (Grand Rapids: Kregel, 2002).

- David Wenham and Steve Walton, *Exploring the New Testament: A Guide to the Gospels and Acts* (Downers Grove, IL: InterVarsity, 2001).

- B. F. Westcott, *An Introduction to the Study of the Gospels* (London: MacMillan, 1895).

GRAMMAR AND SYNTAX

- John Beekman and John Callow, *Translating the Word of God* (Grand Rapids: Zondervan, 1974).

- F. Blass and A. DeBrunner, *A Greek Grammar of the New Testament and Other Early Christian Literature*, trans. and rev. R. W. Runk (Chicago: University of Chicago Press, 1979).

- Constantine R. Campbell, *Advances in the Study of Greek* (Grand Rapids: Zondervan, 2015).

- Constantine R. Campbell, *Verbal Aspect, the Indicative Mood, and Narrative* (New York: Peter Lang, 2007).★

- D. A. Carson, *Exegetical Fallacies*, 2nd ed. (Grand Rapids: Baker, 1996).

- Rodney J. Decker, *Reading Koine Greek: An Introduction and Integrated Workbook* (Grand Rapids: Baker, 2014).

- Rodney J. Decker, *Temporal Deixis of the Greek Verb in the Gospel of Mark with Reference to Verbal Aspect* (New York: Peter Lang, 2001).★

- Buist Fanning, *Verbal Aspect in New Testament Greek* (Oxford: Clarendon, 1990).★

- R. W. Funk, *A Beginning-Intermediate Grammar of Hellenistic Greek*, 3 vols. (Missoula, MT: Scholars, 1973).

- Murray J. Harris, *Prepositions and Theology in the Greek New Testament* (Grand Rapids: Zondervan, 2012).

- Jon Laansma and Randall K. Gauthier, *The Handy Guide to Difficult and Irregular Greek Verbs* (Grand Rapids: Kregel, 2017).

- David L. Matthewson and Elodie Ballantine Emig, *Intermediate Greek Grammar* (Grand Rapids: Baker, 2016).

- C. F. D. Moule, *An Idiom Book of New Testament Greek*, 2nd ed. (Cambridge: Cambridge University Press, 1959).

- Stanley D. Porter, *Verbal Aspect in the Greek of the New Testament with Reference to Tense and Mood* (New York: Peter Lang, 1989).★

- A. T. Robertson, *A Grammar of the Greek New Testament in the Light of Historical Research*, 4th ed. (New York: Hodder, 1923).

- Cleon L. Rogers Jr. and Cleon L. Rogers III, *The New Linguistic and Exegetical Key to the Greek New Testament* (Grand Rapids: Zondervan, 1996).

- Steven E. Runge, *Discourse Grammar of the Greek New Testament* (Peabody, MA: Hendrickson, 2010).★

- Nigel Turner, *Syntax,* vol. 3 of *A Grammar of New Testament Greek*, ed. J. H. Moulton, 4 vols. (Edinburgh: Clark, 1908–76; vol. 3, 1963).

- Daniel B. Wallace, *Greek Grammar beyond the Basics: An Exegetical Syntax of New Testament Greek* (Grand Rapids: Zondervan, 1996).

- G. B. Winer, *A Treatise on the Grammar of New Testament Greek*, 3rd ed. trans. and rev. W. F. Moulton (Edinburgh: Clark, 1882).

- R. A. Young, *Intermediate New Testament Greek: A Linguistic and Exegetical Approach* (Nashville: Broadman, 1994).

- Max Zerwick, *Biblical Greek Illustrated by Examples* (Rome: Pontifical Biblical Institute, 1963).

- Max Zerwick, *A Grammatical Analysis of the Greek New Testament,* 5th ed. trans. Mary Grosvenor (Rome: Pontifical Biblical Institute, 1996).

LEXICAL RESOURCES

- Horst Balz and Gerhard Schneider, *Exegetical Dictionary of the New Testament*, English translation, 3 vols. (Grand Rapids: Eerdmans, 1990–1993).

- Michael H. Burer and Jeffrey E. Miller, *A New Reader's Lexicon of the Greek New Testament* (Grand Rapids: Kregel, 2008).

- F. Danker, *The Concise Greek-English Lexicon of the New Testament*★ (Chicago: University of Chicago, 2009).

- F. Danker, W. Bauer, et al., *A Greek-English Lexicon of the New Testament and Other Early Christian Literature*, 3rd ed. (Chicago: University of Chicago, 2000).

- Gerhard Kittel, ed., *Theological Dictionary of the New Testament*, trans. G. W. Gromiley, 10 vols. (Grand Rapids: Eerdmans, 1964–72).

- G. W. H. Lampe, *A Patristic Greek Lexicon* (Oxford: Clarendon, 1961).

- John A. Lee, *A History of New Testament Lexicography* (New York: Peter Lange, 2003).

- H. G. Liddell and R. Scott, *A Greek-English Lexicon: A New Edition Revised and Augmented Throughout with Supplement*, rev. H. S. Jones and R. McKenzie, 9th ed. (Oxford: Oxford University Press, 1968). Read online at http://stephanus.tlg. uci.edu/lsj/#eid=1&context=lsj.

- J. P. Louw, *Greek-English Lexicon of the New Testament based on Semantic Domains*, 2nd ed., 2 vols. (New York: United Bible Societies, 1999).

- J. H. Moulton and G. Milligan, *The Vocabulary of the Greek New Testament Illustrated from the Papyri and Other Non-Literary Sources* (reprinted, Grand Rapids: Eerdmans, 1976).

- Barclay M. Newman, *A Concise Greek-English Dictionary of the New Testament*, rev. ed. (Stuttgart: Deutsche Bibelgesellschaft, 2010).

- Moisés Silva, *Biblical Words and Their Meaning* (Grand Rapids: Zondervan, 1983).

- Moisés Silva, ed., *The New International Dictionary of New Testament Theology and Exegesis*, 5 vols. (Grand Rapids: Zondervan, 2014).

- Ceslas Spicq, *Theolgical Lexicon of the New Testament*, English translation, 3 vols. (Peabody, MA: Hendrickson, 1993).

- Warren C. Trenchard, *A Concise Dictionary of New Testament Greek* (Cambridge: Cambridge University, 2003).

HISTORICAL–LITERARY–CULTURAL SETTING

- C. K. Barrett, *The New Testament Background: Selected Documents*, rev. ed. (New York: Harper, 1995).

- Craig Blomberg, *The Historical Reliability of the Fourth Gospel* (Downers Grove, IL: InterVarsity, 2001).

- Craig Blomberg, *The Historical Reliability of the Gospels*, 2nd ed. (Downers Grove, IL: InterVarsity, 2007).

- M. Eugene Boring, et al. eds., *Hellenistic Commentary on the New Testament* (Nashville: Abingdon, 1995).

- Gary Burge, Lynn H. Cohick, and Gene L. Green, *The New Testament in Antiquity: A Survey of the New Testament within Its Cultural Contexts* (Grand Rapids: Zondervan, 2009).

- James H. Charlesworth, ed., *The Old Testament Pseudepigrapha*, 2 vols. (New York: Doubleday, 1985).

- Craig A. Evans, *Ancient Texts for New Testament Studies: A Guide to the Background Literature* (reprinted, Grand Rapids: Baker, 2012).

- Craig A. Evans, *Non-Canonical Writings and New Testament Interpretation* (Peabody, MA: Hendrickson, 1992).

- Everett F. Ferguson, *Backgrounds of Early Christianity*, 3rd ed. (Grand Rapids: Eerdmans, 2003).

- Lester L. Grabbe, *Judaism from Cyrus to Hadrian*, 2 vols. (Minneapolis: Fortress, 1992).

- Larry R. Helyer, *Exploring Jewish Literature of the Second Temple Period* (Downers Grove, IL: InterVarsity, 2002).

- James S. Jeffers, *The Greco-Roman World of the New Testament* (Downers Grove, IL: InterVarsity, 2000).

- Craig S. Keener, *The Historical Jesus of the Gospels* (Grand Rapids: Eerdmans, 2009).

- Bruce J. Malina and Richard L. Rohrbaugh, *Social Science Commentary on the Synoptic Gospels* (Minneapolis: Fortress, 1992).

- Victor H. Matthews, *Manners and Customs in the Bible*, 2nd ed. (Peabody, MA: Hendrickson, 1991).

- Martin Jan Mulder, ed., *Mikra. Text, Translation, Reading and Interpretation of the Hebrew Bible in Ancient Judaism and Early Christianity* (Assen/Minneapolis: Van Gorcum/Fortress, 1990).

- Jacob Neusner, *Introduction to Rabbinic Literature* (New York: Doubleday, 1994).

- Jerome Neyrey, *The Social World of Luke-Acts: Models for Interpretation* (Peabody, MA: Hendrickson, 1991).

- G. W. H. Nickelsburg, *Jewish Literature between the Bible and the Mishnah* (Philadelphia: Fortress, 1981).

- S. Safrai and M. Stern, eds., *The Jewish People in the First Century*, 2 vols. (Philadelphia: Fortress, 1974).

- E. P. Sanders, *Judaism: Practice and Belief 63 BCE–66 CE* (London/ Philadelphia: SCM/Trinity, 1992).

- Emil Schürer, *The History of the Jewish People in the Time of Jesus Christ*, trans. and rev. Geza Vermes, et al. 3 vols. (Edinburgh: Clark, 1973–87).

- Michael E. Stone, *Jewish Writings of the Second Temple Period* (Assen/Philadelphia: Van Gorcum/Fortress, 1984).

- H. L. Strack and Günter Stemberger, *Introduction to the Talmud and Midrash*, trans. M. Bockmuehl, 2nd ed. (Minneapolis: Fortress, 1996).

- James C. VanderKam and Peter Flint, *The Meaning of the Dead Sea Scrolls* (San Francisco: Harper, 2002).

- James C. VanderKam and William Adler, eds., *The Jewish Apocalyptic Heritage in Early Christianity* (Assen/Minneapolis: Van Gorcum/Fortress, 1996).

- Michael Wise, Martin Abegg Jr., and Edward Cook, *The Dead Sea Scrolls: A New Translation* (San Francisco: Harper, 1996).

DICTIONARIES AND ENCYCLOPEDIAS

- T. Desmond Alexander, et al., eds. *New Dictionary of Biblical Theology* (Downers Grove, IL: InterVarsity, 2000).

- G. W. Bromiley, ed., *International Standard Bible Encyclopedia*, rev. ed., 4 vols. (Grand Rapids: Eerdmans, 1979–88).

- Craig A. Evans and Stanley Porter, eds., *Dictionary of the New Testament Background* (Downers Grove, IL: InterVarsity, 2000).

- David Noel Freedman, ed., *The Anchor Bible Dictionary*, 6 vols. (New York: Doubleday, 1992).

- Joel Green, et al., eds. *Dictionary of Jesus and the Gospels*, 2nd ed. (Downers Grove, IL: InterVarsity, 2013).

- N. G. L. Hammond and H. H. Scullard, *The Oxford Classical Dictionary*, 2nd ed. (Oxford: Clarendon, 1970).

- Jacob Neusner, ed. in chief, *Dictionary of Judaism in the Biblical Period* (Peabody, MA: Hendrickson, 1999).

- Leland Ryken, et al., gen. eds., *Dictionary of Biblical Imagery* (Downers Grove, IL: InterVarsity, 1998).

- Katharine D. Sakenfeld, ed., *The New Interpreter's Dictionary of the Bible*, 5 vols. (Nashville: Abingdon, 2009).

- Lawrence H. Schiffman and James C. VanderKam, eds. in chief, *Encyclopedia of the Dead Sea Scrolls*, 2 vols. (Oxford: Oxford University, 2000).

- M. Silva and M. C. Tenney, gen eds., *Zondervan Encyclopedia of the Bible*, rev. ed., 5 vols. (Grand Rapids: Zondervan, 2008).

- Kevin J. Vanhoozer, gen. ed., *Dictionary for Theological Interpretation of the Bible* (Grand Rapids: Baker, 2005).

COMMENTARY SERIES

Commentaries are not infallible guides whose views are to be taken as gospel, but students should not assume that their own exegetical prowess renders commentaries unnecessary. Students should consult commentaries as sounding boards—conversation partners to stimulate, challenge, confirm, or sharpen the conclusions they have reached in their own studies.

Devotional and *homiletical* commentaries have a place but the focus here is on commentaries that provide linguistic and historical information for exegetes. Accordingly, expositional, exegetical, and critical commentaries are featured. *Expositional* commentaries may not work directly with the Greek text but their content takes the original language and setting of the text seriously as the basis for discussion. *Exegetical* commentaries work directly with the Greek text and also delve more deeply into historical matters. *Critical* commentaries delve deeply into matters such as tradition history and reception history and tend to be more focused on details than on the message of the text. Commentaries that emphasize *literary* and *theological* aspects of the text are also useful and are occasionally included here.

Commentary series are inevitably uneven—some volumes are more highly regarded than others, and reviewers vary in their assessments of individual volumes. The well-known sets that follow are briefly described in terms of their content and theological leanings.[1]

- Anchor Bible (AB, Doubleday)★
  Uneven critical commentaries; Fitzmyer (Luke) and Brown (John) are helpful.

- Ancient Christian Commentary (ACC, InterVarsity)
  Contains relevant excerpts from early Christian writings.

- Baker Exegetical Commentary on the New Testament (BECNT, Baker)
  Relatively detailed exegesis/exposition based on Greek text and ancient setting.

- Baylor Handbook on the Greek New Testament (BHGNT, Baylor University Press)
  Helpful notes on lexical, grammatical, and syntactical matters.

- Bible Speaks Today (BST, InterVarsity)
  Evangelical exposition of the overall message, not details.

---

1. For wise counsel on serious biblical commentaries, see D. A. Carson, *New Testament Commentary Survey*, 7th ed. (Grand Rapids: Baker, 2013), and John Glynn, *Commentary and Reference Survey: A Comprehensive Guide to Biblical and Theological Resources* (Grand Rapids: Kregel, 2007).

- Evangelical Exegetical Commentary (EEC; Logos Bible Software)
  Recent set, in process, available to Logos software users.

- Cornerstone Biblical Commentary (CBC, Tyndale House)
  Helpful evangelical exposition based on the NLT.

- Exegetical Guide to the Greek New Testament (EGGNT, B&H)
  Helpful notes on lexical, grammatical, and syntactical issues.

- Expositor's Bible Commentary (EBC, Zondervan)
  Exposition based on the NIV with technical details in footnotes.

- Hermeneia (Fortress)★
  Critical, theologically liberal. Luz on Matthew's reception history is helpful.

- International Critical Commentary (ICC, T&T Clark)★
  Critical, theologically liberal. Generally helpful on syntax and setting.

- Interpretation (John Knox Press)
  Theologically moderate to liberal exposition for church ministry.

- IVP New Testament Commentary (IVPNTS, InterVarsity)
  Evangelical exposition and application.

- New American Commentary (NAC, Broadman)
  Conservative evangelical exposition from a Southern Baptist perspective.

- New International Commentary on the New Testament (NICNT, Eerdmans)
  Broadly evangelical exposition with footnotes on technical matters.

- New International Greek Testament Commentaries (NIGTC, Eerdmans)★
  Theologically moderate, detailed critical/exegetical emphasis.

- New International Version Application Commentary (NIVAC, Zondervan)
  Evangelical exposition with bridges to application.

- Pillar New Testament Commentary (PNTC, Eerdmans)
  Detailed evangelical exegesis and exposition.

- *Sacra Pagina* (SP, Liturgical)
  Roman Catholic, relatively brief exegetical treatments.

- Teach the Text (TtT, Baker)
  Attractively formatted synthesis of exegesis, theology, and application.

- Two Horizons New Testament Commentary (THNTC, Eerdmans)
  Hermeneutically based exegetical comments.

- Tyndale New Testament Commentary (TNTC, Eerdmans)
  Evangelical, concise expositions with occasional footnotes on technical matters.

- Word Biblical Commentary (WBC, Nelson)
  Broadly evangelical exegetical-critical approach.

- Zondervan Exegetical New Testament Commentary (ZENTC, Zondervan)
  Evangelical exegetical approach with attention to syntactical structure.

- Zondervan Illustrated Bible Backgrounds Commentary (ZIBBC, Zondervan)
  Attractively illustrated with relevant, concise background information.

COMMENTARIES ON THE GOSPELS AND ACTS

Matthew

- Craig L. Blomberg, *Matthew*, NAC (Nashville: Broadman, 1992).

- Jeannine K. Brown, *Matthew*, TtT (Grand Rapids: Baker, 2015).

- Frederick Dale Bruner, *Matthew: A Commentary*, rev. ed. (Grand Rapids: Eerdmans, 2004, 2007).

- W. D. Davies and Dale C. Allison, *A Critical and Exegetical Commentary on the Gospel according to Saint Mathew*, ICC, 3 vols. (Edinburgh: Clark, 1988–91).*

- R. T. France, *The Gospel of Matthew*, NICNT (Grand Rapids: Eerdmans, 2007).

- David E. Garland, *Reading Matthew* (Macon, GA: Smith & Helwys, 2001).

- Robert H. Gundry, *Matthew: A Commentary on His Handbook for a Mixed Church under Persecution*, 2nd ed. (Grand Rapids: Eerdmans, 1994).

- Donald A. Hagner, *Matthew*, 2 vols. WBC (Dallas: Word, 1993–1995).

- Craig S. Keener, *A Commentary on the Gospel of Matthew* (Grand Rapids: Eerdmans, 1999).

- Ulrich Luz, *Matthew 1–7: A Commentary*, Hermeneia (Philadelphia: Fortress, 1992).★

- Ulrich Luz, *Matthew 8–20: A Commentary*, Hermeneia (Minneapolis: Fortress, 2001).★

- Ulrich Luz, *Matthew 21–28: A Commentary*, Hermeneia (Minneapolis: Fortress, 2005).★

- Leon Morris, *The Gospel according to Matthew*, PNTC (Grand Rapids: Eerdmans, 1992).

- John Nolland, *The Gospel of Matthew*, NIGTC (Grand Rapids: Eerdmans, 2005).★

- Chalres L. Quarles, *Matthew*, EGGNT (Nashville: B&H, 2017).

- H. N. Ridderbos, *Matthew* (Grand Rapids, Zondervan, 1987).

- David L. Turner, *Matthew*, BECNT (Grand Rapids: Baker, 2008).

- David L. Turner, "Matthew," in *Matthew, Mark*, vol. 11 of CBC, eds. David L. Turner and Darrell L. Bock (Carol Stream, IL: Tyndale House, 2006).

- Michael J. Wilkins, *Matthew*, NIVAC (Grand Rapids: Zondervan, 2004).

Mark

- Darrell L. Bock, "Mark," in *Matthew, Mark*, vol. 11 of CBC, eds. David L. Turner and Darrell L. Bock (Carol Stream, IL: Tyndale House, 2006).

- Rodney J. Decker, *Mark 1–8: A Handbook on the Greek Text*, BHGNT (Waco, TX: Baylor University Press, 2014).

- Rodney J. Decker, *Mark 9–16: A Handbook on the Greek Text*, BHGNT (Waco, TX: Baylor University Press, 2014).

- James R. Edwards, *The Gospel according to Mark*, PNTC (Grand Rapids: Eerdmans, 2002).

- R. T. France, *The Gospel of Mark*, NIGTC (Grand Rapids: Eerdmans, 2002).

- David Garland, *Mark*, NIVAC (Grand Rapids: Zondervan, 1996).

- Robert H. Gundry, *Mark: A Commentary on His Apology for the Cross* (Grand Rapids: Eerdmans, 1993).

- William L. Lane, *Mark*, NICNT (Grand Rapids: Eerdmans, 1974).

- Grant R. Osborne, *Mark*, TtT (Grand Rapids: Baker, 2014).

- Robert H. Stein, Mark, BECNT (Grand Rapids: Baker, 2008).

- Ben Witherington III, *The Gospel of Mark: A Socio-Rhetorical Commentary* (Grand Rapids: Eerdmans, 2001).

Luke

- Darrell L. Bock, *Luke*, 2 vols., BECNT (Grand Rapids: Baker, 1994, 1996).

- Darrell L. Bock, *Luke*, NIVAC (Grand Rapids: Zondervan, 1996).

- Martin M. Culy, Mikeal C. Parsons, and Joshua J. Stigall, *Luke: A Handbook on the Greek Text*, BHGNT (Waco, TX: Baylor University Press, 2010).

- Joseph A. Fitzmyer, *The Gospel according to Luke*, 2 vols., AB (Garden City, NY: Doubleday, 1981, 1985).

- R. T. France, *Luke*, TtT (Grand Rapids: Baker, 2013).

- Joel Green, *The Gospel of Luke*, NICNT (Grand Rapids: Eerdmans, 1997).

- Luke Timothy Johnson, *The Gospel of Luke*, SP (Collegeville. MN: Liturgical Press, 1992).

- I. H. Marshall, *The Gospel of Luke*, NIGTC (Grand Rapids: Eerdmans, 1978).

- John Nolland, *Luke*, 3 vols., WBC (Dallas: Word, 1989–1993).

- Robert H. Stein, *Luke*, NAC (Nashville: Broadman, 1992).

- Allan J. Thompson, *Luke*, EGGNT (Nashville: B&H, 2017).

- Allison H. Trites, "The Gospel of Luke," in *Luke, Acts*, vol. 12 of CBC, eds. Allison H. Trites and William J. Larkin (Carol Stream, IL: Tyndale House, 2006).

John

- Thomas L. Brodie, *The Gospel according to John: A Literary and Theological Commentary* (New York: Oxford University, 1993).

- Raymond E. Brown, *The Gospel according to John*, 2 vols., AB (Garden City, NY: Doubleday, 1982).

- Frederick Dale Bruner, *The Gospel of John: A Commentary* (Grand Rapids: Eerdmans, 2012).

- Gary M. Burge, *John*, NIVAC (Grand Rapids: Zondervan, 2000).

- D. A. Carson, *The Gospel according to John*, PNTC (Grand Rapids: Eerdmans, 1991).

- Murray J. Harris, *John,* EGGNT (Nashville: B&H, 2015).

- Craig L. Keener, *The Gospel of John: A Commentary*, 2 vols. (Peabody, MA: Hendrickson, 2003).

- Andreas J. Köestenberger, *John*, BECNT (Grand Rapids: Baker, 2004).

- Leon Morris, *The Gospel according to St. John*, rev. ed., NICNT (Grand Rapids, 1995).

- Herman Ridderbos, *The Gospel according to John: A Theological Commentary*, trans. John Vriend (Grand Rapids: Eerdmans, 1997).

- Rudolf Schnackenburg, *The Gospel according to St. John*, trans. Kevin Smyth, et al. (New York: Crossroad/Seabury, 1980, 1982).★

- Charles H. Talbert, *Reading John: A Literary and Theological Commentary on the Fourth Gospel and the Johannine Epistles* (New York: Crossroad, 1992).

- Urban C. von Wahlde, *The Gospel and Letters of John*, 3 vols. (Grand Rapids: Eerdmans, 2010).★

Acts

- C. K. Barrett, *The Acts of the Apostles*, 2 vols., ICC (Edinburgh: Clark, 1994, 1998).★

- Darrell L. Bock, *Acts*, BECNT (Grand Rapids: Baker, 2007).

- F. F. Bruce, *The Book of Acts*, NICNT, rev. ed. (Grand Rapids: Eerdmans, 1988).

- Martin M. Culy and Mikeal C. Parsons, *Acts: A Handbook on the Greek Text*, BHGNT (Waco, TX: Baylor University Press, 2003).

- James Dunn, *Beginning at Jerusalem* (Grand Rapids: Eerdmans, 2009).

- Joseph. A. Fitzmyer, *The Acts of the Apostles*, AB (New York: Doubleday, 1998).

- Craig S. Keener, *Acts: An Exegetical Commentary*, 4 vols. (Grand Rapids: Baker, 2012–2015).★

- William J. Larkin, "Acts," in *Luke, Acts*, vol. 12 of CBC, eds. Allison H. Trites and William J. Larkin (Carol Stream, IL: Tyndale House, 2006).

- John Polhill, *Acts*, NAC (Nashville: Broadman & Holman, 1992).

- J. R. W. Stott, *The Message of Acts*, BST (Downers Grove, IL: InterVarsity, 1990).

- Ben Witherington III, *The Acts of the Apostles: A Socio-Rhetorical Commentary* (Grand Rapids: Eerdmans, 1997).

BIBLICAL THEOLOGY

Resources that canvass biblical and NT theology more broadly are listed first, followed by works that focus on the individual Gospels and Acts.

Biblical and New Testament Theology

- G. K. Beale, *A New Testament Biblical Theology* (Grand Rapids: Baker, 2011).

- G. K. Beale and D. A. Carson, eds., *Commentary on the New Testament Use of the Old Testament* (Grand Rapids: Baker, 2007).

- G. R. Beasley-Murray, *Jesus and the Kingdom of God* (Grand Rapids: Eerdmans, 1986).

- Brevard Childs, *Biblical Theology of the Old and New Testaments: Theological Reflection on the Christian Bible* (Minneapolis: Fortress, 1993).

- James D. G. Dunn, *Jesus and the Spirit* (London: SCM, 1975).

- James D. G. Dunn, *New Testament Theology: An Introduction* (Nashville: Abingdon, 2009).

- Scott J. Hafemann and Paul R. House, eds., *Central Themes in Biblical Theology: Mapping Unity in Diversity* (Grand Rapids: Baker, 2007).

- John Harvey, *Anointed with the Spirit and Power* (Phillipsburg, NJ: Presbyterian & Reformed, 2008).

- Gerald F. Hawthorne, *The Presence and the Power* (1991; reprinted, Eugene, OR: Wipf and Stock, 2003).

- Richard B. Hays, *Echoes of Scripture in the Gospels* (Waco, TX: Baylor University Press, 2016).

- George E. Ladd, *The Presence of the Future* (Grand Rapids: Eerdmans, 1974).

- George E. Ladd, *A Theology of the New Testament*, 2nd ed. (Grand Rapids: Eerdmans, 1993).

- I. H. Marshall, *New Theology: Many Witnesses, One Gospel* (Downers Grove, IL: InterVarsity, 2004).

- Keith A. Mathison, *From Age to Age: The Unfolding of Biblical Eschatology* (Phillipsburg, NJ: P&R, 2009).

- Frank J. Matera, *New Testament Theology: Exploring Diversity and Unity* (Louisville: Westminster/Knox, 2007).

- Thomas R. Schreiner, *New Testament Theology: Magnifying God in Christ* (Grand Rapids: Baker, 2008).

- Charles H. H. Scobie, *The Ways of Our God: An Approach to Biblical Theology* (Grand Rapids: Eerdmans, 2003).

- Ned Stonehouse, *The Witness of the Synoptic Gospels to Christ* (Grand Rapids: Baker, 1979).

- Frank Thielman, *Theology of the New Testament* (Grand Rapids: Zondervan, 2005).

- Geerhardus Vos, *Biblical Theology: Old and New Testaments*, new ed. (Carlisle, PA: Banner of Truth, 1975).

- N. T. Wright, *How God Became King: The Forgotten Story of the Gospels* (New York: HarperCollins, 2012).

- Roy B. Zuck and Darrell Bock, eds., *A Biblical Theology of the New Testament* (Chicago: Moody, 1994).

Matthew

- David E. Aune, ed., *The Gospel of Matthew in Current Study* (Grand Rapids: Eerdmans, 2001).

- Dale C. Allison, *The New Moses: A Matthean Typology* (Minneapolis: Fortress, 1993).

- David L. Balch, ed., *Social History of the Matthean Community* (Minneapolis: Fortress, 1991).

- R. T. France, *Matthew: Evangelist and Theologian* (Grand Rapids: Zondervan, 1989).

- Matthias Konradt, *Israel, Church, and the Gentiles in the Gospel of Matthew* (Waco, TX: Baylor University Press, 2014).

- Ulrich Luz, *The Theology of the Gospel of Matthew* (Cambridge: Cambridge University, 1995).

- J. Andrew Overman, *Matthew's Gospel and Formative Judaism* (Minneapolis: Fortress, 1990).

- Jonathan Pennington, *Heaven and Earth in the Gospel of Matthew* (reprinted, Grand Rapids: Baker, 2009).

- Anthony J. Saldarini, *Matthew's Christian-Jewish Community* (Chicago: University of Chicago, 1994).

- Graham Stanton, *A Gospel for a New People: Studies in Matthew* (Edinburgh: Clark, 1992).

- David L. Turner, *Israel's Last Prophet: Jesus and the Jewish Leaders in Matthew 23* (Minneapolis: Fortress, 2015).

- Michael J. Wilkins, *The Concept of Disciple in Matthew's Gospel* (Leiden: Brill, 1988).

Mark

- Ernest Best, *Following Jesus: Discipleship in the Gospel of Mark* (Sheffield: JSOT, 1988).

- Ernest Best, *Mark, the Gospel as Story* (Edinburgh: Clark, 1983).

- Daniel J. Harrington, *What Are They Saying about Mark?* (Mahwah, NJ: Paulist, 2005).

- Jack D. Kingsbury, *The Christology of Mark's Gospel* (Philadelphia: Fortress, 1983).

- Ralph Martin, *Mark: Evangelist and Theologian* (Grand Rapids: Zondervan, 1972).

- Willi Marxsen, *Mark the Evangelist*, trans. James Boyce (Nashville: Abingdon, 1969).★

- Stephen H. Smith, *A Lion with Wings: A Narrative-Critical Approach to Mark's Gospel* (Sheffield: Sheffield Academic, 1996).

- W. R. Telford, *The Theology of Mark* (Cambridge: Cambridge University, 1999).

- W. R. Telford ed., *The Interpretation of Mark* (Philadelphia: Fortress, 1985).

- Rikk E. Watts, *Isaiah's New Exodus in Mark* (Grand Rapids: Baker, 2000).

Luke–Acts

- Darrell L. Bock, *A Theology of Luke-Acts* (Grand Rapids: Zondervan, 2012).

- Francois Bovon, *Luke the Theologian: The Interpretation of Luke and Acts 1950–2005* (Waco, TX: Baylor University Press, 2006).

- J. Bradley Chance, *Jerusalem, the Temple, and the New Age in Luke-Acts* (Atlanta: Mercer, 1988).

- Hans Conzelmann, *The Theology of St. Luke*, trans. G. Buswell (New York: Harper, 1960).

- Joseph A. Fitzmyer, *Luke the Theologian: Aspects of His Teaching* (reprinted, Eugene, OR: Wipf and Stock, 2004).

- Joel B. Green, *The Theology of the Gospel of Luke* (Cambridge: Cambridge University Press, 1995).

- I. Howard Marshall, *Luke: Historian and Theologian*, 2nd ed. (Downers Grove, IL: InterVarsity, 1998).

- I. Howard Marshall and David Peterson, eds., *Witness to the Gospel: The Theology of Acts* (Grand Rapids: Eerdmans, 1998).

- Mark Alan Powell, *What Are They Saying about Luke?* (New York: Paulist, 1989).

- Charles B. Puskas, *The Conclusion of Luke-Acts* (Eugene, OR: Pickwick, 2009).

- David Rhoads, et al., eds., *Luke-Acts and Empire* (Eugene, OR: Pickwick, 2011).

- Mark L. Strauss, *The Davidic Messiah in Luke-Acts* (Sheffield: Sheffield Academic, 1995).

- Roger Stronstad, *The Charismatic Theology of St. Luke*, 2nd ed. (Grand Rapids: Baker, 2012).

- Robert Tannehill, *The Narrative Unity of Luke-Acts*, 2 vols. (Philadelphia: Fortress, 1986, 1990).

- Max Turner, *Power from on High: The Spirit in Israel's Restoration and Witness in Luke-Acts* (Sheffield: Sheffield Academic, 1996).

John

- John Ashton, *Understanding the Fourth Gospel* (New York: Oxford University, 1991).

- Gary M. Burge, *The Anointed Community: The Holy Spirit in the Johannine Tradition* (Grand Rapids: Eerdmans, 1987).

- Gary M. Burge, *Interpreting the Fourth Gospel* (Grand Rapids: Baker, 1992).

- R. Alan Culpepper, *Anatomy of the Fourth Gospel: A Study in Literary Design* (Philadelphia: Fortress, 1983).

- R. Alan Culpepper and C. Clifton Black, eds., *Exploring the Gospel of John* (Louisville: Westminster/Knox, 1996).

- Paul Duke, *Irony in the Fourth Gospel* (Atlanta: John Knox, 1985).

- Craig Koester, *Symbolism in the Fourth Gospel*, 2nd ed. (Minneapolis: Fortress, 2003).

- Craig Koester, *The Word of Life: A Theology of John's Gospel* (Grand Rapids: Eerdmans, 2008).

- Andreas J. Köstenberger, *The Theology of John's Gospel and Letters* (Grand Rapids: Zondervan, 2009).

- Robert Kysar, *John: The Maverick Gospel*, rev. ed. (Louisville: Westminster Knox, 1993).

- J. Louis Martyn, *History and Theology in the Fourth Gospel*, 3rd ed. (Nashville: Abingdon, 2003).

- C. Marvin Pate, *The Writings of John* (Grand Rapids: Zondervan, 2011).

- D. Moody Smith, *The Theology of the Gospel of John* (Cambridge: Cambridge University, 1995).

- Marianne Meye Thompson, *The God of the Gospel of John* (Grand Rapids: Eerdmans, 2001).

- Marianne Meye Thompson, *The Humanity of Jesus in the Fourth Gospel* (Philadelphia: Fortress, 1988).

SYSTEMATIC THEOLOGY

The categories are debatable, but this listing includes a variety of evangelical and reformed sources, as well as representatives of Orthodoxy, Roman Catholicism, Anglicanism, Lutheranism, Arminianism, and Pentecostalism.

Orthodoxy

- Daniel B. Clendenin, ed., *Eastern Orthodox Christianity: A Western Perspective*, 2nd ed. (Grand Rapids: Baker, 2003).

- Daniel B. Clendenin, ed., *Eastern Orthodox Theology: A Contemporary Reader*, 2nd ed. (Grand Rapids: Baker, 2003).

- Kallistos Ware, *The Orthodox Church*, 2nd ed. (London: Penguin, 1993).

- Kallistos Ware, *The Orthodox Way*, rev. ed. (Crestwood, NY: St. Vladimir's Seminary, 1995).

Roman Catholicism

- Thomas Aquinas, *Summa Theologica*, 5 vols. (reprinted, Notre Dame, IN: Christian Classics, 1981).

- *Catechism of the Catholic Church*, 2nd ed. (Garden City, NY: Doubleday, 1995).

- Richard McBrien, *Catholicism*, rev. ed. (New York: HarperCollins, 1994).

Lutheranism

- Carl E. Braaten, *Principles of Lutheran Theology*, 2nd ed. (Minneapolis: Augsburg Fortress, 2007).

- Robert Kolb and Timothy J. Wengert, eds., *The Book of Concord: The Confessions of the Evangelical Lutheran Church* (Minneapolis: Fortress, 2000).

- Stephen D. Paulsen, *Lutheran Theology* (London: Clark, 2011).

- Francis Pieper, *Christian Dogmatics* (St. Louis: Concordia, 1968).

Anglicanism

- Edward H. Browne, *An Exposition of the Thirty-Nine Articles* (New York: E. P. Dutton, 1874). Available online.

- Mark Chapman, *Anglican Theology* (London: Clark, 2012).

- Ralph McMichael, ed., *The Vocation of Anglican Theology: Sources and Essays* (London: SCM, 2014).

- John H. Rogers, *Essential Truths for Christians: A Commentary on the 39 Articles and an Introduction to Systematic Theology* (Ambridge, PA: Classical Anglican Press, 2011).

- W. H. Griffith Thomas, *The Principles of Theology*, 6th ed. (London: Longmans, 1930).

Reformed

- John Calvin, *Institutes of the Christian Religion*, 2 vols., ed. J. T. McNeill, trans. F. L. Battles (Philadelphia: Westminster, 1960).

- John M. Frame, *Systematic Theology: An Introduction to Christian Belief* (Phillipsburg, NJ: P&R, 2013).

- Michael Horton, *The Christian Faith: A Systematic Theology for Pilgrims on the Way* (Grand Rapids: Zondervan, 2011).

- Robert L. Reymond, *A New Systematic Theology of the Christian Faith* (Nashville: Nelson, 1998).

Arminian

- James Arminius, *The Works of James Arminius*, London ed., trans. James Nichols, et al. (Grand Rapids: Baker, 1986).

- John Miley, *Systematic Theology*, 2 vols. (reprinted, Peabody, MA: Hendrickson, 1989).

- Roger Olson, *Arminian Theology: Myths and Realities* (Downers Grove, IL: InterVarsity, 2006).

- H. Orton Wiley, *Christian Theology*, 3 vols. (Kansas City, MO: Beacon Hill, 1940).

Pentecostal

- Guy P. Duffield and Nathaniel M. Van Cleave, *Foundations of Pentecostal Theology* (Lake Mary, FL: Creation House, 2008).

- Frank Macchia, *Baptized in the Spirit: A Global Pentecostal Theology* (Grand Rapids: Zondervan, 2006).

- Keith Warrington, *Pentecostal Theology: A Theology of Encounter* (London: Clark, 2008).

- J. Rodman Williams, *Renewal Theology: Systematic Theology from a Charismatic Perspective* (Grand Rapids: Zondervan, 1996).

Evangelical

- Michael F. Bird, *Evangelical Theology: A Biblical and Systematic Introduction* (Grand Rapids: Zondervan, 2013).

- Millard J. Erickson, *Christian Theology*, 3rd ed. (Grand Rapids: Baker, 2013).

- Walter Elwell, ed., *Evangelical Dictionary of Theology*, 2nd ed. (Grand Rapids: Baker, 2001).

- Wayne A. Grudem, *Systematic Theology: An Introduction to Biblical Doctrine* (Grand Rapids: Zondervan, 1994).

- Thomas C. Oden, *Classic Christianity: A Systematic Theology* (San Francisco: Harper, 2009).

- Anthony C. Thiselton, *Systematic Theology* (Grand Rapids: Eerdmans, 2015).

- Daniel J. Treier, *Introducing Theological Interpretation of Scripture* (Grand Rapids: Baker, 2008).

- Kevin J. Vanhoozer, gen. ed., *Dictionary for Theological Interpretation of the Bible* (Grand Rapids: Baker, 2005).

COMMUNICATION

- Ronald L. Allen, *Preaching Luke-Acts* (St. Louis: Chalice, 2000).

- Bryan D. Anderson, *Big Idea in Biblical Narrative* (Maitland, FL: Xulon, 2012).

- Augustine, *On Christian Doctrine.* English translation available online. See also Edmund Hills, trans. and ed., *Teaching Christianity*, vol. 1 of *The Works of St. Augustine: A Translation for the 21st Century*, 2nd rev. ed. (Brooklyn: New City, 1996).

- Bryan Chapell, *Christ-Centered Preaching: Redeeming the Expository Sermon,* 2nd ed. (Grand Rapids: Baker, 2005).

- Fred Craddock, *As One without Authority*, rev. ed. (St. Louis: Chalice, 2001).

- Daniel M. Doriani, *Putting the Truth to Work: The Theory and Practice of Biblical Application* (Phillipsburg, NJ: P&R, 2001).

- Joel Green and Michael Pasquarello, eds., *Narrative Reading, Narrative Preaching: Reuniting New Testament Interpretation and Proclamation* (Grand Rapids: Baker, 2003).

- David R. Helm, *Expositional Preaching: How We Speak God's Word Today* (Wheaton, IL: Crossway, 2014).

- Richard Lischer, *A Theology of Preaching: The Dynamics of the Gospel*, rev. ed. (Eugene, OR: Wipf and Stock, 2001).

- Thomas G. Long, *Preaching and the Literary Forms of the Bible* (Philadelphia: Fortress, 1988).

- Jason C. Meyer, *Preaching: A Biblical Theology* (Wheaton, IL: Crossway, 2013).

- Michael Pasquarello III, *Christian Preaching: A Trinitarian Theology of Proclamation* (Eugene, OR: Wipf and Stock, 2006).

- Haddon W. Robinson, *Biblical Preaching*, 3rd ed., Grand Rapids: Baker, 2013).

- Haddon Robinson and Craig Brian Larson, eds., *Biblical Preaching: A Comprehensive Resource for Today's Communicators* (Grand Rapids: Zondervan, 2005).

- Leland Ryken and Todd Wilson, *Preach the Word: Essays on Expository Preaching in Honor of R. Kent Hughes* (Wheaton, IL: Crossway, 2007).

- Andy Stanley, *Communicating for a Change* (Colorado Springs: Multnomah, 2006).

- John R. W. Stott, *Between Two Worlds: The Art of Preaching in the Twentieth Century* (Grand Rapids: Eerdmans, 1982).

- Donald R. Sunukjian, *Invitation to Biblical Preaching* (Grand Rapids: Kregel, 2007).

- Kevin J. Vanhoozer, *Is There a Meaning in This Text?* (Grand Rapids: Zondervan, 1998).

GLOSSARY

adoptionism. An umbrella term for non-trinitarian Christologies that hold Jesus was adopted as the Son of God at his baptism, resurrection, or ascension.

anarthrous. A term that describes a Greek noun or other construction that does not have an article.

Anti-Marcionite prologues. A term describing short prefaces to the Mark, Luke, and John found in some mss. of the Vulgate. Dated as early as the late second century A.D., they support traditional views of authorship. Only the preface for John is clearly anti-Marcionite. **Marcion** was a second-century gnostic who believed that the God of Jesus was not the God of Moses and the OT.

chiasmus. A literary device, based on the Greek letter *chi* (X), in which elements of the two components are repeated in reverse order, resulted in an inverted (or chi-shaped) structure (e.g., Matt. 7:6; 19:30–20:16). See also *inclusio*.

Christotelic. An approach to the overall biblical story or metanarrative that presents Christ as the goal of history rather than as the center of biblical truth as a system, i.e., Christocentric.

Decapolis. A group of ten Hellenistic cities (including Damascus, Scythopolis/Beth-Shean, Gerasa/Jerash, Philadelphia/Amman, Hippos, Gadara) in northeastern Palestine known as centers of Greco-Roman culture (Pliny the Elder, *Nat.*, 5.16.74; Matt. 4:25; Mark 5:20; 7:31).

Docetism. A heretical Christology, derived from the Greek verb δο-κέω, that affirmed a sort of phantom Jesus who only *seemed* to be human, or to have a human body.

DSS. Abbreviation for the Dead Sea Scrolls, discovered in the Judean desert near Qumran in the mid-twentieth century, with a huge subsequent impact on biblical studies.

epistemological. Relating to various theories of knowledge and the validation of belief-systems.

eschatological. Pertaining to biblical-theological views of the end times.

Ethnarch. Governor or ruler of an ethnic group or homogenous people (2 Cor. 11:32).

etymology. The study of the components or origins of words, an unreliable guide to meaning.

exordium. The beginning or introductory portion of an oral discourse or literary composition.

Feast of Dedication. Hanukkah. An eight-day Jewish festival instituted in 165 B.C. by Judah the Maccabee to celebrate the rededication of the temple after its desecration by Antiochus Epiphanes (1 Macc. 1:41–64; 4:36–39; 2 Macc. 6:1–11; John 10:22).

gematria. Numerology. A system that assigns numerical values to letters of the alphabet, usually involving religious symbolism.

genre. The kind or type of an oral utterance or a literary composition, a major factor in how that utterance or composition conveys meaning.

glossolalia. A word transliterated from Greek that refers to speaking in tongues.

hagiography. A biographical writing about a heroic religious figure, sometimes involving legendary or idyllic passages rather than strictly historical elements.

Hasmonean. Maccabean. The dynasty of Jewish rulers who first revolted against Antiochus Epiphanes in 167 B.C. and ruled Judea more or less independently until 63 B.C., continuing as Roman clients until Herod's rise to power in 37 B.C.

inclusio. A rhetorical or literary technique in which the same words or the same phrase circles or bookends a section of discourse, supplying the theme that ties the section together (e.g., Matt. 4:23; 9:35; Luke 2:40, 52; John 2:11; 4:54).

intertextuality. A literary or rhetorical phenomenon in which an author explicitly or implicitly alludes to a previous (inter)text in order to shape, explain, deepen, or justify the author's agenda in the later text (e.g., Matt. 1:23/Isa. 7:14; Mark 1:2–3/Mal. 3:1/Isa. 40:3).

irony. A rhetorical or literary device in which a text's intended meaning is the opposite of what the text's words apparently mean. In narrative or dramatic irony, the opposite of what the reader might expect to occur actually occurs (e.g., Luke 24:18; John 1:10–11; 3:10).

legate. In NT times, a person from the senatorial class who commanded of a Roman legion under the authority of a provincial governor.

LXX. Abbreviation for the Greek translation of the OT known as the Septuagint due to its legendary origination from seventy translators (cf. the *Letter of Aristeas*).

Masoretic text. Before the discovery of the DSS, the most ancient and authoritative Hebrew text of the OT, dating from the activity c. A.D. 700–1000 of editors known as the Masoretes, whose vocalization and accenting of the text is called the *masorah*.

metanarrative. In general, a grand, overarching narrative that contains and informs episodic or individual narratives. In biblical studies, the unfolding grand story of God and God's plan from Genesis to Revelation.

Muratorian Canon. A list of the NT books found in the muratorian fragment, a Latin ms. discovered by Ludovico Muratori around 1740. The fragment apparently dates from the seventh century, and is generally viewed as a translation of a Greek original dating from the second century.

narrative criticism. Literary methodology which approaches the Gospels as narratives or stories with historical setting, characterization, plot, and editorial point of view.

non sequitur. Describes a logical fallacy in which an assertion "does not follow" from the previous assertion.

paratactic. Etymologically, "placed side by side." A term that describes the coordinate relationship (parataxis) of two consecutive independent clauses in a discourse.

pericope. Generally, in rhetoric or literature, a coherent section or unit of thought. In biblical studies, usually a complete episode or scene in a narrative.

polyvalence. In reader-response literary criticism, the characteristic of having many potential meanings. Most appropriately used in interpreting figurative language, especially parables.

prefect. In NT times, a Roman official with delegated authority for administering civil or military affairs in various provinces. Pontius Pilate was prefect of Judea.

preterition. In reformed theology, God's activity in justly passing over or omitting the non-elect from his efficacious saving grace. Cf. the Westminster Confession 3.7.

procurator. In NT times, a Roman provincial official, often a civilian in charge of civil and financial affairs who served alongside the provincial governor.

proselytes. Gentiles who were full converts to Judaism (Matt. 23:15; Acts 2:11; 6:5), typically distinguished (but cf. Acts 13:43) from pious Gentile "God-fearers" who were more loosely connected to the synagogue. Cf. Luke 7:4–5; Acts 2:10; 10:2, 35; 13:16, 26; 17;4, 17; 18:7; Josephus, *Ant.* 14.110.

proem. A introductory preface or preamble to a speech or a book.

rationalism. An epistemology or worldview that relies solely on human reason, to the exclusion of sensory experience and transcendent revelation.

recension. A revised edition of a text, typically based on careful editorial scrutiny.

redaction criticism. The approach to the Gospels that involves assuming that the authors creatively edited the traditions they received during the composition process.

scholasticism. Narrowly, a medieval European approach to theology that emphasized logic and traditional systems. Pejoratively, applied to scholarship viewed as pedantic and irrelevant.

Second Temple. Narrowly, the edifice rebuilt by the Jews at the behest of Cyrus King of Persia (2 Chron. 36:22–23; Ezra, Neh.; c. 500 B.C.), expanded by Herod the Great (John 2:20), and destroyed by Rome in A.D. 70 (Josephus, *War*). More broadly, an adjective pertaining to the related time period, culture, and literature.

sui generis. The idea that an entity is "of its own kind," or absolutely unique.

synechdoche. A figure of speech in which the part represents the whole or *vice versa* (e.g., "bread" in Matt. 4:4; 6:11; Acts 2:42, 46; 2 Thess. 3:8, 12)

Synoptic, Synoptics. Terms used respectively to describe the common overall perspective of Matthew, Mark, and Luke and to describe Matthew, Mark, and Luke.

targums. Interpretive translations of individual books of the Hebrew Bible into Aramaic, often for liturgical use in synagogues (cf. possibly Neh. 8:1–8).

tautologous. Pertaining to the mere repetition of a previously stated idea without any new evidence for it, or to making an unnecessary argument for something that is already clear.

tetrarch. Etymologically "ruler of a fourth," but in reality a provincial governor (Matt. 14:1; Luke 3:1, 19; 9:7; Acts 13:1) and later four rulers of Rome appointed by Diocletian in A.D. 293.

tradents. Early Christians who passed on eyewitness testimony about Jesus, whether orally or in writing (Luke 1:1–2; cf. 1 Cor. 11:2; 2 Tim. 2:1–2).

triple tradition. Jesus tradition that is common to all three Synoptic Gospels.